GUIDE TO THE VATICAN

Museums and City

EDIZIONI MUSEI VATICANI

I reprint 2007

Texts: Direzione dei Musei, SCV
Photographs: Photographic Archive Vatican Museums
Design: Alessandra Murri
Printed by: Tipografia Vaticana

Editorial staff: Georgina Bernett, Adele Breda, Carla Cecilia,
Ester Console, Guido Cornini, Cristina Gennaccari, Alessandra Murri,
A.M. Daniele Pergolizzi, Maria Serlupi Crescenzi, Sesto Serra, Giancarlo Taraglio

Translation and Editing: Peter Spring

■ Table of contents

■ Guide to the Vatican Museums

■ Guide to the Vatican City

How to use this guide

VATICAN MUSEUMS
including the Sistine Chapel

Each of the chapters of this guide corresponds to one of the traditional sections of the Museums.

References to areas of the Museums, or to works exhibited in these areas, are made as follows:

Lower case letters indicate the main sections, each of which has a corresponding chapter in the guide (for example: f - Pio-Clementine Museum);

Roman numerals indicate further subdivisions of the sections, each of which corresponds to a paragraph in the guide (for example: VIII, OCTAGONAL COURT in the f - Pio-Clementine Museum);

Arabic numerals placed in the margins of the pages refer to the individual works described in the guide; they are repeated on the relevant plan of the section to show the location of the works (for example: the *Laocoön*, which is in the VIII, OCTAGONAL COURT in the f - Pio-Clementine Museum, is indicated by the number 5 in the margin of the page).

COLOURS

In this guide, various colour-keys are used to:

classify works and rooms according to periods or styles. With few exceptions, distinct periods or styles of works correspond to the sections of the Museums. Each period or style is indicated by a colour, which is shown both on the general plan of the Museums (inside cover) and on the topographical plans in the guide. The colours distinguish periods or styles of works as follows (see also pp. 6-7):

- ■ Oriental antiquities (Egypt and Assyria)
- ■ Classical antiquities (Greco-Roman art)
- ■ Etruscan-Italic antiquities (pre-Roman Italy)
- ■ Early Christian and Medieval art (3rd-14th cent.)
- ■ Renaissance (15th cent.) to the 19th century
- ■ Ethnology and history
- ■ Contemporary art (20th cent.)

THE ONE-WAY VISITING ITINERARY

The Vatican Museums include buildings of great historical and aesthetic interest, among which is the original medieval nucleus of the Apostolic Palace, renovated and decorated in the Renaissance (15th-16th cent.), as well as the galleries and museums. They make up a complex of imposing proportions, with more than 42,000 square metres open to the public, and more than seven kilometres of exhibitions.

The various periods and types of buildings, the various uses for which the rooms were originally intended, and the great distances between them, as well as the large number of visitors, have made it necessary to adopt a *one-way visiting itinerary.* This helps visitors to find their way, though it does make it difficult to visit "freely" and selectively. But without this system, visitors would need to be familiar enough with the museum to plan a personal itinerary in order to avoid retracing their steps repeatedly.

RECOMMENDED ITINERARIES

To help the visitor, the museum curators recommend the following two itineraries - one short and one complete - that take into account both the time available and preferences.

Short visit

This itinerary focuses in particular on Renaissance art in the Vatican Palaces (Sistine Chapel and Raphael's Stanze). It also includes a selection of Classical art (sculpture in the Gallery of the Candelabra), tapestries of the 16th and 17th centuries (Gallery of Tapestries); frescoes and decorations of the 16th century (Gallery of Maps), Flemish tapestries and medieval ceramics and mosaics (Apartment of St. Pius V), the frescoes by Fra Angelico (Chapel of Nicholas V) and the sections of the Museums of the Vatican Library.

Complete visit

In addition to the sections in the short visit, this itinerary includes Egyptian art (Gregorian Egyptian Museum), Classical art (Pio-Clementine Museum, Chiaramonti Gallery, Braccio Nuovo, Gregorian Profane Museum and Profane Museum of the Vatican Library), Etruscan and Italic art (Gregorian Etruscan Museum), early Christian art (Pio-Christian Museum), ethnology (Missionary-Ethnological Museum), the masterpieces of the Vatican Pinacoteca (Picture Gallery), the frescoes by Pinturicchio and the Collection of Modern Religious Art displayed in the Borgia Apartment.

Disabled visitors

Wheelchairs available free of charge at the Museum entrance. Availability may vary by season so advance reservation is recommended by calling 06.698.83860.

The list of popes mentioned with the dates of their respective pontificates (p. 234) and the list of artists (p. 236) facilitate the chronological reference to events and works of art mentioned in this guide.

Colour-keys and Signs

Oriental Antiquities
(Egypt and Assyria)

Classical Antiquities
(Greco-Roman Art)

Etruscan-Italic Antiquities
(pre-Roman Art)

Early Christian and Medieval Art
(3rd to 4th cent.)

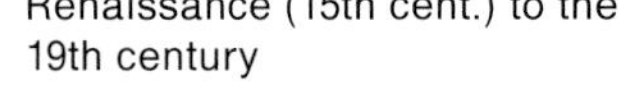

Renaissance (15th cent.) to the
19th century

Ethnology and History

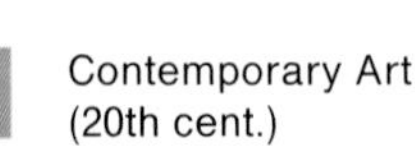

Contemporary Art
(20th cent.)

Information

Coat-check

Currency Exchange

Audio-guide

Cafeteria

Telephone

Post-Office

First Aid

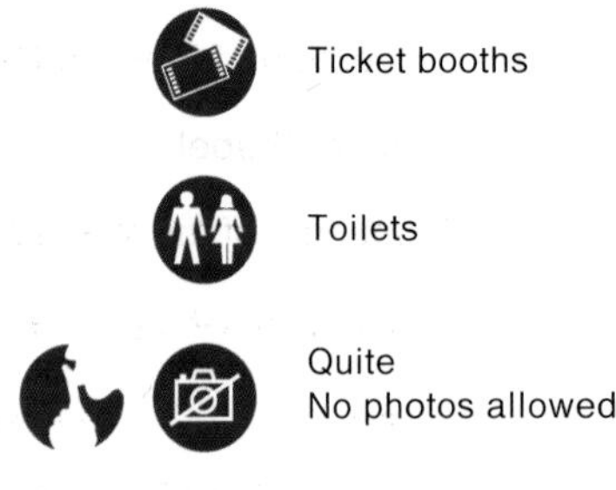

Tours begin here

Escalator

Ticket booths

Toilets

Quite
No photos allowed

Museum store
Book stand

Elevator
Elevator for disabled
Ramp for disabled

Colour-codes for the itineraries

Short visit — Complete visit

○ Visit for disabled

- a - Egyptian Museum
- b - Chiaramonti Museum
- c - Lapidary Gallery
- d - Braccio Nuovo
- e - Cortile della Pigna
- f - Pio-Clementine Museum
- g - Etruscan Museum
- g - Vase Collection (Etruscan Museum)
- h - The Biga Room
- h - Gallery of the Candelabra
- i - Gallery of Tapestries
- k - Gallery of Maps
- l - Gallery of St. Pius V
- m - Sobieski Room, Room of the Immaculate Conception
- n - Raphael's Stanze, Chapel of Urban VIII
- o - Raphael's Logge
- p - Sala dei Chiaroscuri
- q - Chapel of Nicholas V
- r - Borgia Apartment
- r - Collection of Modern Religious Art
- s - Sistine Chapel
- t - Museums of the Vatican Library
- u - Pinacoteca (Picture Gallery)
- v - Gregorian Profane Museum
- w - Pio-Christian Museum
- x - Missionary-Ethnological Museum
- y - Carriage Museum
- z - Vatican History Museum at the Lateran

Recommended Itineraries

Short visit

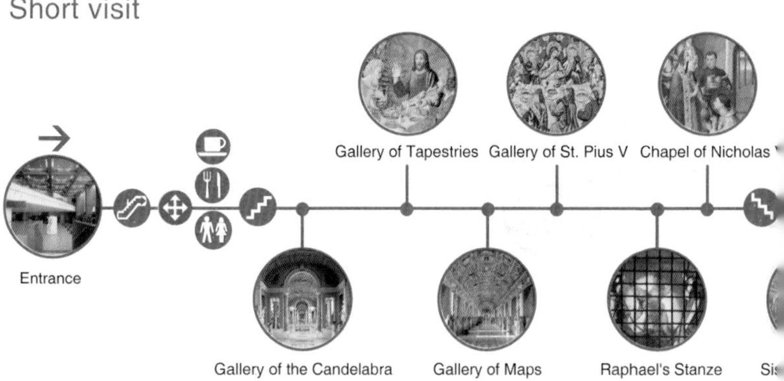

Entrance
Gallery of Tapestries
Gallery of St. Pius V
Chapel of Nicholas
Gallery of the Candelabra
Gallery of Maps
Raphael's Stanze

Complete Visit

Entrance
Pio-Clementine Museum
Etruscan Museum
Egyptian Museum
Cortile della Pigna
Chiaramonti Museum
Braccio Nuovo
Exit
Philatelic Museum
Pio-Christian Museum
Gregorian Profane Museum
Pinacoteca
Missionary-Ethnological Museum
Carriage

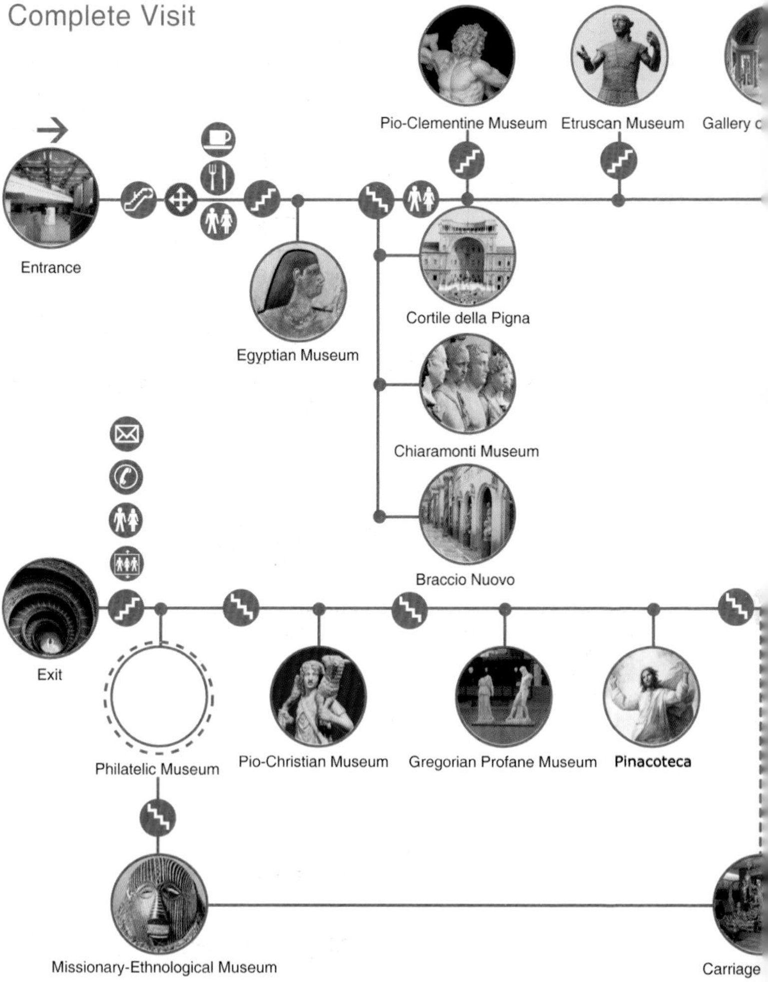

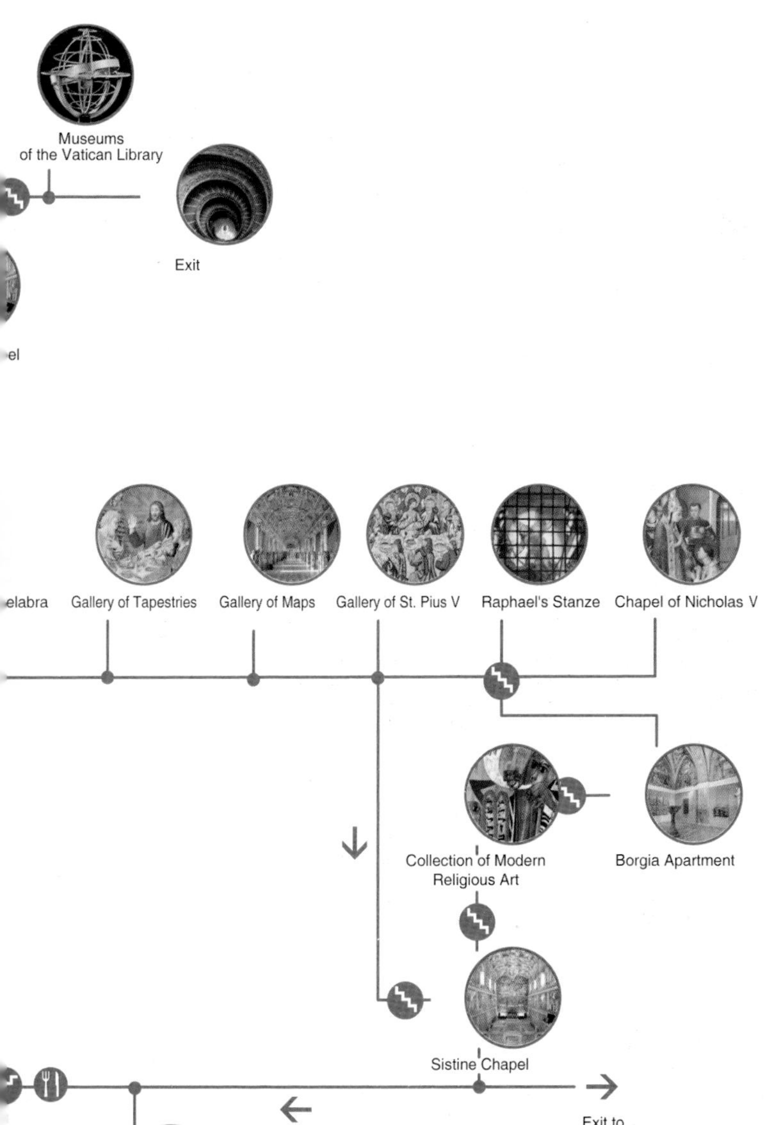

Point of departure

May not be open

Recommended Itineraries

Tour for wheelchair-access

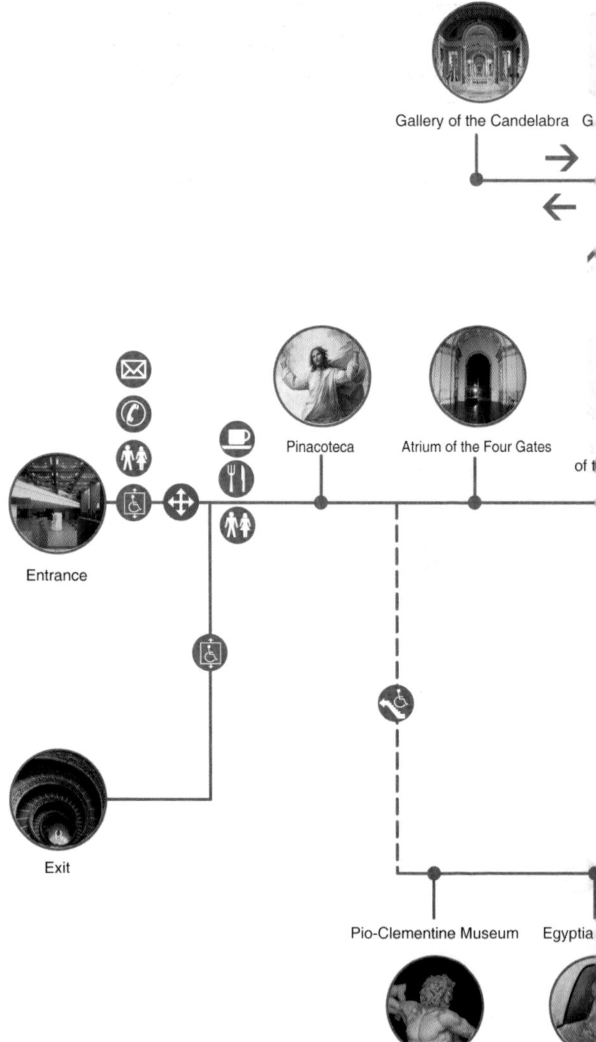

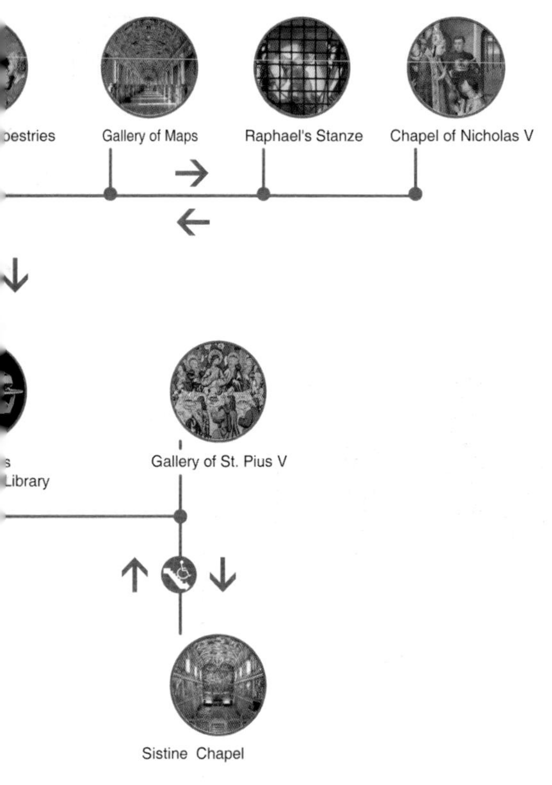

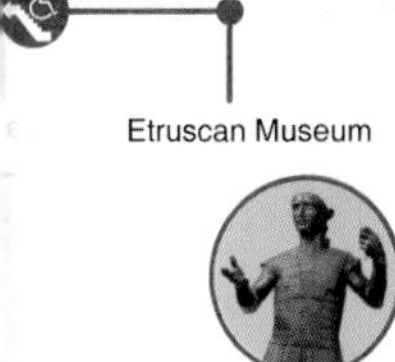

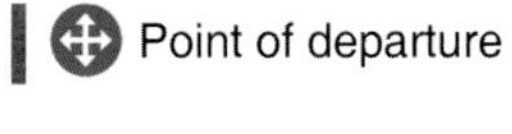

May not be open

Useful information for visitors

VATICAN MUSEUMS
including the Sistine Chapel

The museums are open from Monday to Saturday mornings with seasonal variations for afternoon hours. Please contact the Museums at the following telephone number for exact opening hours: (+ +39)06.698.83860 or consult our website www.vatican.va. The Vatican Museums are closed on Sundays, except the last Sunday of every month (admission is free), unless it falls on Easter Sunday, 29 June, Christmas Day or 26 December. The Museums are also closed on the following holidays: 1 and 6 January, 11 February, 19 March, Easter Monday, 1 May, Ascension Day, Corpus Christi Day, 29 June, 14 (or 16) and 15 August, 1 November, and 8, 25 and 26 December.

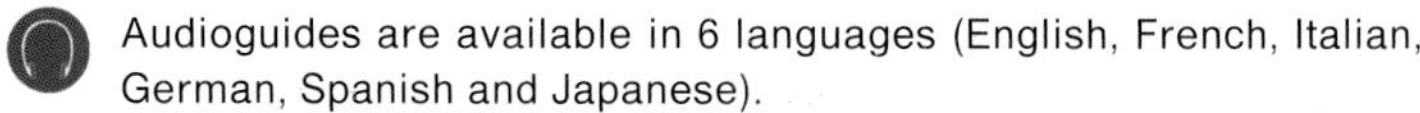

Audioguides are available in 6 languages (English, French, Italian, German, Spanish and Japanese).

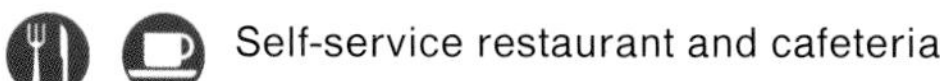

Self-service restaurant and cafeteria.

Post Office.

Two foreign currency exchange offices.

An emergency first aid service is available.

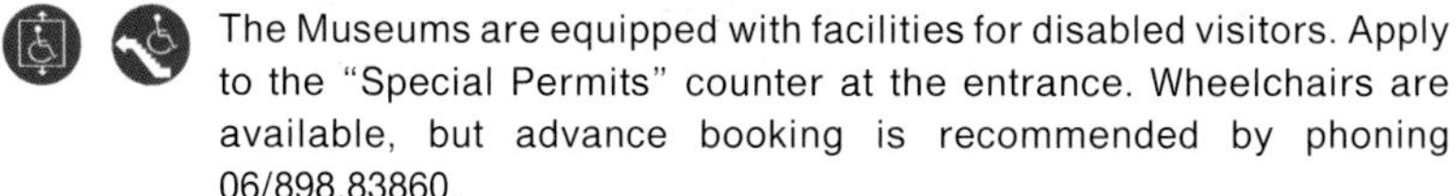

The Museums are equipped with facilities for disabled visitors. Apply to the "Special Permits" counter at the entrance. Wheelchairs are available, but advance booking is recommended by phoning 06/898.83860.

Exhibits and rooms may be photographed with hand-held cameras. The use of tripods requires the permission from the Administration. The use of flash equipment is prohibited during museum hours. It is also prohibited to photograph, film or use video cameras in the Sistine Chapel.

The works of art and entire sections of the Vatican Museums are protected by a closed-circuit television system and by electronic alarm equipment. Visitors are therefore advised to refrain at all times from touching exhibits.

Guided visits to Vatican City and Gardens are available for individual visitors and organized groups. Apply to the "Guided Visits" counter at the entrance to the Vatican Museums (for advance bookings: groups tel. 06/698.83145 – individuals 06/698.84676 – fax. 06/698.85100).

Vatican Museums and Sistine Chapel (approx. 2 hours)
Vatican Gardens (approx. 2 hours)
Vatican Gardens and Sistine Chapel (approx. 3 hours)

PAPAL AUDIENCES

General audiences are usually held on Wednesday morning in the Paul VI Audience Hall (November to February) and at 10:30 a.m. in St. Peter's Square (March to October). Permission to attend may be obtained from the Prefecture of the Pontifical Household (tel. 06.698.83114 or 06.698.83273), whose office is accessible through the Bronze Doors in St. Peter's Square. The office is open on weekdays from 9:00 a.m. to 1:30 p.m.

ST. PETER'S BASILICA

ADMISSION FREE from St. Peter's Square, every day from 7 a.m. to 6 p.m. from October to March and from 7 a.m. to 7 p.m. from April to September.

Members of the *Peregrinatio ad Petri Sedem* (information booth in the hall to the right of the entrance) provide a free guide service (in 24 languages) only to St. Peter's Basilica for the purpose of illustrating its spiritual as well as its historical and artistic significance.

Visit to the Dome

Admission charge. Entrance from the hall on the right side of the Basilica, daily from 8 a.m. to 5 p.m. (October to March) and from 8 a.m. to 6 p.m. (April to September) (lift available up to the terrace over the nave).

Historical Artistic Museum - Treasury of St. Peter's

Admission charge. Situated in the Sacristy of the Basilica, entrance from the left aisle. Opening hours: daily from 9 a.m. to 17:30 p.m. (October to March), and from 9 a.m. to 6:30 p.m. (April to September).

Vatican Grottoes (Tombs of the Popes)

Below the nave and aisles of the Basilica, entrance from the transept crossing. Opening hours: daily from 7 a.m. to 5.00 p.m. (October to March) and from 7 a.m. to 6 p.m. (April to September); admission free.

Pre-Constantinian Necropolis

Below the Vatican Grottoes. Bookings for guided visits must be made in advance at the Vatican Excavations Office , tel. 06.698.85318 Fax 06.698.85518. The office is open on weekdays from 9 a.m. to 5 p.m. Access is through the Arco delle Campane to the left of St. Peter's.

A brief history of the Vatican

THE VATICAN

The urban development of ancient Rome was essentially confined to the left bank of the Tiber River. The right bank, until the beginning of the Imperial period, was limited to wharves and ancillary port facilities, a few small brick kilns and small farms scattered over large areas of uncultivated land, parts of which were marshlands prone to malaria.

Looking across the river from the city, an inhabitant of ancient Rome would have seen a flat strip of land, the *ager vaticanus,* running along the far bank, and, in the background, a range of hills, the *montes vaticani,* lying more or less parallel to the river. Both areas took their names from an ancient place-name, *Vaticanum.* Strictly speaking, the *montes vaticani* were the range of hills stretching northwards from the Janiculum Hill to the present Monte Mario, but the name was sometimes used to refer to Janiculum itself and even to the entire region. The varied use of the name itself indicates that the city had not yet expanded to include the district across the river, a fact also borne out by the vague name of *trans Tiberim* given to the Augustan region XIV of the city, including the Vatican.

Only towards the end of the Republican period did the privileged classes begin to build villas in the *trans Tiberim* for their leisure and amusement. Agrippina, mother of the emperor Caligula (37-41 A.D.), laid out pleasant gardens on the land surrounding her villa in the trans-Tiberine region. Other very extensive gardens were owned by the Domitii family in the same area: inherited by the emperor Nero (54-68 A.D.), they formed the famous *horti Neronis.* Nero completed the circus which Gaius (Caligula) had begun here, and embellished it with an obelisk brought from Egypt (the one now standing in St. Peter's Square). Augustus had already built a *naumachia* (a stadium for naval contests) in the area of these gardens; another was situated closer to the hill. The area, in short, was a large area of parkland dotted with buildings devoted to sports and recreation. It was here that Nero satisfied his every whim and fancy by organising cruel spectacles including the torture of many Christians, then crucified and burnt in the circus (Tacitus, *Annals*, XV, 44).

Among Nero's victims was St. Peter, who was buried not far away from the place of his martyrdom. The Apostle's tomb was given a monumental consecration by the huge Basilica built over it, commissioned by the emperor Constantine in 324, during the papacy of Sylvester I.

But the same emperor downgraded the entire city of Rome when he transferred the capital of the Empire to Constantinople (330). Then came the turbulent times of the barbarian invasions: the Goths of Alaric (410), the Vandals of Genseric (445), and the terrible sieges laid by the Goths of Witigis (537-538) and Totila (545-546). As the old city gradually became smaller, a new, densely-populated quarter developed round the Vatican Basilica. The inhabitants of this unfortified settlement may have counted on the relative immunity that the Christianised barbarians had granted until now to the "holy place". In fact, it was the Saracen invaders of another faith, who finally sacked St. Peter's and St. Paul's in 846, during the pontificate of Sergius II. As a result of this invasion, Pope Leo IV built strong defensive walls around the area surrounding the Basilica, from Castel Sant'Angelo to the western foot of the Vatican hill. From then on, the Vatican was referred to as the "Leonine City".

THE SEAT OF THE BISHOPS OF ROME

Originally, the official residence of the Bishops of Rome was not the Vatican, but the Lateran. St. Peter's was then an out-of-the-way basilica reserved for burials, as was St. Paul's, on Via Ostiensis, and others. For the popes, the initial problem was merely one of finding temporary accommodation at the Vatican when they came to St. Peter's for liturgical reasons. The first to build at the Vatican was Pope Symmachus, who had been forced to abandon the Lateran for the duration of the Laurentian Schism (501-506) and who built two episcopal residences at the sides of the Basilica. In 781 Charlemagne converted a residence for his own use to the north of the Basilica. Eugenius III (1145-1153) then built a 'new palace" on the site, which Innocent III enlarged and enclosed within turreted walls.

Nicholas III (1277-1280) was the first pope to adopt the Vatican as his permanent residence. For this reason he began, but did not complete, a quadrangular fortified residence with corner towers, built round the present Cortile del Pappagallo. He also built a new defensive wall, reinforced with battlements and towers, which probably extended to the north as far as a hill called Monte Sant'Egidio, where two centuries later Innocent VIII would build his Belvedere.

The military nature of the construction work confirms the use of the Vatican is an emergency refuge. The exile of the popes to Avignon (1305-77) and the Great Western Schism (1378-1417) ushered in a period of total neglect for all the buildings in Rome.

Recovery came during the pontificate of Nicholas V (1447-1455), the humanist Tommaso Parentucelli. A new chapter was begun in which the old concept of the Vatican as a fortified palace and papal seat *apud Sanctum Petrum* was enlightened with the spirit of the early Renaissance.

THE VATICAN MUSEUMS

It was this spirit that inspired the creation of two of the most illustrious, humanistic and "secular" institutions of the Holy See: the Vatican Library and the Vatican Museums. But they were never considered profane. Both were the product of a view of Classical (Greco-Roman) culture as the perfect, almost timeless expression of human creativity at its highest levels—both in thought and in art—and as the precursor, at times almost the prefiguration, of Christianity, especially in the West. The origins of the Vatican Museums can be traced back to the courtyard of Innocent VIII's Pallazzetto del Belvedere, which Julius II laid out as gardens and embellished with masterpieces of Classical sculpture: the *Apollo* (consequently known as the "Apollo Belvedere"), the *Venus Felix*, the *Laocoön*, the *Nile*, the *Tiber*, and the *Sleeping Ariadne*. Other pieces of sculpture were used to decorate the Apostolic Palace itself (Raphael's Logge, for instance, in the time of Leo X).

The Vatican Library was officially founded by Sixtus IV in 1475. The first mention of an art collection (or a "cabinet of rarities") in the Library goes back to the prefecture of Marcello Cervini, later Pope Marcellus II (1555).

The spirit of the Counter-Reformation (consider the austere St. Pius V), with its moralistic rejection of the arts of antiquity, soon brought the growth of the Vatican collection to a standstill. However, the new emphasis on the defence of the Faith laid the foundations for a study of the arts of antiquity, approached from both an historical and archaeological point of view, and no longer purely aesthetic.

The 18th century saw the first manifestations of this new approach. In 1756 Benedict XIV founded the Christian Museum of the Library "to increase" – as the inscription over its entrance declares – "the splendour of the City, and bear witness to the truth of religion through sacred Christian monuments". In 1767, Clement XIII founded the Profane Museum in the Library "to preserve the monuments of Roman antiquity".

The responsibility to collect and preserve the heritage of ancient art was threatened by, among other things, the ever-increasing exportation of antiquities. This led Popes Clement XIV, Pius VI and Pius VII to establish the Pio-Clementine Museum (1771-93), the Chiaramonti Museum and the Lapidary Gallery (1807-10) and the Braccio Nuovo (1822). The realization of the new museums involved renewed building activity, considerable financial investment (Monsignor Gian Angelo Braschi, Clement XIV's Treasurer General and successor as Pius VI used lottery proceeds to finance the purchase of antiquities) and the consultation of experts (Johann Joachim Winckelmann, Commissioner of Antiquities of the Papal State 1763-68, and Antonio Canova, Inspector General of Antiquities and Fine Arts 1802-22). Of considerable importance for the preservation of antiquities was the development of legislation, thanks also to the Napoleonic period of French occupation in Rome, regulating archaeological excavations and the trade in antiquities: the Pacca Edict of 1820, which controlled excavations and gave public collections the right of first choice of finds made.

Following intensive excavation carried out in Southern Etruria in the early 19th century, enforcement of the law soon made a new museum of Etruscan monuments indispensable: the Gregorian Etruscan Museum was opened by Gregory XVI in 1837. The deciphering of hieroglyphics (by Jean-François Champollion, 1822) stimulated a similar interest in Egyptian antiquities: the Gregorian Egyptian Museum was opened in 1839.

New space for the Classical antiquities that were continually coming to light in the Papal State was found in the Lateran Palace, where the Gregorian Profane Museum was founded by Gregory XVI in 1844. A significant collection of Christian antiquities was also established at the Lateran by Pius IX in 1854, two years after the creation of the Commission for Christian Archaeology.

With the end of the Papal State (1870) and the resulting reduction of its territorial jurisdiction, two development strategies were open to the Vatican Museums. The first was to continue the critical study and exhibition of their traditional artistic heritage; the second to expand in a direction more in keeping with the nature of the Church's mission in the world. The former led to the foundation of the Pinacoteca (Picture Gallery) (Pius XI, 1932), in which the paintings seized by Napoleon under the Treaty of Tolentino (1797) and returned after the Congress of Vienna (1815) were finally exhibited to the public in a worthy manner, along with other works of art collected in the Vatican. Other developments included the setting up of the Rooms of the Greek

Originals (1960), resulting from a more accurate identification of the specifically Hellenic characteristics of works formerly classified as Greco-Roman (the department was transferred to the Gregorian Profane Museum in 1988); the transfer to the Vatican and subsequent presentation of the former Lateran collections: the Gregorian Profane and Pio-Christian museums (1970), and the Missionary-Ethnological Museum (1973); and more recently the renewed lay-out and presentation of the Gregorian Egyptian Museum (1989, 2000) and Etruscan Museum (1992, 1994, 1996).

The second development strategy led from the foundation of the Missionary-Ethnological Museum (Pius XI, 1926) to that of the Collection of Modern Religious Art (Paul VI, 1973). The Historical Museum (1973), in which old papal berlins (carriages) and arms and uniforms of the Vatican armed forces (disbanded in 1970) became simply historical artefacts, may also be considered an indirect result of this new vision. The Museum was later (1985) divided into the main Historical Museum, located in the Apostolic Palace at the Lateran, and the Carriage Museum.

VATICAN CITY

The majestic complex of the present papal apartments dates to the late Renaissance; it was built by Domenico Fontana in 1589-1590, during the pontificate of Sixtus V. The Baroque period, which radically transformed Rome and lent its own style to the Vatican Basilica and St. Peter's Square, added little to the character of the Apostolic Palace. Its relative neglect was due to the fact that Gregory XIII had built a new papal palace on the Quirinal hill. Later popes, beginning with Clement VIII, preferred it to the Vatican as a residence because of its more salubrious air.

The work of re-fortifying the Vatican had begun about a century earlier under Paul III with a monumental bulwark at the foot of the Belvedere. During the pontificate of Urban VIII the work to give the area of the Vatican a new circuit of walls was completed. They were more extensive and stronger than the earlier "Leonine" walls. These walls and the colonnade of St. Peter's Square now form the boundaries of the modern Vatican State.

The definitive return of the Popes to the Vatican, to the place where Peter, the first Bishop of Rome, had been killed and buried, did not take place until Pius IX, after the unification of Italy and the capture of Rome in 1870.

As a result of these events, the territorial rule of the Papacy came to an end. The Papal State had gradually grown from the 8th century to include the regions of Latium, Umbria, the Marches and Romagna in order to maintain the Pope's independence. When Rome became the capital of the newly formed Italian State in 1870, the Pope withdrew to the Vatican, and his successors have lived there ever since.

In order to guarantee the independence of the Papacy, however, it was necessary to reconstitute some form of temporal sovereignty, even if only minimal. Indeed, with the occupation of Rome the Pope had become, juridically speaking, a private citizen subject to Italian legislation. And although the Italian State, with a law known as *delle guarentigie* passed on 13 May 1871, had guaranteed the Supreme Pontiff a special juridical status, both that law and his freedom to carry out his ministry could be modified or curbed by a unilateral decision on the part of Italy. For this reason, in February 1929, the Lateran Pact was stipulated between the Italian State and the Holy See. This agreement recognized the sovereignty of the Pope over the area of St. Peter's Basilica and Square and the surrounding territory within the Vatican walls, thus creating the Vatican City State. According to the terms of the Lateran Pact, this State is considered neutral territory. The whole of its area, due to its spiritual significance and the treasures of art it contains, was placed under the protection of The Hague Convention of 14 May 1954, which provides for the protection of its cultural patrimony in the event of armed conflict. The Vatican State is thus recognized internationally for its moral, artistic and cultural patrimony, as worthy of respect and protection and as a heritage belonging to all mankind.

Consequently, the Pope is both head of the Catholic Church and sovereign of the Vatican City State. He carries out his primary ecclesiastical functions of teaching and pastoral activity through the organs of the Church, particularly the *Secretariat of State*. Together with the Papacy, these organs constitute the Roman Curia (the central government of the Catholic Church). The Holy See has permanent representatives at the United Nations and in some of its organizations, such as UNESCO, FAO, UNIDO, WHO and the ITU.

In matters concerning Vatican City, the Supreme Pontiff exercises his legislative power through a commission composed of a number of cardinals, whom he appoints for five-year terms (the cardinals, nominated by the Pontiff, are his most important advisors, and it is their task to elect the new Pope when the papal throne becomes vacant.). He exercises his executive power through the Cardinal President of that commission, upon whom depend the various offices of the Governorate that administer to the needs of the tiny State. The Vatican City has about nine hundred inhabitants (including two hundred women), and covers an area of 44 hectares (1045 m x 850 m). It has its own military corps (the Swiss Guard, consisting of about one hundred men, who are responsible for the Pope's security and guard the main entrances to the City); a flag (yellow and white with St. Peter's keys under the triple crown); a national anthem (the Pontifical March by Charles Gounod); its own currency, postage stamps and motor licence plate (SCV, today CV). It also has a post office and telecommunications service, a radio station, a railway station and other services. The first radio broadcast station (1931) was located within the Vatican City, but the present more powerful broadcasting station, built in 1957, is located about 25 km. from Rome at Santa Maria di Galeria. Most of the 1300 employees of the Vatican government do not reside within the Vatican.

In the Vatican City State, justice is administered by a judge, a Court of Assizes, a Court of Appeal, and a Supreme Court, which exercise their powers in the name of the Sovereign Pontiff.

Vatican City State is recognized by the international community as a legal sovereign body, and is a member of various international organizations (Universal Postal Union, International Telecommunications Union, International Union for the Protection of Literary and Artistic Works).

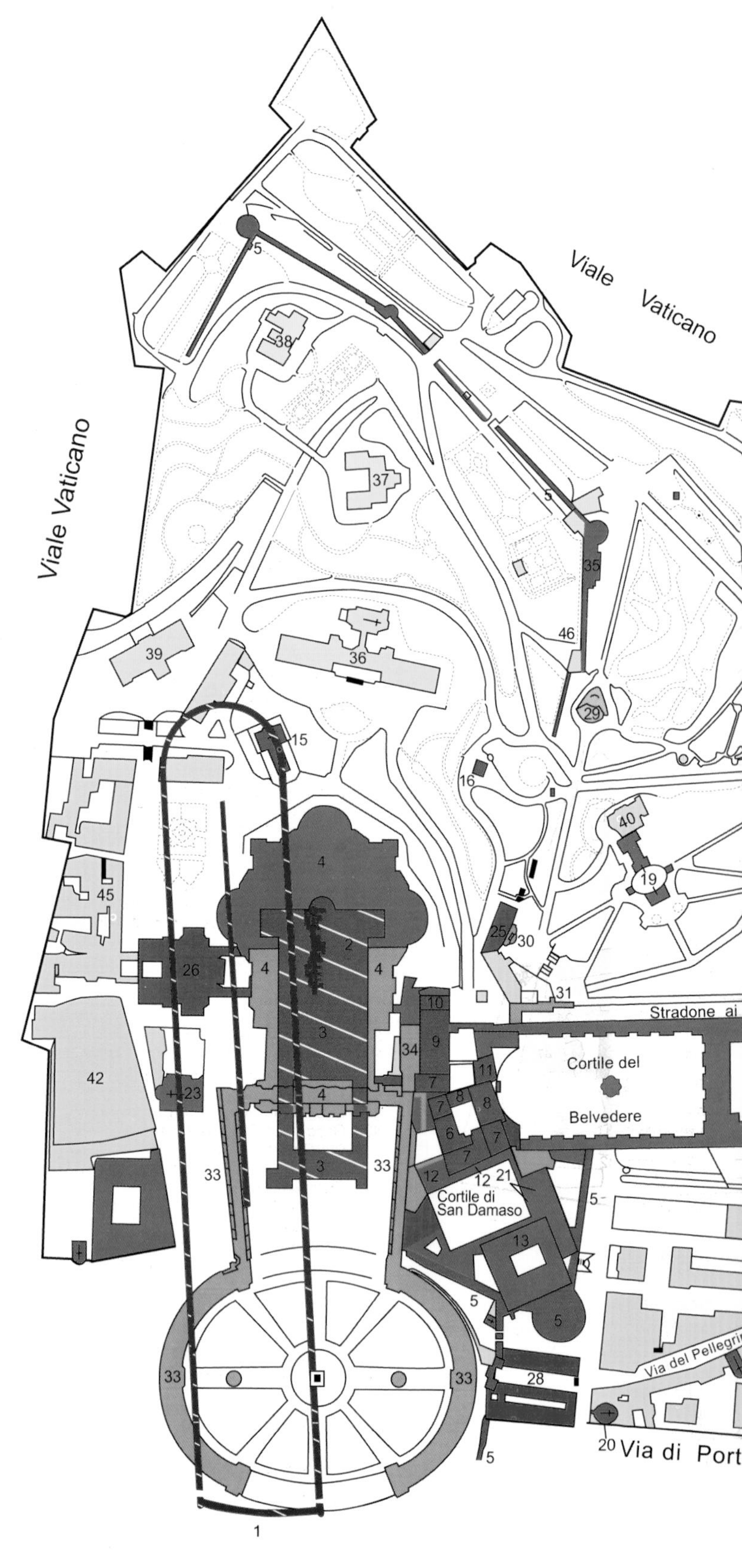

Viale Vaticano
Viale Vaticano
Stradone ai
Cortile del Belvedere
Cortile di San Damaso
Via del Pellegri
Via di Port
1
2
3
4
5
6
7
8
9
10
11
12
13
15
16
19
20
21
23
25
26
28
29
30
31
33
34
35
36
37
38
39
40
42
45
46

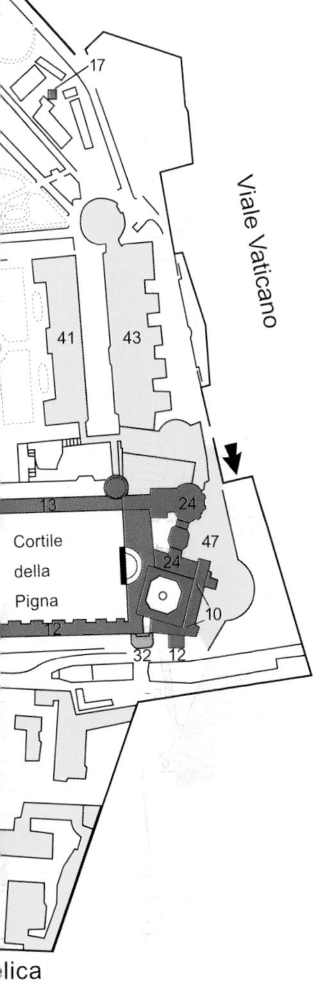

HISTORICAL MAP
OF THE VATICAN CITY

1 The circus of Nero and Caligula
2 Pre-Constantinian Necropolis
3 Constantinian Basilica
4 Present Basilica
5 Walls of Leo IV and Nicholas V

Development of the Apostolic Palace at the end of the 16th century

6 Eugenius III and Innocent III
7 Nicholas III
8 Nicholas V (see also 5)
9 Sixtus IV
10 Innocent VIII
11 Alexander VI
12 Julius II
13 Sixtus V

Buildings of major interest, not mentioned in the Introduction

14 Church of San Pellegrino
15 Church of Santo Stefano degli Abissini
16 House of the Gardener
17 Tower of Innocent VIII
18 Corridor of the west wing of the Court of the Belvedere, built by Pirro Ligorio under Pius IV
19 "Casina" of Pius IV
20 Church of Sant'Anna
21 Logge and Palace of Gregory XIII
22 Palace of the Holy Office (Palazzo del Sant'Uffizio)
23 Church of the Teutonic College
24 Pio-Clementine Museum
25 The Mint (Palazzo della Zecca)
26 Sacristy of St. Peter's
27 Braccio Nuovo (New Wing) of the Vatican Museums
28 Barracks of the Swiss Guards
29 Fountain of the Eagle
30 Fountain of the Sacrament
31 Building of Paul V and Fountain of the Mirrors
32 Fountain of the Galley
33 Colonnade of St. Peter's Square, by Bernini
34 Scala Regia (ceremonial staircase), by Bernini
35 Palazzina of Leo XIII
36 Palazzo del Governatorato (administrative building)
37 Ethiopian College
38 First Vatican Radio station
39 Railway station
40 Pontifical Academy of Sciences
41 Vatican Pinacoteca (Picture Gallery)
42 Papal Audience Hall (Paul VI Hall)
43 Gregorian Profane Museum
Pio-Christian Museum
Missionary-Ethnological Museum
44 Carriage Museum
45 Domus Sanctae Marthae (House of St. Martha)
46 Convent of Mater Ecclesiae
47 New Entrance (Vatican Museums)

➡ Entrance to Vatican Museums

■ Classical Antiquity
■ Medieval
■ 16th century
■ 17th century
■ 18th-19th century
■ 20th century

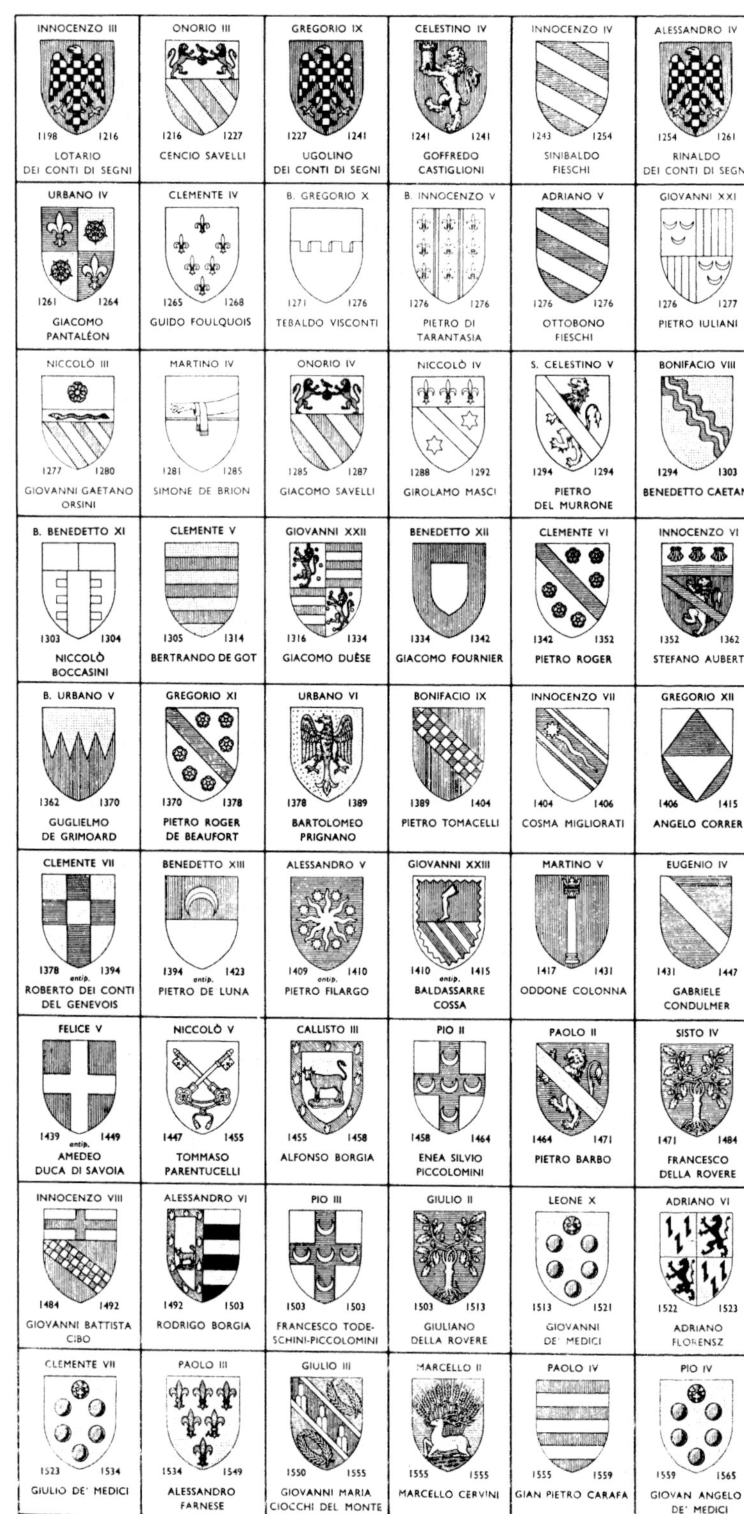
INNOCENZO III
1198 1216
LOTARIO DEI CONTI DI SEGNI
ONORIO III
1216 1227
CENCIO SAVELLI
GREGORIO IX
1227 1241
UGOLINO DEI CONTI DI SEGNI
CELESTINO IV
1241 1241
GOFFREDO CASTIGLIONI
INNOCENZO IV
1243 1254
SINIBALDO FIESCHI
ALESSANDRO IV
1254 1261
RINALDO DEI CONTI DI SEGNI
URBANO IV
1261 1264
GIACOMO PANTALÉON
CLEMENTE IV
1265 1268
GUIDO FOULQUOIS
B. GREGORIO X
1271 1276
TEBALDO VISCONTI
B. INNOCENZO V
1276 1276
PIETRO DI TARANTASIA
ADRIANO V
1276 1276
OTTOBONO FIESCHI
GIOVANNI XXI
1276 1277
PIETRO IULIANI
NICCOLÒ III
1277 1280
GIOVANNI GAETANO ORSINI
MARTINO IV
1281 1285
SIMONE DE BRION
ONORIO IV
1285 1287
GIACOMO SAVELLI
NICCOLÒ IV
1288 1292
GIROLAMO MASCI
S. CELESTINO V
1294 1294
PIETRO DEL MURRONE
BONIFACIO VIII
1294 1303
BENEDETTO CAETANI
B. BENEDETTO XI
1303 1304
NICCOLÒ BOCCASINI
CLEMENTE V
1305 1314
BERTRANDO DE GOT
GIOVANNI XXII
1316 1334
GIACOMO DUÈSE
BENEDETTO XII
1334 1342
GIACOMO FOURNIER
CLEMENTE VI
1342 1352
PIETRO ROGER
INNOCENZO VI
1352 1362
STEFANO AUBERT
B. URBANO V
1362 1370
GUGLIELMO DE GRIMOARD
GREGORIO XI
1370 1378
PIETRO ROGER DE BEAUFORT
URBANO VI
1378 1389
BARTOLOMEO PRIGNANO
BONIFACIO IX
1389 1404
PIETRO TOMACELLI
INNOCENZO VII
1404 1406
COSMA MIGLIORATI
GREGORIO XII
1406 1415
ANGELO CORRER
CLEMENTE VII
1378 antip. 1394
ROBERTO DEI CONTI DEL GENEVOIS
BENEDETTO XIII
1394 antip. 1423
PIETRO DE LUNA
ALESSANDRO V
1409 antip. 1410
PIETRO FILARGO
GIOVANNI XXIII
1410 antip. 1415
BALDASSARRE COSSA
MARTINO V
1417 1431
ODDONE COLONNA
EUGENIO IV
1431 1447
GABRIELE CONDULMER
FELICE V
1439 antip. 1449
AMEDEO DUCA DI SAVOIA
NICCOLÒ V
1447 1455
TOMMASO PARENTUCELLI
CALLISTO III
1455 1458
ALFONSO BORGIA
PIO II
1458 1464
ENEA SILVIO PICCOLOMINI
PAOLO II
1464 1471
PIETRO BARBO
SISTO IV
1471 1484
FRANCESCO DELLA ROVERE
INNOCENZO VIII
1484 1492
GIOVANNI BATTISTA CIBO
ALESSANDRO VI
1492 1503
RODRIGO BORGIA
PIO III
1503 1503
FRANCESCO TODESCHINI-PICCOLOMINI
GIULIO II
1503 1513
GIULIANO DELLA ROVERE
LEONE X
1513 1521
GIOVANNI DE' MEDICI
ADRIANO VI
1522 1523
ADRIANO FLORENSZ
CLEMENTE VII
1523 1534
GIULIO DE' MEDICI
PAOLO III
1534 1549
ALESSANDRO FARNESE
GIULIO III
1550 1555
GIOVANNI MARIA CIOCCHI DEL MONTE
MARCELLO II
1555 1555
MARCELLO CERVINI
PAOLO IV
1555 1559
GIAN PIETRO CARAFA
PIO IV
1559 1565
GIOVAN ANGELO DE' MEDICI

BENEDETTO XVI

2005

JOSEPH RATZINGER
fel. regnante

Chronological index: history of the Vatican Museums

Julius II

1503 The Pope placed the statue of Apollo, subsequently known as the *Apollo Belvedere*, in the inner court of Innocent VIII's Palazzetto Belvedere in the Vatican.

1506 14 January: Discovery of the marble *Laocoön* group on the Esquiline Hill.

Clement VII

*c.*1530 Purchase of the *Belvedere Torso*, formerly in the Palazzo Colonna.

Clement XI

1700-' 21 First plan to collect ancient, pagan and Christian inscriptions, and to found a museum of Christian antiquities.

Clement XII

1730'40 Acquisition for the Vatican Library of 200 so-called "Etruscan" (i.e. Greek) vases, and 328 ancient medals, in addition to precious manuscripts.

Benedict XIV

1740-'58 Foundation of the Christian Museum of the Vatican Library (1756). First director: Francesco Vettori. Arrangement of the lapidary collection in the north end of the Bramante Corridor begun, on the proposal of Giuseppe Bianchini. Ridolfino Venuti nominated Commissioner of Roman Antiquities (1745).

Clement XIII

1764 Johann Joachim Winckelmann appointed Commissioner of Roman Antiquities and *Scriptor* of the Library with the task of directing a future Vatican Museum of Classical Antiquities.

1767 Foundation of the Profane Museum of the Vatican Library.

Clement XIV

1770 Purchase of the Mattei collection of Classical antiquities.

1771-'73 Building of the Clementine Museum. Architects: Alessandro Dori (died 1772) and Michelangelo Simonetti. Commissioner of Roman Antiquities: Giovanni Battista Visconti. Chief restorer: Gaspare Sibilla.

1774 Completion of the lapidary collection by Gaetano Marini.

Pius VI

1776-'84 The Clementine Museum is enlarged with the construction of the Museum of Pius VI and by acquisitions and excavations in numerous parts of the Papal State. By 1784 the Pio-Clementine Museum had been almost completed. Architect: Michelangelo Simonetti; Commissioner of Antiquities: Giambattista Visconti (died 1784), assisted by his son Ennio Quirino. Chief restorers: Gaspare Sibilla and Giovanni Pierantoni.

1785-1788 Enclosure of the Covered Loggia above the south wing of the Library and set up of the Gallery of the Candelabra. Architects: Michelangelo Simonetti (died 1787) and Giuseppe Camporese: Commissioner of Roman Antiquities: Filippo Aurelio Visconti; Chief restorer: Giovanni Pierantoni.

1790 Set up of the first Vatican Pinacoteca (Picture Gallery) in the present Gallery of Tapestries.

1793 Completion of the Atrium of the Quattro Cancelli as entrance to the Pio-Clementine Museum. Architect: G. Camporese.

1797 The masterpieces of the Pio-Clementine Museum transported to Paris in compliance with the terms of the Treaty of Tolentino.

1798-1800 During the French occupation, the Profane Museum of the Library lost forever its collection of gems, coins and medals.

Pius VII

1800 Carlo Fea is appointed Commissioner of Antiquities.

1801 Purchase of Antonio Canova's *Perseus*.

1802 Canova is appointed General Inspector of Fine Arts. Dispersion of the first Pinacoteca within the Vatican Palaces. 2 October: Doria Pamphilj Edict on the protection of works of art.

1807-'10 Set up of the Chiaramonti Museum under Canova's direction. Additions and final arrangement of the collection of inscriptions in the Lapidary Gallery by Gaetano Marini. Foundation of a new numismatic collection (medals).

1814 The tapestries of the *Scuola Vecchia* and *Scuola Nuova* series, based on cartoons by Raphael, are exhibited in the Apartment of St. Pius V.

1815 A series of Etruscan, Greek and Italiot vases are added to the Vatican Library.

1816, 4 January and 11 August: thanks to the provisions of the Congress of Vienna (1815), return from Paris of the masterpieces of the Pio-Clementine Museum, and of the paintings removed from various locations in the Papal State. 21 February: foundation of the Pinacoteca (the Pope ordered that the paintings returned from Paris be displayed in the Borgia Apartment).
1818 Acquisition of the Roman fresco known as the "Aldobrandini Wedding".
1820 The Vatican Library acquires the collection of Agostino Mariotti. 7 April: Pacca Edict, which regulated excavations and the trade in antiquities.
1821 The Pinacoteca is transferred to the Apartment of Gregory XIII (Sala Bologna and adjacent rooms).
1822 Opening of the Braccio Nuovo. Architect: Raffaele Stern (died 1820): work completed by Pasquale Belli.

Leo XII, Pius VIII, Gregory XVI

1827-'36 Excavation and acquisition of antiquities from Etruria and Latium, and of Greek pottery. Excavations at Vulci conducted by the Pontifical Government in association with Secondiano Campanari.

Gregory XVI

1831 The Pinacoteca is set up again in the present Gallery of Tapestries.
1835 2 June: discovery of the "Mars of Todi".
1836 Transfer of the Pinacoteca to the Apartment of St. Pius V.
1836-'37 Excavation and acquisition of the contents of the "Regolini-Galassi" tomb at Cerveteri (Caere).
1837 2 February: inauguration of the Gregorian Etruscan Museum.
Acquisition by the Library of a collection of paintings of the so-called "primitives".
1838 Set up of the Gallery of Tapestries and of the Room of Antique Frescoes in their present sites,
1839 2 February: inauguration of the Gregorian Egyptian Museum.
1844 14 May: inauguration of the Gregorian Profane Museum in the Lateran Palace and of the Lateran Picture Gallery.

Pius IX

1852 Establishment of the Commission for Christian Archaeology to excavate and maintain the catacombs.
1853 The city of Rome donates to the Pope the series of Roman frescoes with scenes from the Odyssey.
1854 Foundation of the Pio-Christian Museum in the Lateran Palace.
1855-'70 Excavations in Ostia Antica; the antiquities found would be displayed in the last two rooms of the Lateran Profane Museum.
1857 The Pinacoteca returned to the Apartment of Gregory XIII.

Leo XIII

1898 Acquisition of the Falcioni Collection of Etruscan and Roman antiquities.

Pius X

1906 The treasures of the Sancta Sanctorum placed in the Christian Museum of the Vatican Library.
1909 19 March: after a series of displacements within the Vatican Palaces, inauguration of the Pinacoteca in its new site in the gallery below the Christian Museum of the Library. Transfer from the Library to the Pinacoteca of the Byzantine and so-called primitive (i.e. early Italian, 13th-15th cent.) paintings acquired by Gregory XVI and Pius IX, and of the picture gallery of the Lateran Palace.

Pius XI

1923 Establishment on a permanent basis of the restoration laboratories.
1925 Inauguration (19 February) of the new set up of the Gregorian Etruscan Museum. Missionary Exhibition in the Vatican: occasion for the founding (21 December 1926) of the Missionary-Ethnological Museum in the Lateran Palace.
1929 Establishment of the Vatican City State.
1932 New entrance to the Vatican Museums from Viale Vaticano. Architect: Giuseppe Momo. Sculptural decoration: Antonio Marsini. Inauguration (27 October) of the new building providing a permanent home for the Vatican Pinacoteca, Architect: Luca Beltrami.
1933 Creation of the Department of Scientific Research.
1935 Donation to the Pope of the Benedetto Guglielmi Collection of Greek and Etruscan vases and bronzes,

Pius XII

1951 Donation to the Pope of the Carlo Grassi Collection of Egyptian minor antiquities.
1955-'60 The Gregorian Etruscan Museum extended to the whole upper floor of the restored Palazzetto Belvedere of Innocent VIII, and to the Upper Hemicycle of Pirro Ligorio's "Nicchione".
1957-'60 Restoration of the *Laocoön*: its original right arm, found by Ludwig Pollak in 1905, was added by Filippo Magi.

John XXIII

1960 Opening of the Rooms of the Greek Originals.
1963 A new buildingis built by the Bros. Fausto, Lucio and Vincenzo Passarelli Architecture Studio to house the three collections formerly exhibited in the Lateran Palace (Gregorian Profane Museum, Pio-Christian Museum and Missionary-Ethnological Museum).

Paul VI

1965 Renovation and rearrangement of the Egyptian Museum begins.
1967 Donation to the Pope of the Teresa and Tommaso Astarita Collection of Etruscan, Italiot and Greek pottery.
1970 Inauguration of the Gregorian Profane and Pio-Christian Museums, formerly in the Lateran Palace, in the new building built for this purpose, designed by the Passarelli brothers.
1972-'75 New arrangement of some works of the Pio-Clementine Museum to facilitate the flow of visitors. Installation of a daytime television control and telecommunications system. Reorganization of visitor services, with new post office, foreign exchange office, writing-room, first aid stations, cloakroom and cafeteria. Construction of a new exit stairway for tour groups from the Sistine Chapel directly to St. Peter's Square.
1973 Inauguration of the Missionary-Ethnological Museum, formerly in the Lateran Palace. Inauguration of the Carriage Museum, and of the Collection of Modern Religious Art. New arrangement of the first three rooms (of the so-called Primitives) of the Pinacoteca.
1976 Re-opening of the first and second rooms of the Egyptian Museum, completely refurbished.
1977 Renovation and rearrangement of the Room of the Greek Originals. Changes to the layout and presentation of the Raphael Room in the Pinacoteca are made. The publication of a *Bulletin of the Vatican Museums* begins. Introduction of selective itineraries for visitors, with routes indicated by a colour-key.

John Paul II

1979 New arrangement of the first three rooms of the Etruscan Museum.
1980 New arrangement of the Cortile della Pigna. The base of the Column of Antoninus Pius moved to the Court of the Corazze. New arrangement of the Profane Epigraphical Collection from the Lateran,
1981 Restoration of frescoes by Michelangelo in the Sistine Chapel begins.
1982 Reorganization of the Restoration and Scientific Research Laboratories.
1984 New rooms of Byzantine icons and of the original models by Bernini in the Pinacoteca.
1985 Historical Museum transferred to the Lateran. Foundation of the Carriage Museum, formerly a section of the Historical Museum.
1987 Introduction of special itineraries for disabled visitors in wheelchairs.
1988 Acquisition of the second part of the Guglielmi Collection for the Gregorian Etruscan Museum. Transfer of the "Greek Originals" from the rooms named after them to the Gregorian Profane Museum.
1989 Reorganization of the first four rooms of the Gregorian Egyptian Museum. Completion of the restoration of the Sistine Chapel ceiling.
1991 Inauguration of the Vatican Historical Museum in the Pontifical Apartment in the Lateran Apostolic Palace.
1992 New arrangement of the first sector of the Gregorian Etruscan Museum.
1994 Completion of the restoration of Michelangelo's *Last Judgement* in the Sistine Chapel. New arrangement of the second sector of the Gregorian Etruscan Museum. Restoration of the Lapidary Gallery.
1996 New arrangement of the third sector of the Gregorian Etruscan Museum. Inauguration of new rooms dedicated to the collection of miniature mosaics and Medieval and Renaissance ceramics.
1997 Restoration of Fra Angelico's frescoes in the Chapel of Nicholas V.
1998 New arrangement of the collection of Borghese-Hercolani religious vestments in the Vatican Historical Museum at the Lateran Apostolic Palace. Completion of the restoration of the fifteenth-century frescoes of Scenes from the Life of Moses and of Christ in the Sistine Chapel.
2000 Inauguration of the new entrance to the Vatican Museums. Re-arrangement of the rooms of oriental antiquities in the Gregorian Egyptian Museum.
2002 Restoration of Pinturicchio's frescoes in the Borgia Apartment begins.
2004 Restoration of the Pauline Chapel in the Apostolic Palace begins.

GUIDE TO THE VATICAN MUSEUMS

From the entrance to the museum collections

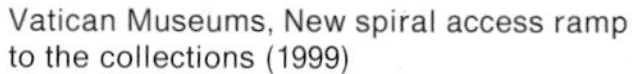
Vatican Museums, New spiral access ramp to the collections (1999)

Giuseppe Momo, Double spiral stairway (1932)

On 7 February 2000 His Holiness John Paul II inaugurated the new entrance to the Museums. Opened in the bastions of the Vatican walls, the new entrance is situated to the left of the previous entrance from Viale Vaticano, which is now used as an exit.

The imposing building project (some 40,000 cubic metres of earth were removed) was made to accomodate the growing number of visitors to the Museums: over the last twenty years they have risen from one and half million per year to roughly three million today. The project consisted not just of a new entrance but also provided for the enlargement and improvement of facilities and services.

The entrance consists of a large and modern building on four floors. The first two floors receive the public. On the ground floor are information and guided visits offices, currency exchange, and a museum store. A monumental polychrome floor mosaic found in a Roman villa on the Via Ardeantina (San Cesareo) graces in the main hall. The design is mainly geometric, but it has a centre scene executed with smaller tesserae representing the head of the Medusa. The lower frieze illustrates perhaps the *Navalia*, the military gate on the Tiber. The mosaic dates back to the mid-1st century B.C. At the end of the museum's itinerary are a pizzeria and cafeteria. For the new entrance two important contemporary works of art were commissioned: the large entrance door, made by the sculptor Cecco Buonanotte, its vibrant bronze surface evoking the theme of the Creation, and the imposing marble sculpture called *Crossing the Threshold* by Giuliano Vangi, which celebrates the themes of the

Vatican Museums, Simonetti Staircase

Pontificate of John Paul II. The ticket offices and cloakrooms are situated on the upper floor. A large spiral ramp takes visitors to the *Court of the Corazze* where they will find all the necessary indications for visiting to the collections or to find museum services (audioguides, post office, currency exchange, shops).

The new entrance has made it possible to create a smoother flow of visitors and has also enabled completion of the one-way visiting itinerary, by separating the entrance from the exit. Visitors now exit through the previous entrance, by way of the double spiral stairway created by the architect Giuseppe Momo in 1932.

From the glass covered Court of the Corazze visitors walk up to the *Atrium of the Four Gates* and from there to the museum collections. The *Atrium of the Four Gates* is a monumental edifice built on a square plan, in the neoclassical style; it is topped by a dome. Built by Giuseppe Camporese in 1792-93, it was originally used as the entrance to the Museums, with access from the avenue to the Vatican Gardens. The interior is decorated with eight life-size statues arranged symmetrically in niches. These are idealized statues and portraits dating to the Roman Imperial period (1st and 2nd centuries A.D.).

The Atrium leads into the *Vestibule of the Four Gates*. Beyond the vestibule, through a gate, is the Cortile della Pigna (see p. 42). It derives its name from the bronze pine cone (*pigna*) formerly kept in the atrium of the Constantinian Basilica of St. Peter, replaced in the 16th century by the present Basilica. It is now installed at the centre of a huge niche at one end of the court (the so-called *Nicchione*), built by Pirro Ligorio during the papacy of Pius IV, developing an exedra formerly designed by Donato Bramante and later modified by Michelangelo).

To the left of the Vestibule of the Four Gates begins the actual VISIT

Vatican Museums, Court of the Corazze

TO THE MUSEUMS. At the top of the first flight of the imposing *Simonetti Staircase,* is a landing leading to the Greek Cross Room, the first of twelve rooms of the Pio-Clementine Museum, described below (see p. 44). This magnificent ceremonial staircase is named after its architect, Michelangelo Simonetti, who built it and the Greek Cross Room in the 1780s, drawing his inspiration from Roman Imperial baths (the barrel vault is supported by antique columns, most of them from the environs of Rome).

From the same landing of the Simonetti Staircase, to the right, is the entrance to the Egyptian Museum.

plan →

a - Egyptian Museum

Painted bas-relief dating from the Old Kingdom.

Founded by Gregory XVI in 1839, the Egyptian Museum was set up by Father L. M. Ungarelli, one of the first Italian Egyptologists. Rooms I and II still contain decorative motifs which imitate Egyptian architecture — cornices, columns and winged solar discs. In Room II note the inscription to Gregory XVI on the cornice, written in hieroglyphics and composed by Father Ungarelli to celebrate the foundation of the museum. Rooms III and IV still retain their original early 19th century decoration, with the walls painted in imitation alabaster and various landscapes evoking Egypt painted by Giuseppe de Fabris.

The collection is made up of Egyptian antiquities acquired by the popes from the late 18th century onwards, but especially of statues found in Rome (and its environs), brought from Egypt in Roman times; also on display are Egyptian-style objects produced in Italy in the 1st and 2nd centuries in imitation of Egyptian originals.

ROOM I I

This room houses a collection of objects and monuments (stelae, statues and other artefacts) with inscriptions, dating from the Old Kingdom to the Christian era.

Of particular interest: 1

Throne of a seated statue of Ramses II (dynasty 19; *c.*1250 B.C.). Inv. 22673.

Two *stelae* (inv. 22775, inv. 22774) and a *bas-relief* from the Old Kingdom (*c.*2400 B.C.). Inv. 22765. 2

A large *stele* celebrating some of the work undertaken in the temple of Karnak by Queen Hatshepsut and her grandson Thutmose III (dynasty 18; *c.*1400 B.C.). Inv. 22780. 3

A *scarab* commemorating the excavation of an enormous lake undertaken by Amenophys III (dynasty 18; *c.*1350 B.C.) near his Malgatta palace on the west bank of Thebes. Inv. 25101. 4

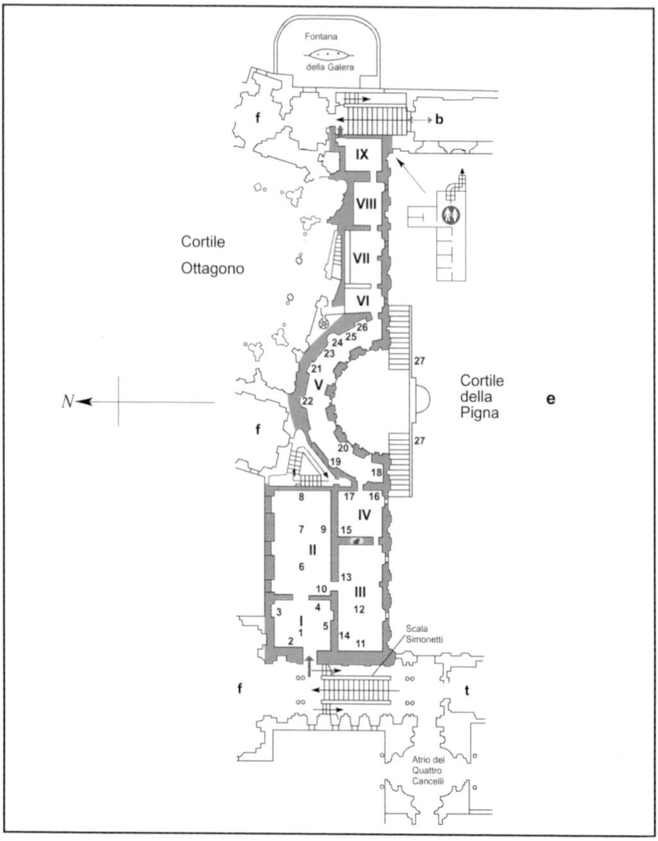

I
5 *Statue of the high priest Udja-Hor-resne* offering a naos (temple), with its inscriptions recalling the conquest of Egypt by the Persian king Cambyses in 525 B.C., some scenes of the conquest and the important role that Udja-Hor-resne played as admiral in critical moments of the history of Egypt. Inv. 22690.

II

ROOM II

6 Objects relating to the funerary cult of the Old Kingdom are exhibited in this room.

7 In the central showcase *painted sarcophagi,* most of them dating to the dynasty 21 (*c.*1000 B.C.), are *two mummies* and a collection of *canopic jars* in which the entrails extracted from dead bodies during mummification were conserved.

8 The other showcases display funerary equipment, including a fine collection of *ushabtis* (statuettes intended to substitute the deceased in their humble labours in the afterlife).

9 Displayed in a special vitrine is the linen cloth painted with a female portrait, the so-called *Lady of the Vatican*; the portrait comes from Antinoe and dates to the 3rd century A.D.

10 On the way out, in the showcase near the door, we can see two *funerary masks* of the Roman period (one in plaster, the other in gilt cartonnage) and a fine painted shroud of the 3rd century A.D. from Antinopolis (Middle Egypt).

ROOM III III

Here we find a reconstruction of the most evocative part of the decoration of the Serapeum of the *Canopus* in Hadrian's Villa, the vast complex built near Tivoli on the outskirts of Rome by the emperor Hadrian (117-138). This building, of complex significance, symbolically represented Egypt submerged by the floodwaters of the Nile and was lavishly decorated with statues of the Hadrianic era, imitating Egyptian statuary.

A *colossal bust of Isis-Demeter* was placed at the base of the 11
monument where a waterfall gushed forth, symbolizing the impetuous floodwater of the Nile.

Water from the Nile then passed under a bridge where a group of 12
statues represented the *ceremony of the awakening of Osiris-Apis,* that is, Serapis (a double bust on a lotus flower) symbolizing the eternal rebirth of the sun in its daily cycle. Gods inside the niches witnessed the scene: note that the two statues placed at the end of the bridge are turned slightly to "look" toward the centre.

Statues of Osiris-Antinous (representation in Egyptian dress of 13, 14
Antinous, Hadrian's favourite, deified after he drowned in the Nile in 130 A.D., during a journey of the emperor in Egypt) completed the scene.

ROOM IV IV

The room contains statues and bas-reliefs that are imitations of Egyptian originals sculpted in Italy in the Roman Imperial period to decorate temples or holy places sacred to Egyptian deities in Rome and its environs.

Apart from the colossal *Nile* in black marble, the following should be noticed:

Fountain-statue of Hapy, the deity of the floodwater of the Nile (late 1st 15
century B.C., or early 1st century A.D.); the water that passed through the body of the statue, and that spouted from its open mouth, was considered the water of the Nile essential for various rituals; the statue undoubtedly comes from the Gardens of Sallust. Inv. 22809.

Statue of Anubis, deity of mummification and the conductor of the 16
dead to the underworld: here he retains a dog's head but is clothed in Roman dress and has the attributes of Hermes with whom he was identified (1st century A.D., from Anzio). Inv. 22840.

Statue of a baboon found in the *Serapeum* of the Campus Martius in 17
Rome. The statue is the "cacco" of the Church of S. Stefano del Cacco (from *macaco*-monkey). Inscribed on its base are the names of the sculptors Ammonius and Phydias (on the right) and the text of the decree of 159 A.D. (on the left) which authorised its place in the temple. Inv. 22833.

ROOM V (HEMICYCLE) V

On display here is the collection of Egyptian statues, some of which come from Rome and its environs.

Note especially:

Head of King Mentuhotep from the dynasty 11 (*c.*2100 B.C.). Inv. 18
22680.

Statue of the lion goddess Sekhmet (other examples are on the 19
terrace of the hemicycle) from the temple of Mout at Karnak where

two series of 365 statues of this deity, protectress of every day and night of the year, were found (age of Amenophis III, dynasty 18 *c.*1350 B.C.) Inv. 22657. Showcase to the right.

20 *Fragment of a bas-relief* from an Old Kingdom tomb (dynasty 6 *c.*2250 B.C.). Inv. 22765.

21 A splendid *torso of King Nektanebos I,* from dynasty 30 (378-361 B.C.), one of the last native pharaohs; the torso was found at Nepi, near Rome. Inv. 22671.

22-25 Group of *four colossal statues* comprising a statue of *Queen Tuia,*
22 mother of Ramses II (dynasty 19 *c.*1250 B.C.), a statue of *Ptolemy*
24 *Philadelphus,* the Greek King of Egypt (283-246 B.C., inv. 22681), a
23 statue of his wife *Arsinoes II* (inv. 22682) and another in imitation of
25 the latter (inv. 22683). The statues were found in the Gardens of Sallust in Rome, and no doubt installed there by the emperor Caligula (37-41 A.D.), whose insanity led him to pose as a pharaoh. Caligula, like Ramses II, was deeply attached to his mother, Agrippina and, like Ptolemy Philadelphus, married and deified his sister, Drusilla, whose statue (a replica of the one of Arsinoes) was probably commissioned by him.

26 Anthropomorphic statue of the sacred bull, *Apis* (3rd-2nd century B.C.), perhaps found in Rome or its environs (Hadrian's Villa?); it was in the collection of the engraver Piranesi before becoming part of the papal collections. Inv. 22808.

VI

ROOM VI

Display of Egyptian bronze artefacts of the 10th to 4th century B.C., formerly in the collection of Carlo Grassi, and donated to Pope Pius XII by his widow Nedda Grassi. In showcase 1 are displayed sacred animals of ancient Egypt, worshiped as apotropaic symbols and charms, representations of popular deities, or amulets. In showcase 2 is a selection of bronze statuettes of deities, which illustrate the various groups of gods in each of the capitals of Egypt (Thebes, Memphis, etc.). In showcase 3 is a series of objects used in rituals; conspicuous among them is a censer used by priests and pharaohs.

VII

ROOM VII

Room VII is dedicated to Alexandria in Egypt and Palmyra in Syria. On the left on entering the room is a portrait of Ptolemy III (264-222 B.C.). The divine Triad of Alexandria (Isis, Serapis and Harpocrates) is represented by a series of bronze statuettes displayed in showcase 1. In showcase 2 is a selection of bronze and terracotta statuettes exemplifying the Alexandrine production of portraits and caricatures diffused throughout the Mediterranean in the age of the Ptolemies (3rd to 1st century B.C.).

The art of Palmyra is represented by funerary reliefs with male and female busts (1st to 3rd century A.D.) bequeathed by Federico Zeri; they are arranged in a niche that schematically reproduces those of the subterranean tombs of the great trading city in Syria.

VIII

ROOM VIII

On the left side are antiquities from Syria and Palestine (pottery, weapons, flint cutting tools, personal objects) that illustrate material culture from the Neolithic to the Roman period (8500 B.C. – 394 A.D.).

On the right side are tablets with cuneiform inscriptions and cylindrical seals from Mesopotamia (Iraq, Iran). Note in particular the large decorative nail from the Ziggurat of King Untash Napirisha (1340-1300 B.C.) at Choga Zanbil (south-western Iran) and, in the showcase of the tablets, the cylindrical seal signed by Nebuchadnezzar II (605-562 B.C.), that celebrates the refounding of a temple in the city of Maradda (southern Mesopotamia).

ROOM IX

IX

Objects displayed in this room are divided into four sections, each dedicated to the reliefs that decorated the palace of a neo-Assyrian sovereign. The first group, to which the winged genius kneeling in adoration of the sacred tree and a winged genius with an eagle head belong, contains reliefs and inscriptions from the palace of King Assrurnasirpal II (883-859 B.C.) at Nimrod; the second, two long inscriptions, an inscribed brick and a head from the citadel of Sargon II (721-705 B.C.) at Khorsabad; the third, reliefs with scenes from military and civilian life from the "inimitable palace" of Sennacherib (705-681 B.C.) at Nineveh; and the fourth, reliefs with scenes of war and deportation from the hunting palace (North Palace) of Assurbanipal (668-631 B.C.), also in Nineveh.

TERRACE OF THE HEMICYCLE (X)

X

On display here are numerous statues of the lion goddess Sekhmet (cf. no. 18 in the Hemicycle) and three sarcophagi from the Late Period (6th to 5th century B.C.).

At the bottom of the stairs and to the side of the fountain below the pine cone, are *two lions in grey granite* from the reign of Nektanebos I (378-361 B.C.; cf. no. 21 in the Hemicycle); both were found in the temple of Isis and Serapis in the Campus Martius. 27

plan →

b - Chiaramonti Museum

Bust portraits of the Imperial period.

Leaving the Egyptian Museum, a landing at the end of the long corridor designed by Donato Bramante connects the Apostolic Palace (floor of the Borgia Apartment) with the Palazzetto del Belvedere, then used as the summer residence of the Pope. To the right, in the direction of the Apostolic Palace, there is an unbroken view through the long corridor that goes from the Chiaramonti Museum and Lapidary Gallery (see p. 38) to the first loggia of the San Damaso Courtyard.

The Chiaramonti Museum, named after the family of its founder Pius VII, has changed little in appearance since it was first laid out by the great sculptor Antonio Canova.

Nearly a thousand pieces of ancient sculpture of every kind are exhibited in this museum: statues of gods, portrait statues, pagan altars, architectural ornaments, urns and sarcophagi. The paintings in the lunettes are by artists of the Academy of St. Luke, commissioned by Canova to commemorate the stimulus the Pope gave to the fine arts. The *Museum Claramontanum Pioclementino adiectum*, founded by Pius VII in the seventh year of his pontificate, is celebrated in a lunette (bay XLI, on the left), painted by Luigi Agricola.

The walls on both sides are divided into bays, each of which is indicated by a Roman numeral (odd numbers on the left, even numbers on the right).

1 I. *Sarcophagus of C. Junius Euhodus and of Metilia Acte*, datable by its inscription to 161-170 A.D. It comes from Ostia. Scenes from the myth of Alcestis, who chose to die in place of her husband, Admetus. The heads of Admetus and Alcestis are portraits of the deceased. Inv. 1195.

2 II. Lower shelf: herm of *Hephaestus,* identified by his *pileus* (conical felt cap). Roman version of a famous statue of Hephaestus by Alkamenes, 430 B.C. Inv. 1211.

3, 4 VII. Above, on the wall: *fragments of relief depicting Aglaurids and*
3 *Horae.* Inv. 1283, 1284. Three *female figures dancing towards the left,* identifiable as the Aglaurid sisters, dispensers of nocturnal dew: Aglauros, Pandrosos and Herse (Inv. 1284). *Figure moving towards*

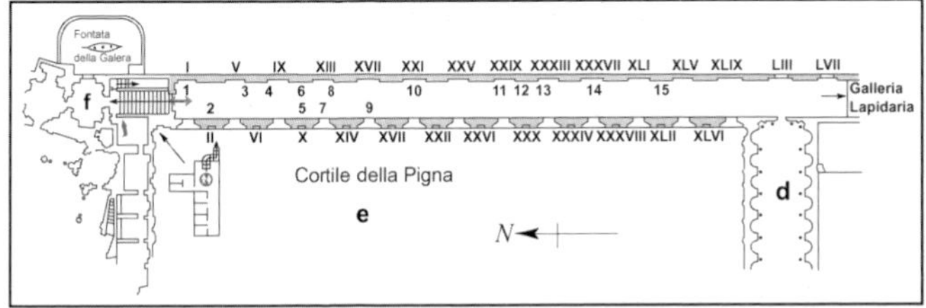

the right, identifiable as a *Hora* (one of the four goddesses of the 4
seasons) (Inv. 1283). Aglaurids and Horae are harmoniously balanced in the composition. Found together on the Esquiline. Neo-Attic copy of the Hadrianic period (2nd century A.D.) based on a 4th century B.C. model.

X. On the floor: *funerary monument of the miller P. Nonius Zethus,* 5
block of marble with conical recesses for cinerary urns. Both the reliefs at the sides of the inscription show that the deceased was a miller and flour merchant (1st century A.D.). Inv 1343.

XI. Lower shelf: head of *Cicero* (106-43 B.C.), probably a Renaissance 6
replica. Inv. 1359.

XII. Above, against the wall: *funerary statue of Cornutus* as Saturn. 7
The statue itself speaks in the inscription: "Here am I, Cornutus, sorrowful, with my eight beloved children". The face is a portrait of Cornutus, but the figure—bearded, mantled, bearing a sickle in the right hand, surrounded by boys bearing fruit—is a typical representation of Saturn, Lord of the Golden Age. Late Roman Imperial period (end of 3rd century A.D.) Inv. 1369.

XIII. Statue of *Ganymede with eagle.* Roman sculpture of the Imperial 8
period. Inv. 1376.

XVI. Colossal head of *Athena,* perhaps intended for a statue made of 9
other material. The restored eyes re-create the vivid gaze characteristic of ancient works. The model of this Roman copy (from the Hadrianic era) is thought to be Phidias' *Athena Promachos* (5th cent. B.C.) Inv. 1434.

XXI. Seated portrait of *Tiberius* (emperor 14-37 A.D.). Type of statue 10
frequently adopted in representations of Jupiter. Inv. 1511.

XXIX. Colossal head of *Augustus* (died 14 A.D.), from Veii. Inv. 1639. 11
—Colossal head of *Tiberius* (emperor 14-37 A.D.), from Veii. Inv. 12
1642.

XXXI. Above, on the wall: relief with the *Three Graces.* The original 13
from which it derives could be one of the reliefs with the same subject in the Propylaea, at the entrance to the Acropolis of Athens, where a cult was devoted to the Three Graces. The original dates back to about 470 B.C., this copy to the late 1st century B.C. Inv. 1669.

XXXVII. Statue of *Hercules* leaning on his club, the lion skin over his 14
left forearm. The original would appear to belong to the school of Lysippos (4th century B.C.) Inv. 1771.

XLIII. On the floor: statuette of *Ulysses,* part of a group representing 15
the Cyclops episode; here the hero offers a drink to Polyphemus. Roman work (1st century A.D.) inspired by Greek models. Inv. 1901.

c - Lapidary Gallery

View of the gallery

The Lapidary Gallery lies beyond the gate at the end of the Chiaramonti Museum, and may be visited on request.

Situated in the Bramante corridor and built to connect the Apostolic Palace with the Belvedere of Innocent VIII (1484-1492), the Lapidary Gallery may be considered an inexhaustible source for the study of the Roman and Christian world, and one of the most significant testimonies of the important role played by enlightened popes and men of letters in the field of collecting and history of epigraphic studies.

The collection, formed gradually during the 18th century, was ordered by Gaetano Marini (1740-1815), who personally supervised the division and display of the inscriptions, of which over 3000 are installed in the gallery. They comprise a large variety of types of inscriptions, mostly pagan but in part Christian (approximately 900), and monuments (panels, pedestals, cippi, urns, altars, sarcophagi, etc.) They are organized by subject in 48 numbered bays, proceeding from the Borgia Apartment, the former entrance at the opposite end of the gallery.

The sectors on the left side concern: Roman deities and priests, emperors, consuls and magistrates, inscriptions from the excavations at Ostia Antica patronised by Pius VII; the army, professions and posts in the imperial household, arts and crafts, Greek inscriptions of all categories, social conditions and relations (patrons, freedmen, brothers, parents, etc.).

The sectors on the right side include especially Christian inscriptions, epigraphs describing social relations and pagan inscriptions of all kinds.

Two large wooden beams are located in the middle of the corridor. They were recovered by Annesio Fusconi from the bottom of Lake Nemi near Rome and belong to the vessels of the emperor Caligula (37-41 A.D.) used as "floating villas". They are among the few surviving remains of the two ships, unfortunately destroyed by fire during the war in 1944.

At the end of the Gallery, we may observe the *trompe l'oeil* perspective, painted in "imitation of Raphael's Logge" by the famous Bolognese "perspective" painter Angelo Toselli in 1814, to create the illusion of the presence of two logge instead of one as the backdrop to the Gallery itself.

d - Braccio Nuovo

North wall

Visitors now enter the Braccio Nuovo ("new wing") from the Chiaramonti Museum.

Pius VII decided to build this new wing in 1806, but it was not until 1817 (after the sculptures Napoleon had "deported" to Paris were returned) that it could be built. The wing was designed by the Roman architect Raffaele Stern; he died on 30 December 1820. The work was completed by Pasquale Belli and was inaugurated in 1822. The reliefs above the niches are by Massimiliano Laboureur. The ancient mosaics (2nd cent. A.D.) set into the floor are from excavations near Tor Marancia, on the Via Ardeatina (note in particular the mosaic representing the *Adventures of Ulysses*).

On the right:

Statue of *Silenus cradling the child Dionysus in his arms.* A Roman copy of a Greek original of about 300 B.C. Inv. 2292. 1

Statue of the *Augustus of Prima Porta,* wearing a *lorica* (leather cuirass). Found in 1863 in Livia's Villa on the Via Flaminia, near Prima Porta, from which the statue takes its name. The portrait head identifies the figure as Augustus, who is represented in the pose of adlocutio: his right arm is raised, and the fact that he is wearing armour suggests that he is addressing his soldiers. The relief decorations on the cuirass are of special interest. The central scene refers to an event that took place in 20 B.C.: a Parthian King (Phraates IV?) returns the Roman military insignia, lost by Crassus in 53 B.C., to Augustus' legate (Tiberius). The whole cosmos witnesses this success of the Augustan policy of pacification: above, *Caelus* raising his outspread mantle, *Sol* on a quadriga, and, in front of him, personifications of *Dawn* and *Dew*; below, *Tellus*, the Roman earth goddess; at the sides, *Apollo*, holding a lyre, on a winged griffin, and *Diana*, holding a torch, on a stag. At the sides of the central scene are two seated female figures, personifications of provinces (*Germania* and *Dalmatia*?). The only decoration on the back of the cuirass is the rough outline of a *tropaeum.* The weight-bearing leg is supported by the figure of Cupid riding a dolphin (an allusion to Venus, progenitrix of the *gens Julia*, to which Augustus belonged). The emperor's bare 2

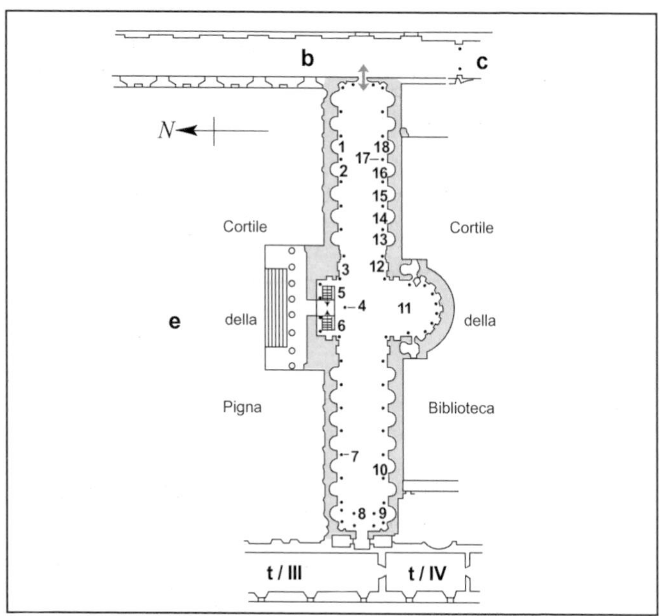

feet are in keeping with the heroic treatment of the subject (the position of the legs was taken from the *Doryphoros*). This is a copy, probably made for Livia after the death of Augustus (14 A.D.), of a bronze statue erected in honour of Augustus shortly after 20 B.C.. Inv. 2290.

3 Statue of *Titus* (emperor 79-81 A.D.) wearing a toga. The toga was the civilian dress of the Roman citizen, and the emperor is presented here as *primis inter pares*. The richly carved drapery with *sinus*, *balteus*, and *umbo* is a characteristic of the Flavian period. Inv. 2282.

4 Head of *Julius Caesar* (assassinated 15 March 44 B.C.) on a bust not belonging to it. It has been so extensively reworked that nothing remains of the original surface (cf. p. 51: VI/10). Inv. 2309.

5, 6 Two *peacocks* in gilded bronze. During the Middle Ages they stood in the first forecourt of Constantine's Basilica of St. Peter. They probably came from Hadrian's mausoleum (Castel Sant'Angelo). Symbol of astral immortality. Inv. 5117 and 5120.

7 Bust of *Pupienus* (emperor in 238 A.D.) wearing a toga. Inv. 2265.

8 Facing the entrance to the Vatican Library: bust of *Pius VII*, founder of the Braccio Nuovo, sculpted by Antonio Canova. Inv. 2301.

On the opposite side of the gallery:

9 Statue of *Demosthenes*, Attic orator, enemy of the Macedonians (died 322 B.C.). Roman copy of a bronze original, by Polyeuktos, installed in the Athenian Agora in 280 B.C. Inv. 2255.

10 Statue of a *wounded Amazon*, copy of a statue by Kresilas. The bronze original dates to 430 B.C.; one of the statues from Ephesos (cf. p. 50: V/10, copy after Phidias). Inv. 2252.

11 Colossal statue of the *Nile*, probably found in 1513 (under Leo X) near the Church of Santa Maria Sopra Minerva (site of the ancient temple of Isis and Serapis). The river god, identified by the sphinxes and

crocodiles, is represented as a dispenser of blessings; the sixteen putti are thought to be an allusion to the number of cubits the level of the Nile rises when it floods, fertilizing the region through which it flows. The reliefs on the base represent life on the banks of the river. 1st century A.D. Roman work, probably based on a Hellenistic original. Inv. 2300.

Statue of *Julia,* daughter of the emperor Titus. Found in the Lateran, 12
together with the statue of Titus opposite (see above: 3). The hairstyle is typical of the Flavian era; about 80 A.D. Inv. 2225.

Statue of the *Giustiniani Athena,* named after its first owner. Athena 13
is identified by the helmet, shield and serpent. Roman version (2nd cent. A.D.) of a Greek bronze of the 4th century B.C. Inv. 2223.

Statue of emperor wearing a toga with a fine portrait of the emperor 14
Claudius (ruled 41-54 A.D.); the head and body do not belong together. Inv. 2221.

Statue of a *resting satyr,* a modest copy of one of the most admired 15
works of antiquity, a statue unanimously attributed to Praxiteles. (Cf. other copies p. 144: II, 37-39, and p. 50: V/7). Inv. 2219.

Portrait head of *Lucius Verus* (died 169 A.D.) placed on a statue of an 16
athlete. On stylistic grounds the latter is thought to be a copy of an original by Myron of the 5th century B.C. Inv. 2217.

Bust of *Philip the Arab* (Emperor 244-249 A.D.) Inv. 2216. 17

Statue of the *Doryphorus* (spearbearer), a Roman copy of a bronze 18
original by Polykleitos of 440 B.C. The expression and attitude are simple and clear, yet conceived with supreme art. One leg carries the weight, while the other is relaxed; one arm is in action, while the other is at rest. Action and inaction alternate and are fused together in this figure, down to the smallest details. Tradition has it that Polykleitos created a model statue called the "Canon" as the perfect embodiment of the theoretical principles of his art. The original of the work before us could well be that statue, as it appears to epitomise the art of Polykleitos. Inv. 2215.

To continue the tour of the Museums, return to the entrance of the Chiaramonti Museum and proceed to the Pio-Clementine Museum (p. 44).

e - Cortile della Pigna

View of the Cortile della Pigna

The Cortile della Pigna forms the northern end of the great Renaissance Belvedere Court that extended from the Papal Palaces to Innocent VIII's Palazzetto del Belvedere and was later divided into three parts with the construction of Sixtus V's Library and the Braccio Nuovo of Pius VII. The present court, which takes its name from the enormous bronze pinecone (*pigna*) set into the huge hemispherical niche ('Nicchione'), is bordered on the south side by the Braccio Nuovo, on the east by the Chiaromonti Gallery, on the north by Innocent VIII's Belvedere and on the west by the galleries of the Apostolic Library.

At the centre of the 'Nicchione':

Colossal bronze pine cone. Cast in the 1st and 2nd century by a certain *P(ublius) Cincius Salvius,* who left his name on the base, it was at one time situated in the Campus Martius, in the area that is still called 'Pigna', where it served as a fountain, water gushing from holes in the scales of the cone. Possibly towards the end of the 8th century, it was moved to the atrium of the medieval St. Peter's, in the centre of a fountain covered by an ornate baldachin, identified in Renaissance drawings. Finally, in 1608, during the construction of the present Basilica, it was dismantled and placed where it stands today. Inv. 5118.

Under the pine cone:

Capital from the Baths of Alexander Severus (222-235 A.D.) with athletes and judges. Placed here as the base of the pine cone under Clement XI (1700-21). Inv. 5119.

At the sides:

Bronze copies of the *Peacocks*, recently moved to the Braccio Nuovo (p. 40: 5,6) for reasons of conservation.

At the centre of the east wing:

Colossal head of Augustus. Found on the Aventine, in the 16th century it became a part of the Mattei collection. It remained in Villa Celimontana until 1801 when it was acquired for the Vatican Museums. It must have formed part of a colossal statue with the bare parts (head, arms and legs) made of marble and the rest of masonry and stucco. The fifteenth-century restoration of the head of hair is worthy of note. Inv. 5137.

At the centre of the court:

Sphere with Sphere by Arnaldo Pomodoro. This sculpted, bronze work, was done by the artist specially for the Vatican Museums in 1990 and has a diameter of 4 metres. It occupies the site where the monument celebrating Vatican Council I (1869-70) once stood. Placed there by Leo XIII in 1885, the monument was moved by Pius XI in 1936 to the Vatican Gardens, where it is still today.

plan →

f - Pio-Clementine Museum

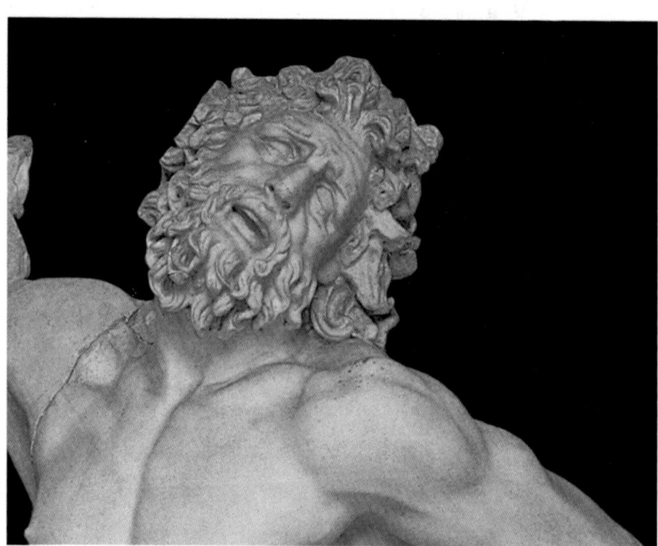

The *Laocoön* group (by the Rhodes sculptors Hagesandros, Athanodoros and Polydoros, 1st century A.D.), detail.

Pius VI added a monumental entrance to the Museum of Sculpture, the only one of its kind, in the form of the Atrium of the Four Gates (Quattro Cancelli) (see p. 29). From there visitors walked up the Simonetti staircase, and, after passing though the Greek Cross Room that served as an entrance hall, entered the Round Room, the Room of the Muses, the Room of the Animals, and from here the old Belvedere Statue Court, now the Octagonal Court. Traffic flow considerations now oblige visitors to follow the reverse route, i.e. from Room XII (Square Vestibule) to Room I (Greek Cross Room).

XII

XII: SQUARE VESTIBULE

This was the entrance-hall of the old Clementine Museum. In fact, the words MUSEUM CLEMENTINUM appear on the architrave of the *trompe-l'oeil* arch on the opposite wall.

1 In the niche in the left wall: *sarcophagus of Lucius Cornelius Scipio Barbatus* (consul in 298 B.C.), in grey tufa; from the Tomb of the Scipioni on the Appian Way. The shape of the sarcophagus indicates Greek-Hellenistic influence. The inscription, in archaic Latin verses, contains a eulogy of the deceased, and a description of his career and achievements. Inv. 1191.

IX Walk through the ROUND VESTIBULE, IX, to enter:

X

X: APOXYOMENOS CABINET

1 The *Apoxyomenos,* Roman copy (1st cent. A.D.) of a bronze original, of about 320 B.C., by Lysippos; it was found in Trastevere in 1849. The athlete has just returned from the palaestra (gymnasium); in his left hand he holds a strigil, with which he cleans the dust and sweat from his right arm (the Greek word *apoxyein* means "to wipe off"). He gazes wearily into the distance. It is an image of a winner, not at his moment of glory, but "in the aftermath of victory, when he is

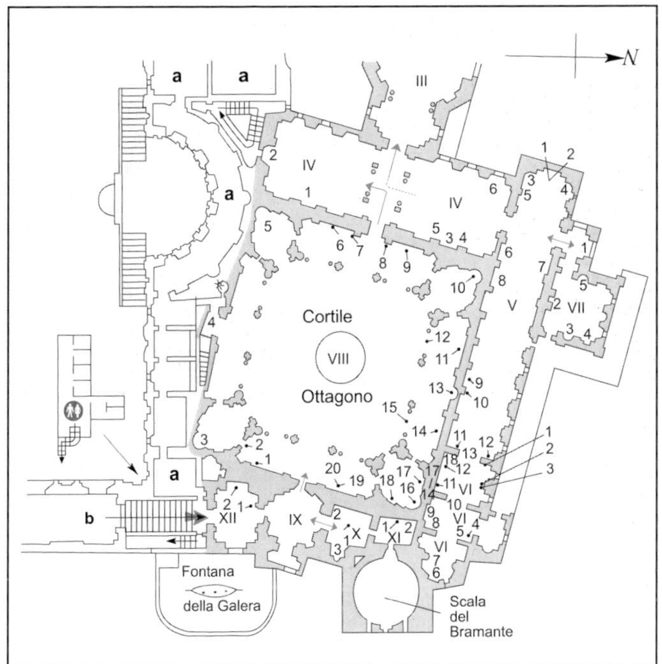

overcome by fatigue. Lysippos, who also made a statue of Alexander the Great, sought to portray men not as they are, but as they appear in the truth of each fleeting moment (Pliny, *Nat. Hist.* XXXIV, 65). Inv. 1185.

On the wall, to the right and left: inscriptions from the Tomb of the Scipioni on the Appian Way. Inv. 1149-61. On a shelf: so-called portrait head of *Ennius,* with laurel wreath, it too from the Tomb of the Scipioni. Inv. 1148. **2**

In front of the window, bust of *Clement XIV*, founder of the Museum. With his acquisition of the Fusconi and Mattei collections in 1770, he founded the new museum in the Palazzetto del Belvedere. **3**

XI: VESTIBULE XI

This small room gives access to the *Bramante Stairway*, built by Julius II in the early 16th century to provide an external entrance to the Belvedere. The spiral stairway is built within a square tower. In accordance with the principles of Vitruvius, the columns are of three types: Tuscan in the first part, Ionic in the second, and Corinthian in the third. At the base of the tower is the *Fountain of the Galley*, so named after the small lead galley (water spouts from its guns) placed there during the papacy of Clement IX. The fountain was made by Carlo Maderno for Paul V.

Above, on the wall: panels of a mosaic from the Aventine with circus and arena scenes. **1**

Large marble niche, part of a funerary tabernacle, from the environs of Todi. Second half of the 1st century A.D. Inv. 975. **2**

Return to the Round Vestibule (IX) and enter the Octagonal Court from the right.

VIII

VIII: OCTAGONAL COURT

The inner courtyard of the Belvedere, originally square and planted with orange trees, is the heart of the museum. It was here that Cardinal Giuliano della Rovere, who was elected Pope as Julius II in 1503, placed his collection of ancient statues. His famous *Apollo Belvedere* was named after this building. He also acquired other significant works such as the *Laocoön* group. In 1772, Clement XIV commissioned Michelangelo Simonetti to build the surrounding portico, which gave the court its present octagonal shape. Antonio Canova had the four corner-bays walled up in the early 19th century; they were re-opened in 1957.

1 On the left side of the portico, against the wall: *fragment of relief with subject from Roman history,* representing a laurel-wreathed attendant (*popa*) leading a large bull to sacrifice; late Republican period. Inv. 996.

2 In the centre, above the entrance: *frieze with Dionysian procession:* Bacchus and followers return from a feast. Late Hellenistic work from Campania, 1st century B.C. Inv. 977.

Also on the left side of the court, proceeding clockwise:

APOLLO BELVEDERE CABINET

3 The *Apollo Belvedere* is a Roman copy in marble of the Imperial period (*c.*130-140 A.D.) of a Greek bronze (*c.*330-320 B.C.), probably by Leochares, which once stood in the Agora of Athens (Pausanias, 1, 3, 4). Already known in the 15th century, the statue was brought by Julius II from his palace near Santi Apostoli to the Belvedere Statue Court. The hands were restored by a pupil of Michelangelo, Giovanni Angelo da Montorsoli, in 1532. The god, "he who strikes from afar", held a bow in his left hand, as a symbol of his role as avenger. In his right hand he presumably held an arrow, taken from his open quiver. The cloak draped over his shoulders and left arm emphasizes his radiant, youthful figure, the utmost expression of the nobility and purity of an Apollonian. "Thus the gods dispose that poor mortals must live in anguish, but they themselves are not touched by pain", writes Homer (*Iliad* 6, 138 and 24, 525). Hölderlin remarked of this statue, "...the eyes observe with silent, eternal light". Johann Joachim Winckelmann wrote, "Of all the works of antiquity that have escaped destruction, the statue of Apollo represents the highest ideal of art". Inv. 1015.

On the south side of the Court, partial reconstruction of the "Fountain of the Tigris", placed by Michelangelo in one of the corners of the Court.

4 Above is a *Reclining statue of a river god* (so-called Tigris) dating to the 2nd century A.D. The head and several other parts have been restored. The statue has been in the Vatican ever since 1536. Inv. 168.

4 Below: *Sarcophagus representing a battle between Greeks and Amazons* (about 160-170 A.D.). Inv. 896. During the Renaissance this served as the tub of the above-mentioned fountain.

LAOCOÖN CABINET

5 The marble *Laocoön* group was found on 14 January 1506 near the "Sette Sale" on the Esquiline Hill (Domus Aurea area). In his *Natural History* (XXXVI, 37), Pliny the Elder, who died in the eruption of Vesuvius in 79 A.D., wrote of this statue that it was the work of the

Rhodes sculptors Hagesandros, Athanodoros and Polydoros, that it stood in the palace of the emperor Titus, and that it was to be preferred to all other representations of a similar subject in painting or in bronze. The Roman writer's authority immediately enabled the statue's importance to be recognized on its discovery. Julius II purchased it on 23 March 1506, and had it brought here.

Laocoön, the priest of Apollo, and his two sons are locked in the coils of two serpents, on the steps of an altar. Laocoön's chest rises and swells as he attempts in vain to tear away the head of the serpent that is about to bite him on the hip. The other serpent has already sunk its fangs into the side of the younger son, who collapses in agony, while the elder son attempts to free himself from its coils. Virgil describes the episode in detail (*Aeneid* II, 199-233): the Trojan priest Laocoön had warned his compatriots against the wooden horse, left by the Greeks as "an offering to Athena", and had hurled his lance at it. This angered Athena, who sent serpents to kill Laocoön. Misinterpreting the omen, the Trojans ignored Laocoön's warning, and dragged the wooden horse into the city. Only Aeneas understood the true significance of the omen, and he and his family saved themselves by fleeing to Italy where Aeneas and his son Alba Longa founded Lavinium. As far back as Caesar's time the legendary Trojan ancestry of the *gens Julia* had been used as a political argument. Indeed, Augustus, made the legend the keystone of his empire, using it to justify his claim to the throne. The *Laocoön* group, which Pliny saw in the imperial palace, was probably commissioned by the emperor in the first half of the 1st century A.D., and was sculpted by the sculptors from Rhodes after a bronze original of the 2nd century B.C. The flexed right arm was discovered by Ludwig Pollak in 1905; it proved to belong to the figure of Laocoön, and was reinstated in the statue during the last restoration in 1957-60. Inv. 1059.

Continuing, above to the left, on the wall: *front of a sarcophagus with columns and three aedicules.* In the centre, the deceased, a lady; at the sides, she takes part in the teaching of philosophers (*c.*240 A.D.). Inv. 871. **6**

At the sides of the exit are two *Molossi,* Roman copies (Imperial period) of Hellenistic originals of the 3rd century B.C. Inv. 872-897. **7, 8**

On the wall: *front of a column sarcophagus* with the representation of a funeral edifice with open door (centre). About 250 A.D. Inv. 866. **9**

HERMES CABINET

Statue of *Hermes* (once erroneously attributed to Antinous). Roman copy of the Hadrianic period of a Greek original in bronze (late Classical period, 4th cent. B.C.), found near Castel Sant'Angelo. The lissom posture, and the travelling cloak thrown hastily over the left shoulder, suffice to suggest a messenger of the gods, confirmed by other copies. Some of these were found in tombs: Hermes as *Psychopompos,* guide of the dead to the underworld. Inv. 907. **10**

Proceeding leftwards: *sarcophagus with battle of Amazons;* in the centre, Achilles with helmet, Penthesilea dying. 3rd century A.D. Inv. 933. **11**

Opposite, in the passageway leading into the court: two *fragments of a large basin-shaped sarcophagus,* with groups of animals in combat on both sides. 3rd century A.D. Inv. 922. **12**

In the central niche, on the left: statue of *Venus Felix,* copy of the *Aphrodite of Cnidos* by Praxiteles (see p. 52: VII-3), with a head portrait reminiscent of the young Faustina, dating to *c.*170 A.D. **13**

According to the inscription on the plinth, the statue was dedicated to Venus Felix by Sallustia and Helpidus.

14 Proceeding leftwards: *sarcophagus of a warrior.* Here the theme of *clementia* or *mansuetudo*, i.e. the clemency or gentleness of the victor to the vanquished, is represented as one of the great Roman virtues (*c.*180 A.D.). Inv. 942.

15 On the opposite side, in the window embrasure: base with scenes from Trojan and Roman legends, the so-called *Casali Altar*, donated by the Casali family to Pius VI. As explained by the inscription in an of oak leaf wreath placed on the front, the monument was dedicated to Ti. Claudius Faventinus. Reliefs: front, Mars and Venus; back, legend of Romulus and Remus; sides, Trojan myths. The character and style of the reliefs suggest a date around 200 A.D. Inv. 1186.

CANOVA'S CABINET

When Napoleon seized the museum's most important works and shipped them to Paris, Pius VII bought three of Antonio Canova's statues (sculpted around 1800) to fill the empty spaces, and exhibited them here:

16 *Perseus triumphant* with the head of Medusa. Inv. 969.

17, 18 The boxers *Kreugas and Damoxenos.* According to Pausanias (8, 40, 3-4), the two engaged in a boxing match at Nemea, the outcome of which was uncertain; Damoxenos then stabbed his opponent in the abdomen, and tore out his intestines. The referee disqualified Damoxenos, and declared the dead Kreugas the winner. Inv. 968, 970.

19 On the entrance wall: *Bacchic sarcophagus in the shape of a tub;* pairs of dancing satyrs and maenads brandishing *thyrsi* (mid-2nd cent. A.D.). Inv. 987.

20 Above, on the wall: *relief from an unusually large sarcophagus,* with representation of a harbour. The heroized figure of the deceased appears at a standing figure in the centre, dominating the scene. His wife, portrayed as Venus, sits in front of him. Both portrait heads are unfinished (mid-3rd cent. A.D.). Inv. 973.

The visit to the Octagonal Court terminates here, cross the court and return to the two Molossi *by the passageway leading to the next room of the museum.*

IV IV: ANIMAL ROOM

This room takes its name from the statues of animals exhibited here. Most of them were so extensively and freely restored by Francesco Antonio Franzoni in the later 18th century that they may almost be considered his own works.

On the floor: ancient mosaics. In the passageway: ornamental mosaic in black and white, with eagle and hare (2nd cent. A.D.). Right and left wings: groups of twelve panels, joined together with plaited ribbons, representing still-lifes (mid-4th cent. A.D.).

South wing (to the left);

1 *Marine centaur with nereids and cupids,* a flat composition with the emphasis placed on its external contour. Perhaps a work of the Tarantine sculptor Arkesilaos (1st cent. B.C.). Inv. 464.

2 Statue of *Meleager,* hero of the Calydonian boar-hunt, with dog and boar's head. Roman version (*c.*150 A.D.) of Greek original of the 4th century B.C., probably by Skopas. Inv. 490.

North wing (to the right):

3 *Mithras group* representing the killing of the primordial bull (symbol of procreative force) by the Persian god Mithras. The shedding of its blood marks the beginning of the Creation. The scorpion, serpent and dog (evil spirits) try in vain to prevent the sacrifice. (2nd cent. A.D.) (cf. p. 159: V/23). Inv. 437.

4, 5 On the wall, two *panels of a mosaic with landscapes,* from Hadrian's Villa (cf. floor mosaics in the Mask Room, p. 51: VII). Inv. 421, 423.

6 *Crab* in green porphyry, an extremely rare stone. Inv. 393.

V: GALLERY OF STATUES — V

This gallery was once an open loggia on the lower floor of Innocent VIII's Belvedere, built by Jacopo da Pietrasanta from a plan by Antonio del Pollaiolo. Under Clement XIV it was converted into a sculpture gallery (1771) by Alessandro Dori (d. 1772). Under Pius VI, in 1776, the gallery was enlarged and joined to the Room of the Animals (which required the demolition of a chapel frescoed by Andrea Mantegna).

1 On the left, in front of the niche at the end of the gallery:

Statue of *Sleeping Ariadne* (once thought to be of Cleopatra). Ariadne, abandoned by Theseus, sleeps and awaits the divine appearance of Dionysus. A much admired copy of a Hellenistic original (of the 2nd cent. B.C.); it dates to 130-140 A.D. Inv. 548.

2 Serving as a base to the above: *sarcophagus depicting a struggle between giants with serpent-like legs, and gods* (the latter not represented here). Late 2nd century A.D. Inv. 549.

3, 4 Two *ornamental candelabra* from Hadrian's Villa near Tivoli (2nd cent. A.D.) On the bases, figures of gods in relief: Jupiter (Zeus) with sceptre and thunderbolt; Juno (Hera) with sceptre; Mercury (Hermes) with ram. Inv. 547. Mars (Ares) with helmet and lance; Venus (Aphrodite) with flower; Minerva (Athena) with parade helmet, shield and serpent. Inv. 551.

Turning our backs to the *Ariadne*, on the right side of the gallery we find:

5 Statue of *Hermes "Ingenui"* (name inscribed on the base, indicating either the sculptor or the dedicator), 2nd century Roman version of a Greek original of the 5 century B.C. Attributes: *kerykeion* (herald's staff), lyre, and wings in the hair, above the temples. Inv. 554.

6 *Eros of Centocelle* (on the Via Labicana). Identified from the marks on the back where wings were once attached. Roman copy of a Greek original (Peloponnesian school, early 4th century B.C. Inv. 561.

7 On the left side of the gallery: statue of *resting satyr,* modest copy of the famous statue attributed to Praxiteles, 4th century B.C. (cf. copies p. 144: II,37-39, and p. 41,15). Inv. 561.

Once again on the right side of the gallery:

8 *Head and torso of a triton* (water deity). Copy of the 1st century A.D. of a Hellenistic original (2nd cent. B.C.) Inv. 765.

9 Statue of *Apollo Sauroktonos* ("the lizard killer"). Roman copy of a Greek original, in bronze, by Praxiteles, of about 350 B.C. From the Palatine. A charming work in which the god is shown blissfully absorbed in his innocent game, perhaps an allusion to Apollo's combat against the monster Python, or to his healing powers. Inv. 750.

10 Statue of *Wounded Amazon.* Copy of a bronze original (the so-called *Mattei Amazon*) by Phidias of about 430 B.C., dedicated to Artemis of Ephesus. According to Pliny the Elder (*Nat. Hist.* XXXIV, 53), this work originated from a competition among artists. (Cf. p. 40:10). Inv. 748.

11 Seated portrait statue of *Posidippus,* famous Greek dramatist (died 250 B.C.), identified from the inscription on the base. Copy from an original of *c.*250 B.C. From the Viminal (found together with the next work, Inv. 588). The face has been extensively remodelled. Inv. 735.

12 On the other side of the passage: seated portrait statue, the so-called *Menander,* found together with the preceding work. Not yet satisfactorily identified. Head extensively remodelled. Inv. 588.

VI

VI: GALLERY OF BUSTS

This room is divided into three sections (indicated by Roman numerals) by three arches, each of which is supported by two columns of precious antique yellow marble.

SECTION I

1 To the left: group portrait (commonly known as *Cato and Portia)* of Gratidia M.L. Chrite and M. Gratidius Libanus, identified from an inscription no longer preserved. Busts of a Roman couple: *dextrarum iunctio.* From a tomb of the late 1st century B.C. Inv. 592.

2, 3 Between the windows: *votive offerings* of the sick; rib-cage and open abdomen. Prayer for recovery, or thanksgiving for "favour received". Inv. 597, 599.

SECTION II

On the left, beyond the small room, lower shelf:

4 Head of the *Young Caracalla* (the bust is modern), son of Septimius Severus and his successor (211-217 A.D.); probably sculpted shortly after 193 A.D. as a portrait of the future heir. Inv. 646.

5 Bust of a *boy dressed as commander-in-chief of the army* (distinguished by the *cingulum* or military belt), probably Diadumenianus (assassinated 218 A.D.), son of the emperor Macrinus. Inv. 648.

SECTION III

6 In the niche on the rear wall: statue of *Jupiter Verospi* (named after the Palazzo Verospi, where it was formerly exhibited). Jupiter is enthroned; in his left hand is a sceptre (reconstruction), in his right a thunderbolt. A work of the 3rd century A.D., it was modelled on the cult statue in the Temple of Capitoline Jupiter (a chryselephantine work—gold and ivory—by Apollonius, made after 83 B.C.). Inv. 671.

7 In front of the statue: *celestial globe* with stars and zodiac. Inv. 784.

SECTION II

Side opposite the window:

8 Lower shelf, on the left: head of *Menelaus* with parade helmet. Copy from the Hadrianic period of the celebrated group representing

Menelaus with the body of Patroclus or Ajax with that of Achilles (2nd cent. A.D.). From Hadrian's Villa near Tivoli. Inv. 694.

Upper shelf, centre: head of *Athena* on a modern bust. Found close to the Castel Sant'Angelo, it is thought to have formed part of the decoration of the mausoleum of the emperor Hadrian (117-138 A.D.). Inv. 612. 9

SECTION I

Side opposite the windows: portraits of Roman emperors.

Lower shelf, from left to right:

Head of *Julius Caesar* (assassinated 15 March 44 B.C.). Inv. 713. 10

Head of *Augustus* (died 14 A.D.), with a wreath of corn-ears, badge of the *fratres arvales*, a religious fraternity. Inv. 715. 11

Head of *Titus* (emperor 71-81 A.D.). Inv. 721. 12

Bust of *Trajan* (emperor 98-117 A.D.). Inv. 724. 13

Upper shelf, from left to right:

Head of *Antoninus Pius* (emperor 138-161 A.D.) on a bust not belonging to it. From Hadrian's Villa near Tivoli. Inv. 703. 14

Bust of *Marcus Aurelius* (emperor 161 -180 A.D.), from Hadrian's Villa. Inv. 704. 15

Bust of *Lucius Verus* (emperor together with Marcus Aurelius from 161 to 169 A.D.). Inv. 705. 16

Bust of *Commodus* (emperor 176-192 A.D.). Inv. 706. 17

Bust of *Caracalla* (emperor 211-217 A.D.). Inv. 711. 18

VII: MASK ROOM VII

The tower of Innocent VIII's Belvedere was included in the museum in 1780. The floor is decorated with four panels of an ancient mosaic with representations of masks, from which the room takes its name. Three of the panels depict theatrical masks, and the fourth an idyllic landscape with grazing animals, and a small sanctuary. They were found in 1779, together with the mosaics in the Animal Room (see p. 48: IV), in Hadrian's Villa near Tivoli, and date back to the 2nd century A.D. The frame, ornamented with heraldic devices of Pius VI, was made at the time the mosaics were brought to this room. On the ceiling are mythological scenes painted by Domenico de Angelis: the *Judgement of Paris*, the *Awakening of Ariadne*, *Diana and Endymion*, *Venus and Adonis*.

In the vestibule, *bust of Pius VI,* who enlarged and completed the museum. 1

Starting from the right, and proceeding anti-clockwise:

Statue of the *crouching Venus,* Roman copy of a famous work by Doidalsas of Bithynia (3rd cent. B.C.) The goddess of love is shown crouching under a spout of water, intent on her ablutions. Inv. 815. 2

Statue of the *Venus of Cnidos,* Roman copy of the famous cult statue (sanctuary of Cnidos) carved by Praxiteles in the mid-4th century B.C. This work was famous in its day (Pliny, *Nat. Hist.* XXXVI, 20), and is known to us through numerous copies, though none of these remotely attains the high artistic standard of the original; above all the splendid 3

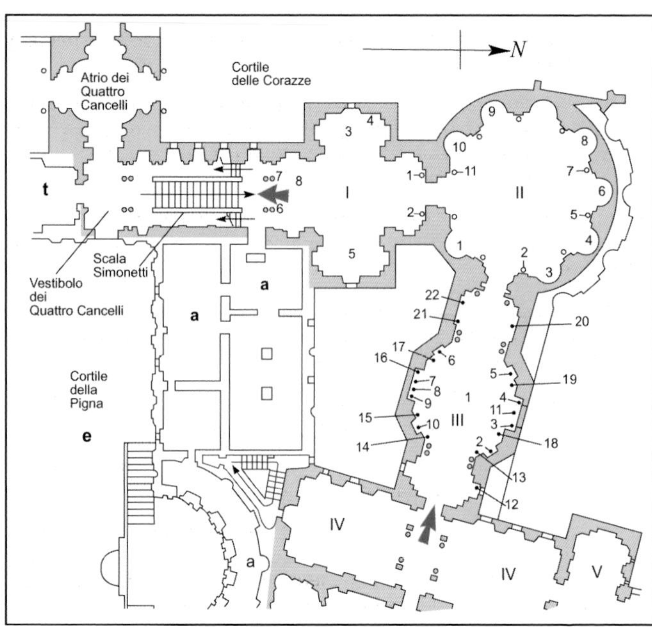

luminosity of the surface texture has been lost. Her clothes draped over the bath, the goddess of love appears in the nude in a cult statue for the first time in history. Serene and imperturbable in her divine essence, she seems unconscious of the presence of any onlooker. Inv. 812.

4 *Group of the Three Graces,* a 2nd century A.D. Roman copy of a late Hellenistic work, whose charm consists of the interplay of variation and repetition. Inv. 810.

5 Statue of *satyr* in red marble; from Hadrian's Villa (2nd cent. A.D.). Inv. 801.

To reach the Room of the Muses, return to the Animal Room and go through the door on the right (opposite the door leading to the Octagonal Court).

III III: ROOM OF THE MUSES

This room was built by Michelangelo Simonetti around 1780. The ceiling frescoes, the work of Tommaso Conca, depict Apollo, the Muses and poets, forming a thematic link with the statues exhibited here (see below).

1 The *Belvedere Torso*, fragment of a neo-Attic statue of the 1st century B.C., was placed at the centre of this room in 1973. The muscular figure is seated on an animal skin spread over a rock, on which are inscribed the words "made by Apollonius, Athenian, son of Nesto". The remaining fragments of the animal's head can be seen on the left thigh. According to the traditional interpretation, this is a lion's head, and consequently the figure ought to be that of Hercules, though the names of Marsyas, Skyron, Polyphemus and Philoctetes have also been suggested. But more recent studies have permitted the real subject of the statue to be identified: *Ajax committing suicide.* Found in the 15th century, the statue was first kept in the Palazzo Colonna, and then moved to the Belvedere statue-court during the papacy of

Clement VII. It was much admired by Renaissance artists, especially by Michelangelo. Inv. 1192.

Against the walls are seven statues, imaginatively restored, of the *Muses*, and one of *Apollo*, the god who presided over the muses. Found near Tivoli in 1774, in the so-called Villa of Cassius, they date back to the 2nd century A.D.

On the right side of the room: *Melpomene* (tragedy), Inv. 299; *Thalia* 2, 3
(comedy), Inv. 295; *Clio* (history, epic), Inv. 291; *Polyhymnia* (mime, 4, 5
song), Inv. 287.

On the left side of the room: *Erato* (hymns, love songs), Inv. 317; 6, 7
Calliope (heroic song, elegy), Inv. 312; *Apollo Citharedos,* "master" of 8, 9
the Muses, Inv. 310; *Terpsichore* (dance), Inv. 308.

Added to the group from other sites: *Euterpe* (flute playing, tragic 10
chorus), Inv. 303; *Urania* (astronomy), Inv. 293. 11

The room also contains Roman copies of portraits of famous Greeks, from other sites. To the right of the entrance:

Less than life-size bust of *Sophocles.* On the lower edge, traces of the 12
inscription bearing the name. Discovered in 1777, in the garden of the Conservatory of the Mendicants (near Constantine's Basilica). The inscription on this portrait made it possible to identify the statue from Terracina exhibited in the Gregorian Profane Museum (cf. p. 145: II,43). Inv. 322.

Head of *Epicurus* (died 270 B.C.) placed on a modern herm; 13
philosopher, founder of the Epicurean school. Inv. 301.

Opposite:

Head of *Euripides* (died 406 B.C.) from an original of about 330 B.C. 14
Inv. 302.

Herm of *Plato* (died 347 B.C.). The inscription "Zenon" is modern. Inv. 15
305.

Socrates (condemned to death 399 B.C.); from the Villa of the Quintilii 16
on the Appian Way. Identified from the Silenus-like features, as described by Alcibiades in Plato's *Symposium.* Inv. 314.

Homer (second half of the 8th cent. B.C.), *Epimenides type.* Identified 17
as Homer from the blindness of the subject represented. Copy of a Greek work of about 460 B.C. Inv. 315.

The following portrait herms of famous Greek poets, philosophers and orators (Roman copies of Greek works) are from the same Roman villa where the statues of the Muses and Apollo were found.

On the right side of the room:

Aischines (died 314 B.C.), famous Attic orator, adversary of De- 18
mosthenes; identified from the inscription. Inv. 297.

Antisthenes (died *c.*365 B.C.), founder of the Cynic philosophical 19
school; identified from the inscription. Inv. 288.

Pericles (died 429 B.C.) with Corinthian helmet of the commander-in- 20
chief of the army (*strategòs*); identified as Pericles from the inscription. Copy of a work by Kresilas (*c.*430 B.C.). Inv. 269.

Opposite:

Periander (7th to 6th cent. B.C.), son of Cypselus, tyrant of Corinth; 21
identified by the inscribed motto, "Practice does everything". Inv. 276.

22 *Bias* (6th cent. B.C.), statesman of Priene, one of the seven wise men of Greece, contemporary of Croesus; identified by the inscribed motto, "Most men are wicked". Inv. 279.

II II: ROUND ROOM

This domed rotunda (external diameter of dome *c.*21.6 m, height *c.*22 m), a Pantheon-inspired masterpiece by Michelangelo Simonetti, was built around 1780. The floor is decorated with ancient mosaics from Otricoli: battle scenes between Greeks and centaurs; marine animals with nereids and tritons. In the centre of the room is a large monolithic basin in porphyry(with a circumference of 13 m.) from the Domus Aurea (Golden House of Nero).

1 In the niche to the left of the entrance: statue of the *Genius of Augustus*, wearing a toga; a fold of the toga covers his head for the sacrificial act; in his left handholds a cornucopia (right arm with patera is restored). Inv. 259.

To the right of the entrance, proceeding anti-clockwise:

2 Colossal head of *Jupiter of Otricoll,* a Roman versionof a well-known Greek representation of Zeus of the 4th century B.C. Inv. 257.

3 Colossal statue of *Antinous* (cf. below: 7) with attributes of the Dionysus-Osiris cult: ivy wreath, band, mystic cist (near the left foot), and pine cone on the head (perhaps better identified as Uraeus, a sacred cobra). Inv. 256.

4 Statue of a goddess, restored as *Demeter,* Roman copy of a Greek work of about 420 B.C. (school of Phidias). Inv. 254.

5 Colossal head of *Hadrian* (emperor 117-138 A.D.), from his mausoleum (Castel Sant'Angelo). Inv. 253.

6 Colossal statue of *Hercules* in gilt bronze, late 2nd century A.D. Discovered in 1864 near the Theatre of Pompey, where it had been carefully buried. The stone slabs by which it had been covered were inscribed with the letters F.C.S. (*Fulgor Conditum Summanium*), indicating that the statue had been struck by lightning, and buried on the spot. Attributes of Hercules: club, lion skin, and apples of the Hesperides. Inv. 252.

7 Colossal bust of *Antinous,* the young favourite of Hadrian; after his death (he drowned in the Nile in 130 A.D.) he was deified by the emperor. From Hadrian's Villa near Tivoli. Inv. 251.

8 Statue of a goddess, the so-called *Hera Barberini;* Roman version of a late 5th century Greek work attributed to Agorakritos, pupil of Phidias. Inv. 249.

9 State of *Claudius* dressed as Jupiter; from Lanuvium. (*c.*50 A.D.). Inv. 243.

10 Statue of *Juno Sospita,* an Italic goddess from Lanuvium. Probably a cult statue of the 2th century A.D. Inv. 241.

11 Colossal portrait statue of *Plotina* (died 122 A.D.), wife of Trajan. The size of the statue suggests that it was sculpted on the occasion of her deification (129 A.D.). Inv. 240.

I: GREEK CROSS ROOM I

This room derives its name from its design in the form of a Greek cross, i.e. a cross with four equal arms. The room was built by Simonetti around 1780, during the pontificate of Pius VI. It was intended to be the entrance-hall of the Pope's museum, the PIUM MUSEUM, which appears in large letters on the architrave above the portal leading from this room to the Round Room.

The passageway between the two rooms is flanked by two *Egyptian-style statues,* architectural supports ("telamones") modelled along the lines of the Pharaoh or Osiris type. They come from Hadrian's Villa near Tivoli. Red granite (2nd cent. A.D.). Inv. 196, 197. **1, 2**

At the centre of the floor: mosaic with bust of Athena, from Tusculum, 3nd century A.D., framed in a flamboyant 18th century décor.

Right wing:

Sarcophagus of Constance, daughter of Constantine; porphyry, 350-360 A.D. From the mausoleum of Santa Costanza on the Via Nomentana. The relief depicts cupids harvesting grapes amid vine scrolls; on the long sides, two peacocks; a ram and a cupid with garland (Dionysian tradition). Inv. 237. **3**

Statue of *Augustus* (in power 31 B.C.-14 A.D.), *from Otricoli,* based on the "Diomedes" model of 5th century B.C. Greek sculpture. Inv. 181. **4**

Left wing:

Sarcophagus of St. Helena, mother of Constantine; porphyry, early 4th century A.D. From the Mausoleum of St. Helena on the Via Labicana (Tor Pignattara). Sculpted with scenes of victorious Roman cavalrymen, and prostrate fettered barbarians. Extensively restored, especially the heads and bust portraits in the upper corners, it was presumably not made for Helena, but for her husband, Constantinus Chlorus. Inv. 238. **5**

At the sides of the exit: two *reclining sphinxes* in reddish-grey granite. Roman Imperial period (1st - 3rd cent. A.D.). Inv. 236, 239. **6, 7**

On the floor, between the sphinxes: *polychrome mosaic with basket of flowers,* modern copy of an 18th century original, now removed to the Cortile delle Corazze. **8**

From here, go through the main entrance to the Pio-Clementine Museum, flanked by the two sphinxes, and return to the Simonetti Staircase. Walk up the second flight of steps to the Gregorian Etruscan Museum.

plan
→

g - Etruscan Museum

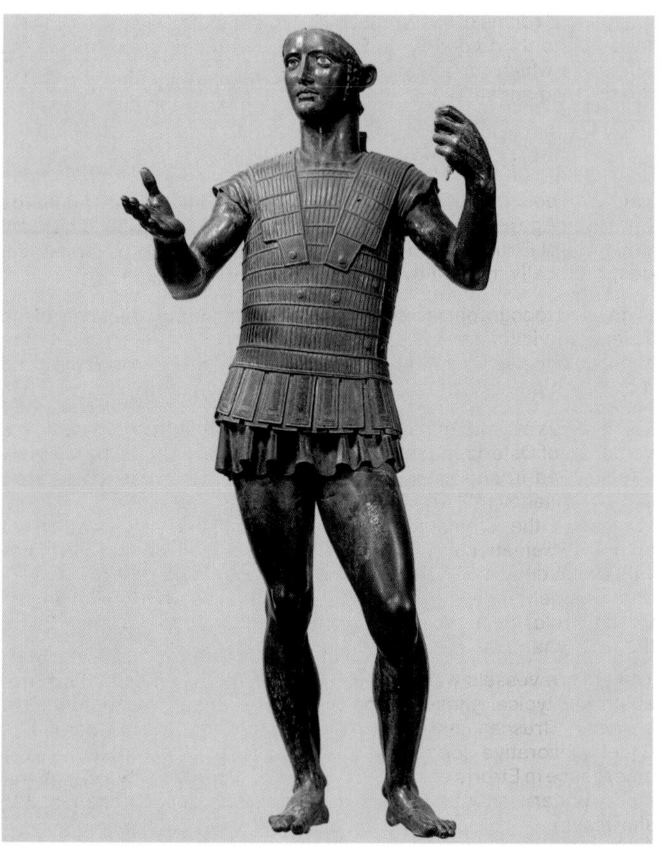

The Mars of Todi (late 5th cent. B.C.)

This museum was founded by Gregory XVI, and inaugurated on 2 February 1837. Most of the artefacts on display came from private excavations carried out in the cemeteries of Southern Etruria in what is now Lazio), with the permission of the Papal Government. They were purchased by the Apostolic Chancellery, on the recommendation of the General Advisory Committee for Antiquities and Fine Arts, and on the basis of the right of pre-emption guaranteed to public collections by the Pacca Edict of 1820. After the end of the Papal State, and of its jurisdiction over Southern Etruria, acquisitions and donations became less frequent; nonetheless, the museum grew in importance with the Falcioni Collection, purchased in 1898, Benedetto Guglielmi's donation to Pius XI in 1935, Mario Astarita's donation to Paul VI in 1967, and the purchase of the Giacinto Guglielmi Collection in 1987.

A collection of Roman antiquities (*Antiquarium Romanum*) from Rome and Latium (see p. 72), and a large collection of Greek, Italiot (from Greek-colonized southern Italy) and Etruscan vases (see p. 74), also form an integral part of the museum. These vases are of great importance for the history of ancient pottery, even though they were removed from their original archaeological site during excavations in the 18th and 19th century, following a practice common at the time. They are exhibited apart, in a separate display in the rooms overlooking the Cortile della Pigna. The rooms are parallel and communicate with the main Etruscan Museum in many places.

The central rooms of the Etruscan Museum (Rooms V-XIII) occupy the second and third floor of the Palazzetto del Belvedere. Rooms I-IV, and those which contain the Vase Collection (XX-XXI) are situated in the building added by Pius IV.

I: ROOM OF THE EARLY IRON AGE I

The first room of the Museum contains artefacts dating back to the Early Iron Age in Etruria and Lazio (9th–8th cent. B.C.). They document the dawn of Etruscan and Latin civilizations of the historical period, geographically marked by the course of the Tiber River.

In an ideal topographical reconstruction- a kind of virtual ascent of the 1
Tiber- the visitor can see the artefacts coming from Etruria in the showcase to the left (an imaginary Etruscan bank of the river), and those from *Latium Vetus* in to the one on the right (the Latian side).

The nucleus of Villanovan material excavated by Filippo Prada in the cemetery of Osteria (Casal di Lanza) at Vulci in the later 18th century is contained in *showcase A*. By common accord, scholars call the period "Villanovan", from Villanova near Bologna, where pit graves containing the cremated remains of the dead in characteristic biconical cremation urns were discovered in 1853. The biconical urn with a single handle (the second handle, if the urn were provided with one, was deliberately broken off during the funerary ritual) and with the particular geometric decoration both incised and impressed, is the most characteristic component of this cultural phase.

The bronze vessels were made of thin hammered sheets of bronze, aping the typical shapes of pottery. However, increasing contacts between Etruscan and Greek civilization favoured the spread of Greek decorative forms, techniques and motifs and led to the emergence in Etruria of local workshops that produced typical wheel-made pottery painted with geometric motifs (upper shelf of the showcase).

Part of *showcase A* is dedicated to the transition to the so-called Orientalizing period, anticipating what is more amply illustrated by the magnificent grave artefacts from Cerveteri (Caere) described in the following Room II. On the middle shelf of *showcase A* the two *Hands made of sheet bronze*, with elongated fingers adorned with small gold studs are worthy of note. They were cut out of a single sheet of bronze, closed at the wrist and slightly bent at the edges. Their most likely place of origin and production is Vulci, since they show an affinity with the sheet-bronze masks of canopic jars from Chiusi, and, more generally, with the first experiments of Etruscan bronze-smiths to depict the human figure, which consisted in the three-dimensional fitting together of parts obtained separately from repoussé-decorated sheet bronze. 7th century B.C. Inv. 11930, 11931.

On the lower shelf of the showcase are a *globular amphora on a tall foot* (inv. 12630) and a chair made of tubular elements of sheet bronze (inv. 12631). The reciprocity between the two objects, or whether they belong together at all, is not clear. The development of the cinerary urn in human form, both in the shape of the body (the ribbon handles taking on the semblance of arms) and shape of the lid for the vase (missing here but it undoubtedly would have reproduced the head of the deceased, more or less schematically), is typical of the region of Chiusi. Often the cinerary urn (the so-called canopic jar) was placed on a chair or, more frequently, on a throne with a circular backrest. Both, together with the accompanying grave goods, were buried in a large dolium (earthenware jar). 7th century B.C.

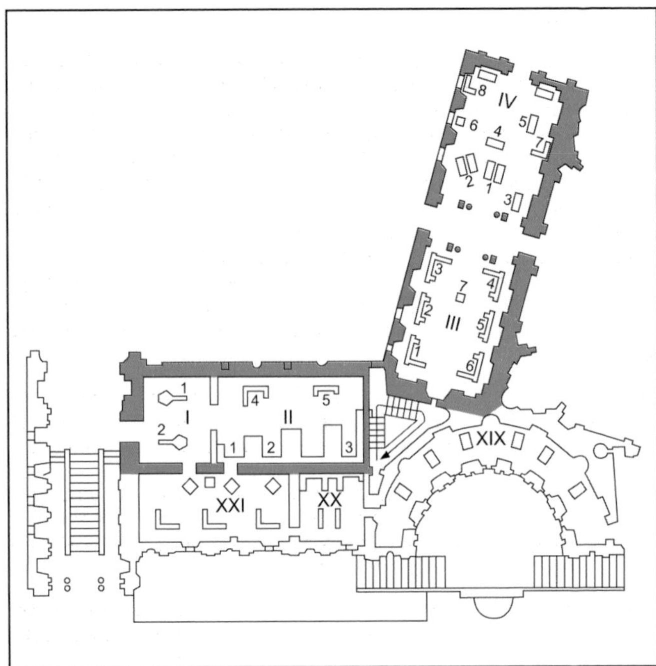

2 *Showcase B* contains artefacts coming from present-day southern Lazio (*Latium vetus*). Conspicuous among them are the grave artefacts excavated between Marino and Castel Gandolfo in 1816-17. The *hut urn* (inv. 15407), adopted together with the Villanovan biconical urn for cremation burials also in Etruria, is a characteristic feature of Iron Age civilization in Lazio, as also are the little vases decorated with chequerboard patterns (inv. 15404) and the so-called *calephatoi* (inv. 15401, 15406). 9th–8th century B.C.

The hexagonal part of the showcase contains the reconstructed archaic bronze war-chariot found in the Casale di Roma Vecchia, on the Via Appia, in the late 18th century, which was once considered a pastiche, if not a fake. 550-540 B.C.

II

II: ROOM OF THE REGOLINI-GALASSI TOMB

In the frieze: scenes from the life of Moses frescoed by Federico Barocci and Federico and Taddeo Zuccari (1563) between stucco caryatids.

The artefacts exhibited in this room form the nucleus of the Gregorian collection, and were found in 1836-37 during the excavation of the Sorbo cemetery south of Cerveteri, by General Vincenzo Galassi and the archpriest of Cerveteri, Alessandro Regolini. Artefacts found by Giovanni Pinza in 1906 in the Giulimondi Tomb during a topographical survey of the necropolis were added to this material, which comes from nine tombs contained in four neighbouring tumuli.

The most lavish grave artefacts come from the centre and oldest tomb of the largest of the tumuli (the Regolini-Galassi Tomb, named after its two discoverers). They are exhibited in the *large showcase A* on the right. The two *smaller showcases B and C* contain grave artefacts from the peripheral tombs, both in the largest tumulus and in the smaller ones.

Showcase A:

All of the main tomb can be dated back to the mid-7th century B.C. and is one of the most splendid testimonies of the mature "Orientalizing" phase in Etruria. During this period, Etruscan cities, especially coastal cities, among which Cerveteri (Caere) was one of the most important, were characterised by extensive urban development. Artistic expression on a monumental scale, imports of luxury goods and decorative and iconographic styles are evidence of extensive trading and cultural links with the Aegean and the Eastern Mediterranean. This extensive process of cultural transformation corresponded to the needs of a fully developed hierarchical society, ruled by an aristocracy with a highly specialised merchant class and craftsmen, which was capable of controlling the resources of vast portions of the hinterland.

The tomb, which can still be visited at Cerveteri, is partly hewn out of the living rock (tufa), and partly constructed of square-hewn blocks of masonry. It is roofed with a false vault constructed of progressively projecting ashlars, and covered with a mound of earth. It consists of a sloping passageway leading from the entrance, a long central cell, an end cell (separated from the central cell by a partition made of blocks of tufa), and, near the partition, of two symmetrical oval side niches, completely hewn out of the tufa.

The objects exhibited here are laid out according to the model represented by the longitudinal section of the tomb reproduced at the back of the large showcase. This reflects the approximate position in which they were found at the time of their discovery. The sequence of the exhibits begins on the right from the entrance to the room.

It is certain that the tomb had two occupants: a woman of noble birth, 1
buried in the end cell, and a man of equally high rank, buried by cremation in the central cell. More problematic is the alleged presence of a third occupant, who was thought to have been buried in the antechamber, laid on the *bed* (an extremely rare example in bronze of a type often reproduced in stone in tombs of the same period, inv. 15052). The funerary cart (inv. 15037) must have been built to the same size; note the remains of its studded iron felloes. The
bronze remains of a throne (no. 20556), and the extremely rich parure 3
of jewels and precious ornaments belong to the woman; she was most likely wearing some of them, while others were attached to or woven into her garments. Of special interest is the enormous *gold fibula* (inv. 20552) with a foliated bow and a disc catchplate. It is a ceremonial piece, jointed at the back to make it less cumbersome to wear, a lavishly decorated version of the simple fibula (or safety pin) known in Italy as far back as the Bronze Age. The miniature freestanding ducks on the bow consist of two embossed pieces welded together; the lions on the disc are also embossed, and were made from a separate plate. Details and ornamental friezes are of the finest granulation (each grain of gold added separately).

The centrepiece of the woven decoration (to which the fragments of 1
gold leaf now displayed on two panels on the lower shelf also belonged) was undoubtedly the *large plate* inv. 20553 (a pectoral or breastplate?); it is punch-decorated with recurrent motifs in concentric rows.

The two-horse chariot (*biga*: inv. 20555) and the rich series of parade 2, 3
shields (inv. 20544-20551) are clear attributes of rank: status symbols denoting a high-ranking warrior.

The vessels found in the tomb are remarkable in their variety. They 1-2
suggest not only functional utility, but also a precise role in the funeral ritual. We may note the significant co-existence of both local and

imported raw materials and decorative motifs. The *silver jug* with gold-plated handle (inv. 20461) is from Cyprus, and is a form often imitated in the local *bucchero* (typical, shiny black pottery produced
3 in Etruria from the 7th to the 5th century B.C.). The *silver gilt cups* decorated with Egyptianizing motifs (inv. 20364, 20367, 20368, 20365)
2 are of Phoenician-Cypriot production. The *small silver amphora with engraved double spiral* (inv. 20464) is an outstanding example of a local form exceptionally rendered in silver. The conical Protocorinthian cup (*kotyle*) is exemplified in its original form (inv. 20285), in local bucchero (inv. 20335) and in silver (inv. 20438, 20440, 20442, 20459, 20460).

3 Among the most important pieces in the entire Gregorian collection is undoubtedly the small *pear-shaped bucchero vase* (inv. 20349): an inkpot with inscribed alphabet around the base, and graffito syllabary on the sides. Writing, here used to decorate perhaps its most emblematic tool, was one of the cultural achievements of the Orientalizing period: it was introduced into Etruria in the late 8thcentury B.C., thanks to the intervention of the Greek colonies in southern Italy.

4 *Showcase B:*

It contains finds from the Giulimondi Tomb, on the Via Braccianese, about 50 metres from the Regolini-Galassi Tomb, excavated by Giovanni Pinza in 1906. It was a chamber tomb with a double-ridged ceiling and a longitudinal channel on top, and two beds hewn into the stone along the walls. The grave artefacts, not all of which can be definitely assigned to one or the other of the occupants, comprise a series of small, spiral patterned impasto or bucchero amphorae (inv. 19961-19965, 19983, 19998: cf. inv. 20464 in the Regolini-Galassi Tomb), and imported Protocorinthian pottery. Among the latter are two globular *aryballoi* (perfume jars), a so-called Thapsos cup, and various ovoid *aryballoi* (inv. 20001-20004). Taken as a whole, the contents of this tomb seem the earliest of those in this room, datable perhaps to the first quarter of the 7th century B.C.

5 *Showcase C:*

It contains artefacts from the Calabresi Tomb. Worth noting here are the splendid bucchero vessels, particularly fine in fabric. They include a *kantharos* (a two-handled drinking cup, inv. 20231), with conical foot and a long, spiral inscription, and an *ampulla* with two busts of horses (inv. 20235) with handle in the form of a charioteer (*c.*625 B.C.).

The same showcase also contains a reddish impasto cinerary urn in the shape of a house with rich orientalizing decoration (inv. 20825-20826). This kind of urn is commonly called a hut urn; in some cases its gabled lid is decorated with reliefs that allude to the roof of a building. This example is called Calabresi after its discoverer, who found it in 1869 in the Banditaccia cemetery at Cerveteri.

III III: ROOM OF THE BRONZES

In the frieze: scenes from the Old Testament (Prophecies of Daniel to Nebuchadnezzar) frescoed by Santi di Tito and Pomarancio, separated by stucco caryatids (1564).

This room contains all the bronze artefacts, statues, votive offerings, grave artefacts and common utensils that the museum following early 19th century excavations in the Papal State. The exhibits are in chronological order except for certain objects grouped together by type (helmets, candelabra, mirrors, cistae, vessels and reliefs) and those few objects that can be assumed to have belonged together on the basis of reliable reports of provenance.

Showcase A, to the left of the entrance: 1

Bronze tripod, probably made at Vulci, striking not least for its imaginative detail. From Vulci, late 6th century B.C. Inv. 12110.

Eleven bronze "bosses" decorated with the heads of lions and Achelous (a mythological figure, later a river god, with the horns and ears of a bull). The original function of this unique class of objects is disputed. They have been variously interpreted as shield bosses, as ceiling decorations (of houses or of tombs having similar architectural features), or – perhaps most plausibly – as bosses to embellish and magically protect the sides of funerary beds. The specimens exhibited here are from a chamber tomb in the cemetery of Monte Quaglieri at Tarquinia. They are magnificent examples of Etruscan bronze work of the late 6th century B.C. In their economy of style, precision of line, and wonderfully stylized details (Inv. 12625 in particular), they bear a strong affinity with the terracotta masterpieces of Veii. Inv. 12461-12463, 12622-12629.

Showcase B: 2

Two cast bronze statuettes of seated boys. Although most "ex voto" temple offerings were made of terracotta, some, such as these, were made of more expensive materials. Identified as offerings from the inscriptions, inscribed before the statues were cast. Inv. 12107 was found at Sanguineto on Lake Trasimene; Inv. 12108 comes from Tarquinia. They date to the late 4th early 3rd century B.C.

Statuette of an haruspex (Etruscan priest who examined animal viscera to interpret the will of the gods). Identified by the tall felt or skin hat, which was tied under the chin to prevent it from falling off (an ill omen) during the ceremony. From excavations close to the right bank of Tiber. 4th century BC. Inv. 12040.

Bronze mirror engraved with scene of an old haruspex, identified by the name of Chalcas, examining the liver of an animal sacrificed to draw omens from it. The legendary Greek soothsayer Chalchas is here represented in an Etruscan iconographic version, with wings. From Vulci, early 4th century B.C. Inv. 12240.

Showcase C: 3

Many helmets are displayed in this showcase. Note in particular Inv. 12304, embossed hemispherical headpiece, reproducing the hair and ears of a silenus. It comes from Atella, and is of undoubted Italiot production, datable to the 4th century B.C.

Showcase D: 4

Bronze mirrors decorated with engraved ornament on the back represent a particularly significant genre of Etruscan art. Chronologically distributed between the 6th and 3rd century, they underwent particular development in the 4th century B.C. Note in particular the following:

Bronze mirror with scene of *Eos* (Aurora) abducting the young hunter Cephalus. The relief technique, with silver-damascened ivy branch, is rare. From Vulci, *c.*470 B.C. Inv. 12241.

Oval *cista* (cylindrical container for woman's toilette articles). The cast handle is of local inspiration, while the embossed decoration (depicting a battle of Amazons) on the body of the vessel reveals clear Hellenistic influence. From Vulci, late 4th century B.C. Inv. 12259, 12260.

Showcase E: 5

The series of bronze candelabra in this case is particularly fine. The largest of them is 1.5 metres high (Inv. 12411). The ornamentation on top consists of isolated figures, or small cast bronze groups, some of a mythological nature, others drawn from the real world, including dancers (inv. 12396), athletes (inv. 12398, 12400), and warriors (inv. 12391, 12395). This is a genre of bronze artefacts of particular prestige and importance, of which the examples exhibited here come mainly from Vulci and date from the early 5th to the mid-4th century B.C.

6 *Showcase F:*

The rich series of bronze articles (craters on tall quadrangular foot, produced by casting, situlae, *oinochoai*, paterae, etc.) come from a chamber tomb near Bolsena, and date to roughly the mid-4th century B.C. The Etruscan word *suthina* ("tomb" or "funerary") appears on many of the vases, denoting their precise role as grave goods. The occupant of the tomb is known from the inscriptions on the situla (inv. 12806) and on the patera (inv. 12787): *Larisal Harenies suthina*, which can be translated as "funerary offering for Laris Harenie".

7 The *"Mars of Todi"* stands in the centre of the room. It is one of the very rare surviving examples of large-scale Etruscan statuary in bronze. Cast in several parts, and then welded together, it represents a young warrior leaning on a lance with his left hand, and in the act of offering, before going into battle, a libation with the cup held in his outstretched right hand. Interesting also for its Umbrian dedicatory inscription *(Ahal Trutitis dunum dede)* on one of the front fringes of his cuirass. The work reflects and combines various Greek influences of the second half of the 5th century B.C. From Todi, where it was found buried between four slabs of travertine. Late 5th century B.C. Inv. 13886.

IV   IV: ROOM OF STONE MONUMENTS

In the frieze: remains of the fresco decoration of the time of Pius IV (1559-1565) with mythological and allegorical scenes, perhaps painted by Orlando Parentini.

Monuments of various genres (sarcophagi, freestanding sculptures, reliefs, cippi, inscriptions, etc.), provenance (Chiusi, Vulci, Cerveteri, Orte, Palestrina, etc.), and periods (from the 6th to the 1st cent. B.C.) are displayed in this room. Their only common denominator is the material of which they are made, the soft local stone—varieties of tufa, travertine, and sandstone—preferred by Etruscan sculptors and stonemasons for the ease with which it could be cut, while its surface defects could be camouflaged by the abundant use of stucco-work and pigment, now almost completely lost.

1 At the centre of the room:

Two *lions in nenfro* (variety of soft volcanic stone), from a tomb at Vulci, where they had been placed to guard the entrance, an act implying a belief in the afterlife of the deceased confined to the tomb itself. Late 6th century B.C. Inv. 14955, 14956.

2 To the left: two *horses' heads in nenfro.* From the entrance to a tomb at Vulci. The belief that the tomb as the home of the deceased that demanded protection from the outside world, here gives way to that of the funeral ceremony and the journey of the deceased to the underworld. 4th–3rd century B.C. Inv. 14953, 14954.

On the opposite side of the room:

3 *Limestone sarcophagus with polychrome relief.* The recumbent figure on the cover represents the deceased. The lid is decorated at both ends like the roof of a house, while the funeral procession is depicted on the two decorated sides of the sarcophagus. Found together with three other sarcophagi made of the same stone, in a

chamber tomb, which originally also had paintings on the walls. From Cerveteri. Second quarter of the 4th century B.C. Inv. 14949.

Displayed at the centre of the room are:

Sarcophagus in nenfro (local variety of tufa) *with scenes of the myth of the Atridae* on the front, and scenes of the *Theban legend* on the back. The lid, which does not belong to the sarcophagus, depicts the deceased lying down (although the position of its limbs is that of a standing figure), holding a scroll. From Tarquinia, 2nd century B.C. Inv. 14561. 4

Sarcophagus in nefro with representations of the *slaying of the Niobids* on the front, battle *of the Centaurs* on the left side; and *Achilles dragging the body of Hector* on the right side. From a large dynastic mausoleum in Tuscania; found together with 26 other sarcophagi (3rd cent. B.C.). Same workshop as Inv. 14561 (see above: 4). Inv. 14947. The lid, with a recumbent male figure, is a plaster cast from the original in the Florence Archaeological Museum. 5

To the left, below the window:

Sandstone figurine of a female figure. The bare breasts suggest that the figure is a representation of a *Lasa* (Etruscan female demon, in this case of the underworld), rather than that of the dead woman. This statuette, from a tomb near Chiusi, is one of the most successful creations of Etruscan sculpture of Hellenistic inspiration; even the unpretentious stone is perfectly in tune with the delicacy and submissiveness of the waiting girl. 3rd-2nd century B.C. Inv. 14951. 6

On the opposite side:

"Bilingual" stele from Todi. Rectangular sepulchral stele in travertine, bearing a text in Latin and Gallic on both faces (the latter written in a special alphabet derived from Etruscan). It mentions the building of the tomb of a certain Ategnatos, son of Drutos, by his younger brother, Coisis. It comes from Todi and is datable to the second half of the 2nd century B.C. Inv. 14958. 7

On the left of the short flight of steps leading to the following rooms: 8

The so-called sarcophagus of the Magistrate, carved out of nenfro. On the front, the last journey of the deceased, who is standing on the chariot, preceded by two figures wearing the toga and bearing *fasces* (bundles of rods: magistrate's symbol). The inscription on the upper cornice gives the name, *cursus honorum* (career path) and age of the dead man, and instructions concerning burial rites. From Tuscania, 3rd century B.C. Inv. 14950.

Walking up the short flight of steps at the centre of the wall at the end of the room, visitors immediately reach the second floor of Palazzetto del Belvedere, built by Pope Innocent VIII (1484-1492) as a place of recreation and meditation. At this point, a brief pause in the tour is recommended to enjoy the wonderful views of Rome from the many windows.

Benches have been placed for those who wish to rest before walking up the new stairway built in 1994 in order to include the vast rooms (V-VIII) located on the third floor of the Belvedere into the museum tour, where architectural and votive terracottas and the important collection of Etruscan gold jewellery are now displayed.

V and VI: ROOMS OF ARCHITECTURAL AND VOTIVE TERRACOTTAS

These rooms, conventionally called the *Rooms of the Terracottas*, are dedicated to the terracotta sculptures that decorated Etruscan temples and to the terracotta figurines used as votive offerings. Room VI is large and well suited to recreating an ambiance in many respects similar to ancient sacred areas, where a perimeter wall (*temenos*) enclosed the tall podium on which the temple was erected and a forecourt full of votive offerings and altars for the performance of religious ceremonies.

A large number of architectural terracottas of various provenance are conserved in the Gregorian Etruscan Museum. Some of them have been reconstructed on supports alluding to the wooden beams of the roof they would have decorated in antiquity. Four different decorative pieces have been selected to exemplify Etruscan architectural decoration as widely as possible; the exhibit is arranged for visitors so that it recalls their original function and layout as closely as possible.

V

ROOM V

1 Entering Room V at the top of the staircase, two antefixes (terracotta ornaments fixed to entablatures) with the head of a Maenad or a Silenus are visible on the eaves of a specially constructed roof. They come from Cerveteri. Mid-4th century B.C. Inv. 13978, 14118.

VI

ROOM VI

1 The terracotta *high reliefs from Tivoli*, set in a partial reconstruction of a pediment, dominate the end wall of Room VI. They must have decorated the triangular pediment of a temple, as is also suggested by the sharp forward projection and sheer size of the figures (to make them clearly visible from below). The presence of the hind legs of a sheepskin hanging from the tree to the side of figure no. 4 reveals a possible reference to the iconography of the Golden Fleece and the myth of the expedition of the Argonauts (inv. 14103, 14014, 14016, 14117, 20820, 20821). Datable to the late 4th - 3rd century B.C.

2 Displayed between the two windows of the room is a corner *acroterion* in the shape of a winged horse, placed in a reconstruction of the eaves of a temple roof. It comes from Cerveteri (ancient Caere) and is datable to the early decades of the 5th century. Inv. 14130.

3 *Four terracotta panels with floral decorations and human heads* (Dionysus? – Ariadne?) are displayed, with the same criterion, to the right of the entrance. They are applied to two horizontal bands alluding to the wooden trabeation on which they would have originally been mounted. Dating to the second half of the 4th century, they perhaps come from Cerveteri. Inv. 14129.

4 A collection of terracotta votive offerings from temples is displayed on the *podium* at the centre of the room and in the *showcases* along the left wall. Most of them come from one or more temples in the Etruscan city of Caere (Cerveteri), and date mainly to the late 4th - 3rd century B.C. The exhibit layout is intended to emphasise not only the artistic quality of the votive offerings (note in particular the materials displayed in the first part of the long showcase below the gallery), but also the great variety and quantity of gifts that were brought to the temple every day (as exemplified by the showcases full of votive offerings above the balustrade). Ancient sanctuaries were normally packed with ex-votos brought by devotees to the gods, either to give

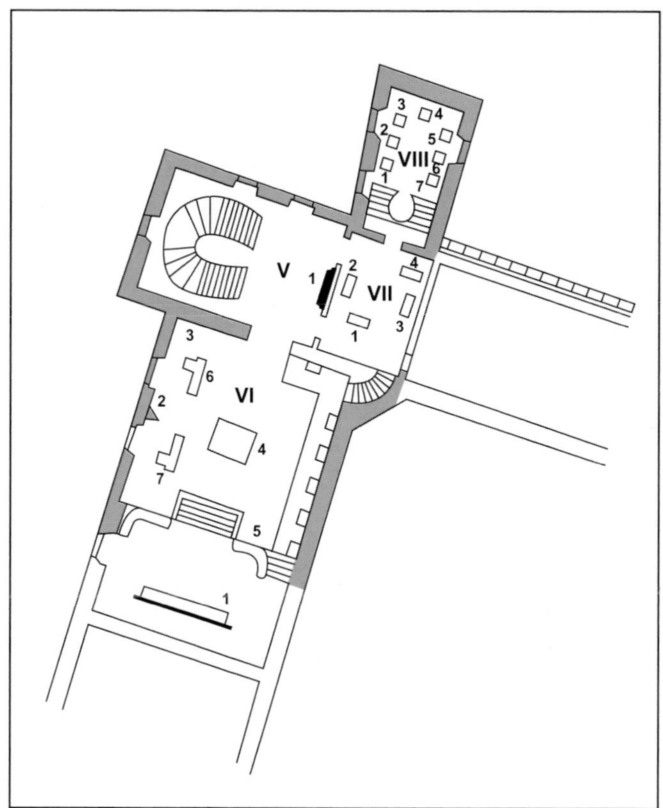

thanks for favours received or to request divine intervention. The gifts normally took the form of small reproductions of cult images, reproductions of various parts of the human body (heads and half-heads, limbs, organs), offerings of food, or images of sacrificial animals.

In the right-hand sector of *showcase A* are displayed a group of antefixes with rich polychromy, alluding to the myth of Orestes, and fragments of a figurative frieze with a mythological subject. From Vulci, excavations of 1835-37. 2nd century B.C. 5

Exhibited in *showcase B* is a magnificent archaic antefix (*c.*500 B.C.) with a female head. It comes from Cerveteri and preserves almost intact its original pictorial finish. Inv. 13883. 6

Showcase C contains an antefix with the head of Achelous (inv. 13828) of the late 6th century B.C., antefixes and other terracotta sculptural decorations of the 4th century B.C. (inv. 14065, 20897, 13748, 13836, 22066); they come from the excavations of 1835-37 at Vulci (cf. showcase A). 7

Leave the large and luminous rooms dedicated to the historical collections of the Museum and enter two rooms with more subdued lighting specially designed for the display of jewellery. They have enabled one of the world's most important collections of Etruscan gold jewellery to become a permanent part of the exhibition once again. Gold jewellery dating from the 7th century B.C. through the Classical and Hellenistic periods, right down to the Roman Imperial period, are displayed in the showcases, arranged both by type and by period.

VII and VIII: ROOMS OF GOLD JEWELLERY

In these two rooms are personal ornaments in gold made with consummate technical and design skills by Etruscan goldsmiths during the ten centuries their civilization existed. An unfaltering taste in the choice of models and precious and semi-precious stones is combined with growing technical virtuosity that made Etruscan jewellery unique and incomparable in the ancient world. The most frequently used techniques were: casting, gold leaf hammering, the making of the most delicate gold wires for twisting into minute strips of gold, finishing with punching or chasing, and lastly granulation. This latter was a particular Etruscan technique that permitted the making of miniscule spheres of gold, sometimes almost infinitesimal in size (almost gold dust), which were fixed to the gold sheet of the jewel by a micro-soldering process to create either continuous granulated surfaces or patterns.

The exhibition follows a chronological order. It begins in the 7th century B.C. (no earlier gold jewellery is found in the Gregorian Etruscan Museum) and continues down to the Roman period. It enables the visitor to follow the course of fashions, traditions and genres of a people that used gold both as a source of wealth to be treasured for its intrinsic worth and as astatus symbol, based on archaeological records and documented by a famous passage in Diodorus Siculus (8,18,1): ".... [the Etruscans] had a kind of supremacy in the opulence of their lifestyle....".

VII

ROOM VII

Showcase A:

1 Pair of miniature gold spiral-shaped hairpins. Late 7th - first half of 6th century B.C.

Gold leech-shaped *fibula* (safety pin) with elongated catchplate inscribed: *mi mamarces artesi* ("I to Mamerce from Arte"). Third quarter of the 7th century B.C. Inv. 13203.

Gold leech-shaped *fibula* (safety pin) with elongated catchplate and rich granulated decoration (inv. 13195). Late 7th - early 6th century B.C.

Gold plaquette with miniature head of the Egyptian goddess Hather (inv. 13548). Final decades of the 7th century B.C.

Gold necklace of globular beads (inv. 13441). Second half of the 7th century B.C.

Silver belt clasps with bas-relief of a woman embracing two men. 600-575 B.C. Inv. 13387-13388.

2 *Showcase B:*

Gold coffer-shaped earrings. Second half of the 6th century B.C.

Gold necklace with granulated pendants in the shape of pine cones, lotus flowers and female heads. First half of the 5th century B.C. Inv. 13327.

Pair of gold earrings with complex disc, set with rock crystal and agate. Late 6th - early 5th century B.C. Inv. 13551-2.

Gold necklace with pendants in the form of lion heads and cylindrical capsules. First quarter of the 5th century B.C. Inv. 13542.

Ivory plaquette with two birds, forming part of the decoration of a casket. From Vulci: 540-520 B.C. Inv. 20446.

3 *Showcase C:*

Silver funerary parure of a woman, early 6th century B.C. Found at Megara Hyblaea (Sicily) in 1896: pair of earrings with granulated ornament; finger ring with glass paste scarab; fibulae with bow decorated with ribbing and granulation; pins.

Gold necklace composed of pendants in the form of ox-heads and acorns. First half of the 4th century B.C. Inv. 13538.

Gold necklace composed of seven figured *bullae* (lockets). The four large *bullae* are decorated with scenes of Hippothoon, Athenian hero, son of Poseidon and Alope, being reared by a mare, and Achilles killing Troilus. The three smaller ones carry representations of Hephaestos (Vulcan) forging the weapons of Achilles. From Vulci. First half of the 4th century B.C. Inv. 13412.

Showcase D: 4

Gold laurel-leaf diadem. From Vulci – second half of the 4th century B.C. Inv. 13471.

Gold leaf ring with figured mount belonging to the *Fortnum* Group. First half of the 4th century B.C. Inv. 13166.

Room VIII VIII

Showcase A:

Series of gold rings and isolated scarabs with Egyptian-style hieroglyphic signs produced at Naukratis (Egypt) in the Saitic period and Rhodian and Phoenician Egyptianizing imitations. Gold Etruscan rings with revolving gemstone scarab incised with figural motifs or mythological scenes. From the late 6 to the 4 century B.C. Note in particular the ring or pendant with incised scarab representing the episode of Achilles receiving weapons from his mother, the goddess Thetis (inv. 13174), a fine work attributed to the so-called Master of the Boston Dionysus, an Eastern Greek intaglio master active in Etruria in the late 6th century B.C. 1

Showcase B: 2

Various examples of pendant earrings, particularly widespread in Etruria in the 4th century B.C. The earrings are displayed here in typological sequence: ranging from the tube or cylinder-shaped specimens of the 5th century B.C. (lower shelf) and the simpler versions of the early 4th century B.C., down to the more elaborate horseshoe-shaped models of the second half of the century (upper shelf).

Showcase C: 3

Gold oak-leaf and laurel-leaf diadem (inv. 13482). Second half of the 4th century B.C. Inv. 13481.

Diadem of gold and enamel lanceolate leaves and enamelware berries. Second half of the 4 century B.C. Inv. 13381.

Little gold ivy-leaf diadem. First half of the 4th century B.C. Inv. 13377.

Showcases D-E: 4, 5

Funerary parure of the mid-4th century B.C., found at Vulci in 1837.

Showcase F: 6

Reconstructed gold necklace with 25 pendants in the form of pomegranates interspersed with little gold pearls. Vulci – Hellenistic period. Inv. 13168.

Gold head of Medusa. Inv. 13664.

Earrings of various types. 3rd - 2nd century B.C.

Series of rings with elliptical settings. 3rd - 2nd century B.C.

Showcase G: 7

Contains gold jewellery of the Roman Imperial period.

Funerary parure of the second half of the 2nd century B.C., found at Artena in 1834: necklace with double gold loop and pendant garnets

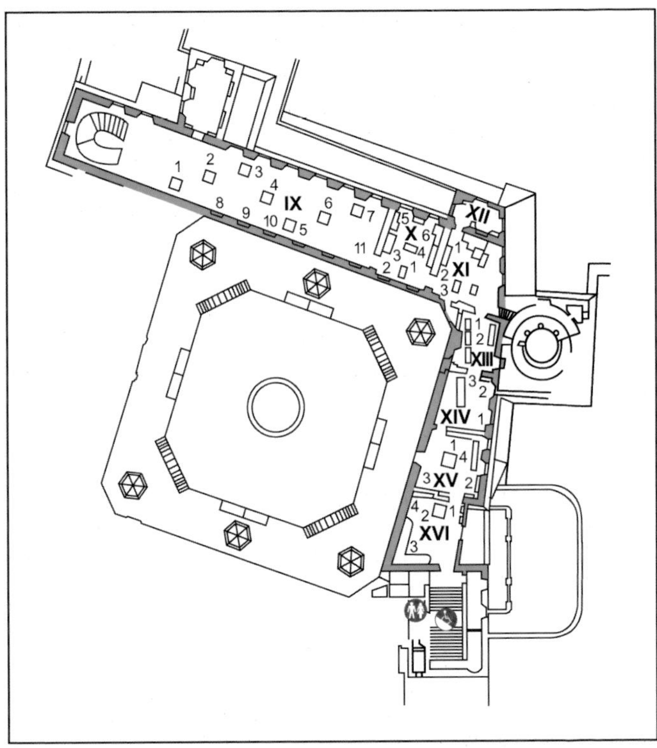

with clasp (inv. 13241 and 13323); gold clasp with amethyst (inv. 13213); gold ring with Eros riding on a sea-horse incised on the setting (inv. 13242); pair of little rings in twisted gold wire (inv. 13212).

Descending the new flight of steps, the visitor finds enters a large room containing the archaeological collection of the Guglielmi family, created in the 19th century following the excavations conducted in the area surrounding the ancient city of Vulci.

IX

ROOM IX: GUGLIELMI COLLECTION

The collection of the *marchesi* Guglielmi of Vulci was one of the last, and richest, private Etruscan collections legitimately owned. Created in the 19th century following the excavations conducted in the estates of Sant'Agostino and Camposcala in the area surrounding of the ancient Etruscan city of Vulci, the collection remained on display in the Palazzo Guglielmi in Civitavecchia until the early y ears of the 20th century, when it was divided into two parts between the brothers Giulio and Giacinto.

The part owned by Giulio was inherited by his son Benedetto, who donated it to Pope Pius XI in 1937. Since then it has been exhibited in the Gregorian Etruscan Museum. The other part, equally rich and prestigious, remained the property of the Guglielmi family until 1987, when it was purchased by the Vatican Museums and finally reunited with the other half of the collection.

The Guglielmi collection consists in all of some 800 objects, including bronze vessels and weapons, Etruscan pottery (impasto, bucchero and painted pottery), and Greek pottery; the latter imported mainly from Attica as part of the close trading relations between Vulci and Greece: Vulci was one of the main markets for Greek pottery in the whole area bordering the Tyrrhenian Sea.

The artefacts on display are heterogeneous in type and cover a time span stretching from the earliest material of the Villanovan period to the typical pottery production of the Hellenistic period. The most sizeable nucleus is undoubtedly that of Attic black-figure and red-figure pottery; the former was more numerous than the latter, conforming to the standard statistical pattern of Attic imports in Etruria.

Showcase A: 1

Protocorinthian, Ionian, Laconian and Attic black-figure pottery.

Attic *kylix* signed by Tleson (inv. 34573): outside: sides A and B – sphinx and signature of the potter: "Tleson, son of Nearchos, made it". Vulci, *c.*550-540 B.C.

Showcase B: 2

Contains Attic black-figure pottery.

Attic black-figure *hydria* (water pot) attributed to the Antimines Painter (inv. 34557); painted with scene of warrior departing on the four-horse chariot. Vulci, *c.*520 B.C.

Showcase C: 3

Contains Attic black-figure and red-figure pottery.

Attic red-figure *hydria* attributed to Euthymides (inv. 34584); a bearded man pours wine into a crater between a male dancer and a musician playing the double flute. Vulci, 520-510 B.C.

Showcase D: 4

Bronze *stamnos* (inv. 39752); Vulci, mid-5th century B.C. Pair of *stamnos* handles of *Kleinaspergle* type (inv. 39705-6); Vulci, 5th century B.C.

Showcase E: 5

Corinthian, Chalcidian and Eastern Greek pottery; Attic black-figure pottery.

Black-figure Attic amphora of the Ptoion Painter (inv. 39515); side A: Judgement of Paris; side B; feast scene; Vulci, *c.*560 B.C.

Tyrrhenian black-figure amphora with Achilles' ambush of Troilus (inv. 39514); Vulci, 570-560 B.C.

Kylix of the Little Masters signed by Gageos (inv. 39545); side A: lioness with inscription: side B: lion with inscription; Vulci, *c.*550-540 B.C.

Showcase F: 6

Attic black-figure amphora by the Amasis Painter (inv. 39518); side A: Dionysus and satyr conversing with a young man; side B: meeting between two warriors; Vulci, *c.*550 B.C.

Showcase G: 7

Contains Attic red-figure pottery.

Central shelf: of particular interest is the Attic red-figure *stamnos* (inv. 39562), the name-piece of the Guglielmi Painter; side A: departure of a warrior; side B: Dionysus between two maenads; from Vulci, 440-430 B.C.

On the lower shelf: Apulian red-figure bell-krater (inv. 39919) attributed to the Lecce 660 Painter; side A: Eros and seated woman;

side B: scene of conversation. Apulian red-figure plate (inv. 39733) attributable to the shop of the Dario Painter; inside: naked youth and woman; outside: seated woman between naked youth to the left and Eros to the right; *c.*330 B.C.

8 *Showcase H:*

Selection of various types and forms of bucchero (typical Etruscan pottery with burnished black surface and black fabric).

Little jug (inv. 36457) with graffito decoration and Etruscan inscription *mi ramuthas kansinaia* in which the vase speaks in the first person and acknowledges its belonging to Ramutha Kansinai; late 7th century B.C.

9 *Showcase I:*

Etruscan pottery.

Etruscan black-figure plate of the so-called *pontic* group (inv. 34600); Vulci, third quarter of the 6th century B.C.

Etruscan black-figure amphora attributed to the mature phase of the Micali Painter (inv. 34604); on the body: Athena and Hercules in the Battle of the Giants; Vulci, late 6th century B.C.

Two Etruscan red-figure *stamnoi* of the Vatican G 113 group (inv. 34626 and 39568); side A: battle of griffins; side B: Nike seated on little pillar; Vulci, *c.*360-350 B.C.

10 *Showcase L:*

Bronze vessels (late 6th early 5th century B.C.).

11 *Showcase O:*

Bronze defensive weapons: helmets (inv. 39749, 39648, 39649) and greaves (inv. 39747-8).

Male votive statuette (inv. 39799) with Etruscan inscription *muras.arnth.thufi.suuris* ("Arnth Muras [gave it] to Thurf and Suri"), Vulci, second half of 3rd century B.C.

ROOMS X-XI: CINERARY URNS OF THE HELLENISTIC PERIOD

The cremation rite, along with the funerary custom of placing the ashes of the deceased in an urn hewn out of stone or modelled in terracotta, is particularly well documented in northern Etruria from the 4th century B.C. and throughout the Hellenistic period.

Large quantities of cinerary urns, with peculiar artistic and typological features, were produced in the main Etruscan cities of this vast area (Volterra, Chiusi and Perugia). The reliefs that adorn the front of the urns are the result of local elaboration of the Greek figurative repertoire. Greek myths and more properly Etruscan themes co-exist, and share the same figurative language, in one of the most characteristic manifestations of Etruscan art. The urns were hewn out of natural stone found in the area: alabaster in Volterra and Chiusi, travertine in Perugia, but other less valuable stones were also used. The surfaces were originally characterised by a vivid polychromy, of which only a few traces have survived.

The figure of the deceased (man or woman), reclining in the classical position when feasting, was ideally represented on the lid of the urns, while the front of the urn itself was sculpted with mythological scenes or scenes connected with the afterlife.

All three main types of cinerary urns produced are exemplified in the Gregorian Etruscan Museum: those of Volterra and Chiusi are displayed in Room X, and those of Perugia in Room XI.

ROOM X X

On entering the room, the visitor is immediately introduced to the 1
production of cinerary urns in Chiusi by an alabaster urn of the *kline* type, bearing the onomastic inscription of the deceased, depicted reclining on the lid. The figure is embellished with ornaments and objects in various precious materials inserted in holes provided for this purpose: a coronet on the head, a ring on the left hand and an object in the right. Inv. 13897, formerly in the Palazzo Giulietti, first half of the 3rd century B.C.

Against the left wall, together with cinerary urns with simple 3
decorations, is the frontal part of a cinerary urn with a relief of Eteocles and Polynices assisted by winged demons (inv. 19016, from Castiglione del Lago, late 3rd century). The theme, though in another iconographic version, would continue to be adopted in terracotta production in the 2nd century B.C., together with that of the hero fighting with the plough, as may be observed in the two showcases on the wall to the right. Four of these urns (inv. 16254-16257) are
displayed in the *first showcase*; they were found, together with grave 2
artefacts, in a chamber tomb at Castiglione del Lago, and belonged to members of the *Ceicna* family. The elaborate surviving polychromy of the urn should be noted.

At the centre of the room is the magnificent alabaster urn, probably 4
made in Volterra. It was found in Todi in 1516 and had perhaps already been used as a reliquary in the Middle Ages (inv. 13887). On the lid: a feasting man and wife (the man is fragmentary). The relief on the body of the urn represents the killing of Oenomaus, King of Pisa in Elis, by Pelops who had defeated him in a chariot race, which the king usually held to challenge the suitors of his daughter Hippodamia. The Etruscan interpretation of the Greek myth and its iconography in a funerary vein is underlined by the insertion of female winged demons: First quarter of the 2nd century B.C.

Urns of Volterran production and various attribution and date (2/first 5, 6
half of 1st century B.C.) follow along the walls of the room. They are decorated with a variety of mythological reliefs (hero with plough inv. 13891), judgement of Paris inv. 13898, abduction of Helen inv. 13888, death of Atteonte inv. 13889, Battle of Centaurs inv. 13890), or with scenes connected with the afterlife, such as the journey to the underworld (inv. 13892, 13893, 13894), scenes of funerary rites (inv. 13896), the apparition of the dead husband to his wife (inv. 13895).

ROOM XI XI

In Room XI contains four urns from the same tomb, discovered at 1
Casaglia near Perugia in 1783. One of them has a Latin inscription. The four represent in some way the typological and stylistic development of cinerary urns in Perugia between the mid-2nd and the
mid-1st century B.C. (inv. 13899-13902) Also in this room are two 2
terracotta sarcophagi from Bomarzo (inv. 14138-14139).

At the centre of the room is the famous funerary monument with the 3
dying Adonis in polychrome terracotta (inv. 14147). The young hunter of mythology lies on a bed, mortally wounded. This scene, imbued

with pathos, is carefully executed. Perhaps it was chosen to suggest some affinity with the fate of the deceased, but, in any case, the Adonis myth was a favourite in Etruscan representations of death and the underworld from the 4th century B.C. on. The intersecting clay partitions inside the monument show that it was not an urn. The holes in the surface were made to ensure uniform ventilation of the clay during firing. From Tuscania, second half of the 3rd century B.C.

XII

ROOM XII: FALCIONI COLLECTION

The frieze is part of the decoration from the period of Julius III (1550-55), executed by Daniele da Volterra and his pupils.

Displayed in this small room is the core of the archaeological collection assembled by Bonifacio Falcioni of Viterbo in the second half of the 19th century. The collection was purchased for the Vatican Museums by Leo XIII in May 1898.

The contents of the showcases reflect the characteristics and eclectic taste of private collections in the 19th century. Artefacts were collected indiscriminately and without any particular logical criteria. So we find among the archaeological finds objects as different as the earliest impasto pottery of the proto-Villanovan period and the early Iron Age, bucchero vessels, Attic and Etruscan painted pottery, artefacts in bronze (vases, statuettes, etc.), votive material and especially gold jewellery, both antique and modern.

The artefacts were for the most part purchased by Bonifacio Falcioni on the art market: only a small part of his collection comes from excavations conducted at the time in some of the major Etruscan sites of upper Lazio, such as Vulci, Tuscania, Bomarzo, Bolsena and Blera.

XIII

ROOM XIII

1, 2 The last glimpse of Etruria during the Hellenistic period is the *terracotta sarcophagi from Tuscania* (inv. 15424-15427), made during the 2nd century B.C. But, in this room, the visitor's attention turns immediately to *Bramante's spectacular spiral staircase*. This jewel of Renaissance architecture was designed in 1504-1505 and completed by Pirro Ligorio in 1564. It now forms the backdrop to the revamped *Antiquarium Romanum*, which opens with a rich selection of bronze artefacts: large-scale statuary, vessels, fittings for furniture, sculptures.

ROOMS XIV-XVI: *ANTIQUARIUM ROMANUM*

The *Antiquarium Romanum* originated from the re-organization of the Gregorian Etruscan Museum between 1855 and 1957. It was the natural result of a more rigorous and thorough archaeological examination of the numerous finds of the Roman period, of various provenance, that had previously been mixed together with Etruscan and Italic artefacts in the Gregorian Etruscan Museum. Later revisions led to the collection's current display, organized by categories of material. It was completed with a section dedicated to the *Ager Vaticanus* (Room XVI).

XIV

ROOM XIV

1, 2 Some fragments of large statues in bronze are exhibited in this room.
The most striking are a male torso of the second half of the 1st century
B.C. (inv. 15055) and a head portrait of the emperor Trebonianus
2 Gallo (251-253 A.D., inv. 15032). *Showcase A* contains bronze

furniture parts, such as a magnificent figured foot of a folding table
(inv. 12194) and a bed backrest (*fulcrum*) (inv. 34926), bronze 3
tableware and the famous silver vases with a dedication to Apollo that
comes from the hot springs at Vicarello, near Bracciano (inv. 12131-
2, 12134, 12137-8, 12148).

ROOM XV XV

A selection of architectural terracottas is presented in this room. They 1, 2
come from Rome and Lazio, and are datable from the 1 century B.C.
to the 1st century A.D. On the walls is the partial reconstruction of the
terracotta decoration of roofs in the Roman period, using original
pieces (antefixes and panels). On the frontal wall, below, are *three*
relief panels from a cycle of the twelve labours of Hercules: the killing 3
of the hydra of Lerna, of the Nemean Lion, and of the Cretan Bull (inv.
14160, 14163, 14477). Showcase B contains a rich selection of
glassware of various periods; the latest examples date to the Roman 4
Imperial period. An ivory doll with jointed limbs (inv. 12224) and
remains of cloth interwoven with gold thread stand out among the
ivory and bone objects. It was found in a girl's sarcophagus of the 4th
century A.D., close to the Basilica of San Sebastiano in Rome.

ROOM XVI XVI

On the wall are two *stucco coffers* of the Flavian period, from a 1
columbarium (collective tomb for cinerary urns within niches)
discovered in the Vigna Moroni on mlVia Appia in 1816 (inv. 14984,
14562): they are decorated with reliefs of *Aphrodite and the dying*
Adonis, and *Alexander-Zeus bestriding the globe between Poseidon*
and Hercules. In *showcase A*: Roman oil-lamps of the 1st century A.D., 2
some of them with theatrical subjects.

Platform and showcase B: During the period of the kings of Rome and throughout the Republican period, the territory on the right of the Tiber was known as *Ager Vaticanus* and stretched to the north as far as the mouth of the Cremera River, and to the south at least as far as the Janiculum. During the Imperial period – beginning in the 2nd century A.D.– the name *Vaticanum* was used and referred to a more limited area, corresponding more or less to today's Vatican City State. During the Roman period the area lay outside the city of Rome and was occupied by villas, by the gardens of Agrippina – mother of the emperor Caligula (34-41 A.D.) – and by huge cemeteries arranged along the main roads. Caligula built a circus (*Gaianum*), later rebuilt by Nero (54-68 A.D.), in the gardens of his mother.

Along the Via Trionfale, that runs north from St. Peter's Square to
Monte Mario, various groups of tombs have been excavated (the
cemeteries of the Annona, Autoparco, Fontana della Galera, and
Belvedere), from which come the *altar of Varia Sabbatis* (inv. 1344), 3
the *infant's sarcophagus with the islands of the blessed* (inv. 1501)
and the objects displayed in showcase B. 4

Leave this sector of the museums located in the east wing of Innocent VIII's Palazzetto del Belvedere, and go partway down the staircase of Julius III (1550-1555), decorated with *grottesche* and the papal coat of arms supported by two angels, perhaps painted by Daniele da Volterra and his pupils. Then return to the large rooms facing the Cortile della Pigna that is part of the private apartment of Pius IV, where the Vase Collection was set up recently (1996).

Rooms XVII-XXII: Vase Collection

Attic black-figure amphora by potter and painter Exekias (c. 530 B.C.) with Achilles and Ajax playing dice, detail.

The original core Vase Collection was acquired by the Vatican in the 18th century and initially adorned the bookcases in the Vatican Library. In 1837 they were transferred to the newly founded Gregorian Etruscan Museum, where they were arranged in the luminous rooms facing the Cortile della Pigna.

Until the beginning of the 19th century, the Greek painted vases were thought to be of Etruscan manufacture. It was during the turbulent period of 19th century excavations in Etruria that they were studied in greater detail and more accurately identified. The discovery in Etruria of so much Greek pottery was the primary reason for the creation of a separate, parallel section of the museum, but that was closely linked to the rest of the Etruscan Museum. The exhibition of the Greek vases in these rooms shows the development of the production of Greek pottery and the great success that these vases enjoyed in Etruria as a result of the flourishing trade between the Greeks and Etruscans.

Numerous masterpieces – signed by or attributed to the great names of Greek vase painting – are contained in the Vase Collection housed in Rooms XVII-XXII, in chronological and typological sequence. The important Astarita Collection (Room XX), donated by Pope Paul VI, was added to it in 1967.

XVII

ROOM XVII

1 *Showcase A.* Corinth held virtually unrivalled supremacy in exports to the markets of the Mediterranean between the late 8th and 7th century B.C., and its finely made pottery was widely distributed in Etruria and Northern Italy. The traditional *olpe* (jug with trefoil mouth)

inv. 16334, is decorated with orientalizing period superimposed friezes: rows of panthers, bulls, deer, herons, sphinxes, and dotted rosettes against an ivory ground. The jug was made by a potter (whose name ison the base of this piece) called "Vatican 73 Painter", and was produced in Corinth *c.*630-615 B.C.

Showcase B. Among later Greek pottery are Laconian wares, represented here by a famous *kylix* (cup) manufactured in Sparta in the mid-6th century B.C. It is painted with a scene of Prometheus and Atlas (inv. 16592). 2

Only between the late 7th and early 6th century B.C. did Athens try to develop an overseas markets by exporting *black-figure* pottery (black figures painted in reserve against a red ground with incised or over-painted details). Production continued until *c.*530 B.C., when the new *red-figure* technique (see further below) radically transformed all of ancient vase painting.

Showcase C. Attic *kylix* of the Phrynos Painter (inv. 16596); on the inside of the cup, scene of Ajax with the body of Achilles, mid-6th century B.C. 3

Showcase D. Attic black-figure amphora signed by the potter Nikosthenes, from Cerveteri (inv. 17716); on the neck: Dionysus and Maenads / Maenads with lions; on the body: battle scene; *c.*530-510 B.C. 4

Showcase E. Black-figure *pelike* (amphora with sagging belly and two handles) from Cerveteri, depicting a scene of the sale of oil. The precious liquid, contained in a vase similar to one used today, is being poured into a smaller container used for unguents (*lekythos*), while the buyer is seated on a *diphros* (folding chair). The inscription in the form of an invocation that accompanies the scene, (= O father Zeus may I become rich!), inspired the conventional name Plousios Painter (from *ploutos* wealth) for the painter of this late 6th century B.C. amphora. Inv. 16518. 5

ROOM XVIII XVIII

Showcase A, which separates the small room from the adjacent Room XVII, contains an Attic black-figure *oinochoe* (jug for pouring or drawing wine) by the Amasis Painter with woman, seated man, lyre-player and youth, from Vulci; *c.*525 B.C. Inv. 17771. 1

Showcase B. Various *hydriai*, large pots for containing and trans-porting water, are contained in this case. Their use is clearly exemplified by the fountain scenes with which they were painted by the Achelous Painters, 530-510 B.C. (inv. 16449) and by Eucharides, 500 B.C. (inv. 17729) 2

ROOM XIX: *Lower Hemicycle* XIX

Bernardino Nocchi (?) painted the frescoes on the walls in 1780, describing the buildings completed under the pontificate of Pope Pius VI.

Showcase B. Panatheneaic amphora (containing the oil awarded to the winning athletes in the Panathenaic Games, inaugurated at Athens under Pisistratos in 566 B.C.), painted by the Berlin Painter, 500-480 B.C., with Athena and scene of an athletic contest (inv. 16559). The painter used the popular traditional black-figure technique, given the symbolic use to which the amphora was destined. Other pots painted by the same painter, in his peculiar style but in the red-figure technique, are displayed in Room XXI (showcase K). 1

2 *Showcase C.* Attic black-figure *hydria* of the Leagros Group (inv. 16450). On the shoulder: scene of a wrestling school. On the body: two horse soldiers in Thessalonian costume, with *patasos* (broad-brimmed hat) and two lances in their hands. The inscriptions indicate their names: *Thrasis* (Courage) and *Arete* (Virtue), and those of two youths: *Olympiodorus* and *Leagros*, each celebrated with the epithet *kalos* (beautiful).

3 *Showcase D.* Two *kylikes* (cups) with black-figure decoration in the inner roundel and red-figure decoration on the outside (inv. 15515, 16584). In *c.*530 B.C., Attic vase-painters began to abandon the black-figure technique, and adopted instead that of red figures painted in reserve on a black background. The change enabled vase-painters to obtain a better definition of the internal details of the figures through painted, instead of incised lines. This reflected contemporary developments in the art of painting. For some time the mixed application of the two techniques would co-exist on the same pot, but gradually the transition to red figures became definitive.

4 *Showcase F.* Black-figure amphora, signed by the potter Exekias (inv. 16757); side A: Achilles and Ajax playing at dice; side B: Castor, with his horse Kylaros, Pollux and their parents Tindaros and Leda. This masterpiece of Attic pottery, found at Vulci and donated to Pope Gregory XVI by the Candelori family in 1834, is dated 540-530 B.C.

5 *Showcase G.* Attic red-figure amphora by the Troilos Painter (inv. 16513): contest for the tripod and procession of musicians; from Cerveteri, early decades of the 5th century B.C. Three red-figure *kylikes* by the Brygos Painter, dated 480 B.C. (inv. 16560, 16582, 16583).

Showcase H. Above, two red-figure *kylikes* (cups) by the Makron Painter, found at Vulci, and dated to the first quarter of the 5 century B.C. (inv. 16576, 16581). Also from Vulci come two *kylikes* by the Epeleios Painter (inv. 16577, 17856), with scenes of wrestling school, datable to *c.*500 B.C. The same date and provenance is shared by the Attic red-figure *hydria* (water pot) by the Eucharides Painter, with the combat between Achilles and Hector. 6

Showcase I. Attic red-figure amphora attributed to the Hector Painter (inv. 16570): Hector performs a libation before battle, taking his leave from his parents Priam and Hecuba; side B: old man between two women, *c.*450 B.C. 7

Showcase K. Two Attic red-figure *kylikes* by Duris. Inv. 16561: a man, rather the worse for drink, is being tended by a girl; on the outside, bucolic scene of five men drinking, singing, making music and playing at *kottabos*, assisted by a flautist and servant; from Vulci, 490-480 B.C. Inv. 16545: Jason, in Colchis to claim the Golden Fleece from King Aietes, is betrayed by the latter and devoured by the monster that guarded the Fleece, hung from the branch of an oak tree. Jason here is rescued by Athena; from Cerveteri, *c.*480 B.C. 8

Attic red-figure *kylix* in the manner of Duris (inv. 16563): Hercules sails towards the island of Erytheia, where he will vanquish the monster Geryon; on the outside: the duel between Achilles and Hector, in the presence of Apollo and Athena; from Vulci (V. Campanari-Papal Government excavations, 1835-37), *c.*480 B.C.

Attic red-figure *kylix* attributed to the Oedipus Painter (inv. 16541): Oedipus, in the guise of a traveller, listens to the enigma proposed to him by the Sphinx; on the outside of the cup: comic scene with satyrs; from Vulci, *c.*480-470 B.C.

ROOM XX: Astarita Collection XX

In the frieze: Atlas, Banquet offered by Saul to Samuel, Banquet of Thyestes and allegorical figures by Orlando Parentini, dating to the pontificate of Pius IV (1559-1565).

The important Astarita Collection, donated to Paul VI in 1967, was inserted in the chronological sequence of the Vase Collection. All the objects on display are of great interest; many are worth special attention.

Showcase I. Large late-Corinthian column-krater (big deep bowl with wide mouth using at banquets for mixing wine and water) (inv. 35525). The front side portrays the mission of Odysseus and Menelaus to Troy to obtain the return of Helen; the two heroes, with the herald Talthybios, sit on the steps of an altar of the sanctuary of Athena and are received by the priestess Theonoe, wife of Antenor, accompanied by three handmaids and by a procession of horsemen, perhaps her sons; *c.*560 B.C. 1

ROOM XXI: *Room of the Sundial* XXI

The name refers to a small room, now incorporated into this far larger room, that once formed part of the Apartment of Cardinal Francesco Saverio de Zelada, Secretary of State under Pope Pius VI, who lived in these rooms until 1801, before they were allocated to the Museums. The room derives its name from the sundial it once contained, together with other astronomical instruments: together they formed the cardinal's observatory.

1 The first *showcase* to the right (*K*) is entirely dedicated to the Berlin Painter, one of the greatest vase painters active in Athens in the period around 490 B.C. The *hydria* (water pot) with Apollo seated on a Delphic tripod as he flies over the sea has been considered, ever since the compilers of the 19th century inventories, one of the finest vases in the Vatican collection (inv. 16568). The figure is portrayed isolated against a background remarkable for its pronounced sheen, in a style peculiar to this master.

2 This is followed, in *showcase I*, by the work of the Achilles Painter, a pupil of the Berlin Painter, portrayed here by his name-piece, an amphora (inv. 16571), found at Vulci, with Achilles and Briseis (?), *c.*450 B.C.

3 *Showcase D.* The introduction of a sober polychromy against the white ground of vases reflects in some way in vase painting the concurrent developments in mural and easel painting. In the calyx-krater of the Painter of the Boston *Phiale* (inv. 16586), pupil of the Achilles Painter (cf. showcase I), a pictorial style emerges that would have been difficult to express by the red-figure technique alone. Yet the same master also expressed himself in this style, as exemplified
4 by the *hydria* inv. 16549 with Thamyras; both vases were found in Vulci and date to 440-430 B.C.

5 *Showcase G.* There are still, however, examples of Late Attic pottery production that are not without freshness and originality, such as this *kylix* of the Jena Painter (inv. 16651), with Triptolemos; it comes from Vulci, and is datable to the final years of the 5th century B.C.

XXII ROOM XXII: *Upper Hemicycle*

The scenic Upper Hemicycle is dedicated to the display of the collection of Italiot vases.

The term Italiot pottery is generally used to denote the vast and varied production of vases painted in the red-figure technique that developed in the Greek colonies of Southern Italy and Sicily between the third quarter of the 5th and the 4th century B.C. The origin of this South Italian production has long been linked to the foundation of the Greek colony of Thurii (Calabria) in 443 B.C. This was followed by the beginning of the activity of the first Italiot potters in Lucania, namely, the Pisticci and Amykos painters (*showcase A*), who were probably of Greek origin; their style seems to depend on contemporary Attic pottery (room XXI) and in particular the followers of the Achilles and Polygnotus Painters.

This room contains examples of the main forms of pottery production in Southern Italy: in Lucania, Campania, Paestum and Apulia, with the sole exception of Sicily. A section is also dedicated to Gnathian -style pottery (from the site of Egnazia near Fasano in Apulia where a large quantity of it was). In its florid style and polychrome technique on a lustrous black ground, Gnathian ware marks the epilogue of ancient vase painting (*showcase M*). The display in the Upper Hemicycle ends with a selection dedicated to the parallel developments of Etruscan pottery (*showcase N*).

From a technical point of view, Italiot pottery is characterised by a lighter fabric and by a less brilliant pigment than the Attic production. The forms, too, reflect the contemporary Greek repertoire; they perpetuate types that had sometimes become obsolete in their places of origin, such as the proto-Panathenaic amphora and the volute-crater that would also assume monumental dimensions, reflecting the tendency of Italiot potteries to increase the size of vases (*showcase L*). The elaboration of local variants is also registered, such as the amphora with handle on the mouth, typically Campanian (*showcase D*), and the *nestoris*, a jar of Messapian origin that would spread in Apulia and Lucania (*showcase B*). Among the subjects are mythological themes of considerable importance. They are usually represented in theatrical settings and are clearly inspired by Greek tragedies. Their solemnity, however, is countered by the scoffing parodies of 'Phylax farces' (from *Phyliax*, a figure in the train of Dionysus), a genre that flourished in Magna Graecia during the 4/3 century B.C., vividly portrayed by the Paestan potters Assteas and Python (*showcase C*). The repertoire of youths, women, heads in profile, satyrs, *erotes* and *nikai*, that characterised Italiot pottery as a whole, represents at the same time a valuable source of information on the customs and daily life of these ancient peoples.

Showcase C. Crater painted by Assteas, painter of Paestum active in *c.*350-325 B.C., with mythological parody: Zeus is courting Alcmene, bride of Amphitryon, under the eyes of Hermes (inv. 17106). A strong inspiration of the Italiot theatrical world is found in the production of Campanian potters. The grotesque hairstyles of the comic actors portrayed here are typical of the popular taste of the Phylax farces that flourished in Magna Graecia during the 4th - 3rd century B.C.

Returning to the floor below, the exit of the Museum is through the Room of the Sun-Dial (XXI).

h - The Biga Room

View of the Biga Room

This domed room is situated above the Atrium of the Four Gates (Quattro Cancelli). It was begun in 1786 by Giuseppe Camporese, but only completed in 1794. Four niches between pilasters and four arched bays form the walls of the small rotunda. The dome is decorated with octagonal coffers. The *biga* (two-horse chariot), from which the room takes its name, is illuminated by the oculus in the ceiling.

1 In the centre: *two-horse chariot,* completed for display in the museum by Francesco Antonio Franzoni (wheels, shaft, one of the horses). The chariot itself was formerly in the church of San Marco, where it served as a bishop's throne. Its form recalls that of an ancient triumphal chariot; the relief decorations (laurel branches) recall representations of the chariots of the gods (Ceres, Tryptolemus). Roman, 1st century A.D. Inv. 2368.

On the right, starting from the entrance:

2 Statue of *Dionysus "Sardanapalos"* (ancient inscription on the hem of the cloak folded diagonally across the chest). An excellent Roman copy (1st cent. A.D.) of a Greek original of the circle of Praxiteles (late 4th cent. B.C.). Inv. 2363.

Five *children's sarcophagi* with reliefs of cupids competing in chariot races at the circus. The race is undoubtedly a symbol of the struggle for survival, the circus is life itself, the finishing-post the goal of life.
3, 4 They date to the 2nd - 3rd century A.D.: Inv. 2364, *c.*140 A.D.; Inv. 2356,
5, 6 *c.*160 A.D.; Inv. 2351, *c.*170 A.D.; Inv. 2348, *c.*190 A.D.; Inv. 2358
7 (opposite), *c.*100 years later.

8 Statue of a *discobolus preparing to throw.* The pose of the young discus-thrower shows his total concentration (the head is also antique but does not belong to the statue). The vigorous forms and balanced forces suggest a model of the Polykleitos school, probably by Naukydes. A fine copy of the early Roman Imperial period (1st century A.D.). Inv. 2349.

Statue of a *discobolus.* The inclination of the discus-thrower's head 9
(correctly restored), the torsion of his chest, the movement of his left leg, and the stretching of his arms show his concentration with unprecedented vivacity and audacity. A Hadrianic copy (2nd cent. A.D.)—as demonstrated by the tree-shaped support—of a bronze original by Myron of about 460 B.C. (the inscription on the tree trunk is modern). From Hadrian's Villa near Tivoli. Inv. 2346.

plan →

h - Gallery of the Candelabra

View of the gallery

Originally (1761) an open loggia, its open arcades were closed by Simonetti and Camporese under Pius VI, and divided into six sections by arches carried on columns and pillars. The gallery was named after the candelabra placed in front of the pillars. The ceiling was painted by Domenico Torti and Ludwig Seitz during the years 1883-87, under Leo XIII.

The six sections into which gallery is divided are indicated in the following description by Roman numerals.

I SECTION I

1 Right: *figurine of a boy* tossing a walnut with his right hand, while his cloak slips off his left arm. This type of motif is typical of the Hellenistic period (3rd - 1st cent. B.C.), when genre scenes of this kind were popular (cf. *Boy throttling a goose*, p. 83: IV/17). Inv. 2419.

2 In front of the statuette: *sarcophagus of a boy;* the reclining figure of the dead child is represented on the lid. At the centre of the frontal relief the boy is portrayed once again, now seated on a throne, as in traditional representations of ancient philosophers, surrounded by plump boys bearing features of the Muses. Roman, *c.*270-280 A.D. Inv. 2422.

II SECTION II

3, 4 Under the arch, right and left: two *candelabra from Otricoli* (for burning oil, wax or resin). Roman, 2nd century A.D. Inv. 2403, 2408.

5 On the left: *Ganymede and the eagle.* Pliny (*Nat. Hist.* XXXIV, 79) refers to a bronze group, by Leochares, portraying Ganymede being abducted by the eagle sent by Zeus. He remarks that the eagle, tenderly grasping the youth by his clothes so as not to harm him, seems well aware of the identity of both the abducted and the abductor. The monumental, mid-4th century B.C. invention by Leochares was used on this occasion as an ornamental motif of what

was once a table leg, the work of Roman copyists of the 2 century A.D. Inv. 2445.

In front of the next niche: *sarcophagus with scenes from the myth of* 6
Protesilaos. Left side: Protesilaos bids farewell to his wife, Laodamia. Front: his death on landing at Troy (he was the first Greek to jump ashore from the ship); Hermes leads him before Laodamia; funeral lament; accompanied by Hermes, he is ferried by Charon across the Styx to the underworld. Right side: Sisyphus, Ixion and Tantalus, the three famous "penitents" of antiquity. From the Appian Way (2 mile). Roman, about 170 A.D. Inv. 2465.

Opposite: *sarcophagus with reliefs depicting scenes from the myth of* 7
Orestes: the slaying of Aegisthus and Clytemnestra; Orestes at Delphi (the Furies). On the sides, sphinxes curled up. Roman, about 160 A.D. Inv. 2513.

Behind the sarcophagus: *statue of the Ephesian Artemis,* a copy of the 8
cult statue with symbols of fecundity and power. 2nd century A.D., from Hadrian's Villa. (Cf. p. 159: V/25). Inv. 2505.

SECTION III III

Under the four arches of this section, left and right: *two pairs of* 9-12
candelabra, found near Sant'Agnese on the Via Nomentana in the 17th century. Trajanic in date (early 2nd cent. A.D.). Inv. 2482, 2487; 2566, 2564.

Set into the walls, ten fragments of Roman frescoes, from Tor Marancia. Mural decoration of the 2nd century A.D.

On the right: *statue of Apollo* and, behind, *base of Semus Sancus.* 13
Contrary to the information given in old catalogues, the statue and base do not belong together. Inv. 2585, 2583. Apollo stands erect, bearing his attributes in his outstretched hands; a classic sculpture rich in archaisms, 2nd century A.D.

SECTION IV IV

On the right:

Statuette of *Nike* (Victory); the head is of Athena, and comes from 14
another statue. Nike leans on a trophy, her right leg resting on the prow of a ship. A monument for a naval victory. Roman Imperial work, based on a Greek model of the 2nd century B.C. Inv. 2721.

Sarcophagus with scenes from the myth of Bacchus. Bacchus and his 15
followers find Ariadne. Roman, late 2nd century A.D. Inv. 2698.

On the left:

Sarcophagus with reliefs of the massacre of the Niobids by Apollo and 16
Artemis, who are shown shooting their deadly arrows at the children of Niobe (right and left of the scene). Roman, *c.*160 A.D. Inv. 2635.

Boy throttling a goose. The little boy, who is about three years old, is 17
squeezing the goose's neck with both hands, using all of his strength to overcome the animal's resistance. Marble copy of a bronze original of about 300 B.C. attributed to Boethos of Chalcedon on the basis of an observation by Pliny: "infans anseren strangulat" (*Nat. Hist.* XXXIV, 84). Inv. 2655.

Opposite: statuette of the *Tyche (Fortune) of Antioch* on the river 18
Orontes, seated on a rock, with a mural crown on her head, ears of wheat in her right hand, and a bust of the river god Orontes at her feet. Roman copy of a Greek original, in bronze, by Eutychides, who made this representation of the city's patron goddess shortly after the foundation of Antioch, in *c.*300 B.C. Inv. 2672.

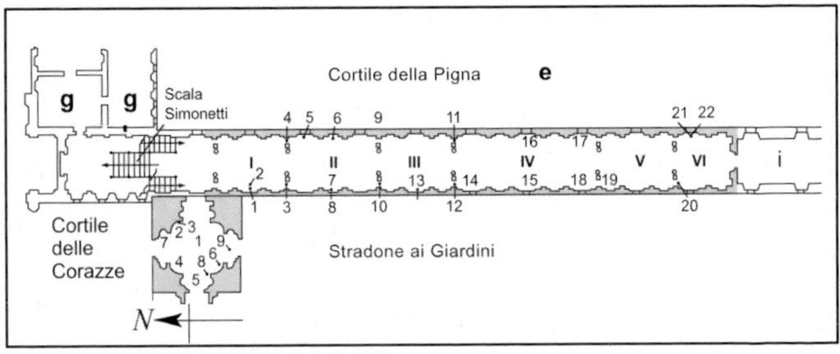

V

SECTION V

19 To the right: statue of a female runner, the so-called *Atalanta*. The palm branch on the support is the symbol of victory. A classic work rich in archaisms, of the circle of Praxiteles, 1st century B.C. Inv. 2784.

VI

SECTION VI

20 To the right: statue of *Artemis* (Diana); identified by the belt that once carried her quiver. Roman version of a work by Kephisodotos (son of Praxiteles) of the early 4th century B.C. The head does not belong to the statue. Inv. 2834.

21 To the left: statuette of a *Persian soldier,* identified by the tiara he is wearing. Copy of a statuette from the group of the so-called small sanctuary of Attalos, which the Pergamenes set up as a votive offering on the Acropolis of Athens in the 2nd century B.C. (the themes are the traditional ones of the Battle of Giants, the Battle of Amazons, and of combats between Greeks and Persians). Inv. 2794.

22 Below the statuette: *sarcophagus with reliefs of the abduction of the daughters of King Leucippus by the Dioscuri,* recognizable by their pointed caps. Castor and Pollux have seized the two girls, and are carrying them away. On the right, a fleeing woman and a warrior (the parents?). On the left, a young warrior prevents a bearded figure from stopping the abductors. On the sides, the nuptials of the abductors with their victims. Since the Dioscuri were transported by Zeus among the stars, they were considered lords of the astral spheres, and for this reason they frequently appear in funerary representations. About 160 A.D. Inv. 2769.

I - Gallery of Tapestries

Tapestry with Christ appearing to the disciples of Emmaus (series of the *Scuola Nuova*, Brussels, 16th cent.), detail

Domenico del Frate and Antonio Marini painted the chiaroscuro decoration of the ceiling with allegorical scenes celebrating the glory of the reigning pope, Pius VI, in 1789. The gallery was originally a picture gallery, but the series of tapestries of the *Scuola Nuova* have been displayed hung here since 1838. They are called the *Scuola Nuova* (New School) to distinguish them from the tapestries of the *Scuola Vecchia* (Old School), now displayed in the Vatican Pinacoteca and woven in the Brussels workshop of Pieter van Aelst from cartoons by Raphael in the time of Leo X. The tapestries of the *Scuola Nuova* were made in the same workshop, but based on designs by Raphael's pupils in the time of Clement VII.

Apart from the Brussels series of tapestries, the walls of the gallery are also hung with a tapestry of the *Conversion of the centurion Cornelius* of Flemish manufacture (*c.*1530), woven for Cardinal Agostino Trivulzio, who died in Rome in 1548), and the series of the *Life of Pope Urban VIII*, woven in Rome between 1663 and 1679. The latter series was produced in the Barberini tapestry workshop established by Cardinal Francesca Barberini, nephew of Urban VIII, in 1627 and closed dawn in 1683, after the cardinal's death (1679).

Wall opposite the windows, from left to right:

Series of the *Scuola Nuova*, woven between 1524 and 1531 (Brussels, workshop of Pieter van Aelst, based on drawings of the school of Raphael. The tapestries represent the following episodes in the life of Christ: *Adoration of the shepherds,* Inv. 43858; *Adoration of the Magi,* Inv. 43860; *Presentation in the Temple,* Inv. 43857; *Massacre of the Innocents,* Inv. 43863; *Massacre of the Innocents*, inv. 43864; *Massacre of the Innocents*, inv. 43865; *Resurrection,* Inv. 3862; *Jesus Appearing to Mary Magdalen,* Inv. 43855; *Resurrection,* Inv. 43861; and *Supper at Emmaus,* Inv. 43856.

Flemish workshop, *c.*1530: *Conversion of the centurion Cornelius,* Inv. 437866.

Flemish workshop, Brussels, 1549: *Death of Julius Caesar,* Inv. 43788.

Wall between the windows, from right to left:

Series of the Life of Pope Urban VIII (Rome, Barberini workshop: *Matteo Barberini graduates from the University of Pisa,* Inv. 43918; *Matteo Barberini controls the level of Lake Trasimene,* Inv. 43919; *Maffeo Barberini is made a cardinal by Paul V,* Inv. 43920: *Matteo Barberini is elected Pope as Urban VIII,* Inv. 43921; *Urban VIII annexes the state of Urbino to the Holy See,* Inv. 43924; *Urban VIII consecrates St. Peter's Basilica,* Inv. 43926; *Urban VIII begins the building of Fort Urban,* Inv. 43926; and *Urban VIII saves the city of Rome from plague and famine,* Inv. 43927.

k - Gallery of Maps

View of the gallery

This gallery was named after the 40 topographical maps of the regions of Italy, and of the Church's territories (32 frescoes each measuring *c.*320 x 430 cm on the two long walls, and 8 smaller ones on the end walls of the gallery). Pope Gregory XIII commissioned the maps between 1580 and 1583. They were based on cartoons by Ignazio Danti, one of the greatest cosmographers of his day. These maps are an extremely important record of 16th century geography and cartography.

The gallery is 120 m. long, and 6 m. wide and has a barrel-vaulted ceiling. It was built between 1578 and 1580 by Ottaviano Mascherino, who also built the Tower of the Winds, which is situated above the north end of the gallery, and is visible from the gardens. The sundial in the tower was also used to demonstrate the inaccuracy of the calendar then in use and the need to make the changes that led to the adoption of our present calendar, called Gregorian after Pope Gregory.

Ignazio Danti used the Apennines as a dividing line to determine where the maps were to be placed on the walls. The regions on the Ligurian and Tyrrhenian seas appear on the wall facing the Cortile del Belvedere, while the regions surrounded by the Alps and on the Adriatic sea are on the wall on the garden side. Opposite the present entrance, there are regional maps and maps of Ancient and Contemporary Italy. Each regional map includes a plan of the main city, often in perspective.

On the short walls, the Tremiti Islands, the Siege of Malta, the Battle of Lepanto, and the Island of Elba, are represented at the north end of the gallery (present entrance wall), while the four great ports of the period: Civitavecchia, Genoa, Venice and Ancona, are represented at the opposite end (south wall).

Girolamo Muziano and Cesare Nebbia co-ordinated and also participated in the work of the large group of artists involved in the frescoes and in the decoration of the barrel vault with stucco work and a series of 80 episodes taken from the history of the Church and the lives of saints; each episode is linked geographically to the region represented below it. In 1631 Urban VIII had the maps "completed" and embellished with additional ornamental elements by Lukas Holste.

plan
p. 94

I - Gallery of St. Pius V

Tapestry with episodes of the Passion (Tournai workshop (?), late 15th cent.), detail of the Last Supper

The gallery, originally divided into three rooms, formed part of the apartment of St. Pius V, together with the two rooms to its left, the chapel at its far end and the so-called Sobieski Room. The chapel (the uppermost of three chapels situated one above the other in the building built for Pius V) is dedicated to St. Michael. It was the Pope's private chapel. All that remains of its original decoration by Giorgio Vasari and Jacopo Zucchi is the ceiling fresco depicting the *Fall of Lucifer and the Rebel Angels.* The frescoes below it were painted in the 19th century.

The gallery now contains a series of tapestries of various periods and provenance. The most valuable are those of Flemish manufacture, probably from Tournai (Belgium), one of the most important and largest centres of high-quality textile production in the 15th century.

Above the entrance door:

Barberini workshop (Rome), 17th century: *two tapestry friezes for the baldachin of Urban VIII.* Inv. 43730, 43732.

Wall opposite the windows, from left to right:

1 Tournai workshop (?), late 15th century: *Episodes from the Passion,*
2 with the Last Supper in the centre, Inv. 43742; *Tapestry of the Credo,* with the Baptism of Christ in the centre, Inv. 43743.

Wall between the windows, from right to left:

3 Brussels workshop, 16th century, from a cartoon by Lambert Lombard based on an invention by Raphael: *Coronation of the Virgin.* It includes the coat of arms of Pope Paul III (1534-1549). Inv. 43852.

4 Brussels workshop (Pieter van Aelst): *Religion, Justice, Charity,* Inv. 43866. This once formed the back of the baldachin over the throne used by Clement VII for Consistories, and is datable to his pontificate (1523-1534).

Faubourg Saint-Marcel workshop, Paris, series of *Scenes from the Life of Coriolanus*, 1610-1620: *Coriolanus in the Presence of the King of the Volsci.*

The two adjacent rooms to the left still have their original coffered 5, 6
ceilings with the Pope's coat of arms and figures of the *Evangelists* in the first and *Doctors of the Church* in the second that are attributed to the painters Ferraù Faenzoni and Ventura Salimbeni. They now contain Medieval and Renaissance Pottery from the Papal Palaces of the Lateran, the Vatican, and the Cancelleria and a selection of so-called Minute Mosaics, a typically Roman form of art that was very popular between the late 18th and 19th century. It was used in particular for decorating small sized personal objects .

plan
p. 94

m - Sobieski Room, Room of the Immaculate Conception

Jan Matejko, The Liberation of Vienna, detail

SOBIESKI ROOM

This room is named after the enormous painting occupying the entire north wall, a work of the Polish artist Jan Matejko. It depicts the victory of the King of Poland, John III Sobieski, over the Turks at the gates of Vienna in 1683. There are more 19th century canvases hanging on the other walls. Above, fragments of a frieze dating to the pontificate of Gregory XIII (1572-1585).

Entering the room, from right to left:

Francesco Grandi, *Martyrdom of the Blessed Johann Sarkander,*1854, Inv. 2607.

Francesco Podesti, *Apparition of Jesus to St. Margaret Alacoque*, inv. 42588.

Ponziano Loverini, *St. Grata gathering the mortal remains of St. Alexander*, 1887, inv. 42614.

Cesare Fracassini, *The Martyrs of Gorkum,* Inv. 2612.

Jan Matejko, *The Liberation of Vienna by Jan Sobieski* (oil on canvas, 458 x 894 cm). This is considered the masterpiece of the Polish artist, who waived the payment of 80,000 florins on condition that the painting be presented to Leo XIII on the occasion of the bicentenary of the victory at Vienna on 12 September 1883 (the scene of the painting's presentation to the Pope is depicted in a fresco on the vault of the second bay of the Gallery of the Candelabra). Inv. 2613.

The floor is Roman and comes from Ostia Antica.

ROOM OF THE IMMACULATE CONCEPTION

The room is situated in the Borgia Tower. Frescoes by Francesco Podesti depict scenes pertaining to the definition and proclamation of the dogma of the Immaculate Conception of Mary by Pius IX in 1854. On the wall opposite the windows, the *Ceremony of the Definition of the Dogma*; above, *Paradise*. On the side walls, the *Pope Censing the Image of the Virgin*, and a *Meeting of Theologians to Discuss the Immaculate Conception*. Between the windows, the Sibyls. On the vault, medallions with biblical scenes and allegorical figures. The floor is Roman and comes from Ostia Antica.

1 At the centre of the room is an elaborate *showcase* (made by Christofle, Paris) displaying ornately bound and decorated volumes, mostly manuscripts, given to Pius IX on the occasion of the solemn definition of the dogma of the Immaculate Conception of Mary. The volumes contain the text of the papal bull proclaiming the dogma (8 December 1854) translated into many different languages and dialects. They were donated by kings, heads of state, bishops, provinces, dioceses, cities, etc., on the initiative of the French priest Marie Dominique Sire, in 1878.

plan →

n - Raphael's Stanze
Chapel of Urban VIII

Raphael, *The School of Athens*, detail (Stanza della Segnatura)

The rooms known as the Raphael's Stanze are part of the apartment on the second floor of the Apostolic Palace, directly above the Borgia Apartment that was used by Pope Julius II della Rovere as his residence, as well as by his successors down to Gregory XIII. Apart from the Stanze, it also included the Room of the Swiss Guards, the Sala dei Chiaroscuri, the Chapel of Nicholas V (his private chapel) and the Logge. Julius II's bedroom (*cubiculum*), now closed to the public, communicated with the chapel and the Sala dei Chiaroscuri. It was preceded by a small antechamber that linked the Sala dei Chiaroscuri with the Stanza di Eliodoro. Julius II lived in this apartment from 1507 refusing to live in the Borgia Apartment, since, as the master of ceremonies Paris de Grassis explained, "*non volebat videre omni hora figuram Alexandri praedecessoris sui*" ("he did not want to see the image of his predecessor Alexander [VI] at every moment".

The Stanze were frescoed by Raphael and his assistants between 1508 and 1524, and the decoration of these rooms marked the beginning of Raphael's success and fame in Rome He began to replace artists who were much better known than he was, including his teacher Perugino and others. Portions of their works were destroyed to accommodate those of the young master; previous paintings done by Piero della Francesca, Bartolomeo della Gatta and Luca Signorelli were completely destroyed.

There are four Stanze with cross-vaulted ceilings. Except for the Sala di Costantino, which forms part of the 13th century wing of the Apostolic Palace, they are situated in the wing built under Nicholas V. They overlook the Cortile del Belvedere to the north and the Cortile del Pappagalloto the south.

To avoid overcrowding, a one-way visiting itinerary takes visitors from the Room of the Immaculate Conception to an outside balcony. Visits to Raphael's Stanze begin from the Sala di Costantino.

I

I: SALA DI COSTANTINO (1517-1524)

This large room, named after the emperor Constantine, was used for receptions and official ceremonies (*caenaculum amplior*) It was decorated by pupils of Raphael, based partly on Raphael's drawings, but painted after his premature death in 1520. Its iconographic scheme is a continuation of the previous one used in the Stanze celebrating the apotheosis of the Church. The subject here is the Church's victory over paganism and its establishment in the city of Rome. The main scenes are painted to imitate tapestries, while allegorical figures, popes and virtues appear at the corners.

The original wooden-beamed ceiling was replaced under Pius IV by the present false vault, decorated by Tommaso Laureti and his assistants in 1585.

1 *Baptism of Constantine.* The setting is the Lateran Baptistery. Pope Sylvester has the features of Clement VII.

2 *Battle of Milvian Bridge.* The fresco depicts Constantine's victory over Maxentius. Some of the details are taken from the reliefs on the Arch of Constantine.

3 *Apparition of the Cross.* The group composed of the emperor and surrounding figures comes from Trajan's Column and from the Arch of Constantine.

4 Constantine's (legendary) *Donation of Rome* to Pope Sylvester (portrait of Clement VII).

At this point those who wish to visit the Sala dei Chiaroscuri and the Chapel of Nicholas V must temporarily leave the Stanze.

II

II: STANZA D'ELIODORO (1512-1514)

It was probably the audience chamber, of the apartment, and Raphael decorated it immediately after the Stanza della Segnatura (see below). Its scheme is political. It is intended to illustrate the miraculous protection granted by God to the Church threatened in its faith (*Miracle of Bolsena*), in the person of its pope (*St. Peter Delivered from Prison*), in its apostolic see (*Meeting of Leo the Great with Attila*), and in its patrimony (*Heliodorus Expelled from the Temple*).

The caryatids on the lower part of the wall were painted by Raphael's assistants, while the small oblong panels were probably painted again by Carlo Maratta. The scenes of the *Sacrifice of Isaac*, the *Burning Bush*, *Jacob's Ladder*, and *God Appears to Noah*on the vaulted ceiling are all by Raphael.

1 The *Expulsion of Heliodorus from the Temple.* It represents the biblical episode of Heliodorus, who was ordered by the King of Syria to plunder the treasure of the Temple of Jerusalem. On his way out, he was assaulted by a horseman and two youths, and driven out of the temple. By choosing this episode from the Apocrypha, Julius II wished to allude to his policy of expelling usurpers from Church lands, and in order to send a clear message, he even had himself portrayed in the scene on the left. The figures in the Pope's entourage

include the litter-bearer in German dress, perhaps Marcantonio Raimondi, engraver and friend of Raphael, while the face of the other litter-bearer is a self-portrait of the artist himself. An inscription on the dado below the fresco records the death of the Constable of Bourbon during the Sack of Rome.

St. Peter delivered from prison. At the centre, over the window, the angel wakes St. Peter, and conducts him out of the prison, past the sleeping guards (right). A soldier with a torch wakes the dumbfounded guards (left). This fresco, one of Raphael's most famous, is remarkable for its masterly representation of the different sources of light. 2

Leo the Great turning back Attila from Rome. The episode took place near Mantua, but Raphael has given it a Roman setting: in the background we can see the Coliseum, an aqueduct, a basilica, and an obelisk. St. Peter and St. Paul, armed with swords, appear in the sky, striking Attila and his barbarian horde with terror. On the left, Leo I, with the features of Leo X, advances on a white horse. The fresco is not entirely Raphael's own work; there are also signs of studio intervention. 3

The *Miracle of Bolsena.* The fresco represents a miracle that took place in 1263. A Bohemian priest, who harboured doubts about the real presence of Christ in the Eucharist, saw blood exuding from the consecrated Host while he was celebrating mass in Bolsena. The miracle gave rise to the Feast of *Corpus Christi* and to the construction of the Orvieto Cathedral. Julius II, kneeling before the altar to the right, is shown witnessing the miracle. The two cardinals of his retinue are Leonardo Grosso della Rovere (the elder of the two) and Raffaele Riario (with clasped hands). The fresco is considered one of Raphael's masterpieces. 4

III: STANZA DELLA SEGNATURA (1508-1511) III

This was the library and study of Julius II. It was the first of the rooms to be decorated by Raphael, and the frescoes here were almost entirely executed by him. The iconographic scheme was undoubtedly established by a theologian *ad praescriptum Iulii pontificis* (at the instructions of Julius II in person). It is intended to illustrate the three highest categories of the human spirit according to the neo-Platonic vision: truth, goodness and beauty. Supernatural truth is represented by the *Disputa*, rational truth by the *School of Athens*; goodness by the *Virtues* and the *Law*, and beauty by the *Parnassus*.

The large medallions set into the ceiling depicting *Theology*, *Philosophy*, *Justice* and *Poetry* are closely linked to the wall paintings. So too are the paintings of *Adam and Eve*, the *Primum Mobile*, the *Judgement of Solomon*, and *Apollo and Marsyas* in the pendentives. The decorative scheme of the ceiling antedates Raphael, and is attributed to Sodoma. The grisaille paintings on the lower part of the walls are by Perin del Vaga and are datable to the pontificate of Paul III; they replaced the wooden panelling by Giovanni Barile and Fra Giovanni da Verona, destroyed during the Sack of Rome in 1527. The inlaid, polychrome marble floor is ornamented with the crossed keys of Nicholas V, the name of Julius II, and emblems of Leo X.

The *Disputa*, or *Debate over the Holy Sacrament.* The title of the fresco ought to be "The Triumph of Religion": above, in the centre, Christ is seated in majesty between the Virgin and St. John the Baptist in Paradise. Above his head is God the Father, below his feet the Holy Spirit in the guise of the dove. The Church Triumphant unfolds at the sides above the clouds: saints, alternating with Old Testament prophets, visually contemplate truth (the Trinity). On earth below is 1

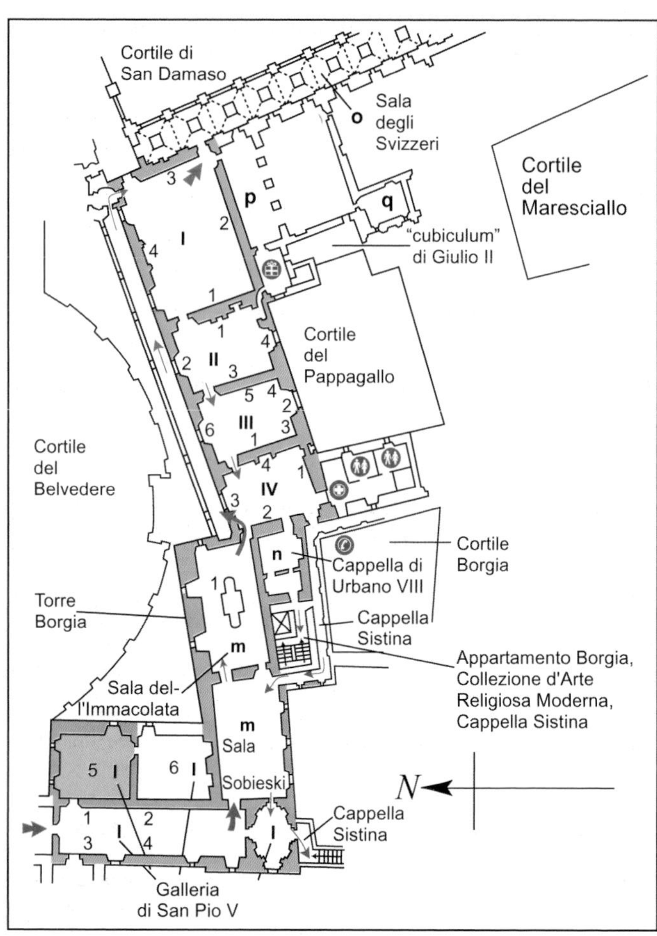

the central altar, with a monstrance on it, the focal point of the composition, flanked by doctors and theologians of the Church Militant who, thanks to the sacrament of the Eucharist, participate in the incarnation of the truth. On the right, in papal vestments, are Gregory the Great and Sixtus IV,and behind him, Dante. Further to the right, his head partly concealed by his hood, is Savonarola. The elderly man looking up, wearing a Dominican habit to the far left is Fra Angelico. The fresco is entirely the work of Raphael, and heralds the artist's full maturity. During the Sack of Rome soldiers left two graffiti on the fresco, one in praise of Luther, the other of Charles V.

2 The *Cardinal and Theological Virtues* (in the lunette). The Cardinal Virtues are represented by women: Fortitude holds an oak branch; Prudence is two-faced and observes herself in a mirror; Temperance holds the reins. The Theological Virtues are represented by cupids: Faith points to the sky, Hope holds a burning torch, and Charity shakes the acorns from an oak-tree. The fresco is by Raphael.

3 *Gregory IX receiving the Decretals* (canon law) *from St. Raymond de Peñafort.* The enthroned Pope has been given the features of Julius II. Next him are Cardinals Giovanni de' Medici, Alessandro Farnese and Antonio del Monte.

Justinian receiving the Pandects (civil laws) *from Trebonian.* This 4
fresco was executed by Lorenzo Lotto, based on Raphael's drawing.

The *School of Athens.* A throng of ancient philosophers and scientists 5
(some of them given the features of contemporary figures by Raphael) converse as they stroll inside an imposing basilica, inspired by Donato Bramante. At the centre, Plato and Aristotle; one points upward to the world of ideas, the other holds his hand open between heaven and earth. On the left, Socrates with his characteristic Silenus-like profile. In front of him, Alcibiades and Alexander the Great, the latter in armour. To the right of centre, Diogenes reclining on the steps. At the foot of the steps, to the left, Epicurus wearing a wreath of vine-leaves. Behind him, Averroes watches Pythagoras, who is writing on a slate. Towards the centre of the foreground is the isolated figure of Heraclitus; the figure was added by Raphael at a later stage, forcing him to alter his original composition. To the right, Euclid (Bramante), bent double as he draws with a compass on a slate placed on the floor; on the neckline of his garment, perhaps is Raphael's signature, "R.V.S.M.". Dressed in white on the far right is a painter, and behind him, Raphael (self-portrait). In the niches of the Basilica: statues of Apollo, god of the Arts, and Athena, goddess of Wisdom.

The *Parnassus.* Apollo is seated in the centre playing a lyre, 6
surrounded by the Muses. On his right is blind Homer (with *Laocoön's* features), flanked by Dante and Virgil. Sappho is seated below (next to the window). On the right, famous Italian poets and writers: Ludovico Ariosto, Antonio Tebaldeo (in profile, bearded) and Jacopo Sannazzaro (dressed in yellow). The fresco was painted after the *Disputa* and the *School of Athens* and marks Raphael's total mastery of his art-form.

IV: STANZA DELL'INCENDIO DI BORGO (1514-1517) IV

This was Leo X's private dining room (*triclinium penitiar*). The kitchens were located in the adjoining room, still used as a service area today. It is the last of the rooms decorated by Raphael, though he left a large part of the actual work to his assistants. The purpose of the scheme of this room was to illustrate the political ambitions of Leo X by depicting events from the lives of two other Popes bearing the same name: Leo III and Leo IV. The decoration of the ceiling with allegories relating to the Holy Trinity is by Perugino, and was completed earlier, in the time of Julius II. The figures below in the corners of the room represent the Egyptian *telamones* (statues of male figures used instead of columns to support an entablature) found in Tivoli before 1504, and now in the Pio-Clementine Museum. The magnificently inlaid doors are the work of Giovanni Barili and Fra Giovanni da Verona.

The *Fire in the Borgo.* According to the *Liber Pontificalis* medieval 1
history of the popes, in 847 Leo IV extinguished a fire blazing in Borgo Santo Spirito, the district extending between St. Peter's and the Tiber with the sign of the cross. The episode is depicted in the background, with the Pope appearing in an open Renaissance loggia in front of the Constantinian Basilica, as it still appeared in Raphael's day. The terrorized crowd is in the foreground and, on the left, the famous pair of figures that clearly refer to Virgil's account of Aeneas' flight from Troy with his father Anchises on his shoulders. The composition, which anticipates Raphael's late style, is largely attributed as his own work.

The *Coronation of Charlemagne* in St. Peter's. Charlemagne has 2
been given the features of Francis I, and Leo III those of Leo X, an

allusion to the concordat reached between France and the Church in Bologna in 1515. Designed by Raphael but executed by his workshop.

4 The *Justification of Leo III.* The fresco depicts the oath sworn in St. Peter's by Leo III to defend himself against the slander of the nephews of Adrian I, while a voice from above admonished, *Dei non hominum est episcopos iudicare.* It alludes to the sanctioning by the 1516 Lateran Council of the principle that the pope is only answerable to God for his actions. Leo III has been given the features of Leo X. The work is by Raphael's assistants.

5 The *Battle of Ostia.* The fresco celebrates the victory of Leo IV, in the likeness of Leo X, over the Saracens, and alludes to Leo X's crusade against the Turks. Among the figures in the retinue behind the Pope are Cardinals Bernardo Bibbiena (to the right) and Giulio de' Medici (to the left). The composition was carefully prepared by Raphael himself with numerous drawings, but was execution by his assistants.

CHAPEL OF URBAN VIII

This small chapel, richly decorated with gilded stuccowork and frescoes, is the work of Pietro da Cortona, and was once the private chapel of Urban VIII. The fresco above the altar depicts the *Deposition.* The altar frontal (inv. 3882; 17th cent.) is from the small Church of San Filippino on the Via Giulia (now deconsecrated), the only Roman church dedicated to St. Philip Neri. The adjacent room contains some preparatory models by Antonio Canova (inv. 4551, 4552, 4546, 4554) and a plaster model of Giuseppe Fabris for the funerary monument of Antonio Canova, which was never made (inv. 4553).

o - Raphael's Logge

Raphael's Logge, Bay 11

The logge may be visited by qualified scholars upon formal request.

Raphael's Logge are situated on the second floor of the building consisting of three orders of superimposed loggias commissioned by Julius II as the façade of the Apostolic Palace overlooking Rome. The construction of this building was entrusted to Donato Bramante in 1508, who was already working on two other Vatican projects: the Belvedere Court and the "new" St. Peter's. By the time he died in 1514, Bramante had only completed the first row of loggias. Leo X then commissioned Raphael, who completed the work in 1519, and also decorated (from 1517) the loggia that bears his name. The decoration of the first-floor loggia, is by Giovanni da Udine, who also did part of the decoration of the third-floor loggia (1560-64), now extensively repainted (these two loggias are closed to the public). Gregory XIII and Sixtus V each added an east wing to the structure, thus creating the present San Damaso Courtyard, which can be seen from the windows.

Access to Raphael's Logge is from Constantine's Room (I) in Raphael's Stanze. The windows opened along the wall illuminate the Sala dei Chiaroscuri (see p. 100), the antechamber of the apartment where Leo X held the "secret consistory", and the Room of the Swiss Guards. A door at the end of the logge, in the same wall, gives access to a ramp (*cordonata*) originally designed to be used on horse-back. It was designed by Bramante and largely built – with alterations – by Raphael to link the three floors of the building with the courtyard known as the Cortile del Maresciallo. The arcades were originally open on the courtyard side, but were closed with large windows in the 19 century to protect the frescoes and stucco-work, which are now in very poor condition, especially the lower sections. Deterioration began just a few years after they were completed and, around 1560, Giovanni da Udine was forced to commission the first restoration.

Michiel tells us that the gallery was "kept closed and reserved for the sole pleasure" of Leo X. He also reports that Leo X placed "many statues, kept in private amongst his possessions" in some of its niches, now destroyed. Leo X's taste for antiques was typical of his age and is reflected in the decoration of the loggia carried out by

Raphael: the grotesques and stucco ornaments of the logge show a series of clearly antique motifs, and prototypes that refer in particular to the *Domus Aurea* (Golden House of Nero) with which Raphael and his school were well-acquainted. Raphael was appointed Superintendent of Antiquities in 1514. Another typically Renaissance element present here is the intermingling of biblical and mythological motifs. In order to carry out this extremely complex decorative scheme, Raphael made use of the collaboration of Giulio Romano, Francesco Penni, and especially Giovanni da Udine and Perin del Vaga. However, the decoration as a whole should not be considered as the work of Raphael's school, but as teamwork, in the modern sense of the word. Minor contributions were made by Pellegrino da Modena, Vincenzo da San Giminiano, Raffaellino del Colle, Tommaso Vincidor, and the very young Polidoro da Caravaggio.

The original majolica floor, by Luca della Robbia the Younger, was removed in the mid-19th century.

There is a great deal of controversy as to the identity of the artists of the individual parts of the loggia decoration. The Roman-style stucco ornaments, made with a mixture of lime, plaster and powdered marble were undoubtedly created and executed by Giovanni da Udine. He also depicted himself and Raphael's studio at work more than once on the pilasters of the first two bays. There is much less certainty as to who painted the biblical scenes on the vaults. They form what has come to be known as *Raphael's Bible*, and are taken from the Old Testament except for the Gospel scenes in the last bay. The emblems of the yoke, ring and feathers placed at the centre of the vaulted ceilings are the heraldic devices of Leo X.

I BAY 1

1-4 *God dividing darkness from light. God dividing the waters. God creating the sun and moon. God creating animals.*

II BAY 2

1-4 *Creation of Eve. Original Sin. Expulsion from Eden. Adam and Eve with their sons.*

III BAY 3

1-4 *The building of the ark. The Flood. Leaving the ark. Noah's sacrifice.*

IV BAY 4

1-4 *The victorious Abraham met by Melchizedek. God's promise to Abraham. The angels visit Abraham. The burning of Sodom.*

V BAY 5

1-4 *God forbids Isaac to go to Egypt. Abimelech learns that Rebecca is the wife of Isaac. Isaac blesses Jacob instead of Esau. Isaac blesses Esau.*

VI BAY 6

1-4 *Jacob's vision. Jacob meets Rachel at the well. Jacob reproaches Laban. Return to Canaan.*

VII BAY 7

1-4 *Joseph relates his dreams to his brothers. Joseph is sold by his brothers. Joseph and the wife of Potiphar. Joseph interprets the Pharaoh's dreams.*

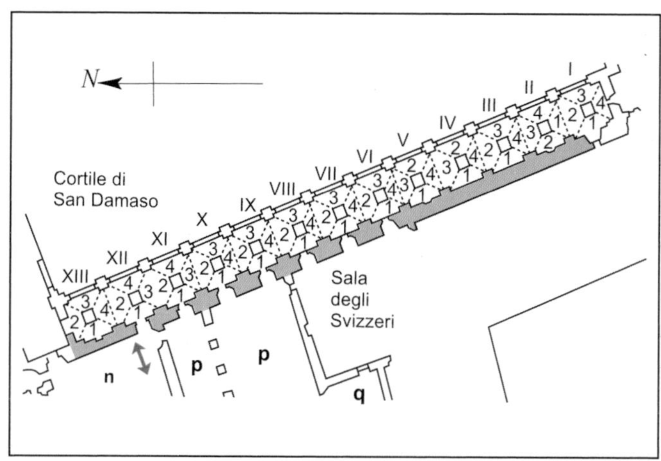

BAY 8 IX

Moses found in the Nile. The burning bush. The crossing of the Red Sea. Moses makes water spring from a rock. **1-4**

BAY 9 IX

Moses receives the tablets of the Law. Worship of the golden calf. God speaks to Moses from a cloud. Moses gives the tablets of the Law to the people. **1-4**

BAY 10 X

The Ark of the Covenant is carried across the Jordan. The capture of Jericho. Joshua stops the sun. Division of the land of Canaan. **1-4**

BAY 11 XI

David is anointed King. David kills Goliath. Triumph of David. David's sin. **1-4**

BAY 12 XII

The consecration of Solomon. The judgement of Solomon. The Queen of Sheba. The building of the temple. **1-4**

BAY 13 XIII

The Birth of Christ. Adoration of the Magi. Baptism of Christ. The Last Supper. **1-4**

p - Sala dei Chiaroscuri

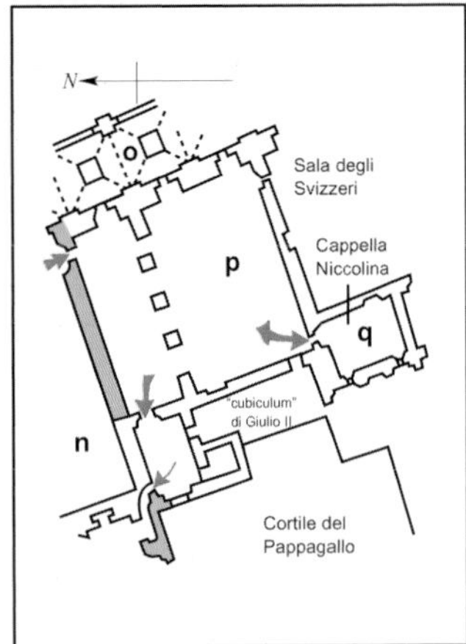

View of the room

The Sala dei Chiaroscuri, also known as the Sala dei Palafrenieri, the vestment room of the papal apartment, was the room where Leo X used to hold the "secret consistory", i.e. meetings with cardinals resident in Rome, and other ceremonies of various nature, both public and private, religious and secular. The room was also known as the Sala del Pappagallo because a caged parrot (*pappagallo*) had been kept in the room ever since the Middle Ages; the name is commemorated by a painting of two parrots, perhaps the work of Giovanni da Udine, on the wall above the door leading to the Sala degli Svizzeri (Room of the Swiss Guards: closed to the public).

The room forms part of the 13th century wing of the Apostolic Palace, and is divided into two by a row of columns that mark the beginning of the 14th century addition, of which Constantine's Room (I) in Raphael's Stanze is a part.

The present decoration dates back to the 16th century. The ceiling was painted during the pontificate of Leo X, based on a design by Raphael. The room is named after the chiaroscuro (or monochrome) figures of apostles and saints, also attributable to the school of Raphael, based on designs by the master himself. Destroyed in part in 1558, they were restored by Taddeo and Federico Zuccari in 1560. Further decorations were added by Giovanni Alberti and Ignazio Danti in 1582, during the pontificate of Gregory XIII (1582), who also commissioned the existing decoration of the Sala degli Svizzeri.

The door bearing the name and coat of arms of Julius II leads to the Chapel of Nicholas V. The door next to it led to the Pope's "cubiculum", now closed to the public.

plan →

q - Chapel of Nicholas V

St. Lawrence receiving the treasures of the Church from Pope Sixtus II, detail

The chapel is named after Pope Nicholas V Parentucelli. It is situated in the Tower of Innocent III, which is the oldest part of the Apostolic Palace. At the end of the 13th century, under Nicholas III, the tower was incorporated into the complex of new buildings that were being added to form the existing papal palace around the Cortile del Pappagallo. In the 15th century Nicholas V chose this room on the fourth floor as the site for his private chapel.

The small chapel has a rectangular floor plan (6.60 x 4 m.), is cross-vaulted and has a barrel-vaulted arch at either end. Entry is from the Sala dei Chiaroscuri through a door opened by Julius II. The original entrance (now walled up and concealed by a door) is next to the present one. It led to a room used by Julius II as a bedroom (*cubiculum*); it was probably originally the small private study of Nicholas V. A low, oblong window in the wall on the left, opened at the end of the 16th century, communicates with the Sala degli Svizzeri. It enabled the occupants of the room to follow the mass being celebrated by the pope in the chapel. The opposite wall has two high, narrow lancet windows .

The decoration of the chapel was carried out by Giovanni da Fiesole, better known as the Blessed Fra Angelico, together with Benozzo Gozzoli between 1447 and 1451. The walls are decorated with frescoes depicting events from the lives of St. Stephen (above) and St. Lawrence (below). The four evangelists with their respective symbols are portrayed against a blue star-spangled vault. The Doctors of the Church are painted on the two barrel-vaulted arches.

Fra Angelico also painted the lost decoration of the above-mentioned study of Nicholas V, and that of the demolished Chapel of the Holy Sacrament.

A series of frescoes on the lower part of the chapel's walls painted to imitate wall-hangings, with the coat-of-arms of Nicholas V, complete the decoration. The painting over the altar is *The Stoning of St. Stephen* by Giorgio Vasari; Benedict XIII installed it in 1725 to replace the lost altarpiece of the *Deposition* that Fra Angelico had originally painted for the chapel. The floor is the original one, and is by Agnolo Verrone, a Florentine marble-worker and contemporary of Angelico.

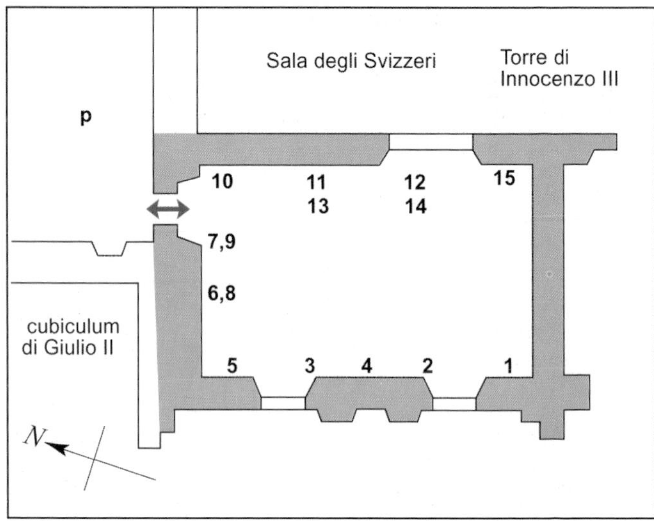

The subjects of the frescoes on the walls and barrel-vaulted arches are as follows (top to bottom):

1 Arch next to the altar, entering on the right : *St. Gregory the Great; St. Anastasius* (repainted in the late 16th cent.).

Right wall, above:

2, 3 The *Ordination of St. Stephen; St. Stephen distributing alms to the poor.*

Right wall, below:

4 The *Ordination of St. Lawrence.* Pope Sixtus II has been given the features of Nicholas V.

5 Arch: *St. Ambrose; St. Thomas Aquinas.*

Entrance wall, above:

6, 7 *St. Stephen preaching; St. Stephen before the Sanhedrin.*

Entrance wall, below:

8, 9 *St. Lawrence receiving the treasure of the Church; St. Lawrence distributing alms.* Pope Sixtus II is a portrait of Nicholas V.

10 Arch: *St. Augustine; St. Jerome.*

Left wall, above:

11, 12 The *Expulsion of St. Stephen;* the *Stoning of St. Stephen.*

Left wall, below:

13, 14 *St. Lawrence before the Emperor Decius;* the *Martyrdom of St. Lawrence.* In the first scene, the boy who looks away, clasping his hands, is St. Roman; further to the right, through a window, scene of St. Lawrence, in prison, converting St. Hippolytus. Further to the right, all but the upper part of the martyrdom scene was repainted in the late 16th century, when the window below it was opened.

15 Arch: *St. Leo the Great; St. John Chrysostom.*

Leaving the Chapel of Nicholas V, go left, through the antechamber of the cubiculum (bedroom) of Julius II to the Stanza di Eliodoro.

plan →

r - Borgia Apartment

View of the Sala dei Pontefici

The Borgia Apartment, which now houses part of the Collection of Modern Religious Art (described in our next chapter), takes its name from the Spaniard Rodrigo de Borja y Doms, who was elected pope with the name of Alexander VI in 1492; he reigned until 1503. The Borgia Apartment only includes the "secret", i.e. private, rooms, which the Borgia pope commissioned Bernardino di Betto, better known as Pinturicchio, to decorate.

The entire papal apartment occupied the whole first floor of the Apostolic Palace, built between the 13th and late 15th century. Its more official part, situated in the wing built between the 13th and 14th century, included the Vestment Room (X), the Sala del Pappagallo, also known as the Room of the Secret Consistory (IX), the Galleriola, or Audience Room (VIII) and the Sala dei Pontefici (VII). Two other rooms facing the Cortile del Pappagallo are located in this same area: the Sala della Falda (XII) and the *cubiculum* or bedroom of Nicholas V (XI). From the Sala dei Pontefici one entered the semi-official area of the apartment, the Borgia Rooms. The Sala dei Misteri (VI), Sala dei Santi (V), and Sala delle Arti Liberali (IV) are in the 15th century wing built by Nicholas V. The Sala del Credo (III) and Sala delle Sibille (I) are in the Borgia Tower, built by Alexander VI during the years 1492-94 to complete the fortifications of the palace. His bedroom (XIII) is next to Room IV, and has two windows looking onto the Borgia Court. The two adjoining rooms probably served as a bathroom and as a treasury (XXVIII).

Pinturicchio decorated the "secret rooms" in 1492-94, assisted by members of his workshop, including Benedetto Bonfigli, Pietro d'Andrea da Volterra, and Antonio da Viterbo, known as Pastura.

After the death of Alexander VI, the apartment was abandoned by the popes, who preferred to live elsewhere, and was used as the residence of the "nephew cardinals", including St. Charles Borromeo, nephew of Pius IV and Secretary of State.

Pinturicchio's frescoes have been restored more than once: especially under Pius VII, when the Vatican Pinacoteca found its second home in these rooms (1816), and again in 1897, when Leo XIII opened it to the public and it underwent extensive restoration. Most of the floors were reconstructed with copies of the very few surviving majolica tiles. Further restoration was done in recent times, when the apartment was chosen to house part of the Collection of Modern Religious Art.

I ROOM I, SALA DELLE SIBILLE

Leaving Raphael's Stanze, the visit to the Borgia Apartment begins from this room situated in the Borgia Tower. Tradition has it that Cesare Borgia, Duke of Valentinois and nephew of Alexander VI, had his brother-in-law Alfonso d'Aragona murdered in this room in 1500, and that Julius II imprisoned him here in 1503. The twelve lunettes are decorated with pairs of prophets and Sibyls, from which the room takes its name. From the wall opposite the window, from left to right: Baruch-Samian Sibyl; Zechariah-Persian Sibyl; Obadiah-Libyan Sibyl; Isaiah-Hellespontic Sibyl; Micah-Tiburtine Sibyl; Ezekiel-Cimmerian Sibyl; Jeremiah-Phrygian Sibyl; Hosea-Delphic Sybil; Daniel-Erythraean Sibyl; Haggai-Cumaean Sibyl; Amos-Europa; Jeremiah-Agrippina.

The astrological symbols of the seven major planets and the influence they were thought to have on mankind are represented in the octagonal panels of the intermediate pendentives: Saturn, with a chariot drawn by dragons and works of charity; Jupiter, with a chariot drawn by eagles, and hunters; Venus, with a chariot drawn by bulls, and lovers; Mercury, with a chariot drawn by deer, and merchants; the Moon, with a chariot drawn by dragons, and fishermen. In the last octagon, astronomers confer beneath an armillary sphere (a globe showing the movements of the planets). The decoration of this room may be the work of Pastura.

III ROOM III, SALA DEL CREDO

Like the previous room, the Sala del Credo is situated in the Borgia Tower. It derives its name from the pairs of prophets and apostles, with cartouches bearing verses of the Credo that appear in the lunettes. Starting from the wall with the window overlooking the Cortile Borgia, from left to right: Peter-Jeremiah; John-David; Andrew-Isaiah; James Major-Zechariah; Mathew-Hosea; James Minor-Amos; Philip-Malachi; Bartholomew-Joel; Thomas-Daniel; Simon-Malachi; Thaddeus-Zechariah; Matthew-Obadiah. The frescoes are again attributed to Pinturicchio's workshop, perhaps by Pastura or Tiberio d'Assisi.

IV ROOM IV, SALA DELLE ARTI LIBERALI

This is the first of the rooms located in the wing built by Nicholas V. It was Alexander VI's study and he also used to dine here; his body was laid in this room when he died. The room's name derives from the Arts of the Trivium and Quadrivium, which formed the seven Liberal Arts in the Middle Ages and are represented here in the lunettes as beautiful enthroned women, each identified by an inscription. Beginning from the lunette above the window, from left to right:

1 *Astronomy;* next to her, the geographer Ptolemy wearing a crown.

2 *Grammar*

3 *Dialectic*

4 *Rhetoric*

5 *Geometry*

6 *Arithmetic*

7 *Music*

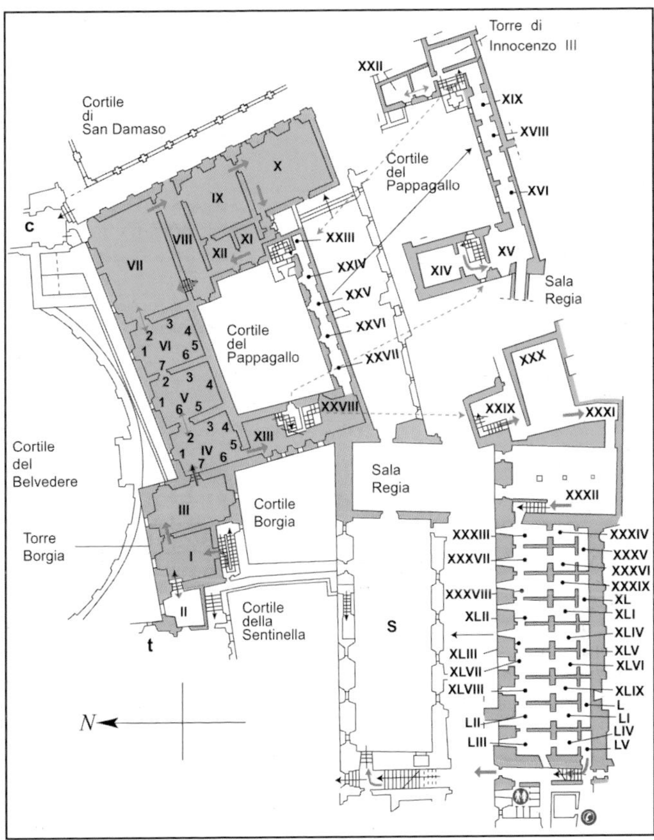

Only part of the frescoes were done by Pinturicchio, whose name appears on the base of Rhetoric's throne. The rest can be attributed to Tiberio d'Assisi or to Pastura.

The five octagons of the large central arch are a 16th century addition or perhaps a restoration. Depicted here: Jacob takes leave of Laban; the Angels save Lot from the destruction of Sodom and Gomorrah; Trajan's justice; Justice distributing gifts.

Two gilt *pastiglia* coats-of-arms and heraldic devices of the Pope adorn the vaulted ceiling.

The 16th century fireplace, carved in *pietra serena* (Tuscan grey sandstone), is the work of Simone Mosca, based on a design by Sansovino; it is traditionally thought to have been brought here from Castel Sant'Angelo.

ROOM V, SALA DEI SANTI V

This is the room in which the work of Pinturicchio is most prominent: not only did he design, but he did most of the frescoes himself. Starting from the lunette above the window, and proceeding from left to right:

Martyrdom of St. Sebastian; in the background, the Coliseum and, further to the right, the Palatine Hill and Church of Saints John and Paul. 1

Susannah and the Elders. 2

3 *Scenes from the Life of St. Barbara;* in the foreground, she is escaping from the tower, and is being hunted by her furious father; in the background, the episodes of her meeting with St. Juliana and the shepherd, who turns her over to her father determined to kill her because she had become a Christian.

4 *St. Catherine of Alexandria* disputing before the emperor Maximinus; in the background, Arch of Constantine. There are many portraits of contemporaries in this fresco. The man with the drooping moustaches, on the left of the throne, is Andrew Paleologus of the imperial family of Byzantium. Behind him is the architect Antonio da Sangallo the Elder, holding a set square, and, on his left, Pinturicchio himself. Prince Djem, guest/hostage of the pope, and friend of Cesare, appears either as the oriental figure on horseback, or as the figure next to the emperor.

5 The *Meeting of St. Anthony Abbot and St. Paul the Hermit.*

6 The *Visitation.*

In the spandrels of the ceiling: scenes from the myth of Isis and Osiris, according to a scheme devised by Antonio da Viterbo; the presence of the bull Apis in the myth is an allusion to Alexander VI (since a bull appears in the Borgia coat of arms). In the cross vault near the window: Osiris teaches the Egyptians to till the earth and to plant vines and apple-trees; wedding of Osiris and Isis. In the other cross vault: Seth (Typhon) kills Osiris; Isis finds the limb of Osiris; Osiris leaves the pyramid in the form of the bull Apis; Apis is carried in triumph by the people.

On the large arch, scenes from the myth of Io and Argus: Mercury lulls Argus to sleep by playing the syrinx; Hera asks Zeus to hand over Io; Io is tempted by Zeus; Isis enthroned between Horus and Mercury; Mercury kills Argus.

Above the door leading to the Sala dei Misteri: *Madonna and Child* by Pinturicchio.

VI ROOM VI, SALA DEI MISTERI

This is the last of the rooms decorated by Pinturicchio, who left a large part of the actual painting to his assistants. The Mysteries of the Faith are depicted in the lunettes. Beginning from the wall opposite the window and proceeding from left to right:

1 *Annunciation*

2 *Nativity*

3 *Adoration of the Magi*

4 *Resurrection*

5 *Ascension*

6 *Pentecost*

7 *Assumption of the Virgin*

Several portraits of contemporaries appear in these frescoes: there is a splendid portrait of Alexander VI kneeling, in the *Resurrection,* the soldier in the centre holding a lance may be a portrait of Cesare Borgia. The figure on the right in the *Ascension* may be Francesco Borgia, chamberlain (*cubicolario*) to the pope.

In the spandrels of the two ceiling vaults: eight roundels with busts of prophets, each identified by an inscription on the frame: Micah, Joel, Jeremiah, Sophonias, Isaiah, Solomon, Malachi and David.

ROOM VII, SALA DEI PONTEFICI VII

The Sala dei Pontefici (Room of the Popes) is the entrance to the official wing of the apartment. Forming part of the 14th century wing of the papal palace, the room was used for formal audiences, banquets, consistories and official functions. The present false vault replaces the original wooden-beamed ceiling, which collapsed in 1500, nearly killing Alexander VI. The ceiling decoration consists of stucco ornaments and grotesques made by Perin del Vaga and Giovanni da Udine, under Leo X. It depicts the twelve signs of the zodiac, the constellations, the seven planets, and, in the centre, dancing angels.

A series of inscriptions above the lunettes celebrates Popes Stephen II, Adrian I, Leo III, Sergius II, Leo IV, Urban II, Nicholas III, Gregory XI, Boniface IX, and Martin V. The room's name presumably derives from these inscriptions.

ROOMS VIII-XIII VIII

Alexander VI's private Audience Room (VIII) is adjacent to the Sala dei Pontefici. Lorenzo Sabbatini and his assistants frescoed the ceiling, with figures of St. Peter and St. Paul and eight episodes from the Acts of the Apostles, in 1576-77. This room communicates with Raphael's Stanze by way of a small stairway (not open to the public) decorated with frescoes by Simone Lagi (*c.* 1630).

One door in the Audience Room leads to the Sala della Falda (XII), XII
and another to Room IX (formerly known as Sala del Pappagallo, later IX
as room of the Secret Consistory, and now as Second Vestment Room; the Sala dei Chiaroscuri, on the floor directly above, was used for the same purpose during the second half of the 16th century). Here the pope donned his vestments, and also met with cardinals, prelates and ambassadors, dealt with day-to-day business, held the secret consistory, and conducted special ceremonies like the Blessing of the Golden Rose, and the Christmas Blessing of the Pontifical Sword. The richly carved and decorated ceiling was added to the room under Pius IV in 1563 and restored under Gregory XIII; the central compartment with the scene of the *Pentecost* is by Girolamo Muziano (1576). The frieze round the top of the walls dates to the pontificate of Pius IV, and is attributed to Giovanni Battista Lombardelli, Paris Nogari and others.

The next room is the Vestment Room (X), so called because the X
cardinals dressed here. The ceiling and frieze are of the same period as those of the previous room.

This room give access to the papal audience halls known as the Sala Ducale and Sala Regia, both closed to the public.

Room XI, the *cubiculum* of Nicholas V, communicates with the XI
Vestment Room, and is adjacent to the Sala della Falda. The coffered ceiling, with a representation of St. Peter in the centre, dates to the pontificate of Nicholas V. The many coats of arms of Sixtus IV suggest that the ceiling was restored during his pontificate.

Alexander VI's bedroom (XIII), where he died, is adjacent to the Sala XIII
delle Arti Liberali. The low, richly carved wooden ceiling is decorated with Borgia heraldic devices in stucco. The small frieze is of a later period.

plan
p. 105

r - Collection of Modern Religious Art

Ben Shahn, *Third Allegory*, detail

No less than fifty-five rooms are dedicated to the display of the Vatican's Collection of Modern Religious Art as part of the visit to the Vatican Museums. Inaugurated by Paul VI in 1973, the Collection comprises some 600 works. Paintings, sculptures and graphic art were collected over the years thanks to the generosity of artists, collectors and public and private benefactors. Most of the donations were the result of direct contacts with the world of art that Pope Paul VI fostered following his meeting with artists in the Sistine Chapel on 7 May 1964. In the address he gave on that occasion, the Pope emphasized the need to re-establish a dialogue between the Church and contemporary art that had been interrupted for far too long, and hoped that the once close and prolific relationship could be revived. It was also a way of contributing to his ambitious project of creating a museum of twentieth-century art in the Vatican collections.
The works collected by Paul VI, and by his secretary Monsignor Pasquale Macchi, thus came to enrich the small body of already existing works, which formed the Vatican Pinacoteca at the time of Pius XII. The collection has been enlarged over the last few decades with the objective of expanding and completing the existing historical sections.
The Collection is displayed along an itinerary leading from the apartments of Innocent III, Sixtus V and Alexander VI Borgia to the Sistine Chapel, enabling visitors to see a representative selection of Italian and international 20th century art through the works of some 250 artists.
The itinerary begins in Room II dedicated to French painting between the late 19th and early 20th century, represented by works of artists like Vincent Van Gogh (*Pietà*, *c.*1890), Paul Gauguin and the artists of the Pont Aven School, Maurice Denis, Odilon Redon and Medardo Rosso.

The rooms of the Borgia Apartment, decorated with 15th century frescoes by Pinturicchio, and the adjacent rooms (Rooms III-XIII) show paintings and sculptures by Italian artists from the 1910's to the 1940's: a collection that, through its main protagonists, permits the visitor to follow the exciting developments of Italian art in the first half of the twentieth century. The paintings of Boccioni (*Mother*, 1907), Balla (*Mother*, 1928), Carrà (*Daughters of Lot III*, 1940), De Chirico, Morandi (*Italian Still Life*, 1957), Rosai, De Pisis (*Piazza Cavalli a*

plan
p. 105

Piacenza, 1937) are only a fraction of the many works that illustrate the many-sided historical and stylistic development of Italian figurative art during this period.
Some of the works in the Collection were divided into groups dedicated to specific cultural situations or schools. The experimental artistic environment of Milan, for example, is exemplified by works of Wildt (*Pius XI*, 1926), Sironi (*St. Martin*, 1941), Casorati, Morlotti (*Women of Warsaw*, 1946), Martini and Fontana. Rome is represented especially by the artists of the so-called "Roman School", Scipione (*Catholic Prince*, 1929-30), Mafai (*Disembowellings*, 1938), Cagli, Pirandello and Mirko (*Girl Neophyte*, 1934-35).
Other rooms exhibit works dedicated to particular themes or particular artists. A selection of 20th century Italian sculpture is displayed in Room V. Francesco Messina is represented by works from 1934 (*Job*) to 1973, when he created his *Horrors of War* after the outbreak of the conflict between Israel and the Arab States. Works by Emilio Greco, Pericle Fazzini, Francesco Nagni and Alfredo Biagini are also on display.
Room VI is entirely dedicated to the works of Marino Marini donated by his wife Marina Marini in 1989. Most of them treat one of the recurrent themes of his oeuvre, the Horse Rider: from the harmonious wooden *Horse Rider* (1936-37) to the synthetic polychrome plaster-casts of 1953 and 1955, to the brilliant revelation of the *Miracle* (1970) and the tragic intensity of the *Cry* (1962).
The section on Italian 20th century art is interrupted in Room VII, which contains an exceptional series of preparatory drawings by Henri Matisse that he did between 1949 and 1952 for the decoration of the Chapel of the Rosary in Saint Paul de Vence in France. The series includes the stained-glass cycle, the *Tree of Life* and the apse decoration with the *Virgin and Child*, as well as some silk *chasubles* and a bronze *Crucifix*.
Before descending to the rooms below the Sistine Chapel, it is worth making a brief detour to Room XIV, the *Chapel of Peace* of Giacomo Manzù. Executed in 1961, it was created by the artist in collaboration with the patron himself, Monsignor Giuseppe De Luca, an erudite and scholarly man who had taken an interest in Manzù's work ever since the beginning when he designed the new bronze door in St. Peter's, the *Door of Death*. Some other sculptures of monumental size are displayed in Room XXXXII; they include Lucio Fontana's stone *Madonna* of 1956.
The rooms that run below the Sistine Chapel display a representative selection of international art, divided by country: the USA (Baskin, Shahn), Latin America (Orozco, Rivera, Siqueiros), Spain (Dalì, Delgado), France (Chagall, Rouault, Manessier), Germany (Kirchner, Nolde, Münter, Beckmann, Ernst), England (Bacon, Sutherland). They lead to the last rooms of the Collection, dedicated to international art in the 1960s, exemplifying the development of various abstract styles and new experiments in communication and expression, also in relation to the possible renewal of contemporary religious art. From Hartung to Capogrossi, from Dorazio to Chillida, from Hantaïto to Azuma, the various styles of abstract art are represented: sign languages, 'informal' art, the use of various materials, and the experimentation with new techniques, have contributed to the continuous development of contemporary art, its contents and the expressive force of the artist through the uniqueness of his own expressive means.

Room XV leads into a loggia overlooking the Sala Regia, formerly used for receiving reigning monarchs and ambassadors and for other ceremonies. Renovated by Antonio da Sangallo the Younger under Paul III, the room is decorated with frescoes by Late-Renaissance artists, illustrating episodes from the history of the papacy.

scheme →

s - Sistine Chapel

View of the chapel

The Sistine Chapel occupies a building situated at the southwest corner of the old medieval section of the Apostolic Palace. It is named after Pope Sixtus IV della Rovere, for whom it was built between 1477 and 1480. Nowadays, entrance to the chapel is through a small door in the wall behind the altar, reached either by descending the stairs from Raphael's Stanze, or by walking up from the rooms of the Collection of Modern Religious Art. But the official entrance to the chapel is through the Sala Regia, the large audience hall (*aula magna*) where the pope publicly received royal and imperial ambassadors. The chapel stands on the site of an earlier chapel (probably 13th century), perhaps of the time of Nicholas III. Some mention of it can be found in documents.

Rebuilt by Giovannino de' Dolci on a plan designed (according to Vasari) by the Florentine architect Baccio Pontelli, the Sistine Chapel was intended to fulfil a dual purpose: religious and defensive. It was to house the new palatine chapel and fortify the Apostolic Palace. The defensive nature of the building is evident from its austere, massive exterior, and battlements (visible from the Sala Sobieski and from the covered passageway linking it with the Stanza dell'Incendio in Raphael's Stanze, and from the Sala degli Indirizzi in the Vatican Library on the lower floor). The building includes an underground vault, a mezzanine floor and the chapel itself, above which is a spacious attic with a galleried sentry walk for the guards on the outside. The mezzanine, which now houses part of the Collection of Modern Religious Art, was once occupied by the offices of the

Magistri Caeremaniarum. They were masters of ceremonies, who also took care of secretarial duties. Among them were personalities such as the German Johann Burchard, who lived at the time of Alexander VI, Paris de Grassis, a contemporary of Julius II and Leo X, and Biagio da Cesena, a contemporary of Paul III. The chapel is still used for pontifical masses and for the conclave to elect a new pope, which was once held in the nearby Chapel of the Holy Sacrament frescoed by Fra Angelico, but later demolished to enlarge the ceremonial staircase (Scala del Maresciallo) under Paul III and replaced by the Pauline Chapel. The Sistine Chapel is built on a very simple rectangular floor plan. It has no apse, and is 40.23 m. long, 13.41 m. wide, and 20.7 m. high. It is covered with a flattened barrel vault, with weight-relieving spandrels over the twelve round-arched windows that illuminate the chapel. The floor is in inlaid polychrome marble. A marble screen with upper grating, a free interpretation of the Byzantine iconostasis, separates the area of the presbytery reserved for the officiating clergy from the congregation. It was originally joined to the singing gallery (*cantoria*), but was moved back in the 16th century to enlarge the presbytery. Both the screen and the singing gallery are embellished with very fine marble reliefs.

The walls were frescoed with scenes from the lives of Moses and Christ and with full-length portraits of the popes by a team of painters originally composed of Perugino, Sandro Botticelli, Domenico Ghirlandaio and Cosimo Rosselli, assisted by members of their respective workshops, including Piero di Cosimo, Bartolomeo della Gatta, and Luca Signorelli: the latter did the last two frescoes of the Mosaic series. Pier Matteo d'Amelia painted a simple, star-spangled sky on the vault. The work was begun in 1481, and completed in 1482. On 15 August 1483, Sixtus IV consecrated the new chapel, dedicating it to the Virgin Mary. Perugino had painted the lost altarpiece of the *Assumption of Mary* and the first two panels of the scenes from the lives of Moses and Christ, later destroyed by Michelangelo to make room for the *Last Judgement*. The only signature found on the frescoes is that of Perugino.

The three popes who succeeded Sixtus IV left the chapel as they had found it. It was only in 1506 that Julius II della Rovere, nephew of Sixtus IV, decided to make some changes to the vault decoration. In 1508 he entrusted the task to Michelangelo Buonarroti, who tried in vain to resist the pope's will. Tradition has it that it was Donato Bramante, envious of his rival's success, who suggested that Michelangelo be commissioned to do the job. On 10 May 1508 Michelangelo began work on the ceiling, initially with the help of assistants such as Jacopo d'Indaco and Francesco Granacci. But as soon as he had learnt the fresco technique - entirely new to him at the time - he dismissed his assistants. By September 1510 he had finished half the vault (from the entrance to the Fall). On 14 August 1511, Julius, impatient to see the work, forced Michelangelo to remove the scaffolding. The ceiling was completed in October 1512, and on All Saints' Day (1 November) Julius II inaugurated it with a solemn high mass. Towards the end of 1533 Clement VII de' Medici commissioned Michelangelo to make further changes to the decoration of the Sistine Chapel, especially by painting the *Last Judgement*. The placing of the *Last Judgement* over the altar is unusual; for liturgical reasons, it was traditionally depicted on the entrance wall. Once again Michelangelo reluctantly accepted the commission, though he did not begin work on the painting until 1535, and only then under pressure from Paul III, Clement VII's successor. It was first necessary to destroy the 15-century paintings on the entrance wall, which was covered with an inclining layer of bricks. Unaided by assistants, Michelangelo began to paint on this surface in the summer of 1536, completing the immense painting (covering 200 square metres with 391 figures) in the autumn of 1541. On 31 October of the same year Paul III, who had impatiently followed the artist's work, celebrated solemn vespers in front of this extraordinary painting which, according to Giorgio Vasari, aroused "the wonder and astonishment of the whole of Rome".

SIDE WALLS AND ENTRANCE WALL

The wall frescoes representing the lives of Moses and Christ are closely related: a Latin inscription above each fresco emphasizes this relationship. The inscriptions sometimes refer to the principal episode in the frescoes, and sometimes to a secondary episode, whose counterpart appears on the opposite wall illustrated by a similar inscription. So, to fully understand the cycle, the two lives should be viewed in conjunction. The complicated iconographic scheme was undoubtedly established by Sixtus IV or one of his court theologians, and has a precise intention: the episodes represented tend to emphasise the continuity of the history of salvation between the Old and New Testament. In the *Charge to St. Peter* (see below: 10), Christ, with a symbolic gesture, hands over the keys to Peter, founder of the papacy; the episode shown in the background- the payment of tribute - alludes to the independence of spiritual from temporal power. That independence was also recognized by the emperor Constantine (whose triumphal arch appears twice in the fresco) with his legendary donation to Pope Sylvester. The fresco with the *Punishment of Korah* (see below: 9) alludes to the divine punishment awaiting those, including persons within the Church, who questioned the authority of the papacy. Similar messages are contained in the gallery of portraits of the first popes (only 28 of them remain, following the destruction of those on the altar wall), which document the historical origins of papal power. The cycle now begins with the two panels at the sides of the altar wall.

1 South wall: the *Journey of Moses*. In the background, Moses takes leave of his father-in-law before returning to Egypt. In the foreground, on the left, the prophet meets the angel sent to punish him for not having circumcised his son; on the right, the Circumcision, the episode to which the inscription of the panel refers. The fresco is by Perugino. The two popes to the side of the window above are: to the
1a, 1b right *Clement I* and to the left *Evaristus*.

2 North wall: the *Baptism of Christ*. The scene is portrayed in the centre, and the inscription refers to the episode. In the background, to the left, a sermon by the Redeemer; to the right, a sermon by John the Baptist. The fresco is by Perugino; his original signature has been rediscovered in the lower left; the one on the marble frame above the tondo of God the Father is a later replica. The popes flanking the
2a, 2b upper window are *Anaclete* (left) and *Alexander I*.

3 South wall: *Events from the life of Moses*. Right to left: Moses kills the Egyptian who had mistreated an Israelite; he flees Egypt; he defends Jethro's daughters from the shepherds, and helps the girls to water the flock; he takes off his shoes and prostrates himself before the burning bush (the inscription refers to this episode); he leads the Israelites out of Egypt. The fresco is by Botticelli. The popes are
3a, 3b *Sixtus I* and *Hyginus*.

4 North wall: the *Temptations of Christ*. The temptations, to which the inscription refers, appear in the background. In the foreground, the Purification of the Leper. There are several portraits among the onlookers; the figure on the far right, with a baton, is Girolamo Riario, the pope's condottiere. The fresco is by Botticelli. The popes are
4a, 4b *Telesphorus* and *Pius I*.

5 South wall: the *Crossing of the Red Sea*. To the left, the jubilant people gather round Moses (the inscription refers to this episode). To the right, the Egyptians are overwhelmed by the waters; in the background, Moses and Aaron before Pharaoh. There are many portraits:

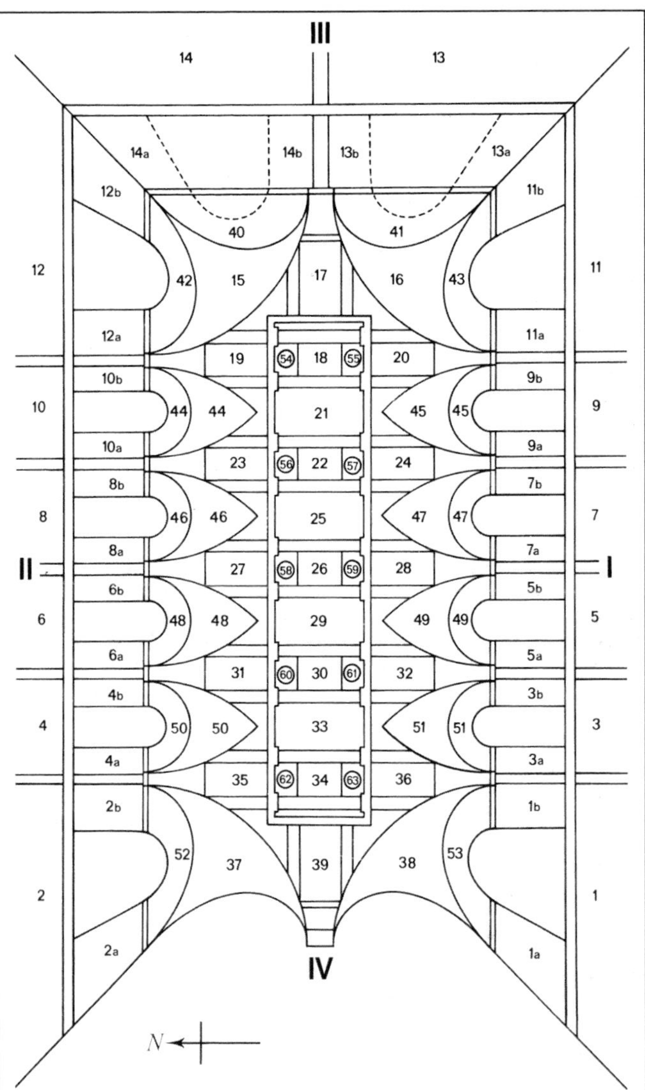

SCHEME OF WALLS AND CEILING

I South wall: life of Moses
II North wall: life of Christ
III East entrance wall
IV West wall with the Last Judgement (see scheme on p. 117)

Ceiling frescoes not mentioned in the guide

The Ancestors of Christ
40 Lunette with Eleazar and Matthan
41 Lunette with Jacob and Joseph
42 Lunette with Azor and Zadok
43 Lunette with Achim and Eliud
44 Lunette and spandrel with Josiah, Jeconiah and Salathiel
45 Lunette and spandrel with Zorobabel, Abiud and Eliakim
46 Lunette and spandrel with Hezekiah, Manesseh and Amon
47 Lunette and spandrel with Ozias, Joatham and Ahaz
48 Lunette and spandrel with Asa, Jehoshaphat and Joram
49 Lunette and spandrel with Rehoboam and Abjijah
50 Lunette and spandrel with Jesse, David and Solomon
51 Lunette and spandrel with Salmon, Boaz and Obeth
52 Lunette with Naashon
53 Lunette with Amminadab

Monochrome medallions with stories from Genesis, Samuel II, and Kings II
54 Joab, nephew of David, kills Abner
55 Bidkar casting King Joram from his chariot
56 Death of Uriah, husband of Bathsheba
57 Jehu destroys the image of the god Baal
58 David before the prophet Nathan
59 Destruction of the tribe of Achab, worshippers of Baal
60 Death of Absalom
61 Medallion with no story
62 Sacrifice of Isaac
63 Elijah ascends to Heaven on a chariot of fire

the old man with a white forked beard holding a monstrance, on Moses' right, is Cardinal Bessarion; the warrior with his back almost turned to the viewer is Roberto Malatesta. The fresco is by Biagio di
5a, 5b Antonio. The popes are *Anicetus* and *Eleutherius*.

6 North wall: the *Calling of the First Apostles.* In the foreground, Peter and Andrew kneel before Christ (the inscription refers to the episode); in the background, their calling, and that of John and James. Among the portraits: the old man in the right foreground is the humanist Argiropolas, and on his right are Giovanni Tornabuoni, the pope's treasurer, with his young son Lorenzo. The fresco is by
6a, 6b Ghirlandaio. The popes are *Soter* and *Victor.*

7 South wall: *Moses receives the Tablets of the Law.* In the centre, above, Moses receives the tablets; below, the people worship the golden calf; foreground, Moses breaks the tablets. In the background to the right, the punishment of the idolaters; left, Moses returns with the tablets of the Law (the inscription refers to this episode). The
7a, 7b fresco is by Cosimo Rosselli. The popes are *Zephyrinus* and *Urban I.*

8 North wall: the *Sermon on the Mount.* In the centre, the sermon, to which the inscription refers; right, the healing of the leper. The fresco
8a, 8b is by Cosimo Rosselli. The popes are *Calixtus I* and *Pontianus.*

9 South wall: the *Punishment of Korah, Dathan and Abiram.* Apart from this episode, the attempted stoning of Moses, to which the inscription refers, is represented to the right. In the background, at the centre, Constantine's Arch; on the right, a classicising portico. The fresco is
9a, 9b by Botticelli. The popes are *Anteros* and *Cornelius.*

10 North wall: *Christ's Charge to St. Peter,* shown in the foreground; further in the background, to the left, is the payment of tribute; to the right, the attempted stoning of Christ, to which the inscription refers. In the background, Constantine's Arch (shown twice). Among the portraits: the second figure from the right is Giovannino de' Dolci, the
10a,10b third Baccio Pontelli, and the fifth, dressed in black, Virginio Orsini.
11 The fresco is by Perugino. The popes are *Fabian* and *Lucius I.*

South wall: the *Testament of Moses,* shown in the foreground, right (the inscription refers to this episode); to the left, Moses gives his staff
11a,11b to Joshua. In the background, right to left: the angel shows Moses the promised land; Moses descends from Mount Nebo; the death of Moses. The fresco was painted by Luca Signorelli and Bartolomeo della Gatta. The popes are *Stephen I* and *Dionysus.*

12 North wall: the *Last Supper,* shown in the foreground, to which the inscription refers; through the windows on the rear wall, scenes of
12a,12b Jesus praying in the garden of Gethsemane, the capture of Jesus and the Crucifixion. The fresco is by Cosimo Rosselli and Biagio di
13 Antonio. The popes are *Sixtus II* and *Felix I.*

13a,13b Entrance wall, south side: *The Archangel Michael Defending the Body of Moses,* by Matteo da Lecce (1571-72). It replaces the lost
14 masterpiece by Signorelli. The popes are *Eutychianus* and *Marcellus I.*

14a,14b Entrance wall, north side: the *Resurrection,* by Henrick van den Broek (1571-72). It replaces the lost masterpiece by Ghirlandaio. The popes are *Marcellinus* and *Caius.*

THE CEILING

Michelangelo's original idea (soon abandoned) was to portray the Twelve Apostles in the spandrels, and a series of architectural elements on the vault. He then decided to represent the history of mankind before the coming of Christ, thus linking the ceiling decoration with that of the walls. The individual scenes are framed and separated by a monumental architectural structure, painted and superimposed over the actual vault.

The nine central panels depict events from Genesis, from the Creation to the Fall, from the expulsion from the Garden of Eden to the Flood and the subsequent renaissance of humanity with the family of Noah. Five sibyls and seven prophets, heralds to the pagan world and to Israel of the future Redemption, are represented in the panels round the edges of the ceiling. The irregular pendentives in the corners contain scenes of the miraculous salvation of Israel, prefigurations of Christ's redemption, by which the ceiling decoration is linked with the 15th century cycle on the walls. In the triangular spandrels and the lunettes below them (the inscriptions on the plaques probably identify the figures portrayed in both) are depicted the Ancestors of Christ (see 42-53, scheme p. 113); the families of Israel, the chosen people, awaiting the Messiah. The nude youths *(ignudi)* to the sides of the panels containing the stories from Genesis have both an ornamental and a symbolic function. They have been variously interpreted as genii of the golden age of Julius II, personifications of various kind, expressions of Michelangelo's neoplatonic ideas, etc. In any case, they have a function similar to that of the tablet-supporting putti (between the lunettes) and to the "bronze" nudes (above the spandrels). Each pair of *ignudi* flanks a monochrome medallion with stories from Genesis, Samuel II and Kings II (see 54-63, scheme p. 113).

Contrary to custom, Michelangelo began painting the ceiling from the entrance end, working towards the altar, probably because the crowded scenes in this area presented fewer technical and compositional problems to an artist as yet unfamiliar with the fresco technique.

From the wall opposite the Last Judgement, *Judith and Holofernes* 15
can be seen in the right corner-pendentive ; Judith lifts a cloth to cover
the head of the dead man, a presumed self-portrait of Michelangelo;
on the right, the decapitated body. In the left corner-pendentive:
David and Goliath; David is about to cut off the head of the giant 16
Philistine. — In the centre, in the triangle between the two pendentives, the prophet *Zechariah* thoughtfully leafs through a book. 17

Central Panel: the *Drunkenness of Noah;* Cam, in the foreground, his 18
head turned away from the viewer, mocks his sleeping father, while
Japheth covers his father's nakedness, and Shem reproaches Cam;
on the left, Noah plants the vine. — On the right, the *Delphic Sibyl,* 19
absorbed in a sudden divination as she reads. The prophet, on the
left, is *Joel,* intent on studying a parchment scroll. 20

Central panel: the *Flood.* Frescoed between December 1508 and 21
January 1509, it was the first of the scenes of Genesis to be painted by Michelangelo. An explosion in the Castel Sant'Angelo in 1797 caused a triangular portion of the right-hand side of the fresco to collapse. In the background, at the centre, the ark represented as a house; in front of the ark, a boat is sinking due to excessive weight; on the right, on a small island, below a tent, the throng of the selfish prevents others from reaching dry land, while on the left, by contrast, an old man "has embraced someone half dead, and is striving his utmost to save him" (Vasari); on the left, in the foreground, the throng of the generous, among whom is a series of famous groups: the embracing lovers awaiting death together, the mother with her terrified children, and the fierce-eyed nude carrying his wife on his shoulders.

Central panel: *Noah's Sacrifice* after the flood. The episode follows 22
the Flood in order of time, but was placed here because it requires
less space. — The prophet is *Isaiah,* distracted by the call from 23

24 heaven. The female figure is the *Erythrean Sibyl,* whose lamp is being
lit by a putto.

25 Central panel: the *Fall.* On the left, Adam and Eve, the most beautiful nudes painted by Michelangelo, are tempted by the devil in the guise of a serpent with a human torso; to the right, the Expulsion from Eden.

26 Central panel: the *Creation of Eve.* Next to Adam, who is "enslaved by
sleep", is the stump of a tree, a symbolic allusion to the Cross. — The
27 wrinkled female figure is the *Cumaean Sibyl,* who searches for a
28 passage in a book. The prophet is *Ezekiel,* wearing a turban; holding
a scroll of prophecies, he is seized by inspiration.

29 Central panel: the *Creation of Adam:* iconographically revolutionary, because it depicts the very moment when the Creator, by the gesture of his outstretched arm, imbues Adam with the pulse of life.

30 Central panel: the *Separation of Land from Water.* — The prophet is
31 *Daniel,* intent on transcribing or annotating a text, his hair and
clothing ruffled by the breeze of the spirit. The elderly female figure
32 is the *Persian Sibyl,* bent with age, and short-sighted.

33 Central panel: the *Creation of the Heavens.* On the right, God creates the sun and moon, while on the left, his back toward the viewer, he creates the plants of the earth.

34 Central panel: the *Separation of Light and Darkness.* — The female
35 figure is the *Libyan Sibyl,* who has just stopped reading and is about
36 to rise from her chair. The prophet is *Jeremiah,* tragic symbol of the
melancholy of knowledge.

37 In the right corner-pendendive (over the altar wall): the *Bronze
Serpent,* with which Moses saved the Israelites from divine pun-
38 ishment. In the left corner-pendentive: the *Punishment of Haman;* on
the right, the reclining Ahasuerus calls Mordecai; on the left, the
council called by the king to decide the condemnation of Haman; in
the centre, the crucified figure of Haman. — In the centre, in the
triangle between the two pendentives, the monumental figure of the
39 prophet *Jonah,* prefiguration of Christ, and symbol of the Faith.

scheme →

THE LAST JUDGEMENT

Conceived as a kind of architecture of human figures, the *Last Judgement* is the masterpiece of Michelangelo's maturity. He was in his sixties when he began the painting, which took about 450 days to complete. For the spectator it's as if the wall had suddenly been flung wide open to reveal, beyond the physical limits of the chapel, the awesome scene of the Last Day. The composition takes from various sources: the Bible, and Ezekiel in particular, the *Dies Irae*, Dante (but only with regard to the presence of Charon and Minas), and the motifs associated with pre-Tridentine religious polemic. The plan is the traditional one, figures arranged in superimposed registers, but the whole composition is absorbed into the dynamic vortex created by the blast of the last trump, and Christ's gesture of judgement.

In the two upper lunettes are the symbols of the Passion borne by
1, 2 angels, including *Gabriel.* Further down, in the centre, *Christ the
Judge,* an anti-classical and anti-traditional image, with Herculean
3 limbs; next to him is the *Virgin,* who turns away her head in pity; at
4, 5, 6 their feet, the patron saints of Rome: *St. Lawrence* with the gridiron,
7 and *St. Bartholomew* with the flayed skin (the head is a sorrowful self-
8, 9 portrait of the artist). On the right: *Peter* with the keys; *Simon of
10 Cyrene* with the cross on his shoulder; *St. Sebastian* with the arrows
11, 12 in his hand; *St. Catherine of Alexandria* with the spiked wheel; *St.*

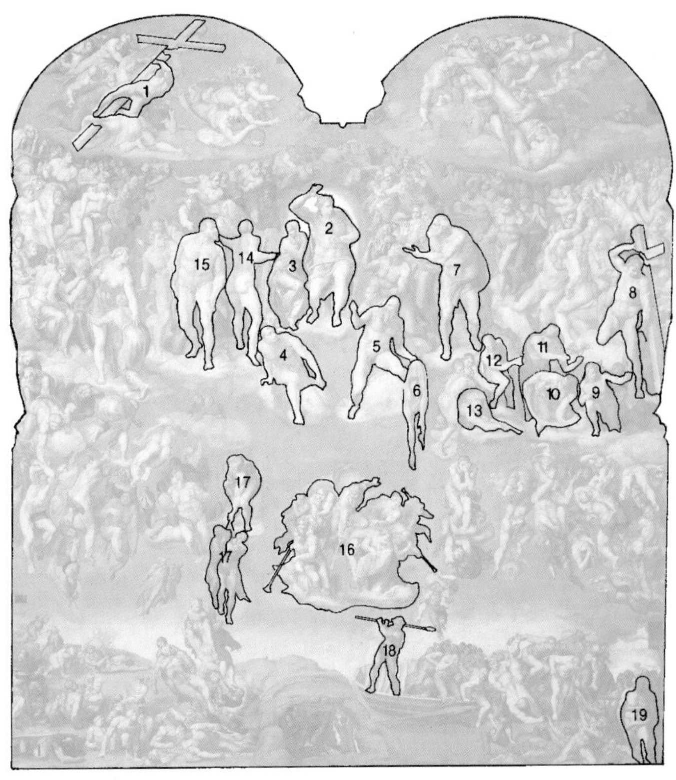

Blaise with the iron combs; *Dismas* (or St. Philip) with the cross; 13, 14
Simon Zelotes with the saw. On the left: *St. Andrew* with the cross;
John the Baptist with camel-skin cloak. In the lower register, at the 15
centre: the *trumpet-blowing angels;* to the right, the damned are 16
hurled down by demons; to the left, the elect ascend to heaven: of
particular interest is the *group of the two redeemed hanging from a* 17
rosary. On the earth below: to the left, the resurrected, whose bodies
are being gradually recomposed; to the right, hell with two Dantesque
figures: *Charon,* who, unlike his counterpart in the Divine Comedy, 18
pushes the damned out of the boat; and *Minos,* to whom Michelangelo 19
gave the features of Biagio da Cesena, the master of ceremonies of
Paul III who had expressed strong criticism of the work.

t – Museums of the Vatican Library

Reliquary-Cross of Paschal I, in gold leaf and enamel (9th cent.), detail; Roman fresco known as the *Aldobrandini Wedding* (1st cent. B.C.), detail; Armillary sphere (17th cent.); Salone Sistino (hall of Sixtus V)

Ever since the first centuries of the Christian era, the Church of Rome had possessed collections of archival documents, both in the form of *volumina* (books) and codices (manuscripts), though always linked to the person of the pope and to the institutional requirements of the Curia. These collections – at first unorganised and lacking the preservation measures that were later taken – were repeatedly dispersed as a result of the vicissitudes of two thousand years of history caught up in the events that plagued the political, religious and civil life of the Christian world. No records exist of the "pre-Lateran" period (i.e. preceding the official settlement of the popes in the papal palace next to the Lateran Basilica, but the ancient papal residence (the *Patriarchio*) certainly included - apart from the private rooms of the pope - a library and an archive, as well as a chapel and the great Triclinium built by Leo III between 756 and 816. So it is only natural that in the following years the collections followed the popes in their movements between the papal seats in Orvieto, Viterbo, Anagni and Perugia, until, in the early years of the 13th century, Innocent III (Lotario of the Conti di Segni, 1198-1216) finally established the papal chancery in the Vatican. The legislative documents that would later constitute the *Regesta* (regests) of the Apostolic See were issued there. In the early fourteenth century, the private library of Boniface VIII (Benedetto Caetani, 1294-1303) was the richest in Italy, but nothing of it has survived, or of the papal collections of the Avignon period (1339-1367). Libraries "*ad usum Pontificis*" (for the use of the pope) were owned by Martin V (Oddone Colonna, 1417-1431) and Eugenius IV (Gabriele Condulmer, 1431-1447). But it was not before the pontificate of Nicholas V (Tommaso

Parentucelli, 1447-1455) that the idea of a Library open to the public began to take shape. Nicholas wanted to establish it in a special section on its own in the Vatican for the common use of learned men ("*pro communi doctorum virorum commodo*"). The Dominican Pope, an accomplished humanist and a passionate collector of books, placed his precious private collection in a room of the new wing of the Apostolic Palace. It was increased with works remaining from the rich Library of Constantinople scattered throughout Europe and the Orient, following its fall to the Turks (1453). A part of the alms that Rome received for the Holy Year of 1450 were used to purchase or commission the illumination of manuscripts; and there is no doubt that the books housed in the Vatican on the death of the Pope (some 1500, of which 807 Latin and 353 Greek) represented the core works of what would soon become the leading library of Europe. Merit for the foundation of the Vatican Library, however, must go to Sixtus IV (Francesco della Rovere, 1471-1484), who formally instituted the new library with his bull "*Ad decorum militantis ecclesiae*", summoning the humanist Bartolomeo Sacchi, called Il Platina (1421-1481), to whom the document attributed the role of *gubernator* and *custos*, to study and safeguard the rich collection (consisting mainly of works of theology, philosophy and patristics). Apart from laying down regulations for the consultation, registration and conservation of the volumes, the bull indicated the main tasks to be fulfilled by the Librarian, and prescribed that assistant librarians respectively for Latin, Greek and Hebrew letters assist him. The same document endowed the Library with its own privileges and its own seat, situated on the ground floor of the wing of the papal palace towards the Belvedere, where Nicholas V had already planned to install the new institution. Under Sixtus IV the structure was divided functionally into three sections, dedicated respectively to the conservation of Latin codices (the *bibliotheca latina*), Greek codices (*bibliotheca graeca*) and papal codices (*bibliotheca secreta*). This was soon followed by the creation of a further section devoted to archival documents (*bibliotheca pontificum*). This division was maintained for over a century, until Sixtus V (Felice Peretti, 1585-1590), prompted by the growing shortage of space in the cramped old rooms, commissioned the construction of a new library building, situated in the transverse wing between the Belvedere Court and the Cortile della Pigna. On the upper floor of the building (which includes on its ground floor the seat of the present Vatican Library) the architect Domenico Fontana built the imposing hall named after the Pope (*Salone Sistino*), where the bookcases placed against the pillars or along the walls still reveal the preciousness of their ancient contents. The choice of the site for the new library proved to be very advantageous, because in the centuries to come the *Libraria* – as it was then called – was able to expand northward and southward, along the alignment established by Pirro Ligorio on the western side of the Belvedere Court, parallel to the Bramante wing. At successive intervals, the entire corridor stretching from the Atrium of the Quattro Cancelli to the Chapel of St. Pius V was equipped to contain bookcases and storerooms, and was continuously extended until it formed a single perspective over 300 metres in length by the end of the 18th century. Material belonging to the original collections of the Sacred Museum (1757) and the Profane Museum (1761) were distributed along it, in dialectical relationship with the collections of the Vatican Museums. Established under Benedict XIV (Prospero Lambertini, 1740-1758) and Clement XIII (Carlo Rezzonico, 1758-1769), these museums were enriched by the acquisition of the collections of Cardinal Gaspare Carpegna (coins, cameos, gold glass and artefacts from the Catacombs), Francesco Ficorini (lead seals and dies), Anton Francesco Gori and Giuseppe Bianchini (Etruscan and Early Christian archaeology), Saverio Scilla (papal numismatics), Alessandro Gregorio Capponi (ancient coins and medals), Pier Leone Ghezzi (ancient cameos and intaglios),

Filippo Buonarroti and Flavio I Chigi (gold glass). These various groups of material were further expanded after 1749 by the collections of Bartolomeo Cavaceppo (Early Christian sarcophagi and inscriptions) and Francesco Vettori (gems, cameos, crystals, intaglios), comprising among other things bronze artefacts, gold glass, ivories, enamelwork, goldsmith's work and painted panels: in the space of a few years a vast collection of antiquities was assembled. It was further increased with the finds from Otricoli (1776-1783) and from the Lateran (1779-1788) under Pius VI (Angelo Braschi, 1775-1799). The collection as a whole was particularly distinguished in the field of carved gems and the sumptuary arts. During the pontificate of Gregory XVI (Bartolomeo Alberto Cappellari, 1831-1846) it was further enriched with important acquisitions of works of carved gems, in part coming from excavations in the catacombs, in part from purchases or private bequests. But it was especially under Pius IX (Giovanni Maria Mastai-Ferretti, 1846-1878) that the study of Christian antiquities was given new impetus, thanks to the foundation of the Pontifical Commission of Sacred Archaeology in 1852 and the creation two years later of the new Pio-Christian Museum (see p. 161). Leo XIII (Gioacchino Pecci, 1878-1903) proceeded to the reorganization of the collections and the recovery of exhibition spaces with the transfer of the library to the lower floor. Pius X (Giuseppe Sarto, 1903-1914) enriched them further with the treasures found in the altar of the chapel of the *Sancta Sanctorum* at the Lateran (1906), decreeing at the same time the transfer of the collections of paintings (the so-called "primitives") to the new Vatican Pinacoteca (1909). At the same time, it became the practice to allocate the gifts that sovereigns and heads of state offered to the pope to the Library as gestures of tribute of filial devotion. Some of the more rare or imposing of these gifts are displayed along the itinerary to the Galleries and Salone Sistino.

The Library Museums were transferred to the jurisdiction of the Vatican Museums on 1 October 1999.

After the adoption of the one-way visiting itinerary in the Vatican Museum, the entrance to the Library Museums is from Room XIII (Room of Tributes to Pius IX), the last of the rooms in which the collections of the Library are displayed.

XIII

XIII, ROOM OF TRIBUTES TO PIUS IX (SALA DEGLI INDIRIZZI DI PIO IX). The room was originally created in 1877 to house the tributes sent to Pope Pius IX by the faithful throughout the world. On the ceiling, coat of arms of Mastai-Ferretti (1846-1878); in the showcases, selection of Byzantine fabrics and liturgical vestments of the 17th and 18th century; they include, on the north wall, silk fragments of Syrian (Byzantine) manufacture from the Chapel of the Sancta Sanctorum, depicting the *Annunciation*, the *Nativity*, *Samson wrestling with the lion*, *Scene of a lion hunt*, and *Lions confronting each other* (8th – 9th cent.). On the east and south walls, altar frontal and pluvial of the *Vestments of Clement VIII* (1592-1605), embroidered by Guasparri di Bartolomeo Papini and based on a cartoon by Alessandro Allori (1593-97). At the centre of the room: showcase containing objects excavated at Pompeii in the presence of Pius XI on 22 October 1849. Of particular interest, in the corners of the room, are the four doors with original inlays by Giovanni Barili and Fra Giovanni da Verona (*c.*1520); they come from the large windows of Raphael's Logge and were transferred here in 1853-54.

XII

XII, CHAPEL OF ST. PIUS V. It is the intermediate of the three superimposed chapels built by Pius V at the southern end of the corridor of Pirro Ligorio (1566-1572). It was decorated by Jacopo Zucchi, based on designs by Giorgio Vasari, with *Scenes from the life of St. Peter Martyr* (1570-71). The showcase contains reliquaries and other precious objects from the Treasury of the *Sancta Sanctorum*, the chapel of the Sanctuary of the Scala Santa at the Lateran, where the most venerated relics were kept in the Middle Ages. By order of Pius X (1903-1914), the objects have been conserved in the Vatican since 1906. Note, in particular: reliquary with *Scenes from the life of Christ* (wood and tempera on wood), a rare Palestinian artefact of the 6th to 7th century; cross-shaped reliquary with *Crucifixion* and *Saints* (wood and tempera on wood), a 13th century artefact from Constantinople; cross-shaped reliquary for the True Cross (chased and inlaid silver and gold), Rome, 817-824 (once containing the gem-studded cross of Belisarius); enamelled case of the Cross of Pasqual I (inlaid silver and gold), Rome, 817-824; Cross of Pasqual I (gold with inlaid enamels), Rome, 817-824; diptych of *St. Peter and St. Paul* (painted panel, 3rd to 4th century; silver reliquary coffer with *Adoration of the Cross* and medallions with busts of *St. Peter* and *St. Paul* (silver with traces of gilding, embossed and chased), Constantinople, first half of the 7th century; silver reliquary coffer (*capsella africana*) with symbolic figural decorations (late 5th early 4th cent.), from Henchir Zirara, Algeria, gift of the archbishop of Carthage to Leo XIII (1889); reliquary of the head of St. Agnes (silver), Rome, late 13th century; reliquary with the head of St. Praxed (incised, embossed and enamelled silver), Constantinople, 11th century and Rome, 1277-80; reliquary of the head of St. Sebastian (silver and gilt silver with *niello* inlays), Rome, 7th to 9th century; box of sandals (silver), Rome 9th century.

There are two other chapels also built by Pope Pius V on the floors immediately above and below, dedicated respectively to St. Stephen and St. Michael the Archangel.

XI

XI, ROOM OF TRIBUTES (SALA DEGLI INDIRIZZI), used under Gregory XVI (1837) to display the collection of icons and so-called "primitive" (or gold ground) paintings (now in the Pinacoteca). The name of the room derives from the fact that it contained, under Pius XI (1922-1939), the tributes sent to Leo XIII and Pius X. Andrea Giorgini and Filippo Agricola frescoed the ceiling under Pius VII with *Patriarchs* and *Doctors of the Church* in neoclassical frames (1818). Along the walls: bookcases in the Empire style designed by Raffaele Stern for the library of Cardinal Zelada. At the centre of the room: grey granite-topped tables dating to the pontificate of Gregory XVI (1831-1846). The room now contains a rich collection of Roman and Early Christian glass, as well as liturgical objects and furnishings in enamel, ivory and precious metals dating from medieval to modern times. Proceeding from the entrance to the rear wall, the cases of the main wall contain:

- Case I: fragments of ancient reliefs and sculptures in ivory and bone; medieval ivories.
- Case II: Gothic and Early Christian ivories; chalices and diptychs.
- Case III: Early Christian and Byzantine diptychs in ivory (including the famous *Rambona diptych*, produced for the monastery of the same name by a northern Italian workshop (*c.*900); ciboria and pastoral horns.
- Case IV: portable ivory Crucifixes (16th - 18th cent.); Niccolò Piper De Arras (active, 1568-1599): *Crucifixion*, *Deposition* and *Burial of Christ* (ivory reliefs on slate).
- Case V: ivory statuettes of the Virgin, Saints and various personages (16th 19th cent.).
- Case VI: bronze Crosses (Italy, France, Spain, 12th 14th cent.).
- Case VII: *Christ in Glory*, *Adam rising from the dead* (inlaid enamels on incised and gilt copper; reliquary case with *Martyrdom of St. Stephen*, reliquary case with *Christ in Glory and Crucifixion*, reliquary case with *Flight into Egypt* and *Holy Sepulchre* (gilt copper, incised and enamelled); series of 6 statuettes representing *Christ* and the *Apostles* (from the altar of the Confession in St. Peter's); Limoges goldsmith's work, 13th century.

- Case VIII: copper panels inlaid with enamels, painted enamels on copper panels (Stories of the Passion): Limoges, 16th century; inlaid enamels on incised and gilt copper (six medallions with busts of *Saints*): Siena, *c.*1320.
- Case IX: medallions and ground crystals (Valerio Belli, Vicenza, 1468-1546), portable altars: pectoral crosses and portable crucifixes (16th 19th cent.).
- Case X: medal of Alexander VII; pastoral horn; enamels, coffers, bronze reliefs, incised plaques, rings (16th to 19th cent.).
- Case XI: Roman and Neapolitan liturgical silverware (18th cent.).
- Case XII: Gold, silver and gilt-silver processional crosses (14th to 16th cent.).
- Case XIII: missals and gospel covers (18th to 20th cent.).
- Case XIV: liturgical silverware (southern Italy, 18th cent.).

On the entrance wall (close to the Chapel of St. Pius V): mosaic fragment with *Head of Apostle* (from the apse mosaic of the Lateran Triclinium, *c.*799); Gentile da Fabriano, *Head of crowned figure* (*David* or *Solomon*), so-called *Charlemagne*, fresco (from the lost cycle in San Giovanni in Laterano, 1427).

The numbering of the cases is resumed on the opposite wall, beginning from the window:

- Case XV: Santi Lotti (Roman silversmith, documented 1629-1659): crosses, ciboria, liturgical objects, Renaissance 'paxes' (liturgical objects for celebrating the Rite of Peace) of Paduan manufacture; monstrances and church furnishings of Sicilian provenance.
- Case XVI : German silverwork (late 16th cent.).
- Case XVII: Roman silverwork (late 16th cent.).
- Case XVIII: French silverware (late 16th cent.).
- Case XIX: French and German silverware (late 16th cent.).
- Case XX: gold, silver, and gilt silver chalices and pyxes (17th 18th cent.).
- Case XXI: lamps, censers and monstrances in silver and gilt silver (17th 18th cent.).

On each side:

- Showcase A: Roman and Early Christian glassware (including the precious glass drinking-cup with incrustations in form of marine animals; it comes from the catacombs of St. Calixtus but was made in Cologne in *c.*300 A.D.).
- Showcase B: pectoral crosses, seals, Early Christian and Dark Age devotional pendants.

In the middle:

- Showcase of the Holy Years (contains mementoes relating to the opening of the Holy Door in the Jubilee Years of 1825 and 1950).

X

X, ROOM OF THE ALDOBRANDINI WEDDING. Built for Paul V by the architect Flaminio Ponzio (1805-08), it was decorated by Guido Reni, with three frescoes depicting the *Stories of Samson* on the ceiling (*Samson lifting the Gate of Gaza*, *Samson killing the Philistines*, *Samson wrestling with the lion*) and restored under Pius VII (1800-1823). Formerly part of the Apartment of Scipione Borghese, the Room takes its name from the famous Roman fresco on the back wall, found on the Esquiline in the early 17th century and long preserved in the villa of Cardinal Pietro Aldobrandini. In 1818, Gregory XVI had the series of mural paintings found in the excavations conducted in the early 19th century transferred to this room; later finds were added under Pius IX in1853.

Rear wall: So-called *Aldobrandini Wedding*, fresco of the Augustan period depicting preparations for a nuptial rite – perhaps alluding to the wedding of Alexander and Roxana, according to an iconographic model created by the painter Aëtion (the fresco was found in the *Horti Lamiani* on the Esquiline). On the side wall: fresco cycle with landscapes and scenes from the Odyssey (*Odysseus among the Laestrygones, Odysseus in Circe's palace, Journey of Odysseus to the underworld*), datable to the 1st century B.C. (from Via Graziosa); cycle of tragic heroines, 3rd century (from Via Laurentina) and *procession of children*, 1st century, from Ostia. Set into the floor: *Achilles dragging the body of Hector*, mosaic of the 3rd century.

IX, ROOM OF THE PAPYRI. Begun under Clement XIV (1771) and IX
completed under Pius VI (1775), the Room was created for Cardinal Librarian Alessandro Albani (1692-1779), a famous connoisseur of antiquities, and decorated in two phases by the painters Anton Raphaël Mengs (1772-73), Cristoforo Unterperger and Antonio Marini (1775). The walls, their lower parts richly embellished with porphyry, are surmounted by a frieze in neo-Classical style; the windows framed with pink granite and the pavement inlaid with polychrome marbles invest the room with the precious intimacy of an 18th to century *cabinet*. On the ceiling: *Allegory of History*, fresco by Cristoforo Unterperger, alluding to the foundation of the Pio-Clementine Museum (1773). In the lunettes on the short walls: *Moses* and *St. Peter*; in those of the long walls: pairs of putti with Egyptian symbols. Along the walls, showcases originally intended for the exhibition of Latin papyri from Ravenna (6th to 9th cent.), now replaced with photographic reproductions. In the four corners: Busts of *Pius II*, *Sixtus IV* (16 century copy of an original by Sebastiano Torrigiani), *Alexander VI* (by Melchiorre Caffà) and *Pius X* (by A. Silva). In the showcases to the sides of the room are displayed in rotation significant groups from the Library's collections; the case to the right (temporarily) contains a group of three terracotta preparatory models by Gian Lorenzo Bernini (the two female figures of *Charity*, studies for the monument of Urban VIII in St. Peter's) and Alessandro Algardi (the *Baptism of Christ*); the case to the left contains a group of five statuettes, also by Bernini, including the preparatory models for the famous statue of *Truth* (Borghese Gallery).

VIII, CHRISTIAN (or SACRED) MUSEUM, founded by Benedict XIV VIII
(1740-1758) to house the 16th to 17th century series of early Christian antiquities among the first discoveries made in the catacombs. with the intention of documenting the beliefs and the living conditions of Christians in the early centuries of the Church (1756). The decoration of the ceiling, representing the *Triumph of the Church* and the *Triumph of the Faith* (Stefano Pozzi, 1757) in allegorical form, also refer to this theme. The collection was further enriched by Pius IX, who added the six showcases and decorated the walls with imitation antique inlays. The varied collections, include objects in glass, both blown and fused, from the 1st to the 4th century (*balsamaria*, flasks, *ampullae*), Roman and Early Christian glassware from Ostia Antica (4th cent.), household pottery, terracotta and bronze lamps with pagan, Jewish and Christian symbols (1st to 4th cent.); sheet silver *ampullae* with figural decoration (4th cent.), amulets, rings, seals and Roman and Byzantine weights (including one with the *effigies of three emperors* (4th to 5th cent.); medieval medals, crosses and pilgrim's insignia . Notable among the metal objects are the *water vessel* of oriental manufacture (8th to 9th cent.), which, according to tradition, was used by St. Lawrence for baptisms; the *incised situla* (4th cent.); the *silver plate with hunting scene* (5th cent.); and the disk with the *earliest representation of the Apostles Peter and Paul* (4th cent.). The icons on display include the *portable icon of St. Theodore,* made of mosaic and probably of oriental origin (12th to 13th cent.). A separate group of artefacts consists of gold glass from the catacombs (3rd 6th cent.); these were vessels such as cups, plates or vases of various types and function, decorated with gold leaf with motifs mainly inspired by the Old and New Testament and preserved by the lime

that fastened them to the funerary niches of the dead. Some portraits capture the features of the deceased and family with great realism, providing some of the most vivid evidence of late Roman life and society. A group of reliefs in steatite and hard stone, of Byzantine and Slav manufacture, complete the collections (11th to 13th cent.). The walnut cases, work of the cabinetmakers Giovan Battista Pericoli and Antonio Ravasi, are masterpieces of neoclassical furniture. They contains bronze busts of the 24 cardinal librarians, made by Luigi Valadier for Cardinal Francesco Saverio De Zelada (1717-1801).

VII, GALLERY OF URBAN VIII (VII). Created under Urban VIII (1624), but decorated under Alexander VII (1658) and Benedict XIV (1757), the gallery has frescoes of Giovanni Angeloni in the lunettes depicting views of the monuments built or renovated by Benedict XIV Lambertini (1740-1758). The entrance to the gallery is through the façade of the Christian Museum (coat of arms and inscription of Benedict XIV, 1756), preceded by paired columns in *giallo antico* (yellow) marble with Corinthian capitals in white marble (coming from the Nicchione of the Belvedere) and flanked by statues of the orators *Lysias* (3rd cent. B.C.) and *Aristides Aelius* (*c.*200 A.D.). In the 17th century, the gallery housed the famous Library of the Elector Palatine in Heidelberg – donated by Maximilian, Duke of Bavaria, to Gregory XV in 1622 – and, later, the equally famous *Biblioteca Urbinate*, founded by Federico di Montefeltro in the later 15th century and acquired for the Vatican Library in 1657. Other important works added in the pontificates of Benedict XIV (*Capponiano* collection, 1746; *Ottoboniano*, 1748), Pius VII (*Cicognara* collection, 1823) and Pius IX (Library of Cardinal Angelo Mai, 1855) made it necessary to display the collections in new bookcases, made and decorated with the Pope's coat of arms (Mastai-Ferretti, 1846-1878). At the sides of the entrance are bronze bells from the Old Basilica of St. Peter's and Santa Maria Maggiore (13th cent.). On the walls and in front of the windows are maps, planetary globes, optical and scientific instruments of measurement, including the portolano of Girolamo da Verrazzano containing the first reported sighting of the Americas (1529), and the one of Diego Ribera (1530). There is also a group of geocentric planetary globes (based on the Ptolomaic model of the centrality of the Earth, in relation to the systems of Mars, Venus, Mercury, Sun and Moon (second half of the 16th cent.); a selection of rare "terrestrial" and "celestial" globes in wood, brass and papier maché made by the geographer Willem Blaeu between *c.*1622 and 1640; the famous *Farnese planisphere*, made in Piacenza in 1725, a gift of the Count of Caserta to Leo XIII; and the *globe painted with personifications of the constellations and planets* on a base with figural carvings in gilt wood, once attributed to Giulio Romano, but now recognized as a work of Giovanni Antonio Vanosino from Varese, commissioned for Cardinal Marco Sittico Altemps (1567). It is also worth mentioning the so-called *Mappamondo Borgiano* (named after its discoverer Cardinal Stefano Borgia). A part of the Cardinal's collection, the planetary map inlaid in copper was made in southern Germany in *c.*1430 and contains references to historical or legendary events drawn from classical and patristic cosmography. It is a unique testimony of geographical knowledge at the end of the Middle Ages.

VI VI, SISTINE ROOMS. Created by Domenico Fontana under Sixtus V to house documents and registers from the papal archives (1585-88), the two rooms – like the following rooms of the library – contain a selection of the gifts offered to the popes over the last two centuries, with particular emphasis on those presented to Leo XIIII (1878-1903) on the occasion of the jubilee of his ordination as priest (1887-88). The walls and the lunettes above the doors are decorated with frescoes by Cesare Nebbia and Giovanni Guerra, illustrating prominent episodes from the pontificate of Sixtus V (1588-90).

Room 1: In the lunettes at the two ends, *View of St. Peter's according to Michelangelo's project* and *Transport of the obelisk to St. Peter's Square in May-September 1586.* Along the walls, to the left: last *fly press* for pontifical lead seals of the Palazzo della Cancelleria (first half of 19th cent.); Bramante's *device* for stamping lead seals from the papal chancery (16th cent.). To the right: *prie-dieu* in ebony wood with enamel, ivory, silver and ormolu inlays, gift of an anonymous donor to Leo XIII (1888); crystal and gilt metal *coffer* with incrustations in jade, pearls, lapis lazuli and precious stones, gift of the city of Milan to Pius XI (1929).

Room 2: In the lunettes at the two ends *Proclamation of St. Bonaventure as Doctor of the Church* (1587) and *Canonization of St. Diego in the old St. Peter's* (1588). Placed against the walls, to the left: *round table* with micromosaic decoration showing a *pair of ducks in flight*, and white marble pedestal with the Mastai-Ferretti coat of arms (from the Room of the Papyri); *round table* with marble and precious stone inlays representing the *Good Shepherd* (with excavated materials from the catacombs of St. Calixtus and Sts. Nereus and Achilleus), donated to Pius IX by Cardinal Costantino Patrizi (1857). To the right: *round table* inlaid with marble with fragments retrieved from the ancient Basilica of Hippo, gift of the bishop of Algiers to Gregory XVI (1843); *round table* with the Mastai-Ferretti coat of arms and inlays of marble and precious stones recovered from the excavations on the Palatine, commissioned by Pius IX from the Ministry of Public Works (1866). At the centre of the two walls: *Mute Swans of Peace*, porcelain and biscuit composition of the Bohem Studios of America, gift of the Archdiocese of New York to Paul VI (June 1976); *showcase of lunar stones*, containing a selection of gifts from heads of state and religious personalities to John XXIII and Paul VI, including: pectoral cross in glass and gilt silver, gift of Orthodox Armenian patriarch Yeghishe Derderian to Paul VI; fragments of lunar rocks retrieved by the Apollo XI mission, gift of the President of the United States Richard Nixon to Paul VI (1969).

V, SALONE SISTINO. Preceded by a little gallery and a vestibule, this V
great hall, originally the Library reading-room, is divided in length into two wide vaulted aisles by six pillars. Built for Sixtus V between 1585 and 1588, it is situated in the large transverse wing erected between the "corridors" of Bramante and Pirro Ligorio by Domenico Fontana, at right angles to the staircase that ascended from what is now the Belvedere Court to the upper terrace, corresponding to the level of the present Cortile della Pigna. The new building was linked to the pre-existing structures through two rooms, to its east and west, corresponding to the present Sala degli Scrittori and the Vestibule of the Salone. Its lavish pictorial ornamentation was completed between 1588 and 1590 by Giovanni Guerra from Modena, and Cesare Nebbia from Orvieto with a large group of assistants, including prominent names such as Andrea Lilio, Giovanni Baglione, Prospero Orso (called Prosperino delle Grottesche), and two Flemish painters: Hendrick van der Broeck and Paul Bril. The complex iconographic scheme, based on the apotheosis of the Book and the glorification of Sixtus V's exploits, was designed by Federico Rainaldi, First Custodian of the Library, assisted by Cardinal Silvio Antoniono, sacristan Angelo Rocca and apostolic protonotary Pietro Galesini. The vaulted ceilings are frescoed with grotesques and are embellished at the top by cruciform panels with allegories and tabernacles with angels in the corbels. At the base of the vaults and in the lunettes above both ends of the two aisles are 18 *views of Rome*, important visual documentation of the transformation of the city during the pontificate of Sixtus V. South wall: scenes of famous Libraries of Antiquity; north wall; scenes of the Ecumenical Councils that paid particular attention to books; on the pillars: figures of real or legendary inventers of the letters of the alphabet. On the left of the door that leads from the end

wall into the Sala degli Scrittori is a canvas by Pietro Facchetti depicting *Domenico Fontana showing his plans for the new Library to the Pope and his entourage*. Bookcases with the insignia of Pius IX stand round the pillars and against the walls. In the centre: pair of *monumental tables* supported by *telamones* in the guise of Hercules, with grey granite tabletops bordered by ornamental friezes in bronze, illustrating the main events of the pontificate of Pius VI (1775-1799), a work by the sculptor Vincenzo Pacetti with the collaboration of the silversmith (and later architect) Giuseppe Valadier and the goldsmith Pietro Paolo Spagna (1789-90). Under the arches (beginning from the first after the vestibule): ARCH II: Crucifix in malachite and gilt bronze, gift of Prince Demidoff of Russia to Pius IX, between pairs of vases in polychrome porcelain, against a blue and gold ground with views of German cities, gift of Frederick William IV of Prussia to Pius IX (Meissen, second half of 19th cent.). ARCH III: monumental case in polychrome porcelain against a blue and gold background with scenes of interlaced flowers, gift of Charles X of France to Leo XII (Sèvres, 1825-27); at the sides, pairs of candelabra in porcelain and bronze (gilding by Pierre-Philippe Thomire, with inlaid wood pedestals painted and gilt by Gabriele Siotto, 1807), gift of Napleon to Pius VII on the occasion of his coronation as emperor in Paris on 22 May 1805 (Imperial Manufactory of Sèvres). ARCH IV: large red granite basin, gift of the Duke of Northumberland to Cardinal Antonelli. ARCH V: *Vase made of the remains of the alabaster sent by Mohammed Ali, Khedive of Egypt, for St. Paul's Basilica*, gift of the viceroy of Egypt to Gregory XVI. ARCH VI: malachite table decoration, crowned by the Mastai-Ferretti coat of arms and supported by gilt bronze *telamones*, gift of Prince Constantine of Russia to Pius IX, between pair of blue porcelain with appliqués in gilt bronze, gift of French president Carnot to Leo XIII (19 February 1893). At the foot of the room: J.J. Kändler (1706-1775), *Crucifixion*, porcelain group on ebony base, gift of King Albert of Saxony to Leo XIII.

IV

IV, PAULINE ROOMS. Rooms furnished under Paul V (1610-11) to house the Greek manuscripts of the Library. The subjects of the frescoes on the ceilings and walls, densely covered with paintings by Giovan Battista Ricci from Novara (1611), are linked to those of the Salone Sistino and their celebratory character. The present bookcases date to the pontificate of Clement XIV (1769-1774).

Room I: In the lunettes at both ends, the *Canonization of St. Francesca Romana*, on 29 May 1608, and of *St. Charles Borromeo*, Archbishop of Milan, on 1 November 1610. On the walls, portrait medallions of scholars and philosophers of Antiquity, interspersed with scenes of the great libraries of the past. Along the corridor: *display case* in inlaid wood with marble appliqués, work of eclectic style signed by the pupils of the Établissement St. Nicolas, Paris (late 19th cent.); Luigi Fontana: *reliquary model* of the Basilica of St. Anthony of Padua (gold and gilt silver with inserts in enamel and lapis lazuli), gift of the diocese of Padua to Leo XIII (c.1888); monumental vase in blue porcelain with gold leaf and appliqués in bronze, gift of French President MacMahon to Pius IX (1873-78).

Room 2: in the lunettes at the two ends, Perspective plans of the cities of Civitavecchia and Ferrara; on the walls, main events of the pontificate of Paul V Borghese (1605-1621) and illustrious men of Antiquity. Along the corridor: marble stele with bronze medallion of John XXIIII, gift of the Government of Austria to the same pope (1961); G.B. Viero di Nove (Vicenza): *prie-dieu* in polychrome porcelain with representation of the *Immaculate Conception*, gift of the diocese of Vicenza to Leo XIII; Giuseppe Bertini (Milan): monumental stained glass with *Madonna Enthroned* in a neo-gothic frame, gift of Cesare Monti to Pius XI (1922); monumental vase in white and pink porcelain (signed: BELET), gift of French President Grevy to Leo XIII.

III, ALEXANDRINE ROOM. It was created by Alexander VIII (1689-1691) to house the prestigious Library of Queen Christina of Sweden (known as the *Reginense* collection), acquired from the heirs of Cardinal Decio Azzolini (1623-1689), to whom the queen bequeathed it (1690). The bookcases of this room date to the pontificate of Clement XIV (1769-1774). In 1818, during the pontificate of Pius VII, the room was decorated with frescoes by Domenico Del Frate illustrating *episodes from the papacy of Pius VI.* In the lunettes at both ends, the *Arrival of Emperor Joseph II in Rome* and the *Meeting between Pius VI and Joseph II in Vienna.* Of particular interest, against the walls: Rudolph Marschall, marble *stele* with bronze relief of the *Good Shepherd*, gift of Franz Josef I of Austria to Leo XIIII (1902); *embroidered linen altar-cloth* of north European manufacture, 11th to 12th century (from the chapel of the *Sancta Sanctorum*); embroidered pluvial (cope) in *opus anglicanum* of English manufacture, 11th century (gift of Pius X); vase in polychrome porcelain with red and gold ground, painted with figure of *Sibyl* in a landscape, gift of Wilhelm I of Prussia to Pius IX (Meissen, second half of the 19th cent.). III

II, CLEMENTINE GALLERY. Commissioned by Clement XII (1730-1740) to house the Library of Cardinal Angelo Maria Querini (1732), the gallery was created by closing the last five arcades of the corridor that Pirro Ligorio had left as an open loggia. Divided into five bays under Pius VI (1793) by a series of porphyry columns from the Abbey of the Tre Fontane in Rome (especially remarkable is the pair in the last bay with porphyry sculpture of figures of *Tetrarchs embracing*), the gallery was given its existing decoration in 1818, with frescoes illustrating *episodes from the papacy of Pius VII,* painted by Domenico del Frate (1818). Of the other objects on display, particular mention should be made of the *View of St. Peter and the Vatican seen from the Janiculum*, pen and watercolour drawing of the Studio Weeser-Krell in Berlin, gift of the diocese of Trier to Leo XIII (1887-88). II

I, PROFANE MUSEUM. Founded by Clement XIII (1758-1769) at the insistence of Cardinal Alessandro Albani, the room has a lavish *antique style* decoration in gilt stuccowork and polychrome marble (1769). The precious bookcases in hardwood from Brazil, designed by Luigi Valadier (1781-1798), contain what remains of the Library's collection of profane antiquities (mainly Etruscan and Roman), transferred to Paris in 1798. On the wall leading into the Clementine Gallery: statue of *Aion Leontocephalus* (2nd cent. A.D.); on the ceiling: *Allegory of Time*, fresco by Stefano Pozzi alluding to the foundation of the Museum (1768); in the four corners: bronze heads of *Augustus*, *Nero*, *Balbinus* and *Septimius Severus* (from Roman originals of the 1st to 3rd cent. A.D.). I

- CASE 1: late-antique and medieval ivories, stuccoes, marbles and mosaic panels, including that of *Deer with birds*, daring to the 2nd century A.D. (from Hadrian's Villa)
- CASE 2: bronze panels and inscriptions (military diplomas, etc.), Roman bronze statuettes (1st to 3rd cent. A.D.)
- CASE 3: ivories, busts and Roman reliefs in bone, marble and alabaster; rock crystal intaglios; fragments of a statue of *Athena* in gold and ivory, perhaps a Greek original of the 5th century B.C.
- CASE 4: Roman ivories, Etruscan bronzes

After completing the visit to the Galleries of the Vatican Library, leave by the stairway located at the end of the Clementine Gallery. It passes below the Atrium of the Quattro Cancelli, leading on one side to the Historical Museum (Carriage Museum) and Missionary-Ethnological Museum, and, on the other, to the exit corridor leading to the rotunda over the spiral staircase.

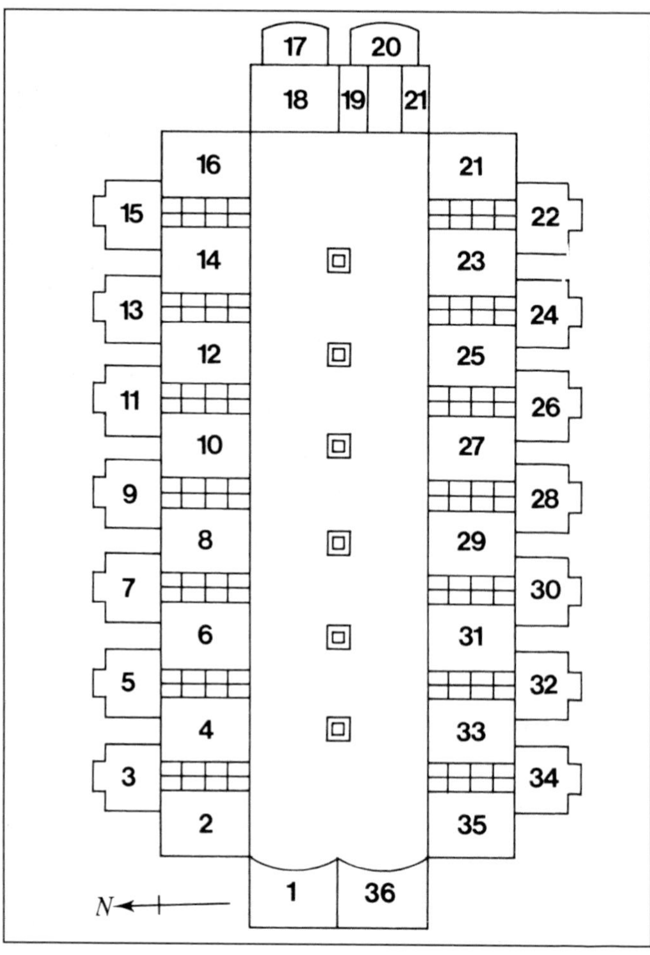

SCHEME OF THE LUNETTES AND WALLS OF THE SALONE SISTINO

In the left aisle:

1 Allegory of the reform of public morals in Rome under Sixtus V
2 Fourth Council of Constantinople (870)
3 Chapel of the Crib in Santa Maria Maggiore (1586)
4 Second Council of Nicaea against the Iconoclasts ((790)
5 Erection of the obelisk in Piazza del Popolo (1588)
6 Third Council of Constantinople (680)
7 Ponte Sisto and the Hospice of St. John Calabita
8 Second Council of Constantinople (553)
9 Erection of the statue of St. Paul above the Column of Marcus Aurelius (1588)
10 Council of Chalcedon (451)
11 Removal of the body of St. Pius V to Santa Maria Maggiore (1588)
12 First Council of Ephesus (431)
13 Obelisk and Square of Santa Maria Maggiore (1587)
14 First Council of Constantinople (381)
15 The Galleys of Sixtus V (1588)
16 Constantine orders the Burning of the Arian books (? 325)
17 Coronation of Sixtus V on the steps of St. Peters (1 May 1585)
18 First Council of Nicaea (325)

In the right aisle:

19 Sixtus V approves Domenico Fontana's plan for the new library (1587)
20 Sixtus V takes possession of the Lateran in a papal cavalcade (1585)
21 The Jewish library founded by Moses
22 Allegory of the fight against the brigands
23 The library of Babylon
24 St. Peter's Square in 1586
25 The library at Athens
26 Allegory of the prosperity produced by the good government of Sixtus V
27 The library of Alexandria, Egypt
28 The erection of the statue of St. Peter above Trajan's Column
29 The Roman library founded by Tarquinius Superbus
30 Papal procession to S. Maria Maggiore for the opening of the 1585 Jubilee
31 The episcopal library of Jerusalem (*c.*250)
32 The new Lateran Palace and the obelisk erected in 1588
33 The episcopal library of Caesarea in Palestine (*c.*230)
34 The "Aqua Felix" in Piazza San Bernardo (1585-87)
35 The Apostolic Library with portraits of St. Peter, Nicholas V, Sixtus IV, etc.
36 Plan of the city of Rome according to the projects of Sixtus V

plan →

u - Pinacoteca

Raphael, *Transfiguration*, detail

The Pinacoteca contains paintings and tapestries dating from the 11th to the 19th century. Each room is devoted to one or more schools of painting, to a period, or to individual artists. In the vestibule, on the left of the entrane, is Enrico Quattrini's bust of Pius XI, who established the Pinacoteca on its present site (see pg. 17, 24-26 for the history of the Pinacoteca). The base of the Antonine Column was recently placed on the terrace adjacent to the Pinacoteca. The Egyptian granite column, *c.*14.75 m. high, was erected at Montecitorio shortly after 161 A.D. in honour of the deified emperor Antoninus Pius by his sons Marcus Aurelius and Lucius Verus. It was found together with its base in 1703, but only the latter has survived. Three of the four sides of the pedestal are carved with high reliefs; the fourth side carries the dedicatory inscription. On the front is the *Apotheosis of Antoninus and Faustina*. The sides are sculpted with carousels, or military parades, held during the funeral.

ROOM I
(Primitives) I

Vittore Cavalli, known as Vitale da Bologna, *Madonna and Child* 1
(tempera on panel, 96 x 68 cm). Signed VITALIS DE BONONIA F. At the bottom left, a group of kneeling monks, members of the confraternity of the *Battuti Bianchi* in Ferrara, who commissioned the painting and used it as a processional banner. Provenance: Church of the Ospedale dei Battuti Bianchi; acquired for the Vatican Library collection in 1841. Inv. 40017.

School of Giunta Pisano, *St. Francis and stories of his life* (tempera on 2
panel, 66 x 86.5 cm). Very similar to two panels in San Francesco in Assisi and San Francesco in Pisa. In the centre, the figure of the saint; at the sides, four of his miracles: the healing of the paralysed child, the healing of the cripple, the possessed woman freed from the devil, and the healing of Bartolomeo da Narni before the altar with the tomb of the Saint. Formerly in the Vatican Library collection. Inv. 40023.

Giovanni and Niccolò, *Last Judgement* (tempera on panel, 288 x 243 3
cm). A work of the Roman school, datable to the second half of the 12th century, the panel comes from the oratory of St. Gregory Nazianzen,

near Santa Maria in Campo Marzio. It was commissioned by two Benedictine nuns, represented at the bottom left, and identified by the Latin inscription *Domna Benedicta ancilla Dei et Costantia abbatissa*. The shape of the panel—round, with a rectangular appendix attached to the base—is unusual. The various scenes are arranged in superimposed registers. In the top register: Christ in majesty flanked by seraphim and angels. In the second register: Christ, with symbols of the Passion, standing behind an altar, surrounded by apostles. In the third: from left to right: the resurrected, led by St. Paul and Dismas, the good thief, the Virgin, the saintly Innocents, St. Stephen, and the Works of Mercy grouped in three episodes. In the register below: the Resurrection of the dead; on the left, those devoured by wild animals and fish; on the right, those buried in the normal way; in the centre, two allegories of classical derivation, of the Sea and the Earth. On the lowest level: Paradise, to the left, and the torments of Hell, to the right. Inv. 40526.

4 Margaritone di Arezzo, *St. Francis* (tempera on panel, 127.2 x 53.9 cm). One of the earliest representations of the saint. Signed at the bottom: MARGARITO DE ARITIO ME FECIT. Formerly in the Vatican Library collection. Inv. 40002.

5 Master of the Life of the Baptist (Rimini, first half of the 14th cent.), *The guardian angel taking the child John the Baptist by the hand* (tempera on panel, 40 x 46.5 cm). The panel probably formed part of a dossal of which other components are now scattered amongst various museums: National Gallery of Art in Washington, Metropolitan Museum in New York, Seattle Art Museum and former Street collection in London. Inv. 40185.

6 Allegretto Nuzi, *Madonna and Child enthroned between St. Michael and St. Ursula* (tempera on panel; central panel 116.2 x 57.8; side panels 83.8 x 33 cm). The triptych is signed in the centre at the bottom: ALEGRITTUS NUTII ME PINXIT A.M. CCCLXV (1365). In the central panel; the group of donors kneeling at the Virgin's feet. The painting comes from the Chapel of St. Lucy and St. Michael the Archangel in the Church of Santa Lucia at Fabriano; it belonged to the Mariotti collection from 1800; in the Vatican Library since 1820. Inv. 40204.

7 Giovanni del Biondo, *Madonna of the Apocalypse with saints and angels* (tempera on panel, 75.4 x 43.4 cm). To the left: Saints Stephen, Anthony, Lawrence and Francis; to the right: Saints Mary Magdalen, Catherine of Alexandria, Clare and Catherine of Siena. Below, in the predella, a skeleton devoured by worms. Formerly in the Seroux d'Agincourt collection, later in the Vatican Library. Inv. 40014.

8 Giovanni Bonsi, *Madonna and Child with saints* (tempera on panel, 166 x 232 cm). At the centre, the Virgin and Child; left, St. Onophrius and St. Nicholas of Bari; right, St. Bartholomew and St. John the Evangelist. The only definitely authenticated work of the Florentine artist, signed and dated (1371): A.D. M. CCCLXXI. IONES BONSI DE FLORENTIA. ME PINSIT. Inv. 40009.

II

ROOM II

(School of Giotto and Late Gothic painters)

1 Giotto, *Stefaneschi Triptych* (tempera on panel; central panel 178 x 88 cm; side panels 168 x 82 cm; predella: central panel 44 x 85 cm; side panels 44 x 82 cm). Painted by Giotto with apprentices for Cardinal Jacopo Caetani Stefaneschi, probably *c.*1320;given the presence of Celestine V among the donors, with a halo (he was canonized in 1313). The triptych comes from the Sacristy of St. Peter's. Commissioned for the high altar of Constantine's Basilica, it is painted on

both sides. *Front side*: central panel, St. Peter enthroned, with angels and donors (Cardinal Stefaneschi offering the polyptych and Celestine V, a manuscript); side panels, to the right St. Andrew and St. John the Evangelist, to the left St. James and St. Paul. *Rear side:* central panel, Christ enthroned with angels and donor (Cardinal Stefaneschi); side panels, to the right Beheading of St. Paul, to the left Crucifixion of St. Peter. Predella of the front side: the central and right lateral panel are missing; the left lateral panel shows three saints including St. Stephen. Predella behind: in the centre, Madonna enthroned, flanked by angels, St. Peter and St. Paul; to the right and left, apostles. Inv. 40120.

Jacopo del Casentino, *Madonna and Child* (tempera on panel, 67 x 2
45.5 cm), central panel of polyptych. One of the few works attributable to this Florentine painter, who was born in 1297 and died in 1358. It comes from the Church of San Prospero at Cambiano; now in the Vatican Library collection. Inv. 40179.

Pietro Lorenzetti, *Christ before Pilate* (tempera on panel, 38 x 27.5 3
cm). Formerly in the Vatican Library collection. Inv. 40168.

Simone Martini, *Blessing Christ* (tempera on panel, 39 x 29 cm). 4
Painted in *c.*1320, it may have formed the gable of a polyptych. Formerly in the Vatican Library collection. Inv. 40165.

Bernardo Daddi, *Madonna of the Magnificat* (tempera on panel, 71 x 5
52.6 cm). The gabled upper part has been restored. Formerly in the Vatican Library collection. Inv. 40174.

Manner of Jacopo di Cione, *Coronation of the Virgin* (tempera on 6
panel, 116 x 64 cm). Formerly in the Vatican Library collection. Inv. 40008.

Giovanni di Paolo, *Christ praying in Gethsemane* (tempera on wood, 7
33 x 32.5 cm), and the *Lamentation* (tempera on panel, 33 x 32.5). They 8
are panels of the predella of a dismembered polyptych, of which other components are now in Philadelphia and Altenburg. Datable to 1440-1445. Formerly in the Vatican Library collection. Inv. 40129, 40124.

Stefano di Giovanni, known as Sassetta, *Vision of St. Thomas Aquinas* 9
(tempera on panel, 25 x 28.5 cm). It originally formed part of the predella of the dismembered triptych commissioned by the Arte della Lana (wool guild) for the guild chapel annexed to the Church of San Pellegrino in Siena (now divided between Siena, Budapest, Melbourne, Barnard Castle and the Vatican), painted 1423-26. Inv. 40234.

Lorenzo Monaco, *Stories from the life of St. Benedict* (tempera on 10
panel, 30 x 65 cm). The Saint frees a monk from the temptations of the devil, and resuscitates a monk killed by a collapsing wall. Formerly in the Vatican Library collection. Inv. 40193.

Gentile da Fabriano, *Stories of St. Nicholas of Bari* (tempera on 11-14
panel): the *Birth of the Saint* (36 x 36 cm); *St. Nicholas gives three* 11, 12
golden balls to three poor girls (35.8 x 36.1 cm); *St. Nicholas revives* 13, 14
three children found cut up in pieces in a barrel (36.5 x 36.5 cm); *St. Nicholas saves a ship from sinking* (39 x 62 cm). The panels belong to the predella of the polyptych painted by Gentile for the Quaratesi Chapel in the Church of San Niccolò, Florence. The other parts of the polyptych are in the Uffizi, Florence, and in the National Gallery, London. Inv. 40247-40250.

Stefano di Giovanni, known as Sassetta, *Madonna and Child* (tem- 15
pera on panel, 54.5 x 73 cm). Inv. 42139.

III

ROOM III

(Fra Angelico, Filippo Lippi, Benozzo Gozzoli)

1, 2 Tommaso di Cristoforo Fini, known as Masolino da Panicale, *Crucifixion* (tempera on panel, 53.1 x 31.6 cm) and *Passing Away of the Virgin* (tempera on panel, 19.7 x 48.4 cm). Inv. 40260, 40245.

3 Guido di Pietro, known as the Blessed Fra Angelico, *Madonna and Child with St. Dominic, St. Catherine and angels* (tempera on panel, 24.4 x 18.7 cm). Datable to *c.*1435, it was formerly in the Bisenzio collection, then belonged to Lord Dudley; in the Vatican since 1867. Inv. 40253.

4 Fra Angelico, *Stories of St. Nicholas of Bari* (tempera on wood, 35 x 61.5 cm each). They formed part of the predella of a triptych painted for the Chapel of St. Nicholas in the Church of San Domenico, Perugia, in *c.*1437; probably commissioned by the bishop, B. Guidalotti. The third panel of the predella and the other parts of the altarpiece are now in the National Gallery of Umbria, Perugia. The two Vatican panels represent the *Birth of St. Nicholas, his vocation, and the alms to the three poor girls*, and the *Meeting with the emperor's messenger and the miraculous saving of a sailing boat.* Inv. 40251, 40252.

5 Filippo Lippi, *Coronation of the Virgin* (tempera on panel; central panel 170 x 95 cm, side panels 164 x 83 cm). The triptych was painted in about 1460 for the Chapel of St. Bernard in the Monastery of Monteoliveto, Arezzo. It was commissioned by Carlo Marsuppini, secretary of the Republic of Florence, who appears, kneeling, in the left panel. Following the suppression of the Order, the triptych went first to the Lippi familiy of Arezzo, and then, in 1841, to Ugo Baldi. It was bought by Gregory XVI for the Lateran Pinacoteca, and later transferred to the Vatican. Inv. 40243.

6 Benozzo Gozzoli, *Madonna of the Girdle* (tempera on panel, 133 x 164 cm). Scenes from the life of Mary are shown in the predella: the *Birth of the Virgin*, the *Betrothal*, the *Annunciation*, the *Nativity*, the *Circumcision*, and the *Passing Away of the Virgin*. The opening at the Virgin's feet appears to have been used for communicating with cloistered nuns. Painted in 1450-52 for the church of San Fortunato, Montefalco. Donated by the Commune of Montefalco to Pius IX in 1848, it was formerly in the Lateran Pinacoteca. Inv. 40262.

IV

ROOM IV

(Melozzo da Forlì, Marco Palmezzano)

1 Melozzo da Forlì, *Sixtus IV and Platina* (fresco transferred to canvas, 370 x 315 cm). The fresco originally decorated one of the rooms of the library of Sixtus IV. Painted in 1477, it represents the nomination of Bartolomeo Platina as prefect of the Vatican Library (1475). The figure dressed as a cardinal is Giuliano della Rovere, nephew of Sixtus IV, and the future Julius II; the others are Raffaele Riario, Girolamo Riario and Giovanni della Rovere. Inv. 40270. This room also contains
2 fragments with *Musical Angels* from the fresco of the *Ascension* painted by Melozzo in the apse of the Basilica dei Santi Apostoli (the central fragment with the *Blessing Christ* is now in the Quirinal Palace). Inv. 40269.14.1-14.

Marco Palmezzano. *Madonna and Child with saints* (tempera on 13
panel, 340 x 226.5 cm). At the foot of the throne are Saints Francis, Lawrence, John the Baptist, Anthony, Dominic and Peter. Painted for the church of the Carmine at Cesena. Formerly in the Lateran Pinacoteca. Signed and dated (1537): MARCHUS PALMEZANUS PICTOR FOROLIVIENSIS FACIEBAT, MCCCCCXXXVII. Inv. 40619.

ROOM V V

(Various 15th century masters)

Ercole de Roberti, *Miracles of St. Vincent Ferrer* (tempera on panel, 1
30 x 215 cm). It formed the predella of the altarpiece painted by Francesco del Cossa for the Griffoni Chapel in San Petronio, Bologna. The central panel of the altarpiece is now in the National Gallery in London; the side panels are in the Brera Gallery, Milan. The following miracles are depicted: the resurrection of a child killed by his insane pregnant mother; the extinguishing of a fire; the rescue of a youth in danger; the resurrection of a Jewish lady; the healing of the crippled woman. Inv. 40286.

Lucas Cranach the Elder, *Pietà* (tempera on panel, 54 x 74 cm). 2
Cranach's monogram, a small winged snake, appears at the base of the tomb. Inv. 40275.

Benedetto Buglioni, *Coat of arms of Innocent VIII Cybo* (enamelled 3
terracotta). It was originally placed over the doorway leading to the apartment of Innocent VIII in the Palazzetto del Belvedere. Inv. 4087.

ROOM VI VI

(Polyptychs)

Carlo Crivelli, *Madonna and Child* (tempera on panel, 148 x 67 cm). 1
Painted for the church of San Francesco at Force, in the Marche. Formerly in the Lateran Pinacoteca. Signed and dated (1482): OPUS CAROLI CRIVELLI VENETI. Inv. 40297.

Carlo Crivelli, *Pietà* (tempera on panel. 105 x 205 cm). Sold to the 2
Vatican by Bernardino Giusti for the Campidoglio in 1831. Transferred to the Vatican by Gregory XVI in 1833. Signed: OPUS CAROLI CRIVELLI VENETI. Inv. 40300.

Niccolò di Liberatore, known as Alunno, *Camerino Triptych* (tempera 3
on panel: central panel 250 x 117 cm, side panels 151 x 84 cm and 157 x 84 cm). It comes from the Valenti Chapel in the Collegiata of San Venanzio in Camerino (Marche). It has been in the Vatican since 1845. In the central panel: Crucifixion, with the two Marys and St. John. Left panel: St. Peter and St. Venantius. Right panel: St. Porphyry and St. John the Evangelist. In the pinnacles: centre, the Resurrection: right, David: left, Isaiah; the missing pinnacles are in the Louvre, Paris. Inv. 40299.

Antonio Vivarini, *St. Anthony Abbot and other saints* (tempera on 4
panel; lower panels 105 x 30 cm; upper central panel 80 x 50 cm; upper side panels 53 x 30 cm). A complex polyptych comprising a wooden statue of St. Anthony, and a series of panels painted with the figures of Christ in the tomb, and Saints Peter, Paul, Jerome, Benedict, Christopher, Venantius, Sebastian and Roch, identified by their attributes. Painted for the church of Sant'Antonio, Pesaro. Formerly in the Lateran Pinacoteca. Signed and dated (1464): ANTONIUS DE MURANO PINXIT. Inv. 40303.

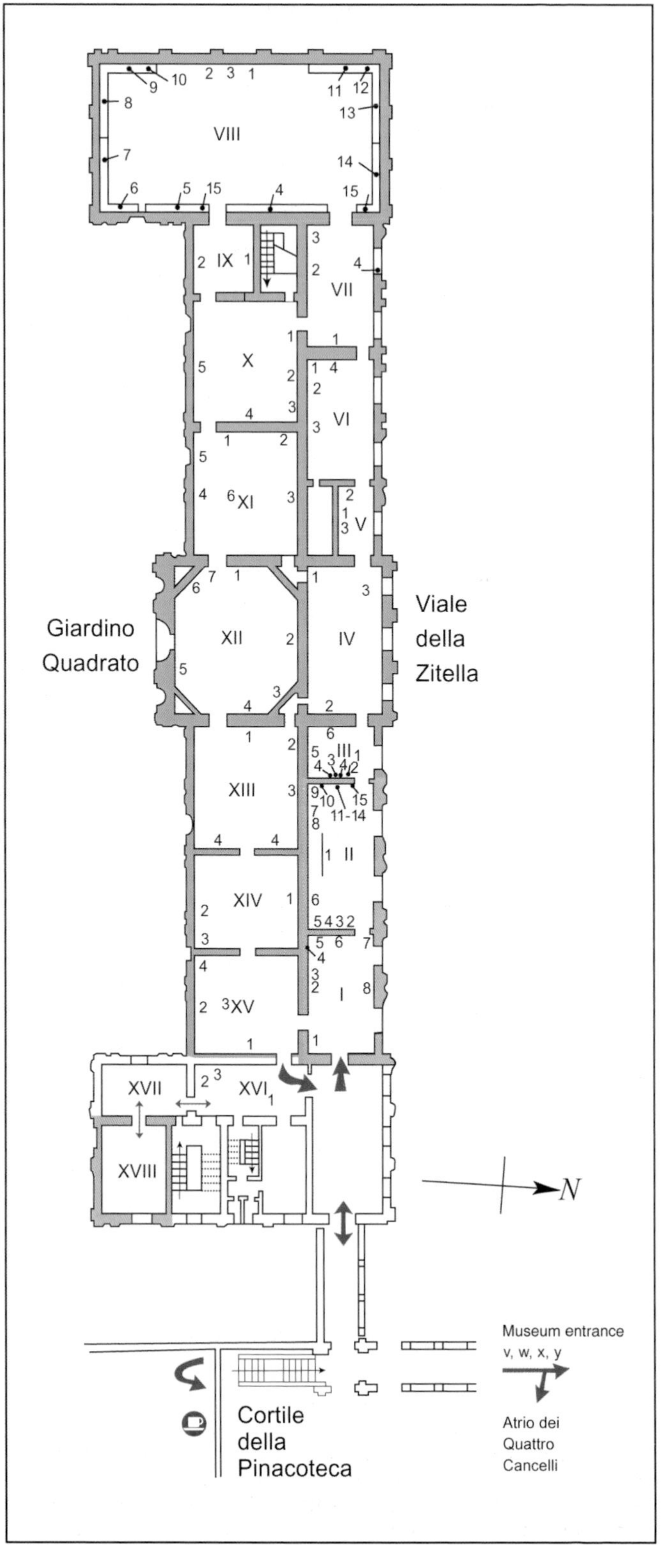

VIII
IX
VII
X
VI
XI
V
Giardino Quadrato
XII
IV
Viale della Zitella
XIII
III
II
XIV
XV
I
XVII
XVI
XVIII
N
Museum entrance v, w, x, y
Atrio dei Quattro Cancelli
Cortile della Pinacoteca

ROOM VII VII

(15th century Umbrian School)

Bernardino di Betto, known as Pinturicchio, and Giambattista Caporali, *Coronation of the Virgin* (tempera on panel, transferred to canvas; 330 x 200 cm). At the Virgin's feet are the apostles, and Saints Francis, Bernardino, Anthony of Padua, Louis of Toulouse, and Bonaventura. Painted in 1503 for the convent of the Observants at Umbertide (near Perugia). In the Vatican since 1826. Inv. 40312. 1

Pietro Vannucci, known as Perugino, *Madonna and Child with saints* (tempera on panel, 193 x 165 cm). Commissioned in 1483, but not completed till shortly after 1495, for the chapel of the Palazzo dei Priori in Perugia. Transported to Paris in 1797. The gable, with representation of Christ in the tomb, is in Perugia, as is the original frame. At the Virgin's feet are the patron saints of the city: Lawrence, Louis, Herculanus and Constant. Signed: HOC PETRUS DE CHASTRO PLEBIS PINXIT. Inv. 40317. 2

Giovanni Santi, *St. Jerome enthroned* (tempera on canvas, 189 x 168 cm.). Painted by Raphael's father, it was a processional banner, and comes from the church of San Bartolo at Pesaro. Signed on the step of the throne: IOHANNES SANTIS DE URBINO P. Inv. 40326. 3

Nicolo Filotesio, known as Cola dell'Amatrice, *Assumption* (tempera on panel, central panel 200 x 133 cm., side panels 115 x 60 cm.). In the lateral compartments of the triptych, to the left St. Lawrence and St. Benedict, to the right the Magdalen and St. Scholastica. Painted for the church of San Salvatore in Force (Ascoli Piceno); then in the Collegiata di San Paolo in the same town. In the Lateran Pinacoteca since 1844. Signed and dated (1515): COLA AMATRICIUS FACIEBAT MDXV. Inv. 40372. 4

ROOM VIII VIII

(Raphael)

Raphael Sanzio, *Coronation of the Virgin* (central panel, *tempera grassa* on panel, transferred to canvas, 267 x 163 cm, predella, *tempera grassa* on panel, 38.8 x 189.3 cm). The apostles, including Saints Thomas, Peter, Paul and John witness the event and are portrayed with their physical features. On the predella: the Annunciation, the Adoration of the Magi, and the Presentation in the Temple. Painted for the Oddi family in 1502-03, it once adorned the Church of San Francesco al Prato, Perugia. Taken to Paris in 1797, and transferred to canvas. Inv. 40334, 40335. 1

Raphael Sanzio, *Madonna of Foligno* (*tempera grassa* on panel, transferred to canvas, 301 x 198 cm). Commissioned from Raphael prior to 1512 by Sigismondo de' Conti, who is shown kneeling before St. Jerome, as an *ex voto* for the saving of his house from a bolt of lightning. Originally placed in the Church of Santa Maria d'Aracoeli, it was removed and transferred by his nephew to the church in the Convent of Santa Anna delle Contesse in Foligno in 1565. Taken to Paris in 1797, it was then transferred to canvas. Inv. 40329. 2

Raphael Sanzio, *Transfiguration* (*tempera grassa* on panel, 410 x 279 cm). Above, Christ between Moses and Elijah, with Saints Peter, John, James and, at the side, Julian and Lawrence, witnessing the event. Below, the Apostles and the episode of the possessed child, whose relatives beg for God's mercy. Cardinal Giulio de' Medici commissioned it from Raphael in 1517 with the intention of donating it to the Cathedral of Narbonne; it was completed shortly before the artist's death in 1520. It is entirely Raphael's work, and any contributions by his apprentices are insignificant. The quality of this 3 painting is superb, and it can be considered the "manifesto" of the artist's late style. The cardinal donated it to the Church of San Pietro in Montorio, Rome in 1523. It was taken to Paris in 1797. Inv. 40333.

4 In the showcases: tapestry of the *Last Supper* (Inv. 43789); its
composition taken from the painting by Leonardo, it was presented by
François I to Clement VII in 1532; and the tapestries of the so-called
Scuola Vecchia series, woven after cartoons by Raphael representing ten episodes from the lives of St. Peter and St. Paul, eight
5, 6 of which are exhibited here: *St. Paul in prison* (Inv. 43875), *St. Paul's*
7, 8 *Sermon in Athens* (Inv. 43876), the *Sacrifice of Lystra* (Inv. 43874), the
9 *Conversion of St. Paul* (Inv. 43872), the *Stoning of St. Stephen* (Inv.
10, 11 43871), the frieze of the *Hours* (Inv. 3878), the *Miraculous Draught of*
12, 13 *Fishes* (Inv. 3867), the frieze of the *Seasons* (Inv. 43867.2.2), the
14 *Healing of the Cripple* (Inv. 43869), and *Christ's Charge to St. Peter*
(Inv. 43868). The tapestries being restored are generally replaced by
the two of the same series kept in store: the *Death of Ananias* (Inv.
43870) and the *Blinding of Elymas* (Inv. 43873). Leo X commissioned
the tapestries from Raphael in 1515 to decorate the side walls of the
Sistine Chapel. The artist painted the full-scale cartoons for them
(now in the Victoria and Albert Museum, London), assisted by his
students, and entrusted the weaving of the tapestries to the studio of
Pieter van Aelst in Brussels. The tapestries were first displayed in the
15 Sistine Chapel on St. Stephen's Day in 1519. Also on show are two
friezes dating from the time of Clement VII (Inv. 43877, 43879).

IX

ROOM IX

(Leonardo and other 16th century artists)

1 Leonardo da Vinci, *St. Jerome* (oil on panel, 103 x 75 cm). Painted *c.*1480. Once owned by the Swiss painter Angelika Kauffmann, then lost. Cardinal Joseph Fesch discovered it divided into two pieces. The saint's torso had been turned into a lid of the coffer in an art dealer's shop, and the head had become the seat of a cobbler's stool. Purchased by Pius IX. Inv. 40337.

2 Giovanni Bellini, *Pietà* (oil on panel, 107 x 84 cm). The dead Christ is depicted together with Mary Magdalen, Nicodemus, and Joseph of Arimathea. This is the gable of the altarpiece painted by Bellini in about 1470-71 for the church of San Francesco, Pesaro. The altarpiece and predella are in the Museo Civico in Pesaro. The *Pietà* was removed by the French and transported to Paris in 1797. After the fall of Napoleon it was returned to Rome in 1816 and has been in the Vatican Pinacoteca since 1820. Inv. 40290.

X

ROOM X

(Titian and 16th century Venetians)

1 Tiziano Vecellio, *The Doge Niccolò Marcello* (oil on canvas, 103 x 90 cm). It is a posthumous portrait. Niccolò Marcello is considered the initiator of the custom for the doge to wear clothes interwoven with gold. Painted *c.*1542. Purchased by Leo XII from the Aldrovandi collection in Bologna. Inv. 40445.

2 Tiziano Vecellio, *Madonna of San Niccolò dei Frari* (oil on panel, transferred to canvas, 388 x 270 cm). At the Virgin's feet are Saints Sebastian, Francis, Anthony of Padua, Peter, Nicholas, and Catherine of Alexandria. The altarpiece was painted in 1528 for the Church of San Niccolò della Lattuga in the Campo dei Frari in Venice; the arched upper part has been lost. Signed: TITIANUS FACIEBAT. Inv. 40351.

3 Paolo Caliari, known as Veronese, *St. Helena* (oil on canvas, 166 x 134 cm). Formerly the property of the Pio di Carpi family, it was purchased by Benedict XIV for the Capitoline Pinacoteca and later transferred to the Vatican. Inv. 40352.

Paris Bordone, *St. George and the Dragon* (oil on panel, 290 x 189 cm), 4
*c.*1525. From the parish church of Noale (Vicenza), the painting was later in Venice and purchased by the Pontifical Government in 1789. Inv. 40354.

Giulio Pippi, known as Giulio Romano, and Francesco Penni, 5
Coronation of the Virgin or *Madonna of Monteluce* (oil on canvas, 354 x 232 cm). Painted in about 1525 for the nuns of the Convent of Monteluce in Perugia. The upper part is attributable to Giulio Romano, and the lower part to Penni. The commission had originally been given to Raphael (1505), but after his death was executed by his two apprentices following his designs. It was taken to Paris in 1797, but returned to the Vatican in 1820. Inv. 40359.

ROOM XI XI

(Later 16th century)

Circle of Girolamo Siciolante da Sermoneta, *St. Sebastian receiving* 1
the crown and palm of martyrdom (oil on panel, 234 x 147 cm), formerly displayed in the Quirinal Palace. Inv. 44275.

Giuseppe Cesari, known as Cavaliere d'Arpino, *Annunciation* (oil on 2
canvas, 290 x 184 cm). Signed and dated (1606): IOSEPH ARPINAS F. Inv. 40365.

Girolamo Muziano, *Resurrection of Lazarus* (oil on canvas, 295 x 440 3
cm). Michelangelo's praise of this work made the artist famous. Formerly in Santa Maria Maggiore, then in the Quirinal; in the Vatican since 1790. Signed: HIERS. MUTIANUS FECIT AC DEDIT. Inv. 40368.

Federico Barocci, *Rest on the Flight into Egypt (Madonna of the* 4
Cherries) (oil on canvas, 133 x 110 cm). Commissioned by Simonetto Anastagi of Perugia in 1573, the painting was given to the sacristy of the Jesuit church in Perugia on his death in 1602. After the Society of Jesus was suppressed, it was brought to the Quirinal in Rome; it has been in the Vatican since *c.*1790. Inv.40 377.

Federico Barocci, the *Blessed Michelina* (oil on canvas, 252 x 171 5
cm.). Commissioned by Alessandro Borignani for the Borignani Chapel in the Church of San Francesco, Pesaro, in 1606; it was taken to Paris in 1797; it has been in the Vatican Pinacoteca since 1820. Inv. 40378.

Pierino da Vinci, *Cosimo I dei Medici founding the University of Pisa* 6
(Carrara marble, 74 x 108 cm.). After 1549. Originally the property of the Salviati family, later in the Cavaceppi collection. Bought by G.B. Visconti for the Pio-Clementine Museum in 1771, it has been in the Vatican Pinacoteca since 1984. Inv. 742.

ROOM XII XII

(Baroque)

Jean de Boulogne, known as Valentin, *Martyrdom of St. Processus* 1
and St. Martinian (oil on canvas, 302 x 192 cm.). Painted for an altar in St. Peter's, where it was later replaced by a mosaic copy. Formerly in the Quirinal, it was taken to Paris in 1797; it has been in the Vatican Pinacoteca since 1820. Inv. 40381.

Domenico Zampieri, known as Domenichino, *Communion of St.* 2
Jerome (oil on canvas, 419 x 256 cm.). Painted for the church of San Gerolamo della Carità in 1614, it was removed to Paris in 1797. Signed and dated (1614): DOM. ZAMPERIUS. BONON. FA. MDXIV. Inv. 40384.

3 Michelangelo Merisi, known as Caravaggio, *The Deposition* (oil on canvas, 300 x 203 cm.). Commissioned by Pietro Vittrice, it was painted for the Vittrice Chapel in the church of Santa Maria in Vallicella (Chiesa Nuova) in Rome in 1604. Taken to Paris in 1797. Both Rubens and Cézanne painted copies of this painting. Inv. 40386.

4 Guido Reni, *Crucifixion of St. Peter* (oil on canvas, 305 x 171 cm.). Commissioned by Cardinal Scipione Borghese for the Church of San Paolo alle Tre Fontane, Rome, it was later transferred to the papal palace at the Quirinal. Taken to Paris in 1797, it has been in the Vatican Pinacoteca since 1820. Inv. 40387.

5 Giovan Francesco Barbieri, known as Guercino, *St. Mary Magdalen* (oil on canvas, 222 x 200 cm.). Painted in 1622 for the demolished Church of Santa Maria Maddalena delle Convertite on the Corso in Rome. Formerly in the Quirinal, it has been in the Vatican Pinacoteca since 1820. Inv. 40391.

6 Nicholas Poussin, *Martyrdom of St. Erasmus* (oil on canvas 320 x 286 cm.). Commissioned by Cardinal Francesco Barberini, it was painted in 1628-29 for the left tribune of St. Peter's where it was later replaced by a mosaic copy. Perhaps Poussin's largest painting. Signed: NICOLAUS PUSIN FECIT. Inv. 40394.

7 Guido Reni, *St. Matthew and the Angel* (oil on canvas, 85 x 68 cm.). Painted in 1635-40, it was donated to the Pinacoteca by A. Castellano in 1924. Inv. 40395.

XIII

ROOM XIII

(17th and 18th century)

1 Pietro Berrettini da Cortona, *The Virgin appearing to St. Francis* (oil on canvas, 227 x 151 cm.). Inv. 405. A mature work of the artist; there is a copy of it in Leningrad. Inv. 40405.

2 Orazio Gentileschi, *Judith and her handmaid with the head of Holofernes* (oil on canvas, 123 x 142 cm.), *c.*1611-12. Donated to the Vatican by A. De Angelis-Gammarelli in 1938. Inv. 41059.

3 Nicolas Poussin, *The Battle of Gideon* (oil on canvas, 98 x 137 cm.). An early work, painted soon after the French master moved to Rome *c.*1624. Inv. 40815.

4 Gerard Seghers and Jan Wildens, *St. Francis Xavier* (oil on canvas, 316 x 214 cm.) and *St. Ignatius Loyola* (oil on canvas, 345 x 215 cm). Painted for the Jesuit church of the Gesù in Rome. Inv. 40775, 40790.

XIV

ROOM XIV

(Various subjects)

1 Erasmus Quellinus and Daniel Seghers, *Garland of flowers with Madonna and Child* (oil on canvas, 118 x 85 cm.). Inv. 40416.

2 Pietro Navarra (?), *Flowers and fruit* (oil on canvas, 135 x 98 cm.). Inv. 40427.

3 Giovanni Battista Salvi, known as Sassoferrato, *Madonna and Child* (oil on canvas, 133 x 98 cm.). Painted by the artist *c.*1650. Donated by Pius IX to the Vatican Pinacoteca. Inv. 40396.

ROOM XV XV

(Portraits)

Thomas Lawrence, *George IV of England* (oil on canvas, 292 x 204 2
cm.). Signed at the bottom of the curtain: SIR THO. LAWRENCE PI. Donated by George IV to Pius VII. The letter sent by the pope to the king lies open on the table. On the king's left leg, the ribbon of the Garter. Inv. 40448.

Giuseppe Maria Crespi, *Benedict XIV* (oil on canvas, 260 x 180 cm.). 2
Painted for Prospero Lambertini while he was still a cardinal and archbishop of Bologna. When he was elected the new Pope, the cardinal's robes were repainted as papal vestments. Inv. 40458.

Donato Creti, *Astronomical observations (Sun, Moon, Mercury,* 3
Venus, Mars, Jupiter, Saturn and a comet) (oil on canvas, 51.5 x 35 cm. each). The series was commissioned by Luigi Marsigli in 1711 and donated to Clement XI to induce him into founding an astronomical observatory in Bologna. Inv. 40432, 40439.

Carlo Maratta, *Clement IX* (oil on canvas, 145 x 116 cm.). From the 4
Rospigliosi Gallery; donated by Louis Mendelssohn of Detroit. Painted in 1669 and signed: CARLO MARATTA. Inv. 40460.

ROOM XVI XVI

This room contains a series of paintings by Wenzel Peter, a German 1
artist specialized in painting flora and fauna. They were purchased by Gregory XVI to furnish the Sala del Concistoro in the Vatican Apostolic Palace in 1831.

Wenzel Peter, *Adam and Eve in the Garden of Eden* (oil on canvas, 2
247 x 336 cm.). The English collector Lord Bristol commissioned another version of the same work. Inv. 41266.

Wenzel Peter, *Self-Portrait* (oil on canvas, 75 x 71 cm.). Signed and 3
dated (1813): *Wenceslaus Peter se pinxit.* Inv. 40449.

Wenzel Peter, *Combat between a lion and a tiger* (oil on canvas, 136 x 130 cm.). Inv. 41262.

ROOM XVII- This room contains original clay models for Bernini's bronze sculptures for the Chapel of the Sacrament in St. Peter's (kneeling angel) and for the *Cathedra Petri* (standing angels and heads of Doctors of the Church), both in St. Peter's.

ROOM XVIII- The Vatican's Byzantine icon collection is displayed in this room. The 115 paintings, tempera on panel, dating from the 15th to the 19th century are mainly of Slav and Greek provenance, but also include a group of pseudo-icons produced in the West. They represent biblical scenes, evangelical calendars and saints.

plan →

v - Gregorian Profane Museum

View of the museum

This museum contains the collection of antiquities formerly housed in the Lateran Museum. The collection was installed in the Lateran Palace by Gregory XVI, and inaugurated on 14 May 1844. Under John XXIII it was transferred to this new building and re-opened to the public in 1970.

Most of the material in the museum comes from excavations and finds made in the Papal State. The main sections of the museum are: Greek originals, copies and versions made during the Roman Imperial period (1st to 3rd cent. A.D.) of Greek originals of the Classical Age (5th to 4th cent. B.C.); miscellaneous Roman sculptures arranged in chronological order: historical portraits and reliefs, urns, funerary monuments, sarcophagi, cult statues, and ornamental sculpture.

1 On the wall to the left of the entrance: *inscription* commemorating the foundation of the three former Lateran museums (Gregorian Profane, Pio-Christian, Missionary-Ethnological). Just inside the entrance, on the right: marble bust of *Gregory XVI,* founder of the Gregorian
2 Profane Museum; cast-iron bust of *Pius IX,* founder of the Pio-
3 Christian Museum, with commemorative plaques of the same period.

I

SECTION I

(Greek originals)

In the late 1950's, the small fragments of original Greek statues and reliefs of the 5th to 4th century B.C., which had until then been dispersed throughout the Vatican Museums, were brought together on the top floor of the Palazzetto del Belvedere, at the end of the Gregorian Etruscan Museum and the *Antiquarium Romanum.* A new layout of the collection was inaugurated at the entrance to the Gregorian Profane Museum in 1988.

4 On the wall facing the entrance: *funerary stele of a youth*; tall and slender, it once stood on top of a burial mound, crowned with a palmette, and placed over a pedestal with inscription. The dead youth is shown raising his arm in greeting; a boy is carrying objects used in

the palaestra: a globular *aryballos* and a strigil. The stele dates to *c.*450 B.C. Inv. 559.

To the right of the stele are three marble fragments of the original sculptural decoration of the Parthenon in Athens, built between 448 and 432 B.C. and the result of the combined efforts of Pericles, the patron, of Iktinos, the architect, and of Phidias, the sculptor.

Fragment of a horse's head from the western pediment of the 5
Parthenon. A drawing by Jacques Carrey dated 1674 shows how the pedimental decoration appeared before it was destroyed in 1687. Athena and Poseidon were shown competing for dominion over Attica. Both deities were riding in war-chariots, each drawn by two horses. As the heads of three other horses have been preserved, this must be the fourth, i.e. the one belonging to the front horse of Athena's chariot; this is confirmed by its appearance, size and stylistic features. Inv. 1016.

Fragment of relief with the head of a boy from the north frieze of the 6
Parthenon. This frieze, 160 m long, surrounds the cella (inner sanctum) of the temple. It represents the procession of the Panathenaea, a festival in honour of Athena held every four years. Over three hundred men and two hundred animals are represented in the frieze. This fragment with the head of a boy, who carries a tray of votive cakes (*skaphephoros*), is from the fifth panel of the north wall. Inv. 1014.

Bearded head from the sixteenth metope of the south side of the 7
Parthenon frieze. The identification is based on Carrey's drawing, and is consistent with the material, size and style of the fragment. The 92 metopes of the Parthenon were decorated with scenes representing the battles of the gods and primordial heroes to establish world order. On the south wall is the Battle of the Centaurs, and at its centre, on the sixteenth metope, is a figure presumed to be that of Erechtheus, legendary King of Athens; it is his head that appears on the fragment exhibited here. Inv. 1013.

Continuing in a clockwise direction:

Head of Athena. It formed part of an acrolith, i.e. a statue made of 8
other material (e.g. wood covered with precious metal leaf) but with stone extremities. The inserted eyeballs are in chalcedony, the irises and pupils (lost) in vitreous paste; the eyebrows are of thin bronze foil. Jewels were affixed to the ear lobes. The holes on the forehead and temples were for attaching a helmet, which Athena was the only goddess to wear. The head presumably belonged to a cult statue in Magna Graecia dating to the period around 460 B.C. Inv. 905.

Fragment of relief with horseman, part of a funerary monument *c.*440- 9
430 B.C. It recalls the horseman frieze of the Parthenon. Inv. 1684.

Votive relief: three *male figures clad in a "himation"*(mantle); the two 10
bearded figures are unidentifiable heroes, the youth is making a votive offering. Late 5th century B.C. Inv. 9984.

Relief with representation of a horseman, altar and devotee. Attic, *c.* 11
400 B.C. Inv. 1900.

Large votive relief with *Aesculapius enthroned, Hygeia and the* 12
children of Aesculapius, and devotees (on a smaller scale). Attic, 4th century B.C. Inv. 739.

Crowning-piece of a funerary monument; the dead woman is shown 13
emerging from an acanthus plant. Attic, 3rd century B.C. Inv. 886.

Fragment of relief with representation of a Theoxenia: a banquet in 14
homage to the god Dionysus, who is also present. Votive relief, 2nd century B.C. Inv. 1346.

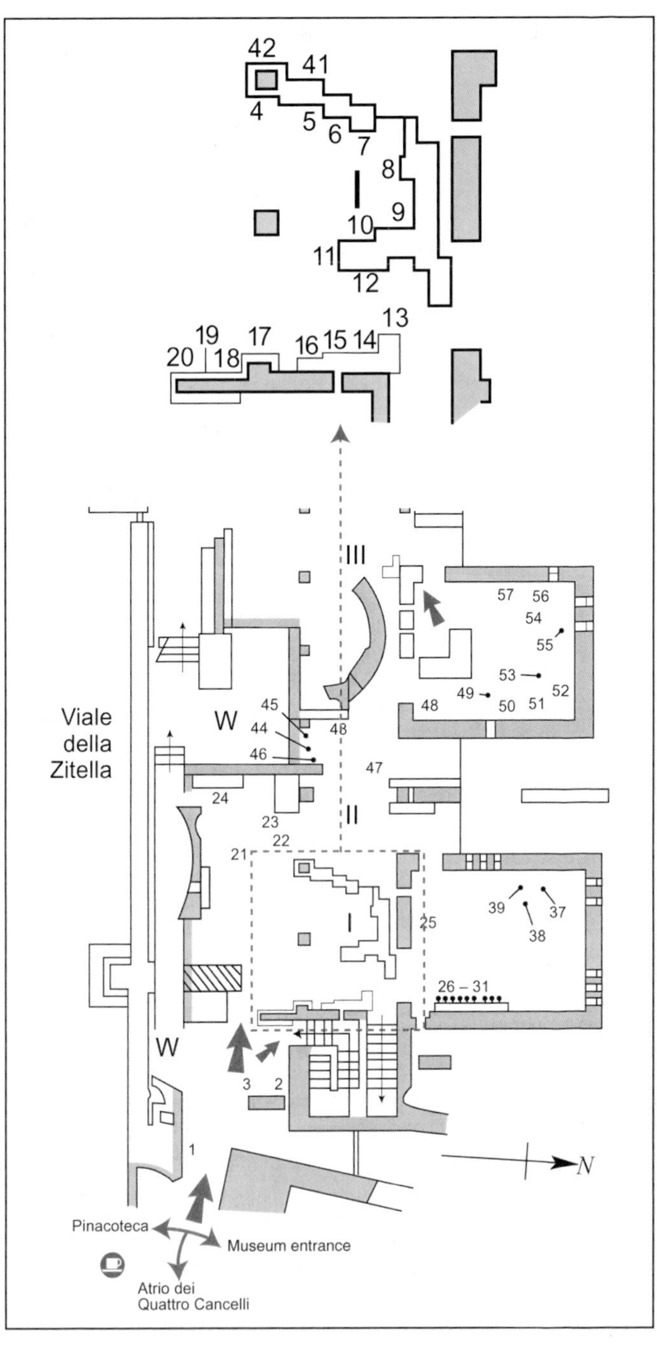

15 *Relief with funeral banquet.* Hades (with a crown, a sign of divinity) on a "kline" (couch); at his feet are Kore-Persephone and a group of worshippers. Attic, second half of 4th century B.C. Inv. 1348.

16 Votive relief: *Aesculapius enthroned with Hygeia* and the dedicator (the smaller figure). It probably dates to the late 5th century B.C., as the Aesculapius cult was only introduced in Athens in the second half

of the 5th century; in any case, Hygeia's hairstyle and the manner in which the heads are carved tend to rule out an earlier dating. Inv. 799.

Fragmentary relief with the seated Penelope. The portrayal of Ulysses' wife, who remained alone for twenty years, pensive and sad, is a subject known from numerous replicas; it is unquestionably identified by the inscriptions that accompany some of them, as well as by the constant repeating of the motif. The fragment, thought to be part of a Boeotian funerary relief (*c.*450 B.C.), actually comes from the tomb of Claudia Semne on the Via Appia. First half of the 2nd century A.D. Inv. 1558. 17

Figure of seated woman with head covered in sign of mourning: Electra at the tomb of her father, Agamemnon, as she awaits her brother Orestes, the avenger. From Taranto, 4th B.C. Inv. 2050. 18

Aphrodite, leaning against a female herm crowned with *polos*. Attic, early 4th century B.C. Inv. 9561. 19

Votive relief dedicated to the *Nymphs,* three of whom dance in a circle. About 400 B.C. Inv. 1345. 20

SECTION II II

(Roman Imperial copies and versions of Greek originals, 1st to 3rd century A.D.)

Turning one's back to the museum entrance, a series of torsos of ephebes can be seen on the left. They are early Roman Imperial copies and versions of Greek originals of the Classical Period (5th to 4th cent. B.C.).

Opposite the entrance at the end : copies of Myron's famous bronze group of *Athena and Marsyas* and a cast of Myron's Lancellotti
Athena. Statue of *Marsyas,* from the Esquiline, Inv. 9974. Torso of 21
Marsyas, from Castel Gandolfo, Inv. 9975. *Fragment of the head of* 22, 23
Athena, completed in plaster, Inv. 9970. The bronze group of *Athena and Marsyas*, the work of Myron of Eleutherai, is lost but can be reconstructed on the basis of two ancient literary sources: Pausanias (I, 24, 4) and Pliny (*Nat. Hist.* XXXIV, 57), and with the help of numismatic evidence. Placed as a votive offering on the Acropolis of Athens in the mid-5th century B.C., the group has only been partially preserved in Roman copies in marble. The Silenus Marsyas, drawn by the sound of the pan pipes, tries to snatch the musical instrument that Athena has just invented and discarded, but the peremptory gesture of the goddess prevents him.

Among a group of heads on the left: *basalt head,* copy of a Greek celebratory statue known as the *Idolino*; it represents a young athlete, victor at the Olympic or Delphic games, offering a libation with a sacrificial *patera*. The head is in the style of Polykleitos, and based on a prototype dating to *c.*440 B.C. Inv. 10134. 24

Go back through the section of the Greek originals to enter the Room of the Asaroton Mosaic; on the wall to the left of the entrance:

Hellenistic relief, perhaps of the 1st century B.C., with figures of a woman and a poet holding a theatrical mask; in the centre, between them, a table on which two other comic masks are placed. It has been suggested that the poet is intended to represent Menander, the greatest exponent of the "new comedy" (i.e. Attic comedy of the 4th cent. B.C.); the female figure may be a Muse or a personification of Comedy. Inv. 9985. 25

Set into the floor: large floor mosaic reconstructed from fragments found in an ancient building on the Aventine. The central part has been lost and only parts of the two framing friezes have survived. The inner one is decorated with figures of Nilotic fauna set against a black background. The outer frieze, against a white ground, represents the unswept floor of a dining room, scattered with the remains of a sumptuous banquet (note the mouse gnawing a nut). This still-life genre is known by the Greek name of *asaroton*. On one side, a row of six theatrical masks and other objects are set into the white frieze; below them is the artist's signature, in Greek: "made by Heraclitus". However, the mosaic is not by Heraclitus, but is a copy of the famous Hellenistic mosaic by Sosus, in Pergamum. We know from Pliny the Elder (*Nat. Hist.* XXXVI, 14) that the centre of the mosaic contained a bowl and doves, a scene similar to that of the well-known mosaic from Hadrian's Villa, now in the Capitoline Museum, (first half of the 2nd cent. A.D.) Inv. 10132.

To the right: gallery of herms. Originally, herms (*hermae*) were tapering pedestals terminating in a head or bust of the god Hermes
26-29 (Mercury), who was the guardian of roads and city gates in ancient
30 Greece, but the word is now used more generally to indicate any
31-34 pedestal-shaped statue with the head of a deity or demigod. *Bearded* god (Dionysus?), Inv. 10120, 10119, 10068, 10069. *Apollo,* Inv. 10070. *Hercules* (identified by the hero's headband), Inv. 9800, 10118. *Dionysus,* Inv. 10121. *Hercules,* Inv. 10067.

35 Colossal statue of *Poseidon* (Neptune). The god of the sea rests his right foot on the bow of a ship; a large dolphin serves as support for the statue. The downcast eyes suggest that the statue once stood in an elevated position. The statue is remarkable for its grandeur; the head framed by the god's flowing locks expresses nobility and dignity. The face shows controlled passion. The prototype of this statue was probably a bronze of the 4th century B.C. (perhaps by Lysippos?)and well-known, since it was reproduced on silver coins of the Hellenistic period (the dolphin was added by the copyist). Inv. 10315.

36 *Triangular base* with reliefs depicting Dionysian festivals. The form of the base is similar to that of Athenian bases used to support votive tripods offered by the winning chorus of the drama competitions held during the Dionysian Festival. A neo-Attic work in Pentelic marble of the 1st century B.C., inspired by a Greek original of the 4th century B.C., the base is remarkable for the delicacy of its reliefs. Inv. 9987.

37-39 *Dionysiac figures.* Replica of the satyr relaxing against a tree attributed to Praxiteles, one of the most famous and most frequently reproduced works of the great Attic sculptor of the 4th century B.C. Only its pointed ears, and perhaps the woolly hair and cunning expression of eyes and mouth , reveal the satyr's animal nature. (Cf. the copies p. 41: 15, and p. 50: V/7). Inv. 9980, 5330 and 10292.

40 Just outside the room: relief with *Medea and the daughters of Pelias.* On the left, the scene shows the witch Medea in the act of throwing a magic concoction of herbs into the cauldron that one of Pelias' daughters is preparing, while another daughter stands by, pensively holding the sword with which she will cut their father into pieces and boil him in the cauldron in order to rejuvenate him, following the deceitful advice of Medea. But the scheme is actually designed to restore Medea's husband Jason (winner of the Golden Fleece) to the throne usurped by his uncle Pelias. The whole relief is charged with dramatic tension. Three-figure reliefs of this type, the most famous of which is the relief of Orpheus and Eurydice, are linked to the dramatic trilogies performed in Athens during the Festival of Dionysus. They are thought to have been votive offerings for success in the drama competitions. Neo-Attic copy of the 1st century B.C. of a late 5th century Greek original. Inv. 9983.

plan ←

Leaving the room, on the metal trellis to the left:

Head Portrait of Demosthenes (died in 322 B.C.), Athenian orator and politician. The head, found in the Lateran, is a Roman copy of a bronze original sculpted by Polyeuktos for the agora in Athens *c.*280 B.C. (cf. p. 42: 9). Inv. 20725. 41

Head of Achilles, part of a group showing the hero in combat with Penthesilea, a Hellenistic work of the 2nd century B.C. Inv. 4632. 42

On the opposite side is a *statue of the Athenian tragic dramatist Sophocles* (496-406 B.C.); found at Terracina in 1839, and donated to Gregory XVI by the Antonelli family. Inv. 9973. 43

On the metal trellis to the left: *head portrait of Sophocles,* Inv. 4528.

The identification of the statue from Terracina is confirmed by the small bust with inscriptions in the Room of the Muses (see p. 57: III/12). Both are Roman Imperial copies of Greek originals in bronze. Literary sources mention two portraits of Sophocles, one commissioned after his death by his son Iophon (*Vita Sophoclis*, 11), and the other, in bronze, commissioned, together with portraits of Aeschylus and Euripides, by the orator Lycurgus for the 110th Olympiad (340-336 B.C.; Pseudo-Plutarch, *Vita X oratorum*, Lycur., p. 841). They are probably the portraits that Pausanias saw in the Theatre of Dionysus in Athens (I, 21, 1). On stylistic grounds, the Terracina marble is thought to be a copy of the portrait formerly in the Theatre of Dionysus, while the headportrait , inv. 4528 (known as the Farnese type because of a copy formerly in the Farnese collection), is thought to derive from the portrait commissioned by Iophon. The dramatist is shown in his prime, composed and self-confident, his cloak thrown casually round his shoulders, his gaze fixed on something in the distance. The headband indicates his status as priest of the cult of Aesculapius; when the cult first appeared in Athens, Sophocles introduced it into his own household. After his death he was given heroic status by the Athenians. His contemporaries called him "favourite of the gods" (*theophilés*) and "blessed" (*eudaimon*). Only seven of his 123 plays have survived, but they suffice to show that he was capable of penetrating to the depths of human passion. 44

On the same trellis:

Fragmentary portrait herm of *Homer* (for this type, cf. p. 53: 111/17). Inv. 7112. 45

To the left: portrait of the Greek lyric poet *Anacreon* (*c.*572-487 B.C.). This is a marble copy of a portrait statue that Pericles probably commissioned from Phidias for the Athenian Acropolis in 440 B.C.. Inv. 4563. 46

In the room with the glass wall, to the right of the statue of Sophocles: *mantle-clad male torsos.* Roman copies or versions of Greek statues of heroes or gods. It is possible that Roman head portraits were added to them to signify the divine or heroic status of the person represented. 47

Facing the reconstruction of a circular tomb near Vicovaro (see below), is the entrance to a second room (Room of the Chiaramonti Niobid), where Roman copies of female statues, based on Greek originals of the Classical period can be seen.

To the right: upper part of a statue of *Artemis* in the "severe style"; traces of a goat are visible on her left arm. Inv. 9833. 48

Headless figurine with peplos. The outstretched right hand probably held a sacrificial *patera.* The original was probably of the "Diana of Ariccia" type, dating to 430-420 B.C. Inv. 9569. 49

50 Torso of a statue of *Athena, of the Rospigliosi type.* The original is associated with the work of Timotheos (*c.*360 B.C.). Inv. 5377.

51 *Female head* in the "severe style". Inv. 10313.

52, 53 Two *draped female statues of Aurae* (personifications of the softest breezes). Formerly installed on the roof of the Round Room (Pio-Clementine Museum), they were removed in 1956. They are thought to come from Palestrina. Originally, they served as ornaments (acroteria) placed at the corners of a temple tympanum. Neo-Attic Hellenistic works of the 1st century B.C., based on classical models of about 400 B.C. Inv. 15046, 15047.

54 *Chiaramonti Niobid.* The statue represents one of the daughters of Niobe, wife of Amphion, King of Thebes. She had seven sons and seven daughters and boasted of her many children to Leto, who had only two, Apollo and Artemis. The two gods, angered by the insult to their mother, killed all of Niobe's children (Niobids) with their infallible arrows. The statue here represents one of Niobe's daughters, and can be identified because its main features are similar to those of a statue in the Uffizi Gallery in Florence, which was identified as a Niobid when it was discovered. Pliny the Elder (*Nat. Hist.* XXXVI, 28) speaks of a group of dying Niobids (*Niobae liberos morientes*), the work of Skopas or Praxiteles, displayed in the Temple of Apollo Sosianus in Rome. It is probable that an echo of this 4th century B.C. group is preserved in the *Chiaramonti Niobid.* The figure, with chiton gathered tightly round the waist and hand pressed to her hip, was presumably copied as an isolated sculpture – without her sisters or mother. (Cf. the representation of this myth on the sarcophagi, p. 155: IV/9, and p. 83: IV/16). Inv. 1035.

55 *Head of a Muse* with ivy garland, in the style of Praxiteles. It was sculpted to be inserted in a separate statue. Found near the Lateran. Roman copy of a 4th century B.C. original. Inv. 9969.

56 *Portrait of Cleopatra VII,* the famous Egyptian queen who reigned between 51 and 30 B.C. The head was detached from a statue to which it did not belong, displayed in the Room of the Greek Cross (Pio-Clementine Museum), and exhibited here since 1987. Inv. 38511.

57 Torso of a statue of *Diana* (Artemis) the huntress. The swift forward movement of the figure is accentuated by her flowing drapery. Roman copy of a Greek original of the 4th century B.C. Inv. 9567.

A new section now begins that is devoted to Roman sculpture, arranged in chronological order.

III

SECTION III

(Roman sculpture from the late 1st century B.C. to the early 2nd century A.D.)

The first part of this section consists of Roman portraits from the late Republic and early Empire.

1, 2 Two *portraits of the same person.* It has been suggested that the subject is Virgil, though there is unfortunately no proof. Inv. 10162, 10163.

3-5 Three *funerary reliefs* with portraits of the families of Roman
3, 4 freedmen, of the 1st century B.C.: the *gens Numenia* (Inv. 10490), the
5 *gens Servilia* (Inv. 10491), and, further along the trellis, the *gens Furia* (Inv. 10464).

6 *Round altar dedicated to Pietas* (Piety), decorated with garlands of fruit, interspersed with ten-stringed citherns. Under each garland,

four attributes of Hephaestus (Vulcan): hammer, tongs, anvil and pileus (cap worn by artisans, and associated with Hephaestus). The altar is a copy of the one dedicated by Scribonius Libo, in the Forum Romanum, known from coins of the Emilia and Scribonia *gentes* (families). In the delicacy of its carvings and the accomplished composition of its ornaments, it is reminiscent of the magnificent festoons of the *Ara Pacis* of Augustus. (From Veii; 1st century A.D.). Inv. 10455.

Idealized statue with mantle round the hips, and portrait of Germanicus (15 B.C.-19 A.D.), brother of Emperor Claudius. Excavated at Veii, 1811. Inv. 10434. 7

Twenty-one marble fragments of a *round tomb near Vicovaro* have been assembled so as to give a general idea of the appearance of the original structure. The surviving pieces include four fragments with palmette frieze from the upper edge of the drum; eight fragments of the decorated cornice at the top of the drum; and nine roof blocks. The latter are arranged in an alternating horizontal and vertical pattern. Their outer surface is decorated with reliefs: *bucrania* (ox skulls) and festoons. The diameter of the roof, and therefore of the drum and cornice, has been estimated at about 10 metres. The ornaments and shape of the tomb suggest that it was built during the reign of Tiberius or Claudius (*c.*20-40 A.D.). 8

Sculptures of the 1st century A.D., found in the area of the Roman municipality of Cerveteri (ancient *Caere)* in 1840-46, are arranged inside and in front of the hemicycle formed by the Vicovaro Tomb.

Pair of *sleeping sileni;* their heads rest on a wineskin that probably served as a fountain (from the theatre of Caere). Roman copies of Hellenistic originals. Inv. 9949, 9962. 9

Toga-clad statue with portrait of an ordinary citizen. Inv. 9951. 10

Draped female figure. Copy of a Greek original of the 4th century B.C. The head is modern. Inv. 9954. 11

Reliefs with personifications of three Etruscan cities: Vetulonia, Vulci and Tarquinia (their names are inscribed)*:* a man standing under a pine-tree, with an oar on his left shoulder; a veiled woman sitting on a throne, holding a flower (?) in her right hand; a man standing, wearing a toga, his head covered (possibly Tarchon, mythical founder of Tarquinia). These figures, evidently copied from statues, were placed side by side without any relation to each other; the only element that links them is the garland held above them by a putto. On the back, small altar with a boar in front of a laurel. The relief was found together with other statues of members of the Julio-Claudian imperial family; it probably adorned an altar for the imperial cult. The altar, whose preserved fragment constituted half of the left side, was decorated with personifications of the peoples of the Etruscan League, which was originally formed of twelve cities, but it was re-founded and extended to include fifteen by imperial decree in the period between Augustus and Claudius. Inv. 9942. 12

Colossal seated statue of the emperor *Claudius* (41-54 A.D.) of the Capitoline Jove type. It is unlikely that the head originally formed part of the statue. The head of Claudius is crowned with oak leaves. Inv. 9950. 13

Plaster cast of the *head of Augustus* in the Louvre (MA 1246). The original, together with other imperial portrait statues from Cerveteri, was found in 1840. However, since it was not acquired by the Papal State, it remained in private hands; as part of the Campana collection it ended up in Paris. The portrait belonged to a seated statue similar to those of Tiberius and Claudius (nos. 13, 16); identified only recently, its cast was put on display in 1988. 14

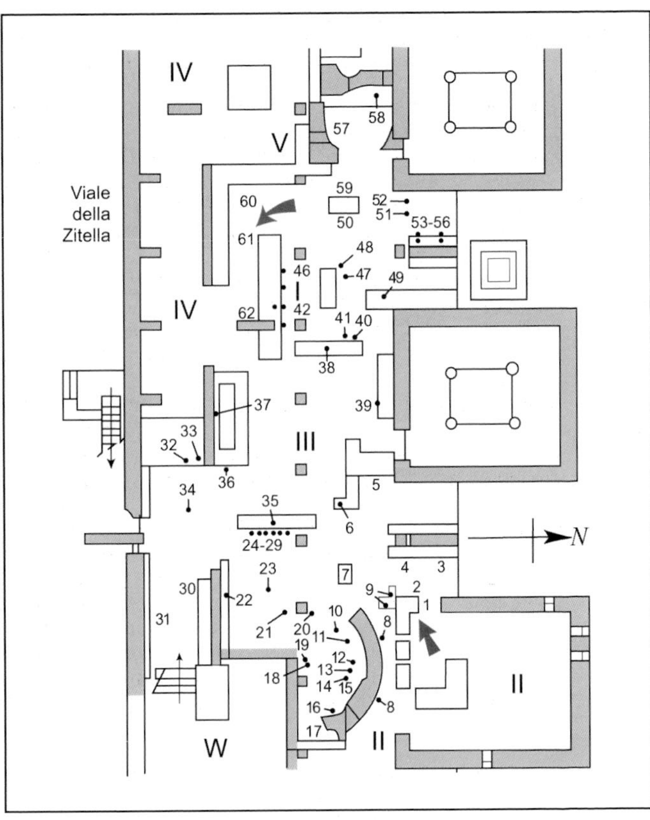

Colossal head of *Augustus* (31 B.C.-14 A.D.); found at Cerveteri in 1846, it probably adorned the theatre of Caere. Inv. 9953.

15 Colossal seated statue of the emperor *Tiberius* (14-37 A.D.), of the Capitoline Jove type, with civic crown of oak leaves. From Cerveteri. (Cf. below: 29). Inv. 9961.

16 *Toga-clad statue with portrait head not belonging to it,* probably representing a member of the Julio-Claudian family. Inv. 9955.

17 On the metal trellis: inscriptions, from the area of the Theatre of Caere, in honour of Augustus, Germanicus Caesar, Drusilla, Agrippina the Younger and Claudius.

In front of the hemicycle:

18 *Altar dedicated to C. Manlius,* censor of Caere, by one of his clients. Front: the sacrifice of a bull (the inscription is above the garland). Back: a female deity sits on a rock, surrounded by devotees. The deity may be Fides. On each side: a *lar* (household god) dances between two olive trees. (1st century B.C.). Inv. 9964.

19, 20 Two *statues with lorica* (leather cuirass): one headless, and of high accomplishment, the other with the portrait possibly of *Drusus* (38-9 B.C.), brother of the emperor Tiberius. Inv. 9948, 9963.

19, 20 *Draped female statue* with the portrait possibly of Agrippina the Younger (15-59 A.D.), wife of the emperor Claudius, and mother of Nero. The hairstyle is typical of the early Empire, and the face bears a strong resemblance to members of the Julio-Claudian family. The body, copy of a Greek original of the 5th century B.C., idealizes the empress by giving her the appearance of a goddess. Inv. 9952.

Opposite the Caere group, at the back: relief known conventionally as 22
the *Altar of the Vicomagistri.* Found in the Campus Martius area (on the site of the present Palazzo Cancelleria) in 1937-39, the relief, of which only two non-adjacent portions remain, probably decorated the base of a large altar of the early Imperial period. It represents a sacrificial procession: two consuls accompanied by lictors, trumpeters, three sacrificial animals – ox, bull and heifer - accompanied by attendants; flautists and cithern-players; five veiled youths; figures wearing togas and laurel wreaths interpreted as *vicomagistri.* The youths preceding the *vicomagistri* hold figurines in their left hands: one represents two dancing *lares* with drinking-horn, the other a toga-clad figure, the *genius augusti*, a sort of tutelary spirit of the emperor. The duties of the *vicomagistri* included guarding the *lares compitales* in each of the *vici*, the small districts into which Rome was divided. One of the changes made by Augustus in the period 14/13-7 B.C. was the introduction of his own Genius into the cult. In fact, the large number of *vicomagistri* in the relief, the fact that they wear patrician footwear in contrast with the humble social extraction from which they were usually drawn, and the importance of the sacrifice at which even consuls (the highest-ranking Roman magistrates) are present, all lead one to suppose that the *lares* in question are those of Rome itself, whose temple was in the vicinity of the Forum Romanum. So the high priests represented here are probably those responsible for this important central cult of the Roman state. The reliefs date to the Tiberian-Claudian period (*c.*30-40 A.D.). Inv. 1156, 1157.

Opposite the Altar of the Vicomagistri is the *Altar of Augustus Pontifex* 23
Maximus (12 A.D.). All four sides are decorated with reliefs. Front: winged Victory with round shield, on which appear the words. 'The Senate and people of Rome have dedicated this altar to the emperor Augustus, son of the divine Caesar, as Pontifex Maximus". Back: apotheosis of Caesar. Sides: a sacrifice to the *lares*, and the prophecy made to Aeneas regarding the sow of Lavinium. Inv. 1115.

On the next trellis: *portraits of the Julio-Claudian period* (first half of 24-29
the 1st cent. A.D.). From left to right:

Portrait of *Livia,* second wife of Augustus; born in 57 B.C., she died at 24
the age of 86 in 29 A.D. and was deified under Claudius in 41 A.D. Inv. 10204.

Colossal head of *Augustus,* from Veii. Born 63 B.C., adopted by his 25
great-uncle Caesar in 44 B.C., he became emperor in 31 B.C. (date of the naval victory at Actium), proclaimed "Augustus" by the Senate in 27 B.C., died at Nola at the age of 76 on 19 August 14 A.D. This is a posthumous portrait (cf. above: 15, and. p. 39: 2). Inv. 10222.

Princes of the Julio-Claudian family. Inv. 10194, 10198, 10221. 26-28

Tiberius, stepson and successor of the emperor Augustus (14-37 29
A.D). (Cf. above: 16). Inv. 4060.

Behind the wall of the Vicomagistri relief: funerary urns and altars of the 1st century A.D. In the rite of cremation the incinerated remains were placed in urns of various shapes—round, square, rectangular, with lids in the form of a ridge roof—, or in ossuaries in the form of an altar. Most of the funerary altars exhibited here were found in the Volusii columbarium on the Appian Way, near the Vigna Ammendola, in 1825.

30 They comprise the *cinerary urn in the form of a richly decorated altar* (to the left, in the area below the stairs). Two candelabra (or censers) are depicted at the corners. The head of Medusa and a large festoon are centrally placed on the front of the altar, bearing the tablet with inscription. Below is a charming genre scene: the end of a cockfight organized by two cupids; the winning cock, holding a wreath with its claws, taken from a table on which other victory crowns and palms are depicted, is embraced by its master; the other cock is carried away in disgrace under the arm of a weeping cupid. On the other sides: festoons, and nests with newly hatched birds being fed by their parents; below, other cupids (1st century A.D.). Inv. 9820.

31 At the outer wall: *cinerary urn with scene of vintage;* on the front, between herms, two men press grapes in a vat. Inv. 10531.

Turning away from the area below the stairs:

32 *Funerary altar of Claudius Dionysius* together with his wife: husband and wife are shown standing, holding hands (mid-1st century A.D.). Inv. 9836.

33 *Funerary relief showing the same Claudius Dionysius* lying in bed, his wife sitting beside him. The woman's hairstyle is typical of the Claudian period (mid-1st century A.D.). Inv. 9830.

34 *Altar of Gaius Julius Postumus.* The reliefs suggest that the deceased was a child. On the front: a boy feeds grapes to a hare held in his tunic; next to him, a taller boy wearing a toga. On the right side: a boy plays with a dog. Left side: a child in a miniature carriage drawn by a boy. Until 1925 this altar was used as a holy water stoup in the Church of Santa Maria in Domnica, on the Caelian Hill (1st century A.D.). Inv. 9934.

35 Leaving the section devoted to cinerary urns and funerary altars, on the trellis to the right: *ornamental reliefs with Bacchic scenes* represented among leaves and saplings; finely carved reliefs, evidently used as wall decorations (1st century A.D.). Inv. 10111-10117.

36 To the left: *base of a column* from the Basilica Julia in the Forum Romanum; an example of the precision achieved in the carving of marble architectural ornaments in the early Flavian period. Inv. 9788.

37, 38 The two large reliefs displayed in the following zone were found in the Campus Martius, under the Palazzo Cancelleria, in 1937-39 and are therefore known as the *Cancelleria Reliefs*.

37 Left: *Frieze B, with the "adventus" (arrival) of the emperor Vespasian* (69-70 A.D.) in Rome. The emperor can be clearly identified as the noble-looking, toga-clad figure with the typical features of Vespasian, on the right-hand side of the frieze. Standing before him is a magistrate, also clad in the toga, who receives him on the outskirts of the city of Rome, on Vespasian's return from Palestrina after having been acclaimed emperor in 70 A.D. Among the emperor's retinue are a winged Victory, holding a wreath of oak leaves over his head, and lictors. In the entourage of the magistrate are the Genius of the senate and the Genius of the people; the latter rests one foot on the boundary stone. Vespasian's greeting is addressed not only at the magistrate but also at the personified Rome, enthroned on the left, surrounded by Vestal Virgins. Inv. 13392-13395.

Right: *Frieze A, with the "profectio" (departure) of the emperor* 38
Domitian (Nerva). The emperor is dressed in a tunic and *paludamentum* (travelling-cloak), and is surrounded by deities, genii, lictors and soldiers. He is preceded by Minerva, Mars, lictors, and Victory, whose left wing is visible at the edge of the relief (about a metre of the left panel is missing). Virtue leads the emperor by the arm. The Genius of the Senate and the Genius of the people, both behind the emperor, bid him farewell. They are followed by a commander and soldiers. The emperor holds a scroll in one hand, and raises the other hand in a gesture of command. The head of Domitian (81-96 A.D.) is recognizable from the hairstyle; but his face was later eliminated, and replaced with that of Nerva, his successor (96-98 A.D). In fact, after Domitian's death, his face and his name were removed from all public monuments by decree of the Senate (*damnatio memoriae*). Inv. 13389-13391.

On the wall, on the right: fragment of a portrait of the emperor *Titus* 39
(79-81 A.D). A large part of the upper skull, the nape of the neck, and part of the forehead and right eye are missing. What remains of the face reveals a splendidly modelled portrait, untouched by the hand of the restorers. Inv. 4066.

Beyond Frieze A of the Cancelleria Reliefs we come to an area in which almost all the fragments (some forty) from the Tomb of the Haterii are displayed. It was excavated on the Via Labicana, near Centocelle, in 1848. Further excavations conducted in early 1970 resulted in the discovery of new epigraphic and sculptural material
(now the property of the Italian State). A description of *some of the* 40-48
Tomb of the Haterii fragments follows.

On the opposite side of the trellis on which Frieze A of the Cancelleria
Reliefs is exhibited are: *aediculae with the busts of a man and woman* 40, 41
of the Haterii family, in almost perfect condition. The man has an expressive face, short, curly hair, combed forward, and prominent, bristly eyebrows. The bust is naked, but for the mantle thrown over his left shoulder. Below, a writhing serpent takes the place of the base of the bust, an allusion, perhaps, to the heroization of the deceased. Inv. 10025, 10026.

On the trellis on the right:

Fragmentary relief with lemons and quinces, and, above, frieze with 42
masks. Inv. 10024.

Relief representing five buildings of ancient Rome. They have been 43
identified as follows, from left to right: 1) Arch with three barrel-vaults and the inscription *Arcus ad Isis.* This was the monumental entrance to the Temple of Isis and Serapis in the Campus Martius. Known in the 11th century as the Arch of Campigliano or Arch of Camillo, it stood at the corner of the Via del Piè di Marmo in what is now the Piazza del Collegio Romano, and was probably erected to commemorate the victory over Judaea. 2) The Flavian Amphitheatre, known as the Colosseum (begun by Vespasian 70-76 A.D., and dedicated by Titus in 80 A.D.), with a reproduction of the main entrance, an arch surmounted by a quadriga. 3) Triumphal arch, generally identified as the one erected 80-81 A.D. in honour of Titus at the east entrance to the Circus Maximus; the *Magna Mater in Circo Maximo* can be seen through the central passage enthroned between lions. 4) Triumphal arch with the inscription *Arcus in Sacra Via Summa.* This is the arch erected, in honour of Titus, on the Via Sacra, at the highest point of the Velia. 5) Temple of Jupiter Tonans at the entrance to the Capitoline Hill. Behind the altar is a cult statue of the god, with thunderbolts and sceptre; similar representations appear on contemporary coins. The temple was destroyed by fire in 80 A.D., and reconstructed during the time of Domitian. This relief from the Tomb of the Haterii is now

interpreted as follows: the tomb was built by a building contractor for himself and his family (this theory is supported by the presence of a crane in the relief Inv. 9998, see below: 46) who had been involved in the erection or reconstruction of the edifices represented in the reliefs, all of the Flavian period. Inv. 9997.

44 *Relief* (in two pieces) *with scene of laying out of the body of the deceased lady and mourners.* Lamps and torches are arranged round the large funerary bed, placed in the atrium of a house. Behind the bed, wailing-women; below, mourning servants and a flautist. Inv. 9999.

45 *Fragment of a portal with busts of the four gods of the underworld*: Mercury, Proserpine, Pluto and Ceres. The underside, which would have been visible from below, is also decorated. Inv. 10018.

46 *Relief representing a mausoleum and crane.* The temple-like building stands on a high podium; it is articulated with columns and pilasters, and is richly decorated with reliefs and with the busts of three children in circular niches and, on the pediment, the bust of a woman, probably the deceased. The scene above the building shows the inside of the tomb, with the dead woman lying on a funerary couch. Below, an old woman performs a sacrifice at a burning altar, with three children playing in front. On the right, is a small shrine with a statue of Venus; three portrait masks crown the small chapel. Below the stairs of the podium are a canopied altar and what is probably an *ustrinum*, or place of cremation. The crane, on the left, extends to the top of the relief; the machine was operated by the force of the weight of the workmen inside the wheel. Inv. 9998.

On the floor, in front of the trellises:

47 *Quadrangular cinerary urn;* the decorations show water spouting from a shell, with fish, dolphins and ducks; at the corners, ram-heads. Inv. 10000.

48 *Pillar of the roses.* Two sides are embellished with the same motif, a candelabrum with rose branches and olive branches below. Above, two long-tailed birds (parrots?). One of the finest examples of Roman decorative art. Inv. 10029.—This concludes the description of the major finds from the Tomb of the Haterii.

49 In the first window compartment, on the right: *bust of L. Iulius Ursus,* friend of the emperors Domitian and Trajan; it was he who prevented the execution of the empress Domitia Longina (Cassius Dio, LXVIII, 3, 1; 4, 2); made consul for the third time in 100 A.D. Identified from another bust portrait with inscription, property of the Duke of Wellington. Inv. 10210.

50 A little further, on a separate trellis: *relief with procession of Roman magistrates in front of a temple.* The magistrates are accompanied by lictors. The upper part of the relief, with the columns and pediment of a temple, is a cast of the original fragment, which is now in the Museo Nazionale Romano. The myth of Rhea Silvia, with the wolf and the twins Romulus and Remus, is represented on the temple pediment. The head of Trajan, the second figure, is a restoration by the Danish sculptor Bertel Thorvaldsen. Inv. 9506.

Second window compartment:

51, 52 In front: *two ancient columns,* decorated. Inv. 10096, 10097.

Behind the columns, on the wall:

53 On the right, above: *fragment of a tomb relief.* The central slab with inscription is missing. Left, toga-clad figure offering a libation. Below, a man asleep in a grotto (or inside a tomb), possibly a representation

of the deceased; he is holding a poppy pod. Above, a cockfight and cupids carrying garlands (*c.*100 A.D). Inv. 9822.

Below: *tomb relief with circus races.* The circus is seen sideways from above. A four-horse chariot races along the *spina* (wall separating the two tracks). On top of the *spina* are several *metae* (signposts), an obelisk, two columns with statues, and, between the statues, a shrine with four dolphins on the roof. A victor holding a palm leaf leans against the group of *metae* on the left. The large figure on the left is the deceased, dressed in a toga, and holding a scroll in his left hand. His right hand is extended towards his wife (*dextrarum iunctio*). The races are in honour of the dead man (*c.*100 A.D). Inv. 9556. 54

On the left, above: *fragment of a pediment* of a funerary monument on the Appian Way. Cupids support the bust of Claudia Semne (identified by the circumstances of its discovery). The bust is meant to be the spirit of the dead woman. Inv. 10528. 55

Below: *tomb relief of Ulpia Epigone.* The deceased woman is shown lying on a couch, supporting herself on her left hip, a sewing box at her feet, a lapdog under her arm. The hairstyle is typical of the Flavian/Trajanic period. Inv. 9856. 56

Leave this room and enter a small semicircular room on the right:

Colossal statue of a barbarian prisoner. His costume and facial features identity him as a Dacian (a Balkan people conquered by Trajan). Trajan's Column, though the most celebrated monument of the Dacian campaign, was not the only one. This unfinished statue, together with other similar statues used in the Arch of Constantine, comes from some other monument celebrating the same event. It was excavated on the Via dei Coronari in 1841 (early 2nd cent. A.D). Inv. 10534. 57

Fragment of relief with military insignia. The thunderbolt on the shield at the top of the standard identifies the legion to which it belonged: namely, the 12 *Fulminata.* The fragment clearly comes from a military scene (2nd to 3rd cent. A.D). Inv. 9508. 58

On the trellis in front of the hemicycle: *fragment of relief with standard-bearer.* The insignia is that of the Praetorian Guards; it appears frequently on the columns erected by Trajan and Marcus Aurelius. Standard-bearers are always shown with their heads covered with an animal skin. This fragment was clearly part of a military scene, perhaps from a triumphal arch (2nd cent. A.D). Inv. 9507. 59

Most of the architectural fragments are from Trajan's Forum.

Proceeding to the right, on the trellis: *two fragments from the same architectural frieze,* probably from Trajan's Forum. The two pieces fit together to form a scene that was probably repeated along the frieze. A neo-Attic amphora, decorated with reliefs representing a satyr and two maenads, is flanked by two cupids, each watering a griffin. Their legs are transformed into acanthus leaves and spirals; the cupids are elegantly fused into the luxuriant floral decoration (early 2nd cent. A.D). Inv. 9700, 9648. 60, 61

Above the passage leading to Section IV: *fragment of architectural frieze* with acanthus spirals. Despite the abundant foliage, the basic ornamental design is clearly visible (early 2nd cent. A.D). Inv. 9715. 62

IV

SECTION IV
(Sarcophagi)

The reliefs in the Gallery of the Sarcophagi are arranged by subject. The ones with mythological themes are first

On the left:

1 Below: *fragment of sarcophagus with the labours of Hercules:* the capture of the Cretan bull; the killing of the mares of Diomedes; the victory over Geryon. Inv. 9803.

2 Above: *sarcophagus frontal with scene of Meleager killing the Caledonian boar.* Inv. 10404.

On the right, in front of the trellis:

3 *Sarcophagus with scenes of the myth of Adonis.* To the left: the young hunter Adonis takes leave of Aphrodite, who sits on a throne surrounded by cupids. To the right: the boar is about to attack; Adonis falls, mortally wounded. Centre: Adonis enthroned, with a physician who tries in vain to treat his wounds, next to Aphrodite. The goddess, inconsolable for the loss of her beloved youth, begs the god of the underworld to let Adonis spend six months of the year on earth—a reference to the theme of life after death. The faces of Adonis and Aphrodite are portraits. (*c.*220 A.D). Inv. 10409.

4 *Lid on the Adonis sarcophagus with scenes from the myth of Oedipus* (lid does not belong to the sarcophagus). Left to right: the sacrifice of Laius, King of Thebes, before the Delphic Apollo; Laius and the exposure of Oedipus; Oedipus flees from Corinth. A pilaster separates the two series of scenes. The second series should be read from right to left: Oedipus kills Laius (in the chariot); the riddle of the Sphinx, and its interpretation by a Theban shepherd. Inv. 10408.

On the other side of the pillar:

5 To the left: *sarcophagus frontal with the myth of Adonis.* Adonis takes leave of Aphrodite; departure for the hunt and combat with the boar. (Cf. above: 3; the style and treatment are different: *c.*300 A.D). Inv. 9559.

6 To the right: *sarcophagus* (with fragments of the original lid) *with scenes from the myth of Phaedra and Hippolytus.* Left to right: Phaedra, wife of Theseus, and stepmother of Hippolytus, reveals her love for the youth through his nurse. Hippolytus, departing for the hunt, rejects the advances of his stepmother. On the right, Hippolytus hunting a boar; he is accompanied by a female figure wearing a helmet, a personification of courage. On the fragments of the lid, hunting scenes. Left side, sacrifice to Artemis; right side, hunters on horseback (*c.*220 A.D). Inv. 10400.

7-9 The next three *sarcophagi* (inv. 104450, 10443 and 10437) to the left at the back of the gallery were found together in a tomb near the Porta Viminalis in 1839. Tiles from this mausoleum bear marks dated 132 and 134 A.D.

7 To the left: *sarcophagus with scenes from the myth of Orestes.* From left to right: Orestes and Pylades at the tomb of Agamemnon, who appears as a shadowy figure below the vault; death of Aegisthus, whom Orestes strips of the royal cloak; murder of Clytemnestra, and two Furies with serpent and torch; Orestes' purification at Delphi, to which the tripod, laurel and omphalos allude. Right side: a seated Fury (Eumenide). Left side: the shadowy figures of Aegisthus and Clytemnestra on Charon's boat. Lid: Orestes and Iphigenia in Tauris. Inv. 10450.

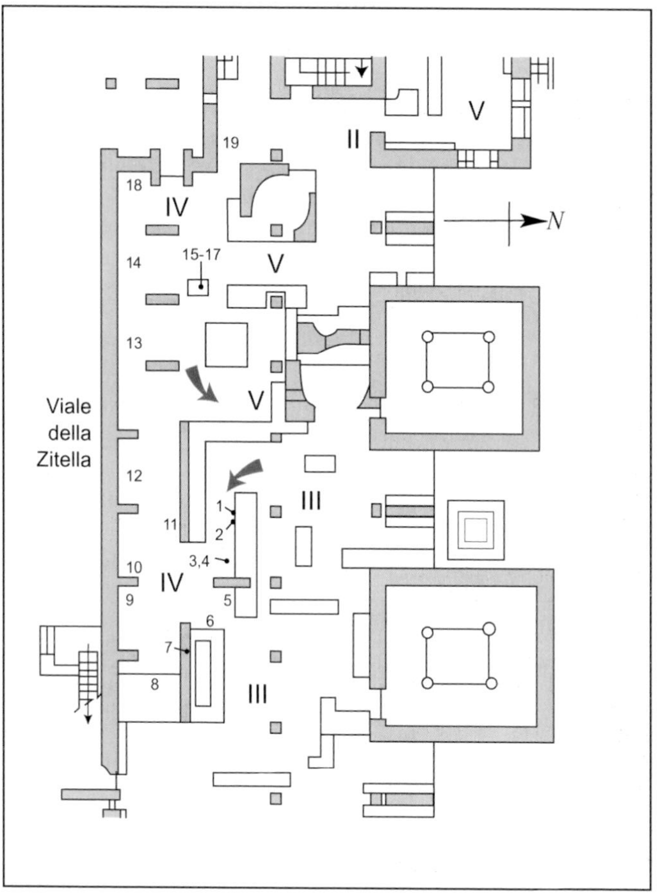

On the right: *Sarcophagus with two Gorgon masks and festoons of fruit* supported, at the centre, by a small satyr, flanked by cupids. On the sides of the sarcophagus, lighted candelabra with pairs of griffins. On the lid, racing contests between cupids riding various animals. Inv. 10443. **8**

Sarcophagus representing the massacre of the Niobids. Lid: the very small figures at the sides are Apollo and Artemis who shoot arrows at Niobe's helpless children to avenge their mother Latona. The parents are forced to watch, powerless to intervene. Amphion, his shield raised, in the left corner, and Niobe, her cloak billowing in the wind behind her head, in the right corner. Shorter side to the left: herdsman with oxen in a rocky landscape with nymph. Shorter side to the right: Niobe and Amphion at their children's tomb. (Cf. p. 146: II/54). Inv. 10437. **9**

On the external wall of the next compartment: *sarcophagus frontal with myths of Mars and Rhea Silvia* (left), and *Selene and Endymion* (right). In the first myth, a girl is found worthy of the love of a god; in the second, a youth is found worthy of the love of a goddess: the two parallel episodes express the participation of mortals in the lives of the gods. The heads of Mars and Rhea Silvia are probably portraits; those of Selene and Endymion, unfortunately, are restorations (*c.*250 A.D). Inv. 9558. **10**

11 Opposite: *sarcophagus with Bacchic scene.* Two satyrs, in the centre, symmetrically arranged, support a shield designed to contain the inscription. Left, Dionysus (Bacchus) in a chariot drawn by two centaurs; right, Ariadne in a similar chariot. Both are accompanied by their retinue. The sarcophagus is in excellent condition, as is its lid, decorated with Bacchic scenes and two satyr-heads. It gives an excellent idea of a Roman sarcophagus preserved in its original state (2nd cent. A.D). Inv. 10425.

12 In the next compartment, in front of the external wall: *sarcophagus with Bacchic scene.* The triumphant Dionysus (Bacchus) returns from his conquest of India (this legend was introduced into the myth after Alexander the Great's eastern campaigns). Nike (Victory) crowns the god, who stands on a chariot drawn by two elephants. The lion, panther and giraffe (visible in the centre, above Silenus) add an exotic touch to the otherwise traditional retinue. The various elements are successfully combined into a lively composition. Both the workmanship and state of preservation are excellent (3rd cent. A.D). Inv. 10428.

This is followed by sarcophagi with cupids: with masks and festoons (left wall); with scenes of grape-harvesting (in front of the pillar); and with medallions (next compartment). Of special interest among these:

13 *Sarcophagus with the Seasons.* At the centre, two cupids hold a medallion bearing the rough portrait of a woman. Below, a cupid disguises himself with a large mask of Silenus to frighten his small companion. On the right and left, four more cupids, two on each side, appear as traditional representations of the Seasons. However, the characteristics of each season are no longer distinct , as was often the case in the late Imperial period when their original significance had been forgotten (3rd cent. A.D). Inv. 10411.

14 In the next compartment, on the outer wall: *frontal of a large sarcophagus with philosophers.* The master of wisdom is enthroned in the centre. He reads from a scroll to a man and two veiled women. The attitude of the woman on the left recalls the traditional representation of Polyhymnia, one of the nine Muses. The other woman holds a closed scroll. Bearded figures facing outward appear at both sides of the central scene. On the right, traces of a sundial. The particularly imposing character of the central figure suggests that it may be the philosopher Plotinus, who came to Rome from Alexandria in 244 A.D, and died at Minturnum in 270. The assumption is interesting, but there is no evidence to support it. (*c.*270 A.D). Inv. 9504.

In front of it:

15 *Fragment of an oval sarcophagus.* On the right side, bearded philosopher, and the hands of a cloaked figure holding a scroll. Inv. 9524.

16 To the left: *fragment with lion-hunt* (traces).

17 The *fragment of a lid* with representation of a cockfight may belong to the same sarcophagus (above: 15). Inv. 9523.

18 At the end of the Gallery of Sarcophagi, to the left of the glass door: *sarcophagus of a boy depicting athletes* engaged in boxing, wrestling and *pancratium* (combination of boxing and wrestling), and paying tribute to the winner. The bearded figures holding palms are the judges. On the left a victor is being crowned. A herald blows his trumpet to announce the victory (*c.* 210 A.D). Inv. 9495.

This the section describing the sarcophagi ends with the *sar-* 19
cophagus with representations of the cultivation and processing of wheat (left, in front of the stairs). The rough-hewn relief is divided into two levels. In the upper part: a peasant works a plough drawn by two oxen, and another digs the ground; on the right, the harvest. In the lower part, right to left: a cart takes the wheat to the mill; two workmen turn the millstone; the baking of bread. In the centre, portrait of the deceased dressed in a toga holding a scroll. On the lid: the name of the deceased and an ironic Latin verse (from a Greek epigram), in which he dismisses Hope and Fortune, for whom he has no further use, leaving them to make fools of others (3rd cent. A.D). Inv. 10536.

SECTION V V

(Roman sculpture of the 2nd and 3rd century)

Return to the area where the capitals are exhibited.

The Ionic and Composite capitals in the centre are probably from Trajan's Forum.

On the wall (the Dacian statue is displayed behind the wall): three 1-3
fragments of a large historical frieze of the Hadrianic period (Inv.
9916, 9922, 9921). The *figure dressed in the toga* and patrician boots 2
(Inv. 9922) is probably the emperor Hadrian (117-138 A.D). An image
of what he looked like is furnished by the *portrait* displayed nearby
(Inv. 4068). A *portrait of a member of his retinue* appears on the left 4
(Inv. 9921). He is probably one of the Caesernii brothers, who are 3
known to have been in Hadrian's suite and whose presence has been
recognized in the two Hadrianic roundels incorporated into the Arch
of Constantine.

Proceeding leftwards:

Statue of Antinous. Though the original head has been lost (the 5
present one is a restoration), the statue is probably a representation of Hadrian's young favourite, in the guise of Vertumnus, a god who presided over spring and orchards (cf. p. 54: II/3 and 11/7). Inv. 9805.

Portrait of bearded man with Greek helmet. The facial type, and the 6
treatment of the eyes, suggest a work of the late Hadrianic period; it probably comes from a statue of Mars. Inv. 10150.

Fragments of relief with two wrestlers. Sculpted in high relief, the 7, 8
figures are remarkable for their three-dimensionality and are almost completely detached from the base. The relief probably decorated a large monument. It was known to Raphael, who made a drawing of it (now lost), filling in the missing parts. Antique-style Renaissance work . Inv. 9504, 9502.

On the opposite side of the trellis: *funerary relief.* This heavily 9
restored relief represents a young warrior on horseback greeting a woman sitting on a throne; in the background, a slave holding his master's spear. The laurel and serpent are an allusion to the heroization of the deceased. Inv. 9977.

Left: *fragments of toga-clad statues, in porphyry.* This precious stone 10-13
(quarried in Egypt) was reserved for representations of Roman emperors. Inv. 10478, 10480, 10481, 10483.

Right: *torso wearing a military cuirass.* Carved from porphyry, of 14
extraordinary quality, it probably represented Trajan or Hadrian. It comes from the area of the Hospital of San Giovanni in Laterano (1896). Inv. 10482.

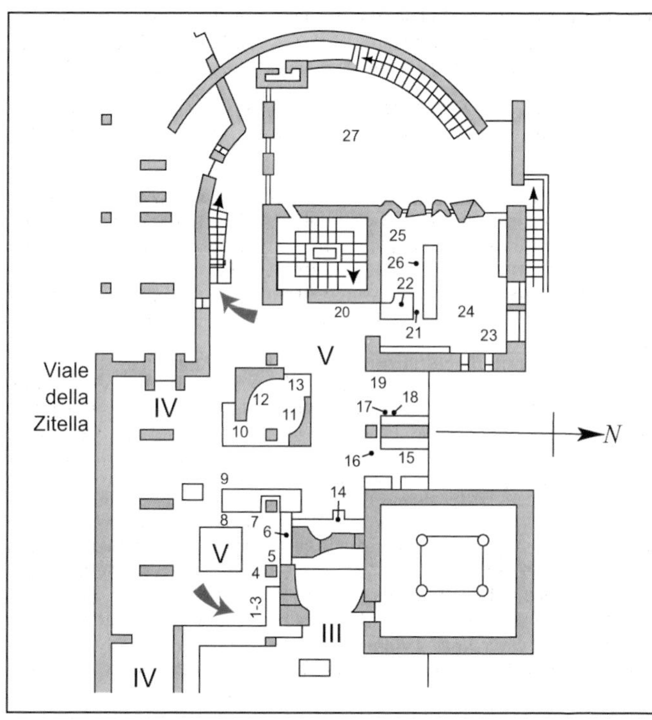

15 In the first window compartment, on the left: *relief from so-called Fountain of Amalthea.* A nymph offers a large horn-shaped vessel to a young satyr, inviting him to drink. Young Pan plays his syrinx in a grotto nearby. Water gushed from the hole in the drinking horn. A Roman-Hellenistic work of the 2nd century A.D. Inv. 9510.

16 In front of the partition that separates the two windows: eight Roman portraits of the first half of the 3rd century A.D. They include the *young Caracalla* (211-217 A.D.), son and successor of the emperor Septimius Severus. Inv. 19627.

In the second window compartment:

17-18 Right: two *richly decorated fragments of a pillar facing.* A vine grows from a vase, filling the whole panel with its foliage and fruit; the foliated ornament is interspersed with cupids and animals. Inv. 10087, 10089.

19 Opposite: *statue of Omphale* with head portrait . The statue recalls Aphrodite, though the club and lion-skin identify the subject as Omphale, the Lydian queen whom Hercules was ordered to serve, depriving him of his traditional role. The portrait dates to the early 3rd century A.D. Probably a funerary statue. Inv. 4385.

On the left wall, before entering the next room:

20 Toga-clad statue of *Dogmatius* (Galus Caelius Saturninus), presumably on its original base. The inscription lists the offices held by Dogmatius, a consul and intimate of the emperor Constantine. Stylistically, the portrait itself corresponds to the period 323-337 A.D. though the style and treatment of the toga are typical of the Hadrianic period (2nd cent. A.D). The erection of the statue can therefore be dated to the period between 323 and 337 A.D. The portrait corresponds stylistically to this period, while the toga, in form and

workmanship, seems to belong to a much earlier period (Hadrianic, 2nd century A.D). It is likely that an earlier statue clad in a togue was used and a head portrait of Dogmatius added *c.*330 A.D. Inv. 10493.

Turn right for the *Room of the Statue of Mithras* where Roman sculptures associated with chthonic and mystery cults are displayed.

Omphalos wrapped in bands, attribute of the Delphic Apollo. Apollo received the *omphalos* (sacred navel-stone) from the goddess of the Earth, the original mistress of Delphi, and it remained a feature of the chthonic cult of the Earth goddess until the Roman Imperial period. The impression of a right foot on the upper surface presumably formed part of a statue, as may be seen in the following relief. Inv. 9978. 21

Triangular base of a candelabrum. All three sides are decorated: Poseidon with cloak and trident, one foot resting on a mound of earth (see the *omphalos* above): Pluto with cornucopia; goddess with peplos and sceptre. Produced in a neo-Attic workshop, the work is of the Roman Imperial period and of Classical inspiration. Inv. 9967. 22

Mithraic group. Mithras slays the bull (Taurus). The god, in Persian dress, is shown plunging his sword into the bull's neck. Followers of the Mithras cult believed that life on Earth originated from the death of the primordial bull. The five ears of corn on the tail are symbols of the energy of the plant world. The dog seizes the soul by drinking the blood; the serpent and scorpion, forces of Darkness and Evil, try to impede the Creation by devouring the bull's life-giving blood and semen (3rd cent. A.D.: cf. p. 49: IV/3). Inv. 9933. 23

Altar with the Twelve Labours of Hercules. The inscription explains that Publius Decimus Lucrio has fulfilled a vow to Hercules by erecting this altar. The three-line inscription is divided by a relief depicting Hercules and Minerva standing at an altar. Below, the Labours of Hercules, from left to right: the Nemean lion, the Lernaean Hydra, the Erymanthian Boar, the Hind of Cerynela, the Stymphalian birds, the cleaning of the stables of Augeas, the victory over the Amazons, the horses of Diomedes, the Cretan bull, the fight against triple-headed Geryon, the capture of Cerberus the dog of the underworld, the apples of Hesperides (1st cent. A.D.) Inv. 9811. 24

Diana of Ephesus. Her attributes symbolize her power to influence growth. She is an Asian deity, of the type of the Great Mother of the gods. The Acts of the Apostle (19:23 ff) attest to the greatness and power of her cult: "Great is Diana of the Ephesians!" shouted the people, enraged by the attempts of Paul to convert them. And the town clerk of Ephesus insisted: "What man is there who does not know that the city of the Ephesians is temple keeper of the great Diana and of the sacred stone that fell down from the skies?". (Cf. p. 83: II/8). From the Lancelotti collection. The head is ancient, but much of the body is the result of a 17th century restoration. Inv. 10410. 25

Statue of *Asclepius* (Aesculapius), identified by the staff with a snake coiled round it. He is shown leaning on his staff, his long cloak thrown over his left shoulder, his chest bare. The representation probably goes back to an original by Bryaxis, known through literary sources. The statue is of the Trajanic period (2nd century A.D.) Inv. 9910. 26

In a semicircular court outside this room is one of two *floor mosaics* discovered in two exedrae of the central room of the Baths of Caracalla in 1824. There is a good view of the first mosaic from the top of the stairs. It is divided by a continuous band that twists and turns into a series of squares and rectangles, containing representations of Roman referees or "coaches" (toga-clad figures) and athletes (nude figures), who are holding their characteristic objects: boxing baskets, 27 disc, sword and palm of victory. Some squares contain representations of objects that allude to the training exercises that went on at these baths: a strigil, an ointment jar, weights, discs, a crown, and a palm. It is possible that the mosaic is a 4th century remake of the original mosaic dating to the first half of the 3rd century A.D.

JEWISH LAPIDARIUM FORMERLY IN THE LATERAN

The catacomb of Monteverde (probably the oldest Jewish catacomb in Rome) was discovered by Bosio in 1602, but was only fully explored by Müller in 1904-1906. Most of the tombstones exhibited in this lapidarium were found there (but occasional pieces come from Porto and Capua), as well as other objects and material of pagan origin used in the Jewish catacomb, such as roof tiles and bricks used to close the *loculi* (tomb niches). The marks on these tiles and bricks enable us to date the period of use of the catacomb from the 1st to the 3rd century. The epitaphs, many of which begin with the formula *enthàde kèitai* ("here lies...") and end with the words *en eirène he kòimesis autù* ("may your rest be in peace"), reveal to us the name of communities (*Augustesi*, *Agrippesi*, etc.), political or religious functions and kinship with the deceased. There are also many traditional Jewish symbols, such as the seven-armed candelabrum *(menorah)*, the ram's horn *(shofar)* or the sacred ark of the law *(torah)*. The language of the inscriptions suggest that the Jews of Rome spoke Greek (75%), Latin (22%) and Aramaic (3%).

Beyond the end of the corridor is a semicircular balcony, the Belvedere. The Pio-Christian Museum begins here.

28 From the Belvedere there is an view from above of the *second mosaic from the Baths of Caracalla,* it too decorated with figures of athletes and referees (cf. above: 27).

plan →

w - Pio-Christian Museum

The Good Shepherd, detail

This museum contains the collections of Christian antiquities housed in the Lateran Palace until 1963.

It was founded by Pius IX in 1854, two years after he set up the Commission for Christian Archaeology with the task of "conducting excavations in the catacombs and assuming responsibility for their maintenance". Those monuments which could not be preserved *in situ* were placed in the museum. The museum was organised by Father Giuseppe Marchi and G. B. De Rossi. It consists of two sections, the first devoted to sculpture, mosaics and architectural fragments, the second to inscriptions. The first section, the only one now open to the public, places special emphasis on the collection of sarcophagi, divided by subject (as far as possible) and by type. The second section contains historical inscriptions pertaining to public monuments and places of worship, poems of Pope Damasus I, tomb inscriptions furnished with consular dates, or pertaining to Christian dogmas or the ecclesiastical hierarchy, and inscriptions accompanied with symbols. In consideration of its more specialistic character, this second section is only opened on request.

This is the end of the itinerary through the Gregorian Profane Museum. Visitors may now visit the Pio-Christian Museum in the opposite direction, i.e. by beginning from the Belvedere above the Baths of Caracalla mosaic.

Of exceptional importance among the Christian epigraphs displayed 1
in the Belvedere is the *cippus of Albercius,* Bishop of Hieropolis in Phrygia in the time of the emperor Marcus Aurelius (161-180 A.D.). Two fragments, now reassembled, were discovered in 1883 by W. Ramsay at Hieropolis, near Synnada, in Phrygia (Turkey). One was presented to Pope Leo XIII by the Sultan, and the other by Ramsay. The inscription on the fragments was immediately identified as part of a metrical epigraph dictated by the bishop before his death, and
recorded in the *Vita S. Abercii* in the *Acta Sanctorum* (to the left of the 2
fragments is an attempt at a *plaster reconstruction of the cippus).* Albercius, who in the early part of the text proclaims himself "disciple of the pure shepherd who leads his sheep to graze on the hills and plains...", mentions his journey to Rome in these surviving fragments, where he saw "the palace and the queen in golden raiment and

golden shoes; and [...] a people that possesses a radiant seal". Having mentioned other travels, he adds: "Wherever faith led me, and set before me as food the fish of the uncontaminated [...] spring, that is caught by the virgin undefiled, and each day she [faith] invites her friends to eat of it, together with excellent wine which she offers mixed with bread". If the Christian interpretation of the text is correct (as now seems accepted), then the Cippus of Albercius is one of the most important Christian inscriptions of a eucharistic character, and the earliest one datable with certainty.

3 A narrow passageway follows. Just beyond the stairway on the left and the mould of the statue of Hippolytus, on the wall opposite the large window, is: the frontal panel of a *sarcophagus* from San Lorenzo fuori le Mura. It represents a young, beardless Christ in short tunic and mantle among the twelve bearded apostles (the first two are Peter and Paul). The fifteen sheep in the foreground symbolize the Christian flock. At the corners, two shepherds in dress similar to that of the Good Shepherd. From an iconographic point of view, the figure of the Good Shepherd, which is reminiscent of classical models, is not a Christian invention: the iconography of the shepherd was known in the Mediterranean area as far back as the 7th century B.C. (e.g. the famous *moskophoros* in the Acropolis Museum, Athens). But here the way it is treated is new: no longer is the devotee bearing his offering to the temple, but the Good Shepherd himself: *Luke* 15:4-5: "And when he has found it (the lost sheep), he lays it on his shoulders, rejoicing"; *John* 10:11: "I am the good shepherd. The good shepherd lays down his life for the sheep"; and *John* 10:10: "I came that they [the lost sheep] may have life, and may have it abundantly". Inv. 31534 (ex 177).

4 Leaving the narrow passageway the statue of the *Good Shepherd* can be seen on the left beyond the window. This statue was acquired by the Sacred Museum in the 18th century and later transferred to the Lateran. The figure is that of a young, beardless shepherd with long curly hair, covering his ears. His head is turned to the right. He is dressed in a sleeveless tunic, and carrying a bag across his shoulders. There is very little freestanding early Christian sculpture, perhaps because of an ideological prejudice towards statues as a potential source of idolatry. The statue was extensively restored in the 18th century. Inv. 28590 (ex 103).

5 Next to the statue is a *sarcophagus decorated on all four sides,* found near the Cemetery of Pretestatus, on the left side of the Appian Way. Front side: three shepherds standing on ornate pedestals; the shepherd in the centre is bearded, and holds a ram on his shoulders; the two at the sides are beardless, and each holds a sheep. The short tunics, leggings, ankle-boots, staffs and sacks complete the conventional representation of the shepherd. The background is filled with a crowded scene of grape harvesting showing winged putti climbing the vine shoots, picking bunches of grapes, and putting them into a vat to be pressed (below, on the right). On the right a small Psyche offers grapes to a resting putto. Below, on the left, another putto milks a goat. The decorations on the ends of the sarcophagus are on two levels, with scenes of country life symbolizing the four seasons. The back is decorated with triangular motifs (second half of the 4th cent.). Inv. 31554 (ex 191 A).

6 Just beyond, on the left: *sarcophagus in the form of a bath,* found in 1881 on the Via Salaria near the mausoleum of Lucilius Poetus, and purchased by Leo XIII in 1891. In the centre, a shepherd with a ram on his shoulders, and two other rams at his feet. Left, a bearded man, in philosopher's dress, seated between two listeners. Right, three women, one of whom is seated. The scene is enclosed at either end by two large rams. The frieze is faithful to the compositional convention of placing all the heads at the same level, regardless of

the height or attitude of the various figures; as a result, the two seated figures, probably the occupants of the tomb, are decidedly larger (probably mid-3rd cent.) Inv. 31540 (ex. 181).

In front of a small niche in the outer wall (to the right): *sarcophagus with lid,* found in 1818 at Tor Sapienza on the Via Prenestina, on an estate of the Massimi family. It is in very good condition, and is the only one in the collection that still retains traces of its original pigment (blue, red, gold). On the lid: at the centre, *tabula inscriptionis,* with three B's written in red; to the left, hunting scenes; to the right, female bust placed against a background of drapery (*parapetasma),* supported by putti. On the frontal of the sarcophagus: to the left, a bearded shepherd carrying a ram on his shoulders (and therefore not the Good Shepherd); to the right, a woman in prayer against a *parapetasma*; at the centre, a lively agricultural and pastoral scene (late 3rd early 4th cent.). Inv. 31485 (ex 150). 7

Down a few steps,about halfway along the following gallery, on the outer wall (to the right): *frontal of a sarcophagus with lid* (they may not belong together) from the Cemetery of St. Calixtus. On the sarcophagus, from the left: resurrection of Lazarus; multiplication of the loaves and fishes; miracle of Cana; praying woman between Peter and Paul; healing of the woman with a haemorrhage; Peter taken prisoner; miracle of the pool of Bethesda. On the lid, to the left of the *tabula inscriptionis,* the manger scene; right, scenes from the Book of Jonah. The long metrical inscription on the upper edge and on the *tabula* states that Crescens was buried here after only four months of marriage, and that his widow had him placed here against the wishes of her father-in-law, and with the help of her mother-in-law (early 4th cent.) Inv. 31484 (ex. 148). 8

At the end of the gallery is a large, dimly lit room. On the right is the large so-called *"dogmatic" sarcophagus,* found in the foundations below the baldachin in the Basilica of san Paolo fuori le Mura. Only the frontal is decorated, with two rows of reliefs. The busts of the dead couple, in the central clipeus (medallion), are only rough-hewn. Top row, from the left: God creates man and woman; Christ gives Adam a sheaf of corn, and Eve a lamb, symbols of their condemnation to work for their food and clothing; behind Eve is the tree of the knowledge of Good and Evil. To the right of the clipeus: the wedding at Cana; miracle of the loaves; resurrection of Lazarus. Bottom row, from the left: Adoration of the Magi; healing of the blind man; Daniel in the lions' den; foretelling of Peter's denial; Peter taken prisoner; miracle of the pool of Bethesda (first half of the 4th cent.) Inv. 31427 (ex 104). 9

On the left side of the same room: *cast of the sarcophagus preserved in the Basilica of Sant'Ambrogio, Milan.* All four sides are decorated with reliefs. The various scenes are set against a background representing the city walls of the heavenly Jerusalem. Front: Christ and the Apostles. Right side: Elijah ascending to Heaven before the eyes of Elisha (Second Book of Kings, 2:11-12); Noah leaving the ark; below, the smaller figures of Adam and Eve below the tree of knowledge of Good and Evil. Rear side: Christ and the Twelve Apostles. Left side: sacrifice of Isaac, and four Apostles. The rear corners of the roof-shaped lid are decorated with sculptures of heads; at the centre, two winged putti support a clipeus containing bust portraits of the dead couple; to the right, the Epiphany; to the left, the three young Judeans, Shadrach, Meshach and Abednego, refuse to worship the statue erected by Nebuchadnezzar (Daniel 3:1 ff.), or, according to another interpretation, the Magi before Herod. On the right tympanum of the lid, the manger scene; left tympanum, monogram of Christ within a laurel wreath; doves and the two apocalyptic letters Alpha and Omega, (late 4th cent.). 11

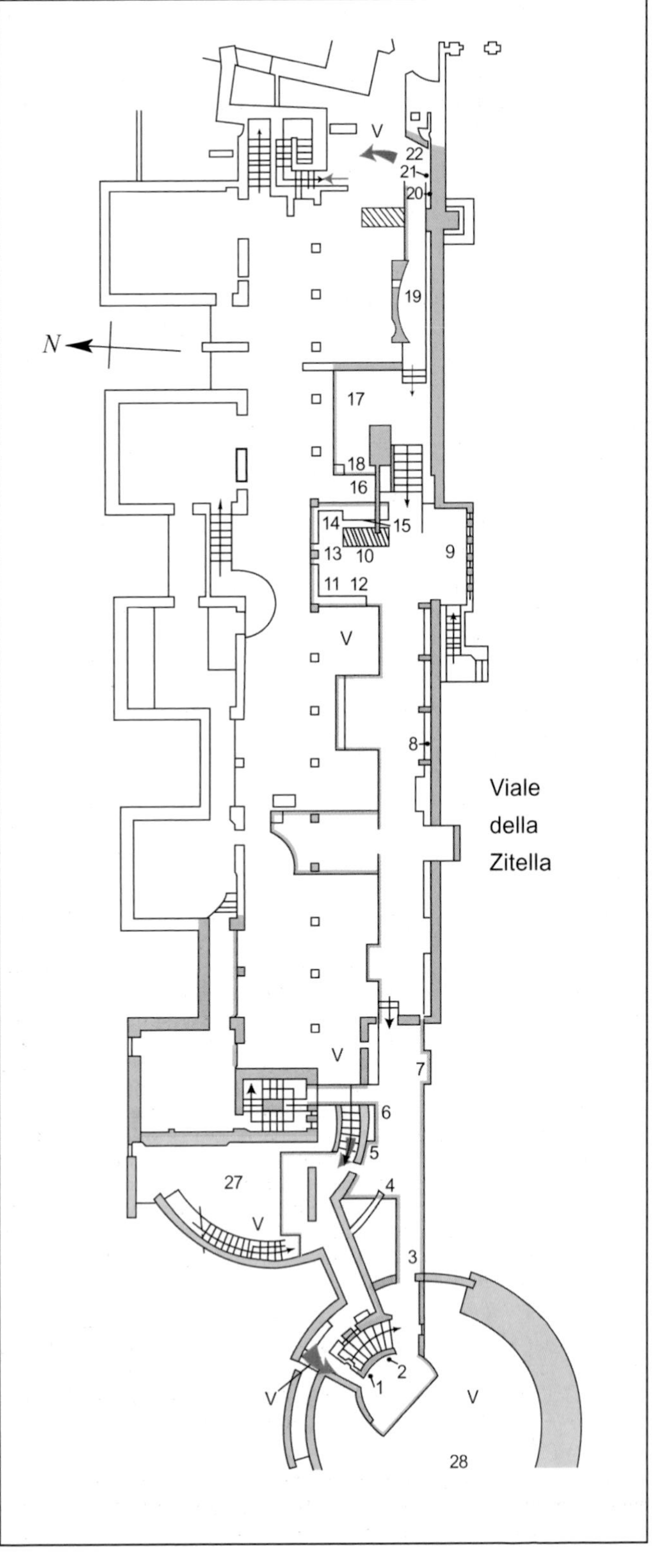
V
22
21
20
19
N
17
18
16
14
15
13
10
9
11
12
V
8
Viale
della
Zitella
V
7
6
5
27
4
V
3
2
1
V
V
28

On the metal trellis marking the left side of the room, proceeding clockwise:

Frontal of a sarcophagus with two rows of reliefs representing scenes from the Old and New Testament. In the centre, shell niche with portrait of the buried couple (300-320). Inv. 31532 (ex 175). 12

Frontal of a sarcophagus with two rows of reliefs, from the Basilica of San Sebastiano. In the central shell niche, portrait of the buried couple. Reliefs: scenes from the Old and New Testaments (mid-4th cent.) Inv. 31535 (ex 178). 13

Frontal of a sarcophagus with two rows of reliefs, found near the Basilica of San Sebastiano. In the centre, shell niche with portrait of the buried couple. In the upper register, from the left: Christ's entry into Jerusalem; Christ between Adam with the sheaf of corn, and Eve with the lamb (cf. above: 9); Moses receives the tablets of the Law. To the right of the central shell: the hand of the angel of the Lord stops the sacrifice of Isaac; resurrection of the youth from Nain; multiplication of the loaves. In the lower register, from the left: miracle of the pool of Bethesda; Peter taken prisoner; foretelling of Peter's denial; Daniel in the lions' den; healing of the man with palsy, the man born blind and the woman with a haemorrhage; miracle at Cana (first half of the 4th cent.) Inv. 31551 (ex 189). 14

Frontal of a sarcophagus with two rows of reliefs, friezes and medallion, from Palazzo Carpegna. In the central clipeus, busts of man and wife: the beardless husband, in tunic and toga, holds a scroll; his wife is dressed in a tunic and cloak. Top row, from the left: Miracle of the loaves; the foretelling of Peter's denial; Moses receives the Law on Sinai. To the right of the clipeus: sacrifice of Isaac; healing of the man born blind; resurrection of Lazarus. In the unfinished lower register: praying woman between Apostles; Peter taken prisoner; three winged putti symbolizing the seasons (roughly-hewn, perhaps part of an initial decorative scheme that was later abandoned); Daniel in the lions' den; miracle at Cana; healing of the man with palsy; miracle of the pool of Bethesda (first third of 4th cent.) Inv. 31546 (ex 184). 15

Going down the stairs, on the left: *sarcophagus with decorated ends,* lid and inscription, from the Vatican Necropolis. The inscription reads: "To my dearest wife Agapene who lived with her husband 55 years, one month and five days, and who was laid to rest on 23 December. Crescentianus made [this sarcophagus] when he was still alive". After his death, the following was added in less careful lettering: "buried 30 August at the age of 101". The front of the sarcophagus is divided into seven niches by spiral fluted columns supporting alternating tympana and arches. From the left: sacrifice of Isaac; Moses receives the Law on Sinai; Christ heals the man born blind; Christ foretells Peter's denial; healing of the woman with a haemorrhage; multiplication of the loaves; miracle of the pool of Bethesda. On the left shorter side: Original Sin. On the right shorter side: the three youths in the furnace. This subject is repeated on the lid, to the left of the *tabula inscriptionis*; on the right, scenes from the Book of Jonah (second half of 4th cent.) Inv. 31489 (ex 152). 16

At the bottom of the staircase, in the centre of the large raised podium: *cast of the sarcophagus of Junius Bassus.* The original was found in 1595, under the "Confession" of St. Peter's, and is now displayed in the Room of Junius Bassus in the Treasury of St. Peter's. The cast is exhibited here because of the exceptional iconographic importance of the monument. 17

At the left end of the podium: *sarcophagus with five niches,* from the hypogeum of the "Confession" of San Paolo fuori le Mura. In the centre, a cross: on the vertical bar, the monogram of Christ within a 18 laurel wreath; on the crossbar, two doves. At the sides, two sentinels; one is sleeping, while the other contemplates the symbol of Christ triumphant over death. In the other niches formed by olive branches, from left to right: God with Abel and Cain; Peter taken prisoner; martyrdom of Paul; Job, rebuked by his wife for his patience, is comforted by his friends (second half of the 4th cent.) Inv. 28591 (ex 164).

19 Descending a few steps, to the left, in the centre of the niche: *sarcophagus with the Crossing of the Red Sea.* On the left, Pharaoh and the Egyptian army pursue the people of Israel, who pass "into the midst of the sea upon the dry ground, while the waters were a wall unto them on their right hand and on their left" (*Exodus* 14:22). On the right, Moses stretching his hand over the sea, and the waters close in around the Egyptian army. Further on, Miriam, prophetess and sister of Aaron, singing a hymn of victory and thanksgiving (late 4th cent.) Inv. 31434 (ex. 111).

Further ahead at the end of the (yellow) external wall are various fragments of sarcophagi depicting the Nativity and the Epiphany. The Epiphany was the most commonly represented theme in early Christian art from the 3rd century onwards. St. Augustine (Sermon 203, 3) explains the reason for this: "The Magi were the first pagans to know Christ our Lord, and these first of the Gentiles deserve to symbolize all peoples". The Magi are depicted in short tunics and Phrygian caps, and are accompanied by their camels. St. Matthew (2:2-12) writes that the Magi came from the East, led by a star, to the Temple of Herod in Jerusalem. Herod directed them to Bethlehem, where they found the Messiah and worshipped him, offering him gifts of gold, frankincense and myrrh. Irenaeus, Bishop of Lyon in the 2nd century, explains the significance of the threefold gift of the Magi (*Adversus Haeres*, III, 9) as follows: "Myrrh, because He came into the world to die and be buried for mortal man; gold, because of His kingdom there shall be no end (*Luke* 1:33); frankincense, because God revealed himself in Judah (*Psalms* 76:1-2) and showed himself to those who had not sought him".

Worth noting among these fragments:

20 *Front of a sarcophagus lid.* From the left: the enthroned Madonna holding the Child, to whom the Magi are offering gifts with their camels in the background. Next: the manger scene between two palms; the swaddled Child in a wicker cradle, an ass and an ox. Centre: Daniel in the lions' den. Next: the deceased (Crispina) is shown reading a codex bearing the engraved monogram of Christ, the *Lex Christi*, which was given to her at her baptism, and which guided her through her earthly life. On the right side: the miracle of the loaves (a youthful Christ in tunic and cloak); Peter taken prisoner; the miracle of the pool of Bethesda (mid-4th cent.) Inv. 31552 (ex 190).

21 *Fragment of the front of a sarcophagus lid*, with the star at the corner of the stable roof (cf. *Matthew* 2:9: "... and Lo, the star, which they saw in the east, went before them, till it came and stood over where the young Child was"). Inv. 31563 (ex 204).

22 *Front of a sarcophagus lid,* with the theme of the Epiphany occupying the right side: the first of the Magi offers the Child a golden crown with his left hand, and points to the star with his right (late 4th cent.) Inv. 31463 (ex 126).

Philatelic and Numismatic Museum

The museum is located at the foot of the staircase leading to the Missionary-Ethnological Museum.

Following the signing of the Lateran Treaty between Italy and the Holy See of 11 February 1929, a new sovereign territorial entity was created, the Vatican City State, surrounded by the city of Rome with a surface area of 44 hectares and a resident population of 600 .

The State's form of government is an elective monarchy. The Head of State is the Sovereign Pontiff, who is elected for life and is invested with full powers: legislative, judicial and executive. During the period of "vacant seat", i.e. after the death of a Pope and prior to the election of his successor, these powers are exercised by the Sacred College of Cardinals.

The Vatican City State adopted the euro as its official currency on 1 January 2002. It also issues its own postage stamps in euros (including stamped postcards, aerogrammes, etc.).

Ordinary Vatican euro currency, by virtue of the existing Monetary Agreement stipulated between the Holy See on behalf of Vatican City State and Italy on behalf of the European Community, has legal tender and debt-paying power in the territories of the States of the euro area; vice versa, Vatican currency minted for numismatic collections only, also in euros, has legal tender and debt-paying power exclusively in the territory of the Vatican City State, by mutual agreement with the other States of the euro area.

Obviously, banknotes in euros also have legal tender and debt-paying power within the territory of the Vatican City State.

The Monetary Agreement currently in force prescribes a ceiling for the coining of Vatican metallic coins in euros, to which the Vatican City State must abide.

Vice versa, issues of postage stamps are not subject to any particular limitations, except for the provisions laid down in the bilateral agreements with Italy concerning postal tariffs and in the international agreements which the Vatican City State has signed.

The postage stamp collection, including stamped postcards and aerogrammes, issued by Vatican City State from 1929 to the present, is generally divided by pontificate and displayed in chronological order. Of particular value is a whole sheet (100 stamps) of each denomination of the 1934 overprinted series , the so-called "provisional" series.

There are also some showcases in the Museum that contain numerous plates, cylinders, plaquettes, and other similar typographical material used for the copperplate printing of Vatican stamps. Some original designs for the stamps are also displayed in the main room.

The Museum also contains a number of showcases dedicated to numismatics. They contain not only the coins issued by Vatican City State from 1929 to the present day, but also plaster-casts and casts in bronze, all of them "unique pieces", necessary for producing the minting dies from which new coins are struck. There are also find some showcases in the Museum dedicated to the Papal State, with some philatelic rarities such as the sheet of 100 stamps "not issued" of 1868. This postage stamp was prepared to satisfy the French postal tariff; the events linked to the Franco-Prussian war prevented its issue. We will also find, the postal values (new and cancelled) of the philatelic issues of 1852, 1864, 1867 and 1868, and a large collection of stamped envelopes with cancellations and other postmarks that commemorate important historical events linked to the period 1852-1870.

plan →

x - Missionary-Ethnological Museum

Ceremonial mask of the Baluba tribe, Zaire

The Missionary-Ethnological Museum was first established by Pius XI in the Lateran Palace, and inaugurated on 21 December 1926. John XXIII transferred it to the Vatican in this new building. The museum contains objects associated with non-European cultures. They come from the Missionary Exhibition (1925), the Borgia Museum, and from donations made by various missionary congregations and private donors.

The museum is divided into two sections with a main and a secondary itinerary. The former is designed for the general public, and comprises objects illustrating the various forms of religion in countries outside Europe. The secondary itinerary includes ethnographical collections, and is intended for scholars.

In view of the didactic nature of the exhibits, visitors are advised to follow the itinerary indicated by the arrows.

ASIA

CHINA

At the entrance, two Takuchai (guardian lions) in enamel, from Beijing; the male lion faces the entrance, the lioness the interior. They represent the two essential principles of Chinese philosophy and religion—*yang* (male, sky, round, perfect) and *yin* (female, earth, square, imperfect), which combine to form *tao* (supreme law, order, universe).

To the right, model of the Temple of the Sky, in the southern suburb of Beijing. It was built in wood in 1420, and rebuilt in marble in 1755. During the winter solstice, the emperor, standing on the upper platform of the altar (left), would make a sacrifice to his ancestors, i.e. the Sky and former emperors of his dynasty, while a dignitary on the lower platform would make a sacrifice to the sun, moon, constellations, wind and rain. The last sacrifice took place in 1916. During the summer solstice a similar ceremony was held in honour of the earth in the Temple of the Earth, situated in the northern suburb of Beijing (model unavailable).

To the left, in *showcase A1:* objects associated with the cult of the 1
dead, funerary gifts from the time of the Chin (221-206 B.C.), Han (206 B.C.-220 A.D.), and Tang (618-906 A.D.) dynasties. Note also the two fine porcelain statuettes of the Qing dynasty (1644-1912), one of which is dedicated to the Buddhist goddess Kwanyin, goddess of infinite compassion.

In the niche on the right: model of a pagoda in the region of Fujian.

Follow the arrows to the red altar of Confucius. The altar, which 2
comes from the Pagoda of Confucius at Küfu (where he was born and buried), is a faithful reproduction of the original, made by Chinese artists by permission of the descendants of Confucius in 1924-35.

The next section of the museum is devoted to Chinese Buddhism. In 3
showcase A3: Buddha and two of his satellites; in front, three sacred vases from a Buddhist temple in Beijing. Outside the showcase, wooden statue of Kwanyin, the most popular Bodhisattva in China. She was an ancient fertility goddess who, thanks to Chinese religious syncretism, occupied an important place in the Buddhist pantheon.
This is followed by *Showcase A* 4 with various representations of 4
Buddha (left side) and Kwanyin (right side). Outside the showcase, various stone sculptures of Buddha and Kwanyin. Of special interest are the head of a monk, from Lohan, and the statue of a Buddhist monk (Ming dynasty, 1368-1644).

Opposite to the right, set apart, *showcase A5:* Chinese pottery 5
bearing Arabic inscriptions documenting the presence of Islam in China. Next to the Islamic showcase: copy of the large stone stele erected in 781, China's first Christian document (in Nestorian form). It was unearthed near Sianfù, in the province of Shensi, in 1625. This faithful copy, made *in situ* was presented to Benedict XV by Fritz Holm in 1916.

Entering the small block of showcases, there is a Christian altar in the Chinese style (Fu-yen, Beijing). Near the altar is the bronze statue of Father Marcellus Sterkendries (ancient bronze vases were melted down to make the statue). This missionary saved the city of King Chow from extermination in 1911-12; to show their gratitude, the Christian converts of the city sacrificed their most valuable vases to have the statue made. Beside it, against a red screen, is a Chinese bronze *Madonna and Child* donated to Paul VI by the episcopate of Taiwan.

Now turn around, and with the Islamic showcase on the left, turn right to enter the documentary section on China, followed by Japan.

JAPAN

At the entrance, B1, two "Chinese lions" in gilt wood, guardians and 6
protectors against evil spirits.

In *showcase B2,* a model of a Shintoist temple (*jinja*), situated in the 7
ancient capital of Nara.

In *showcase B3,* against the wall: three small Shintoist garden- 8
temples; in front, sacrificial vases (for wine, water, rice, perfume), a mirror (symbol of the sun goddess, Amaterasu), and foxes (symbols of the god of rice and riches).

In *showcase B4,* against the wall, are several ritual and theatrical 9
masks; worth noting are nos. 10068 and 10069, carved in the ancient manner from sacred "Sughi-di-Dohi" wood.

Outside the showcase is a large, metal perfume-burner (the wooden base is a restoration) with scenes and statuettes depicting figures

8 from Shintoist mythology; a scene of Amaterasu, the sun goddess (ancestor of the Japanese imperial family), fighting the moon and Earth is in the upper part of the medallion in the middle (18th cent.).

Over the centuries, Shintoism, a religion of Japanese origin, often merged with Buddhism imported from China (6th cent.).

Above, in the large showcases: thirteen Kakemono representing the thirteen Buddhas or Bodhisattvas, commemorated on the anniversaries of the dead (from the seventh day after death till the thirty-third year).

Below, outside a showcase, a lacquer screen.

10 In the separate *showcase B5:* objects pertaining to Japanese Buddhism. Worth noting is the monk (mannequin) in ceremonial dress. Eight prayer scrolls are exhibited on a special support; they are a copy of the book of Hokekyo (Buddhist prayers). The original was written in Kansho in 1289, and is preserved in the Temple of Nyohoji.

11, 12 In the large block of showcases: two Butsudan (household altars), in *showcases B6 and B7* containing sacrificial vases, statues of Buddhist and Shintoist deities, ancestral tablets, etc. These Butsudan provide an excellent example of the religious syncretism of Japan.

13 *Showcase B8,* in the same group of showcases (proceeding to the right): paintings of the Japanese martyrs killed in Nagasaki in 1597 (painted by Okayama Shunkyo of Kyoto) and wooden tablets with persecution edicts.

KOREA

14 *Showcase C1* contains objects representing some deities, such as the mythical founder of the Korean people, reproduced in the watercolour painting, or the goddess, guardian of order and security, sculpted in dark stone. Other objects are associated with the world of shamanism, such as the hat and painted fan, or with Won Buddhism.

15 Facing it is *showcase C2* containing objects associated with the cult of the dead and the cult of ancestors, such as the little paper tablet or the linen mourning suit.

16 *In showcase C3* are several masks of the Hahoe theatre, made of carved and painted wood.

17 A special *showcase, C4* is dedicated to the presence of Christianity in Korea. The exhibits include the typographical matrices to print the first catechism in Korean and the two little tablets with the Ten Commandments, one written in Chinese, the other in Korean.

TIBET AND MONGOLIA

18 *Showcase D1* contains objects pertaining to Lamaism (Tibetan and Mongolian form of Buddhism), and in particular to the original Tibetan Bon-pö religion: representations of spirits; drums made from human skulls; flutes made from human bones (shamanistic influence).

19 In the following *showcase D2* there are typical monk cowls, representing the two sects of Lamaism: the Yellow Hats and the Red Hats.

20 In the following *showcase D3* are various statues, Lamaistic reliquaries, cult implements and vases. Of special interest are the two brass statues of Kwanyin (or Avalokitesvara) (Chinese, Ming dy-

nasty). A tent used by a Mongolian lama on his journeys lies behind.

In the centre of the room is a model of the Lamasery of Tch'uo-yang-Hien (Eastern Mongolia). The monastery was founded in 1700 by the lama Tchuo-eul-tsi, disciple of the Dalai-Lama of Lhasa, who had sent him to Mongolia. The first temple (from the entrance) is the "Pagoda of the four guardians of the four main parts of the world"; the second the "Pagoda of prayer" (liturgical assemblies were held here on important feast days); and the third the "Pagoda of beneficence", where daily rites were celebrated at dawn and dusk.

Showcase D4, in the rear part of this section, contains a selection of 21
Tibetan paintings (*thanka*) and some objects representative of the Tibetan world: figures of deities and a monk's ceremonial costume At the back, in *section D4,* are Tibetan standards and religious books.

SOUTH-EAST ASIA

To the left, *showcase E1,* cult of the dead: rice baskets for tomb 22
offerings, a wooden enclosure with ancestral figures, and two vases for secondary burials (Vietnam).

Next to it is a model of a Buddhist monastery (Vietnam).

In *showcase E2,* against the wall, note the sacred book with case 23
(Thailand, 17th cent.), and statuettes of Buddha made from the ashes of Buddhist monks (Tibetan influence, Thailand).

The *large showcase E3* is next: it contains altars with tablets 24
dedicated to ancestors (Vietnam).

In *showcase E4* to the right: statuettes of Buddhas and Bodhisattvas 25
from various countries in South-East Asia. Note the white marble statuette of the "Sleeping Buddha", found in the ruins of the Temple of Ara, Myanmar (16th to 17th cent.).

Outside the showcase: large Christian sedan chair in gilt wood, manufactured in 1846; it was used in the procession of the Madonna of the Rosary, and needed ten men to carry it (Tonking, Vietnam).

In Showcase E5: Christian statues in the Annamite style (Vietnam). 26

INDIAN SUBCONTINENT

In *showcase F1,* to the left against the wall, are displayed some 27
vessels for ritual use (central India). Outside the showcase, five funerary stelae carved out of wood (central India).

The main religion of India is now Hinduism. The two main branches of this religion are illustrated in the museum: Shivaism (Shiva is the supreme god) and Vishnuism (Vishnu is the supreme god).

At the entrance to the large Indian room, on the right: votive ox *(nandi),* Shiva's legendary means of transport (India, Chamanarayngore, 18th cent.) On the left: small votive temple dedicated to Shiva, and wooden door with carved stones.

In the large *block of showcases, F2,* on the right: painting of Shiva and 28
Kali, his consort, the giver of life; next to the painting, a collection of statuettes of Shiva and Kali.

Further on *showcase F3,* containing objects pertaining to Vishnuism: 29
a painting of Vishnu, preserver of the universe, and several statuettes connected with his cult.

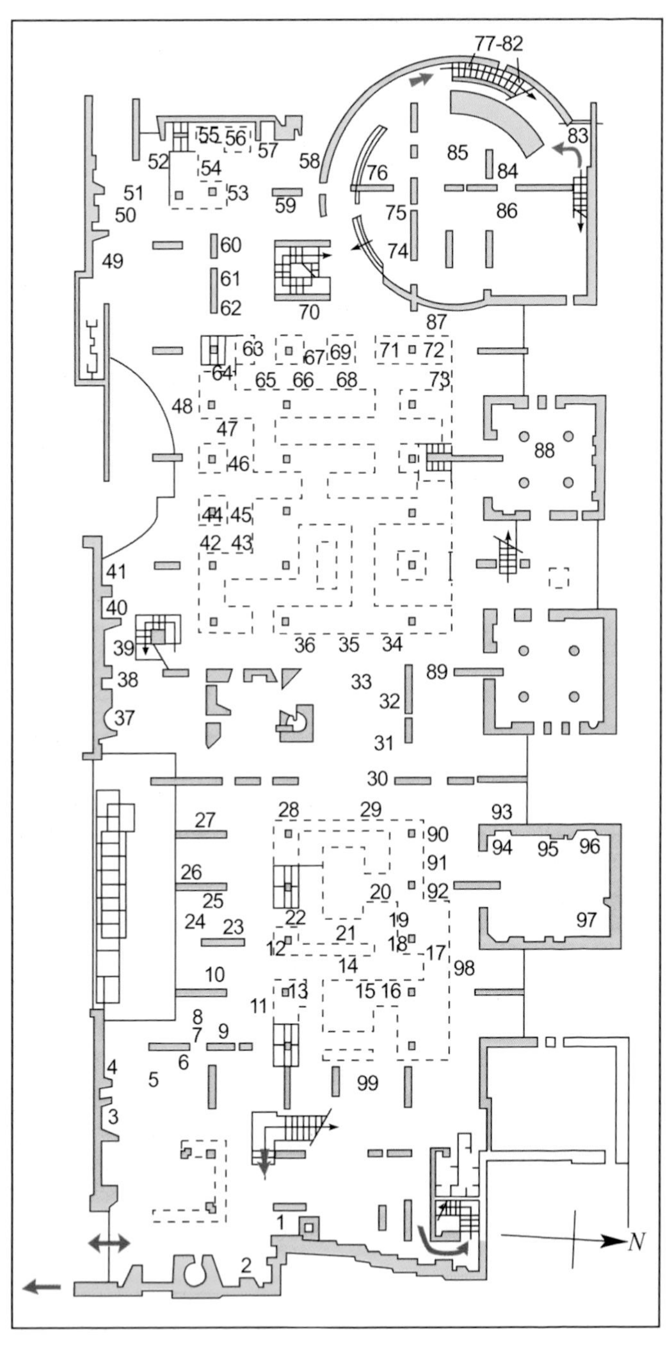

Close by, *showcase F4*: two magnificent household altars with 30
representations of Vishnu, at the centre and, on the sides, his various incarnations (17th cent.)

Showcase F5: ceremonial masks. Used in ritual dances in various 31
magic rites, these masks combine elements of both Hinduism and primitive religions (Sri Lanka, southern India). Note the tripartite mask of Maha Kola, the demon of the eighteen diseases. Below the large portal (Baroda, Shivaistic) is a statue of Bhima, protector against serpents (India, Pulaya).

Show-case F6 (against the wall): various Hindu cult objects: rattles, 32
knives, vases, domestic altars, etc.

The small *showcase F7* (set apart) contains a model of the Golden 33
Temple at Amritsar (northern India), spiritual centre of the Sikhs.

Showcase F8 is devoted to Buddhism, widespread in the Indian 34
subcontinent in the last centuries before Christ, but now essentially limited to Sri Lanka.

Showcase F9 is devoted to Islam, widespread in the Indian sub- 35
continent from the Middle Ages up to the British conquest of India. It is still professed in Pakistan, Bangladesh and some parts of northern India. In the showcase: a Koran (Agra, 19th cent.); jewels with inscriptions from the Koran; and alabaster model of the Taj Mahal (Agra).

Showcase F10 is devoted to Christianity: statues of the Madonna and 36
saints (India, Sri Lanka; Portuguese influence, 17th to 18th cent.), several ex-votos from the Sanctuary of the Madonna at Verapoly (Syrian-Malabar rite) and several modern paintings.

Turning back, on the left, is a large wooden urn. Scenes from Hindi mythology are carved on its base; inside, about a hundred small statues of Hindu gods, exemplifying the populous Hindu pantheon.

On one side, to the right, a carved wooden coffer is adorned with other scenes of Hindu mythology.

Go round the urn and enter the section on the right dedicated to Indonesia and the Philippines.

INDONESIA

To the left, on the wall, is one of the 24 bas-reliefs that form part of the Asian collection exhibited outside. These bas-reliefs depict the life of Buddha from his birth to his first sermon. The originals are situated in Borobudur, Java (9th cent.).

A scale model of the Temple of Borobadur is placed close to the bas-relief.

Showcase G1 (against the wall) contains objects pertaining to the cult 37
of the dead and ancestors, and various sculptures and masks of a mythical and ritual nature: a basket for offering rice to the dead; a model of a tomb; wooden statuettes of ancestors.

Outside the showcase are carved and incised wooden poles and shields from Irian-Jaya; they reflect the myths and rituals of the local populations.

In the centuries before Christ and up to the arrival of Islam, a large part of Indonesia was under the influence of Hinduism.

38 *Showcase G2:* iron and bronze statuettes of Hindu-Buddhist deities (Java). The Hindu influence in the region is also testified by the shadow theatre (Wayang), common throughout Indonesia, displayed
39 in *showcase G3* (Java, Bali).

40 Hinduism is still professed on the island of Bali. *Showcase G3* contains painted wooden statues of the chief Hindu deities (Shiva, Vishnu, Kali, etc.)

41 Islam, now the principal religion of Indonesia, is illustrated in the first section of *showcase G4* (against the wall). Examples of vessels for everyday use are also displayed (Borneo, Java, Philippines). The end section of *showcase G5* illustrates Christianity in this cultural zone.

On the right, a large Christian altar, the earliest example of Christian monumental art in Indonesia. It was produced by the Javanese sculptors Iho and Adi, from a design by Giulio Schmutzer (1926).

OCEANIA

POLYNESIA

The objects exhibited in the block of showcases on the right pertain to
42 the cult of the dead. *Showcase H1:* two boats for the conveyance of souls to the afterlife (Marquesas), an ancestral casket (Tuamotu), and various mourning wreaths. To the side, diadems, pectorals, necklaces and bracelets testify to ritual use and the social status associated with objects of this kind.

43 *Showcase H2:* magnificent wooden and stone statues of ancestors and Polynesian gods (Marquesas, Tahiti, etc.). Note the two wooden statues of the god "Tu" and of the god "Rongo" (the former with four legs and the only one of its kind in the world) (Mangarewa Islands), genuine masterpieces of Polynesian sculpture.

44 In the large *showcase H3* (set apart) are various ritual objects carved out of wood: axes, oars, clubs, etc. The picture representing the Hawaiian cosmology painted by a local artist should also be noted.

45 The presence of Christianity in Polynesia is documented in *showcase H4.* It contains objects once belonging to Father Damien de Veuster (1840-89) and Father Nicouleau, both of whom dedicated their lives to the care of lepers, and died of leprosy themselves.

MELANESIA

To the left, not in a showcase, are large sculptures in wood from New
Caledonia. They form part of an architectural structure framing the
entrance to some huts and represent the spirits of the ancestors,
46 protectors of the village. To the right, in *showcase I1*, are a series of objects pertaining to the cult of the dead and ancestors. The small hut supported on a sculpted wooden pillar was placed over the place of cremation of a tribal chief for the offering of sacrifices in honour of the deceased (Solomon Islands). The statues represent deified ancestors (Solomon Islands, New Caledonia). On the wall are funeral mats (New Hebrides).

47 *Showcase I2:* ceremonial masks representing ancestors or protective spirits. Note the fine tripartite mask with the carved figures of an ancestor and mythological birds (New Ireland).

Turning to the right, in *showcase I3*, are various objects either for ritual use or for social identification: ceremonial stone sceptres that symbolise the strength and power of the chief and tribe (New Caledonia); ritual paddles of painted wood (Solomon Islands); drums, shields, etc. 48

Christianity in Melanesia is represented by three crucifixes (New Ireland, Solomon Islands, New Guinea) and a painted wooden statue of the Madonna, the earliest Christian sculpture of the Solomon Islands.

The two large masks (left) of the Tubuan (New Britain) secret society introduces the second part of Melanasia, i.e. New Guinea, famous for its wooden sculptures. In the centre of this area is the *tambaran*, the ceremonial hut that forms the social and religious centre of New Guinean villages. These huts are built to honour the group's ancestors(real or mythical), and to perform rites associated with male initiation. Entrance to women and children is strictly forbidden.

The *tambaran* huts are built with great care by the men of the village. Pillars, supports and architraves are often richly carved. Some tribes build the huts on the ground, others on piles. The hut displayed here was reconstructed from original pieces from central New Guinea. Over the entrance are five skulls of deceased villagers, modelled in clay and painted.A large oval mask and a projecting figure complete the architrave. The clay figure on the rooftop represents the spirit of the house.

Inside the hut, at the back: large wooden statue of the god of war, and a mythological heron decorated with feathers. To the left: hand drums, wooden horns for giving signals, skull mask with boar face, instruments of torture (for initiations), and stone shields. To the right: stools and headrests, plumed lances, painted human skulls, various masks, and sacrificial pots. To the left of the main supporting post is the hearth, where sacrifices to the spirits were prepared.

To the left outside are two showcases that contain artefacts exemplifying the art of New Guinea. In the first of these, *showcase I4*, are 49
various sculptures of ancestors and spirits (Buna, Nor, Kanengara,
Korawari, Tuo, etc.). *Showcase I5* contains various ritual masks also 50
representing ancestors (Ambot Kanengara) and spirits (Nor, Buna,
etc.). In the separate *showcase I6* we see a wonderful and very rare 51
headdress of coloured feathers used for ritual dances (Papua - New Guinea).

AUSTRALIA

Outside the section, ten carved and painted tomb poles (Northern Territory, Melville Islands).

Showcase J1, in front: thirteen paintings on stone, representing 52
mythological motifs (sun, rain, ancestors, totemic animals, etc.) of the Australian aborigines (Drysdale). At the back, various cult implements (funerary wreaths, tjuringa, shields, etc.) (Western Australia, Northern Territory).

Leave the Australia section and enter the area of the museum devoted to Africa.

AFRICA

NORTH AFRICA

53 In the foreground of *showcase K1* are various statuettes of the ancient religion of Egypt.

54 *Showcase K2* to the left: Christian objects including lamps, altar cloths with Coptic inscriptions, sacred images, terracotta moulds for making the host (Coptic, 9th to 12th cent.), and two stamps from the Catholic mission of the Friars Minor.

55-56 In the large *showcase K3 - K4* to the right are objects illustrating Islam, the main religion of North Africa. In the first section (left), fragments of painted terracotta vases of Arab manufacture (Egypt, 9th 16th cent.); typical Arab ornaments (Algeria), and vessels for everyday use, with inscriptions in Arabic (Algeria, Morocco). On the back wall, a Turkish inscription, in Arabic characters, invoking the protection of Allah (from a fortress in Algeria, 1830). Showcase K4 also contains objects of sub-Saharan Islamic cultures (camel saddle, dagger with sheath, shields, containers, amulets).

UPPER NILE

57 The *cubical showcase L1* containing ornaments and objects associated with everyday life and with ritual purposes. On the right, plaster statue of Cardinal Guglielmo Massaia (1809-89), apostle of Ethiopia.

58 *Showcase L2* (placed apart) contains objects associated with Coptic Christianity from Ethiopia: a processional cross (the shaft is missing), an iron lectern, a cross-shaped altar-stone, censers, etc.

Showcase L3 contains objects pertaining to the animistic cults of the area.

59 Four Ethiopian icons (copies made in ancient Ethiopia) are exhibited in the small, adjoining room.

After passing the elephant tusks, we enter the Madagascar section.

MADAGASCAR

To the left (not in a showcase): six tomb stelae carved out of wood and painted white: white is a symbol of death (Betsileo).

60-62 To the right, the *showcases M1, M2, M3* (against the wall) are dedicated to the cult of ancestors and the dead: two ancestral statuettes of soldiers who died in Europe in World War One; and models of tombs (Betsileo).

WEST AFRICA

63-66 *Showcases N1, N2, N3 and N4* contain exhibits testifying to voodoo cults, widespread throughout West Africa.

Showcase N1: a group of figurines in painted terracotta; they represent priests, and devotees of the voodoo cult. *Showcase N2:* a collection of iron objects; these sculptures of ancestors and totemic animals are used for tomb ceremonies (Ewe, Togo). *Showcases N3* and *N4* contains a series of vessels and sculptures used for the cult of ancestors and for offerings to the gods. *Showcase N5:* ceremonial masks, some complete with costumes and musical instruments (drums).

CENTRAL AFRICA

Not in showcases: several wooden masks and sculptures introduce the Central Africa section.

To the right, *showcase O1* contains a series of wooden sculptures 68
used for ritual and magical purposes: they represent superhuman beings and ancestors, musical instruments (drums), nailed fetishes with reliquaries closed by mirrors. This particular use of mirrors recalls the reliquaries with inset mirrors incorporated in the statues
of Christian saints, introduced into the area by the Portuguese in the 55-56
17th century.

In *showcase O2* are some reliquaries of the Kota tribe in the Congo 69
area. The three metal-plated wooden figures represent ancestors.

In showcase *O3* are various ceremonial masks from Central Africa. 70

EAST AFRICA

In *showcase P1* the small straw hut was used for the cult of ancestors. 71
These huts were situated in the bush, and, in times of calamity, sacrifices to appease the spirits of ancestors were performed in them. Wooden statuettes of ancestors, and various cult implements attest to the magical and religious beliefs of the populations of this area.

Various types of amulets are displayed at the back of the same showcase. The amulets made of horn contain special herbs and other ingredients believed to possess magical powers as a form of lifelong protection against lightning and disease, for example, or against enemies, and also as a means of protection against problems arising from the return of the dead.

SOUTHERN AFRICA

Showcase Q1 contains various sculptures testifying to the cult of 72
ancestors and rituals connected with female fertility (clay figures adorned with pearls). Other objects: ceremonial masks, protective amulets, necklaces for oracles, batons of command for those officiating the rites.

In *showcase Q2* are , among other things, articles from the trousseau 73
of a Zulu bride.

Turn back, leaving this block of showcases, descend two steps, and enter the section devoted to African Christian art.

AFRICA: CHRISTIANITY

In *showcase R1* are several statuettes carved out of ebony forming a 74
nativity scene (the figurine of the infant Christ is carved out of ivory). The figures reveal a strong European influence (Zaire). There are two other groups of statuettes in painted metal that also form nativity scenes (Burkina Faso).

Showcase R2 contains various statuettes of the Madonna. Those in 75
ivory are simple imitations of European art. The others show a complete africanization of Christian sculptural styles.

Showcase R3 contains four groups of brass figures (scene of 76
martyrdom; story of the prophet Jonah; the Good Shepherd; the Orant). These groups, reminiscent of the scenes on Roman sarcophagi and in frescoes, are nevertheless represented in an in-

digenous style. In the same showcase are various representations of Christ, especially as the Good Shepherd, a favourite motif in African sculpture.

AMERICA

SOUTH AMERICA

77-82 The six *showcases, S1* to *S6* placed against the wall , contain feather ornaments of the indigenous populations of South America (diadems, crowns, ankle ornaments, bracelets, hairpins, belts). At the end of the flight ofstairs is a small room with masks made of bark and animals skins from Terra del Fuego and Brazil (showcases S7 – S9).

83 It is followed by a semicircular room containing Pre-Columbian artefacts from South America. At the entrance are four sculptures (plaster copies) representing the goddess Bachue (Chibcha, Colombia) and two Inca gods (Huaraz, Peru).

84 *Showcase S10* to the left contains representations of various Colombian gods, and some examples of Colombian goldsmith's work (copies).

85 The *central showcase, S11,* contains artefacts (vases, fragments of sculptures) illustrating the Pre-Columbian religions of Peru (Nasca, Tiahuanaco, Trujillo plateau). Of particular interest is the large funerary urn decorated with painted geometrical designs and an anthropomorphic figure in relief.

On the wall is a bas-relief (copy) representing the five lunar nights (Chavin de Huantar, Peru).

Turn left to enter the room devoted to Central America.

CENTRAL AMERICA

At the entrance: two plaster reliefs; the one on the left represents the god of destructive fire, and a man dancing with a skeleton; the one on the right shows a seated tribal chieftain (Guatemala, Maya). On the wall: above, relief (copy) portraying Quetzalcoatl, god of the wind (Chichen Itza, Yucatan); below, a relief model of the ruins of the Temple of Copan (Honduras). Next, a sculpture in grey stone (palm style), symbol of the sun (Mexican plateau). Next, cast of a richly carved column found in the ruins of Copan (Stele II, Copan, Honduras).

On the right: two relief models. The first is of the so-called Temple of the Cross, decorated with Mayan mythological figures and hieroglyphs; on the sides, figures of mythological birds, and priests offering sacrifices (Yucatan, Mexico). The second model is of the Pyramid of Papantla (Gulf of Mexico, Totonacos).

86 To the left, *showcase T1* contains pre-Columbian sculptures from Mexico.

In the centre of the room is a splendid sculpture, in reddish stone, representing Quetzalcoatl (Mexican plateau, classical Aztec style). Next, five fragments of stone statues of gods. Against the wall, four statues (copies) of the main Aztec gods, including Tlaloc, god of the rain; Quetzalcoatl, god of the wind; and Chalchiuthlicue, goddess of water.

plan ←

To the right of the wall, plaster cast of the "Cross of Teotihuacan" (Mexico, Tula). Below, model of the so-called "Temple of the Shields and Jaguars", dedicated to the goddess Kukulkan (Yucatan, Toltec).

Next, two casts of the cornerstones of the pyramid of Monte Alban (Mexico, Oaxaca), and a model of the Temple of Xochicalco, dedicated to the goddess of rain and fertility (Mexican plateau, Aztec).

At the exit of the Central American sector (to the right) are two casts: the one of a fragment with hieroglyphs relating to Mexican cosmology, the other of a drum (Teponatztli) (Mexico, Aztec). In the centre is a large ceremonial cylindrical brazier for sacrificial fire, in the form of an ape bearing a vase on its back (Guatemala, Maya).

AMERICA: CHRISTIANITY

87

At the corner of the large block of showcases are objects associated with Christianity in the Americas (lecterns, sculptures, liturgical implements), *sections S, T, V.* Note in particular: the wooden lectern, decorated with shell-shaped mounts in mother-of-pearl, once belonging to Fra Bartolomeo de Las Heras, Christopher Columbus's chaplain during his voyages to America (made by the Caribs of Cuba); a metal bell used by the first missionaries to Mexico; two silver flasks found in the ruins of a Christian church in Parana (Brazil).

Proceed along the corridor to the room dedicated to North America.

NORTH AMERICA

The objects displayed in this section *(U)* were sculpted by Ferdinand Pettrich. He was a disciple of the great Danish neoclassical sculptor Bertel Thorvaldsen. Acting on the master's advice, Pettrich went to the United States in 1835. There he prepared small-scale models for his sculptures, which he later executed in life-size proportions during his long stay in Brazil. He later donated them to Pius IX.

At the entrance we see a bas-relief representing a war dance of the Sauk-Fox and Mississippi Sioux tribes. Next, a statue of a young hunter.

Next, a bas-relief representing a battle between two hostile tribes: the Winnebagos and the Creeks. The representation is an imaginative reconstruction by the artist based on the accounts of the Indians themselves; but the figures are taken from real life. Next to the relief is the statue of the dying Te-cum-seh, the famous chief of all the western Indian tribes, when he was wounded during the Battle of Thames in 1813, shown leaning on one elbow encouraging his warriors.

This is followed by a bas-relief representing a buffalo hunt; the numerous portraits were drawn from real life at Campden, near the Delaware River. The large statue on the left is of Tahtapesaah (Raging Hurricane), a Sioux chief of the Mississippi river area.

The busts along the wall represent various chiefs, counsellors and priests of the Sioux, Sauk-Fox, Winnebago and Creek tribes.

In the centre, a bas-relief taken from real life, representing the council held in Washington in 1837, between US government representatives and the chiefs of the Sauk-Fox and Mississippi Sioux tribes, for the sale of the lands, which by right belonged to the two tribes.

Proceed to the section dedicated to Persia (V).

ASIA

PERSIA

In the showcases along the wall, Persian and Oriental glazed majolica from the La Farina Collection, Palermo.

89 Of special interest is the cross-shaped majolica, with a verse from the Koran around the edges. It reads, "In the name of the compassionate and merciful god"; the other pseudo-cufic letters are meaningless arabesques. All the majolica comes the collection of the Imam Zadeh, Veramin (13th cent.). Of exceptional beauty is the square tile with metallic reflections depicting the mythological Persian bird, the simurgh (Persia, 13th 14th cent.).

Leaving this section, a picture composed of vitreous enamelled tiles with travel scenes (Persia, 17th 18th cent.)can be see on the right; above, a large arch with fourteen human figures on glazed terracotta tiles (hunting scenes) (Teheran, 17th 18th cent.).

Pass through the arch to enter the Middle Eastern section.

MIDDLE EAST

90-92 To the right of the block of *showcases W1 - W3* are objects associated with the ancient cultures of the Middle East (all the artefacts come from the area). Note in particular: a necklace made of seals representing Oriental gods; a clay tablet with cuneiform writing (2000 B.C.); and fragments of stone bearing Hittite hieroglyphs (1400 B.C.). They are followed by artefacts of Hellenistic and Roman influence: reliefs, statuettes, vases, lamps, glassware, etc.

93 Objects of Islamic culture are exhibited opposite.

Turn left to enter the room dedicated to the religions of the Middle East today.

94 The first *showcase W4* is dedicated to Jewish religion: a scroll (1400) of the Torah with wooden case (17th cent.); a candlestick associated with the Hanukkah, festival of lights (from a synagogue, early 19th cent.); and two versions of the *Meghillat Esther* (Story of Esther), one in a silver gilt case (a wedding gift to a bride).

95 *Showcase W5* is dedicated to Christianity in the region: small icons, silver crucifixes, and a representation in mother-of-pearl of the Last Supper and the Resurrection. On the wall, a reproduction of a mosaic with a map of the Holy Land (the original, dating to the second half of the 6th century, is in a Christian church at Madaba in Jordan).

96 *Showcase W6* is dedicated to Islam, the predominant religion of the Middle East, exemplified by various objects of common use.

CHRISTIAN ART IN MISSION COUNTRIES

The last section of the museum contains works representative of Christian art in mission countries.

97 A magnificent altar of richly carved and gilded wood (from Japan) can be admired in the Middle Eastern room.

Showcase X1 contains examples of religious decorative arts from China: enamelware altar furnishings; liturgical vessels; wooden and enamelled candlesticks; crosiers, etc.

98 The *tabernacle X2,* in lacquered and gilded wood, was made in Vietnam, after European models.

Among the Christian paintings on display, note in particular the magnificent representation of the *Last Judgement*. The anonymous artist has made use of both European and Buddhist elements to create a vision of the end of the world (Vietnam, 17th cent.).

The painting of the *Last Supper*, in Chinese ink on white silk, is a typically Chinese product (Wang-Su-Ta). The two panels representing the Virgin are by the same artist. The last painting of this series represents the introduction of Christianity into Japan with the arrival of St. Francis Xavier; his sermon; the martyrdom of the Christians of Nagasaki; and the Madonna as Queen of Japan (Japan, Luca Hasegawa).

y - Carriage Museum

19 century carriage

The Carriage Museum is a branch of the Historical Museum, installed in the Papal Apartment of the Apostolic Palace at the Lateran since 3 March 1991.

Founded by Paul VI in 1973, the Carriage Museum was laid out in a long corridor-like room (105 x 14 m), built below the so-called Square Garden in 1963-64. The collection contains vehicles, accessories and memorabilia associated with the pope's transportation and travel needs, such as saddles, sedan chairs, carriages, automobiles, models, accompanied by photographs and paintings.

There is a *bronze bust of Paul VI* by the sculptor Guarino Roscioli in the vestibule (inv. 39952). On a table is a *small model of the first locomotive* (inv. 45593) that entered the Vatican City on the new railway branch line built in 1929, following the Lateran Pacts. Also on display: documentation of the protocol for the berlin *gran gala* cavalcade.

The museum proper begins with a wonderful 17th century *model of the papal berlin* (inv. 44585). On the right side of the long room are black *"mezza gala"* harnesses, and *"gran gala"* harnesses in red velvet, saddles, trappings, cushions, travelling-bags, reins and the like. Note in particular: a *cavalcade saddle* (inv. 45590), complete with all its parts, saddle-both embroidered in gold and silver and the coat of arms of Clement XIV (1769-1774). On the opposite side of the room is an *English type saddle* (inv. 45591), donated by an emir complete with all its parts, and covered in red velvet with floral decorations in white thread; its brown saddle-cloth is gold embroidered and has glass inserts and silver-plate brass fittings.

We come to the red damask-upholstered *sedan-chair of Leo XIII* (inv. 45587), presented to the Pope by the faithful of Naples in 1887, on the 50th anniversary of his priesthood. The other sedan chairs in the collection are in the Historical Museum in the Lateran.

On the walls, a small iconographic collection includes the large painting of Julius Blaas representing the *Eucharistic Congress of Vienna in 1912* (inv. 42776).

There are 13 carriages in the museum. They are the most important part of the collection. Placed in rows on the two sides of the room, in the centre is the magnificent *"gran gala" four-seater berlin* (inv. 45551) of Pope Leo XII (1823-1829). On the right side is the *four-seater gala berlin* (red and gold) of Cardinal Lucien Louis Bonaparte (1829-95), later donated to Pius IX. On the left side is the *four-seater travelling carriage* (inv. 45572) that Ferdinand II King of Naples donated to Pius IX on his return to Rome (1850) after his exile in Gaeta.

The papal carriages were all made according to a particular protocol that took into account the important functions they were required to perform on certain occasions. The carriages of the popes thus possess, in a peculiar manner, a seat that could also serve as a papal throne and the image of the Holy Spirit, in the form of the image of a dove with rays situated on the ceiling. Facing the throne are two seats that, depending on circumstance, could carry two cardinals, the majordomo and *maestro di camera*, or two privy chamberlains. The papal carriages are red with gilt metal inlays and fittings. The interior is upholstered in red silk and velvet, with matching carpet.

At the end of the room are three historic papal automobiles belonging to Pius XI (1922-1939): a *Mercedes Benz* (inv. 30564); a *Citroën Lictoria Sex* (inv. 30565), which is fitted inside like a carriage ; and a *Graham Paige* (inv. 30565), famous because it was used by Pius XII when he went to the Basilica of San Lorenzo fuori le Mura during the war and declared Rome an open city.

z - Vatican History Museum
Lateran Apostolic Palace

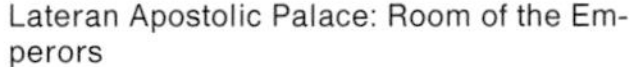

Lateran Apostolic Palace: Room of the Emperors

Lateran Apostolic Palace: Sala della Conciliazione

Open to the public everyday except Sunday from 9:00 a.m. to 12:00 p.m. The entrance to the museum is in the atrium of the Basilica of St. John Lateran.

The Vatican Historical Museum consists of two large sections. Each section is located in a separate building: the Historical Museum is situated in the Apostolic Palace at the Lateran, adjacent to the Basilica of St. John Lateran, while the Carriage Museum can be found in the Vatican Museums.

The Historical Museum was founded by Paul VI in 1973. It was initially located in a building constructed under the Square Garden, but it was later transferred to the first floor of the Lateran Apostolic Palace in 1987 and inaugurated on 1 March 1991.

The palace was built by the architect Domenico Fontana during the pontificate of Sixtus V (1585-1590).The newly elected pope immediately ordered the demolition of the old run-down residence of the Popes, and replaced it with a building that was more appropriate as the seat of the Bishop of Rome. The museum itinerary includes a visit to both the papal apartment and the Historical Collections.

The Papal Apartment consists of four large halls and eight rooms, all of them richly decorated with late Mannerist frescoes. They are decorated with tapestries of various periods and schools (Gobelins of French manufacture and some from the Barberini and San Michele workshops in Rome), which come from the papal collections. There are also some wooden sculptures, dating from the 13th to the 18th century, historical paintings and papal memorabilia. The Ante-Chapel room of the contains liturgical vestments of the Borghese-Hercolani Collection.

The Historical Collections also contain a series of portraits of Popes (papal iconography), from the 16th century to the present, testimonials of the Pontifical Military Corps, records of the papal chapel and household and documentation with relics of papal ceremonial no longer in use.

The section with papal carriages and automobiles is still in the Vatican Museums (see above: Carriage Museum).

Vatican History Museum
Lateran Apostolic Palace

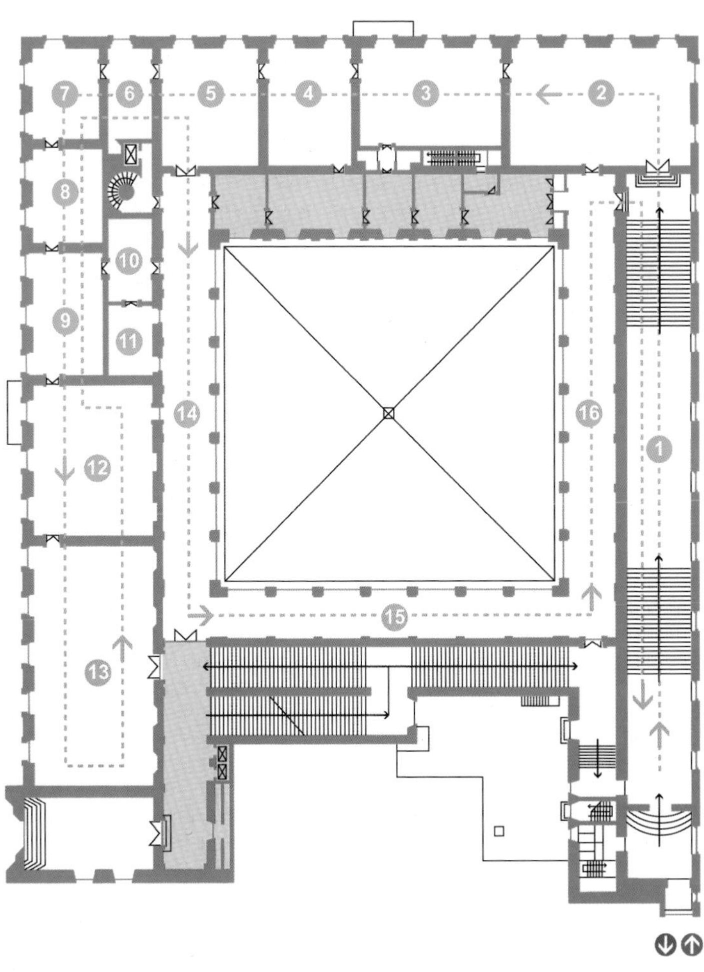

closed areas

museum itinerary

entrance

exit

1 Papal staircase
2 Room of Constantine
3 Room of the Apostles
4 Room of the Four Seasons
5 Room of Daniel
6 Room of Eliah
7 Room of Solomon
8 Room of David
9 Room of Samuel
10 Antechamber - Borghese-Hercolani Collection
11 Chapel
12 Room of the Emperors
13 Room of the Conciliation
14 Gallery of Papal Iconography
15 Gallery of the Papal Ceremonial Court
16 Gallery of the Pontifical Armed Corps

GUIDE
TO THE VATICAN CITY

plan
→

ST. PETER'S SQUARE

St. Peter's Square

St. Peter's Basilica was completed in 1614 with the construction of its façade, in a period when the dramatic and theatrical Baroque style had become popular. The elliptical and similarly Baroque piazza is enclosed by
1 quadruple colonnades with 284 columns, built by Gian Lorenzo Bernini from
2 1656 to 1666 during the papacy of Alexander VII. Joined to the atrium of the Basilica by two straight but outward-splayed corridors, the colonnades appear to embrace all who enter the square and, metaphorically, all of mankind.

Along the balustrade overlooking the forecourt of the Basilica and the square itself there are one hundred and forty statues, each 3.20 m. high; they were sculpted by artists of the 17th and 18th century.

3 The *Egyptian obelisk* at the centre of the square was placed there in 1586 by Domenico Fontana. It previously stood to the left of the Basilica (see p. 191: 8), marking the site of the *spina* in the centre of the circus where early Christians were martyred by the emperor Nero (see 1, plan pp. 20-21). The
4 *fountain on the right* was originally designed in 1490 but remodelled by Carlo
5 Maderno (1613), while the *fountain on the left* was added by Bernini in 1675, during the papacy of Clement X. Two porphyry disks in the pavement of the square, between the obelisk and the fountains, mark the foci of the radii of the colonnades. A marble-inlaid circle in the pavement all round the obelisk indicates the names and directions of the various winds and signs of the zodiac.

At the centre of the Basilica's façade by Carlo Maderno (1607-1614) is the
6 *Loggia delle Benedizioni*. It is from the balcony of this loggia that the Pope imparts his first *Urbi et Orbi Blessing* after his election and on other solemn occasions (such as Easter). The façade is crowned by thirteen statues, each 6 m. high, with the exception of Christ the Redeemer at the centre, which is 7.50 m. high They were sculpted under the direction of Ambrogio Buonvicino between 1612 and 1614: Christ in the centre, St. John the Baptist and eleven Apostles (excluding St. Peter because his statue is located in front of the staircase leading up to the entrance).

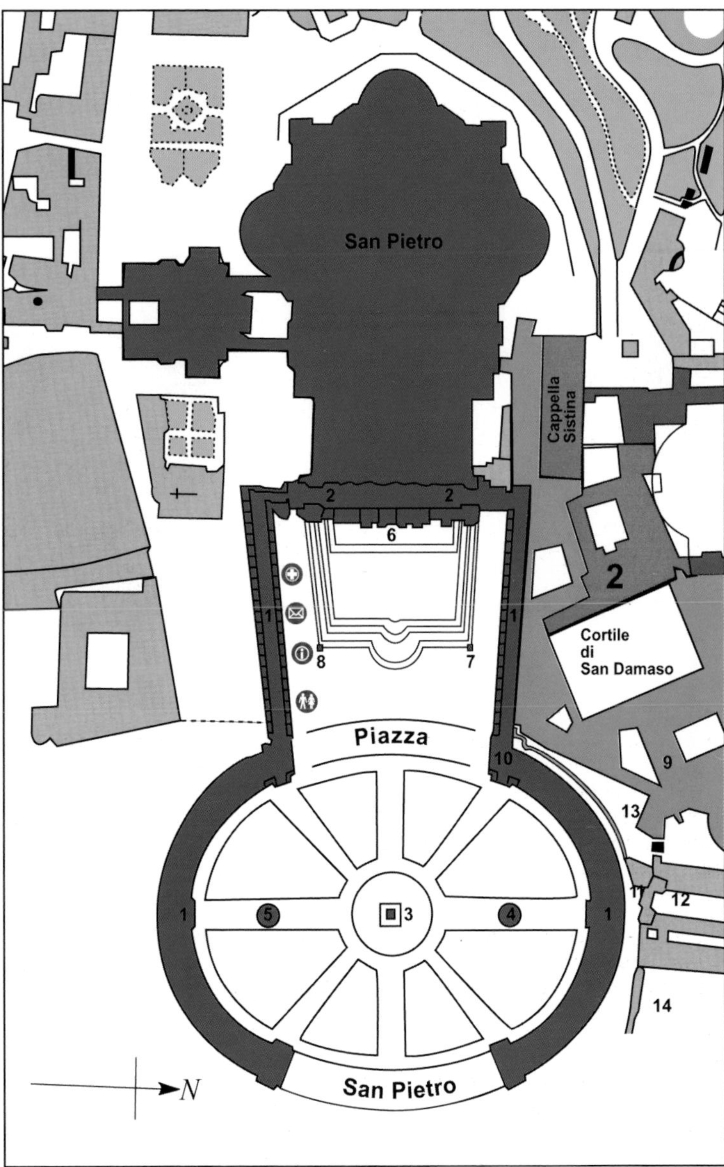

ST PETER'S SQUARE

1 Bernini's colonnade
2 Atrium of St. Peter's Basilica
3 Egyptian obelisk
4 Maderno's fountain
5 Bernini's fountain
6 Loggia delle Benedizioni
7 Statue of St. Paul
8 Statue of St. Peter
9 Papal residence
10 Bronze Doors (*Portone di Bronzo*)
11 St. Peter's Gate (*Porta di San Pietro*)
12 Courtyard of the Barracks of the Swiss Guard
13 Chapel of the Swiss Guard
14 Corridor between the Papal Palace and Castel Sant'Angelo called "il passetto".

- Areas of the Papal Palace not open to the public
- Areas of the Papal Palace included in the visit to the Vatican Museums
- Vatican Museums
- St. Peter's Square and Basilica
- Restrooms
- First aid station (during public audiences)
- Post Office
- Information Bureau

Aerial view of St. Peter's

7 Later, in the 19th century, the *statue of St. Paul* on the right (by Adamo
8 Tadolini) and the *statue of St. Peter* on the left (by Giuseppe de Fabris) were placed at either end of Bernini's stairway in front of the facade.

Behind the colonnade to the right of the Basilica stands the Apostolic Palace.
9 The *papal residence* is on the third floor. The penultimate window to the right is that of the Pope's study. It is at this window that the Pope appears every Sunday at midday and recites the "Angelus" together with the faithful. The
10 *Bronze Doors* are at the end of the right colonnade (going towards the Basilica) . This is the main entrance to the Papal Palace, which is guarded by the Swiss Guards.

11 Behind the colonnade to the right is *St. Peter's Gate (Porta di San Pietro),* constructed by Alexander VI on the site of the medieval entrance to the Vatican. Beyond the arched gateway, which is usually closed, is the
12 *courtyard of the Swiss Guard Barracks,* which corresponds to the last portion of the Via Francigena, the main pilgrims' road leading from northern
13 Europe to Rome in the Middle Ages. The *Chapel of the Swiss Guard,* built by Pius V (1566-1572) and dedicated to St. Martin and St. Sebastian, is located on the ground floor of the Apostolic Palace to the left of St. Peter's Gate. On either side of the gate is the high medieval wall of the original ramparts of the
14 Vatican. A *corridor* inside linked the Apostolic Palace with Castel Sant'Angelo. It was a convenient escape route and enabled the popes, as in the case of Clement VII, to find refuge in the great fortress on the banks of the Tiber in moments of danger.

VATICAN CITY AND GARDENS

South quarter

Entry to the Vatican City is through the *Arch of the Bells (Arco delle* 2
Campane) to the left of the Basilica, guarded by the Swiss Guards (wearing early 16th century uniforms). This famous military corps was founded by Julius II (1503-1513), and is still entrusted with the surveillance of the entrances to the Vatican City and the *Apostolic Palace* (see p. 199). The 3
remaining Vatican territory is guarded by the Vatican's own police force, the *Corpo della Gendarmeria*. In 1527, when Rome was sacked by the troops of Emperor Charles V, almost all the Swiss Guards were killed in the area that is now the Teutonic College cemetery (5). Their sacrifice enabled Pope Clement VII (1523-1534) to flee his palace in the Vatican and seek refuge in Castel Sant'Angelo. This event occurred on May 6, and a memorial service is held every year on this date in their honour, together with the swearing-in ceremony for new recruits.

At the opposite side of the Arch of the Bells is a sentry-post of the guards of the *Corpo della Gendarmeria*. Behind the sentry-post is a huge square, called *Piazza dei Protomartiri Romani.* To the right is the side of the Basilica 4
and to the left the Teutonic College of Santa Maria in Campo Santo. A memorial plaque on the wall reminds us that it is the site of Caligula's circus (see 1, plan pp. 20-21), where so many Christians (including St. Peter) met their death under Nero (64 A.D.). This is why the square is dedicated to the protomartyrs, the first martyrs of the Church.

The *Teutonic College* (originally a hostel for Frankish pilgrims built by 5
Charlemagne) was formally established by Pius IX in 1876 for priests from the territories of the former Holy Roman Empire. The adjacent cemetery (early 9th century) was the burial place of pilgrims from the northern countries who died in Rome, and is still in use today. The 15th century church of the cemetery, dedicated to the Virgin Mary, has recently been restored.

Beyond the Teutonic College, on the left at the far side of the square, is the 6
Domus Sanctae Martae or *St. Martha's Hospice,* belonging to the French nuns of St. Vincent. Built in the Holy Year 1900, it was recently enlarged and refurbished (1996). It serves as a hostel for clergy serving in various Vatican offices, and a residence for bishops and cardinals during their visits to Rome.

Behind the Teutonic College rises the great curved white travertine vault of
the *Papal Audience Hall,* built by Pier Luigi Nervi and inaugurated by Paul VI 7
on June 30, 1971. Prior to the construction of this building, papal audiences were often held in St. Peter's and even now, whenever the number of pilgrims exceeds the capacity of the hall, the audience is held there or (weather permitting) in St. Peter's Square. The new hall has seating for 6300 and standing room for 4000. It has a concave shape, so that everyone may see the Pope on his podium. Behind the podium is a large relief sculpture of the Resurrection of Christ by Pericle Fazzini, installed in 1977.

Facing the Arch of the Bells (2) is the large domed Sacristy of St. Peter's. The 8
left part of the building contains the residential quarters of the canons (the priests who regularly perform the divine services in St. Peter's). Designed by Carlo Marchionni and built between 1776 and 1784, the Sacristy was commissioned by Pius VI, who had been a canon himself before being elected Pope. On the right side of the building, set into the paving of the square, is a granite disk commemorating the original site of the obelisk (placed at the centre of Caligula's circus) now in St. Peter's Square. In the small square between the two arches that join the sacristy to the Basilica is

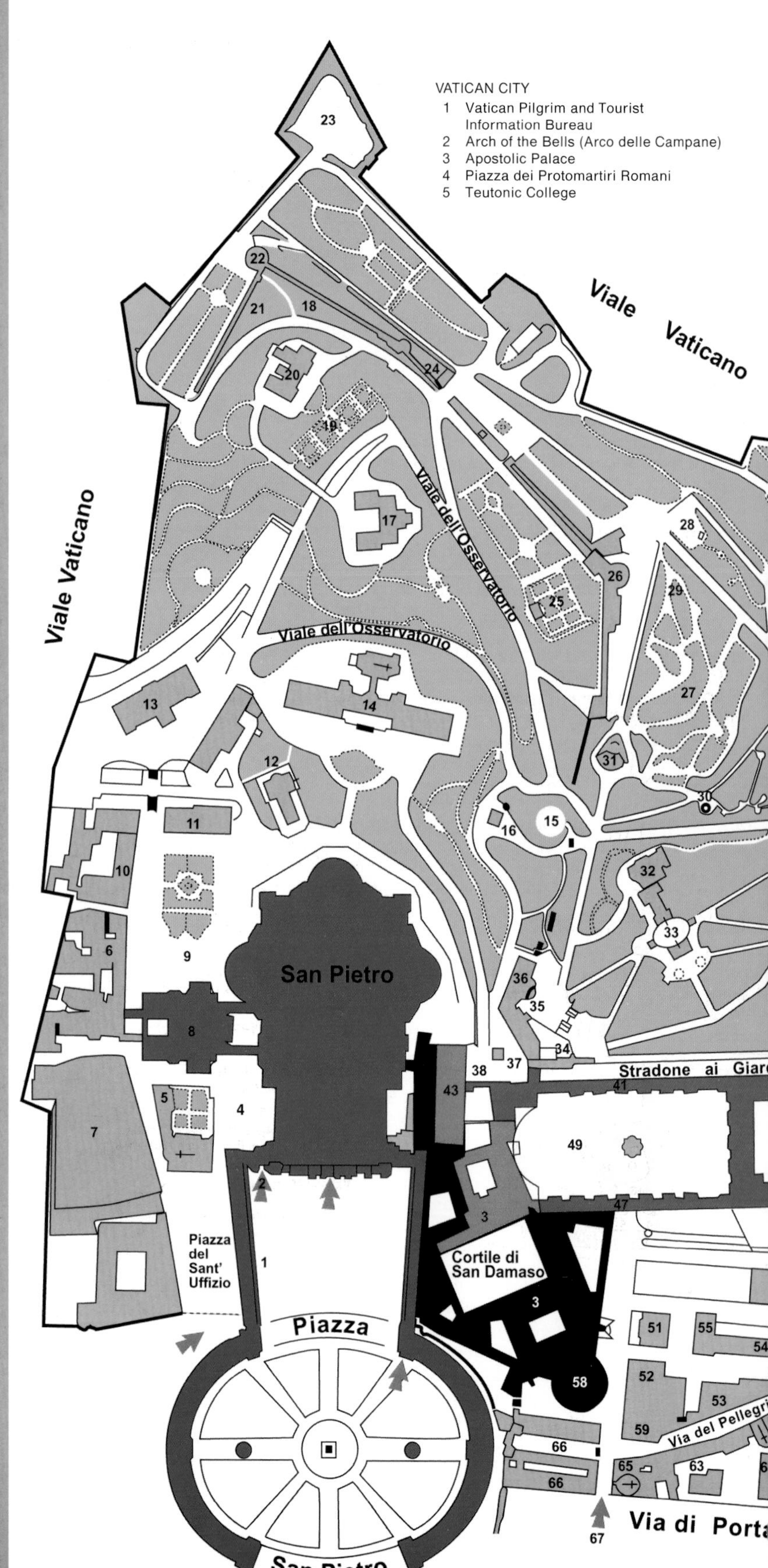
VATICAN CITY
1 Vatican Pilgrim and Tourist Information Bureau
2 Arch of the Bells (Arco delle Campane)
3 Apostolic Palace
4 Piazza dei Protomartiri Romani
5 Teutonic College
Viale Vaticano
Viale Vaticano
Viale dell'Osservatorio
Viale dell'Osservatorio
San Pietro
Stradone ai Giar
Piazza del Sant' Uffizio
Cortile di San Damaso
Piazza
San Pietro
Via del Pellegri
Via di Porta

6 *St. Martha's Hospice*
7 Papal Audience Hall
8 Sacristy of St. Peter
9 Piazza Santa Marta
10 Palazzo San Carlo
11 Palazzo del Tribunale (courthouse)
12 Church of Santo Stefano degli Abissini
13 Railway Station
14 Palazzo del Governatorato
15 Bronze statue of St. Peter
16 House of the Gardener
17 Ethiopian College
18 Crenellated wall (ramparts of Leo IV and Nicholas V)
19 Italian garden
20 First building of Vatican Radio
21 Muretto (ramparts of Leo IV and Nicholas V)
22 Tower of St. John
23 Heliport
24 Grotto of Lourdes
25 Rose garden
26 Offices of Vatican Radio
27 English Garden
28 Chapel of the "Madonna della Guardia"
29 Statue of St. Peter in Chains
30 Chinese pavilion
31 Fountain of the Eagle
32 Pontifical Academy of Sciences
33 "Casina" of Pius IV
34 Building of Paul V and Fountain of the Mirrors
35 Fountain of the Sacrament
36 Palazzo della Zecca (mint)
37 Piazza del Forno
38 Arch of the Sentinel
39 Cortile della Pigna
40 Vatican Pinacoteca
41 Secret Archive of the Vatican, Vatican Library, galleries of the Vatican Museums
42 Torre dei Venti
43 Sistine Chapel
44 Fountain of the Galley
45 Bramante's spiral staircase
46 Palazzetto del Belvedere, now part of the Vatican Museums
47 Bramante's Corridor, now part of the Vatican Museums
48 Atrium of the Quattro Cancelli (Four Gates)
49 Belvedere Court
50 Car-Park
51 Post and Telegraph office
52 Tipografia Vaticana and Libreria Editrice Vaticana
53 Grocery stores
54 Pharmacy
55 Vatican health services
56 Mechanical workshops
57 Central heating plant
58 Tower of Nicholas V
59 Sentry-post of the *Corpo della Gendarmeria*
60 Church of San Pellegrino
61 Seat of *L'Osservatore Romano* and *L'Osservatore della Domenica*
62 Residential quarters of the personnel of the Corpo della Gendarmeria
63 Tapestry restoration workshop
64 Refectory
65 Church of Sant'Anna
66 Swiss Guard barracks
67 St. Anne's Gate (Cancello di Sant'Anna)

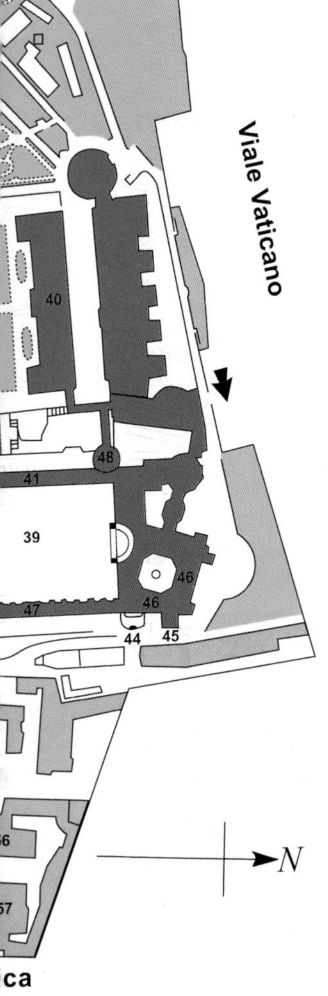

MAIN ENTRANCES TO THE VATICAN CITY

from left to right:

Gate of the Holy Office *(Cancello del Sant'Uffizio)*
Arch of the Bells *(Arco delle Campane)* (entrances to the Papal Audience Hall)

Entrance to St. Peter's Basilica

Bronze Doors (*Portone di Bronzo*) (entrance to the Apostolic Palace and to the Prefecture of the Papal Household)

St. Anne's Gate *(Cancello di Sant'Anna)* (entrance to the north quarter of Vatican City)

ENTRANCE TO THE VATICAN MUSEUMS

Buildings in the Gardens and in the urban quarter

Restricted areas of the Apostolic Palace

Areas of the Apostolic Palace included in the itinerary of the Vatican Museums

Vatican Museums

St. Peter's Square and Basilica

a plaque that marks the site of the demolished Church of Santo Stefano degli Ungheresi, with its adjoining hospice for Hungarian pilgrims.

9 Through the second arch is a large square (*Piazza Santa Marta*) with a
garden in the centre. The layout of the square - like most of the City - is post
1929, the year the Vatican City State was established. The left side of the
10 square is occupied by *Palazzo San Carlo,* now used for offices and
apartments. To its left (in Palazzo di Santa Marta) is the *Mosaic Workshop*,
which is under the supervision of the *Reverenda Fabbrica* of St. Peter's and
is responsible for training artists in mosaic art and the preservation of the
mosaics in the Basilica. The workshop dates back to the late 16th century, but
was formally established by Benedict XIII in 1727. On the opposite side of the
11 square is another large building, the *Palazzo del Tribunale,* which also
houses the apartments of the penitentiaries, i.e. the religious who administer the sacrament of Confession in the Basilica, the Ufficio della
Gendarmeria (security and surveillance office) and the Vatican courthouse
where law enforcement in this small State is administered.

12 To the right of the Palazzo del Tribunale is the *Church of Santo Stefano degli Abissini,* originally annexed to a hospice for Abyssinian pilgrims. The foundations of the church can be traced back to St. Leo I (440-461). Entrusted to Coptic monks in 1479, it was extensively rebuilt under Clement XI in the early 18th century and restored between 1931 and 1933. Worth noting is the 11th century portal decorated with scrolled foliated ornament. Fragments of inscriptions and sarcophagi walled into the exterior provide evidence that the cemetery discovered under St. Peter's extended this far (see p. 230).

13 Further uphill is another square (Piazza della Stazione) with the railway station built by Giuseppe Momo and inaugurated in 1930. Built into the station's façade are two bas-reliefs by Eduardo Rubino, representing the *Miraculous Draught of Fishes* and the *Prophet Elijah and his Chariot of Fire.* The railway is used for freight transport and is linked to the Italian State railway system. It was from here that John XXIII set out on 14 October 1962 for his first pilgrimage to Assisi and Loreto, on the occasion of the forthcoming Second Vatican Council. It was the first time the Vatican railway was used for passengers. Later, it was also used by Pope John Paul II.

To the right of the station square is another large square, where the *Palazzo*
14 *del Governatorato* is located: the building in which the main administrative
offices of Vatican City State are housed. It too was designed by Giuseppe
Momo and built in 1930. The sloping ground between the square and the
apse of St. Peter's are laid out with flowerbeds, in a pattern that forms the
coat of arms of the reigning Pope.

Gardens

The Vatican Gardens extend beyond the Palazzo del Governatorato. They occupy about a third of Vatican territory. They consist of lawns anabounding with artificial grottos, pavilions, monumental statues and fountains.

Almost at the centre of Vatican territory, in the midst of a palm grove, is a
15 *bronze statue of St. Peter.* It was once part of the monument standing in the
centre of the Cortile della Pigna (39) to commemorate the First Vatican
Council (1869-1870).

To the right of the statue of St. Peter is a small turreted building called (the
16 name is self-explantory) the *House of the Gardener.* It was probably one of
the buildings built inside the Leonine walls by Innocent III (1198-1216).

Turn left and go up to the top of the Vatican Hill. On the left is the *Ethiopian*
17 *College,* built by G. Momo. It was built to accomodate seminarians from
Ethiopia. Germany and Ethiopia are the only countries to have colleges
inside the Vatican walls.

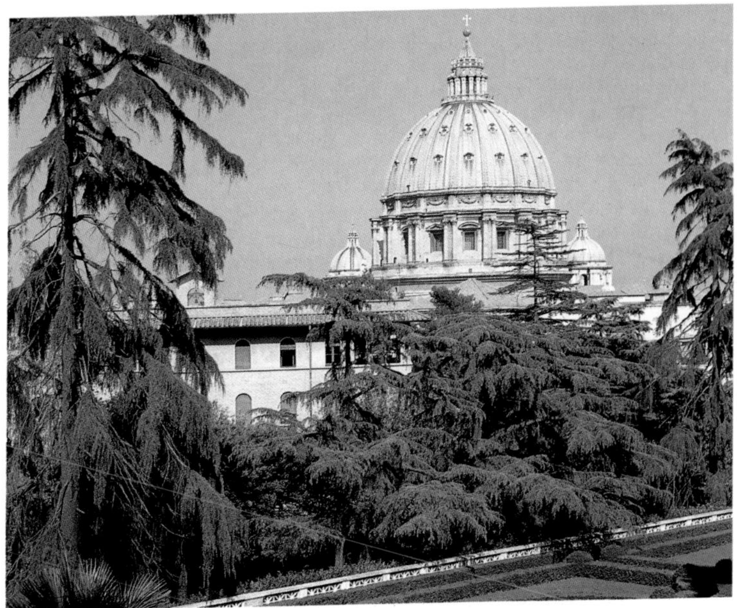

The *Cupola* seen from the Vatican Gardens

From the top of the hill, walk along a stretch of crenellated brick wall, part of the Vatican's original ramparts (see 5, plan pp. 20-21) built by Leo IV (847-855) to protect the ancient Basilica and the Vatican Hill (the original nucleus of the present city), and restored by Nicholas V in the 15th century. 18

On the left is the *Italian garden* with shrubs and flowerbeds symmetrically laid out and trimmed. Nearby is the building of the *first Vatican Radio transmitting station,* designed by Guglielmo Marconi and inaugurated in 1931. 19 20

Continue to the left along a low wall. During the papacy of Pius XII, it was covered by a transparent roof. This enabled the Pope to take his customary one-hour stroll after lunch in any kind of weather. 21

Pass the wall and turn right to reach the highest point of the Vatican Hill (78.5 m.) and the Leonine walls, dominated by the medieval *Tower of St. John,* which was adapted as a temporary summer residence for Pope John XXIII (1958-1963). The tower has provided accommodation for many illustrious guests, including Athenagoras, Patriarch of Constantinople, who visited the Vatican in 1967. More recently it also provided temporary accommodation for John Paul II during renovation work in the Pope's private apartment. 22

Further on, the *heliport* is situated on top of the outermost western bastion of the Vatican walls. 23

Descending along the edge of the imposing bastions built in the 16th century (delimiting the territory of Vatican City), we come to the grotto of the Madonna of Lourdes. Here is a concrete reproduction of the *Grotto of Lourdes* (Massabielle) where the Immaculate Conception appeared to St. Bernadette Soubirous in 1858. The Bishop of Tarbes, the diocese that includes the city of Lourdes, donated it to Leo XIII. Images of the Pope and donor are represented in mosaic above the grotto. The original altar of the Grotto of Lourdes, donated to Pope John XXIII, is still used on special occasions. 24

25 From here continue on foot to a *rose garden* where there is a magnificent
view of the apse and dome of St. Peter's visible through the rose pergolas.
Behind is a medieval tower, called the Leonine Tower, rising from another
part of the fortified wall built by Leo IV and Nicholas V. This tower and the
villa below it were used by the Vatican Observatory between 1908 and 1936.
The Observatory was moved there from the Torre dei Venti (42) and later
transferred to the pope's summer residence at Castel Gandolfo in the Alban
26 Hills. The medieval tower and the villa below it now house the *Administration of Vatican Radio.* The unassuming villa was once the summer
residence of Leo XIII (1878-1903), the Pope who lived longest in the Vatican
in the period between 1870 and 1929 (when the popes never left the Vatican
due to the still unresolved questions of relations with the Italian State).

27 Beyond the villa of Leo XIII is the *English garden,* where the vegetation is allowed to grow naturally.

28 In a clearing along the upper border of the garden is the little *Chapel of the "Madonna della Guardia",* with a reproduction of the statue that overlooks the entry to the port of Genoa; it was donated by the people of Genoa to their fellow-citizen, Benedict XV (1914-1922).

29 Among the trees of the English garden stands a *statue of St. Peter in Chains,* sculpted in 1887 by Amalia Dupré (the first woman artist represented in the Vatican). The statue is an allusion to the fact that the successor of St. Peter was prevented from leaving the Vatican in the decades following the occupation of Rome by the new Italian State (1870-1929). Like most of the statues in the garden, it is dedicated to Leo XIII.

30 At the lower end of the English garden is a *Chinese pavilion* (donated by
Chinese Catholics to Pius XI in 1933, on the 19th centenary of the death of
Christ). John XXIII was fond of sitting in this pavilion. From this point we can
40 see part of the Vatican Museums complex, including the *Vatican Pinacoteca,*
built by Luca Beltrami in 1930.

After descending through one of the most attractive and shady areas of the
gardens, dotted with little fountains and benches, and embellished here and
31 there with ancient marbles, we come to the 17th century *Fountain of the Eagle*
by the Dutch artist Jan van Santen. Like all the fountains in the Vatican, the
water comes from the Lake of Bracciano, about 40 km. north of Rome. The
eagle and the griffin are the symbols of the Borghese family of Paul V (1605-
1621), who commissioned the fountain.

Further down on the left is the villa constructed by Pius XI to house the
32 *Pontifical Academy of Sciences,* where scientists from all over the world
meet. It is now also the seat of the Pontifical Academy for the Social
Sciences.

Next to it is one of the finest and best preserved architectural complexes in
33 the Vatican: the *"Casina" of Pius IV,* begun in 1558 by Pirro Ligorio and
completed between 1560 and 1562. It is composed of two buildings facing
each other across an elliptical courtyard: the villa with a richly decorated
stucco façade to the west, and the loggia with fountain and grotto to the
east.

Facing the Casina of Pius IV, on the other side of a broad avenue (*Stradone
ai Giardini*) separated from the gardens by a railing, is the long wing of the
41 Apostolic Palace. The lower floor houses the *Vatican Secret Archive,* and an
41 annex the School of Palaeography and Diplomatics. The middle floor houses
the *Vatican Library* where courses in librarianship are also held, while the
41-42 *Galleries of the Vatican Museums* occupy the upper floor. The tower known
as the *Torre dei Venti* rises above from this building; until 1908, it served as
the seat of the Vatican Observatory, founded by Gregory XIII. Observations
made from this tower contributed to the modification of the calendar (in
October 1582), now called the Gregorian calendar after this Pope. Later
moved to the tower of the villa of Leo XIII (see above: 26), the Observatory
was then transferred by Pius XI to the papal villa at Castel Gandolfo. Queen

Christina of Sweden lived in the Torre dei Venti in 1655. The Library and the Secret Archive are among the most important cultural institutions of the Holy See. The Library, notwithstanding its ancient origins, was officially founded by Nicholas V (1447-1455) and owes its organization to Sixtus IV (1471-1484), who appointed the first librarian. It has a collection of over two million printed books, of which 8,000 *incunabula* (early printed books), 150,000 manuscripts, and a rich collection of prints and drawings. The Secret Archive is responsible for the conservation of important collections of archival documents of the various offices of the Holy See, including (since 1660) the correspondence of the Secretariat of State (the Vatican's foreign ministry). Both Archive and Library are open to scholars of all nations.

Proceeding in the direction of the machicolated building that houses the
Sistine Chapel, on our left is a *building* built *by Paul V* (1605-1621) to connect **34**
the Apostolic Palace with the gardens. At the foot of the building is the
Fountain of the Mirrors, probably built by Martino Ferrabosco for Paul V in **34**
the early 17th century. It is in the form of an elegant pedimented tabernacle with side entrances and two small fountains, one inside and one outside, unfortunately without water. It is magnificently decorated on the inside with blue and gold mosaic, inspired by the mosaics of the fountains of Pompeii.

On the tree-lined square is the monumental *Fountain of the Sacrament* (so **35**
called because its jets of water resemble a monstrance surrounded by six
candles), built on the site of an old entrance to the Vatican. This too is the
work of Jan van Santen (who also designed the Fountain of the Eagle). Two
griffins, emblems of the Borghese family, perch on the crenellated towers,
which flank it (perhaps reflecting the fortified elements of the ancient
entrance). The fountain is right against the rear wall of the *Palazzo della* **36**
Zecca, the mint where the currency of the Papal State was once coined.

Founded by Eugenius IV (1431-1447), the Palazzo della Zecca was reconstructed by Pius VI in the late 18th century. Its opposite side faces *Piazza* **37**
del Forno, so called because the bakery (*forno*) where bread was made until
recently for the inhabitants of the Vatican was situated on the area of the new
building overlooking the piazza. Towering over the piazza is the heavily
fortified building built by Sixtus IV in the second half of the 15th century to
protect St. Peter's and the Apostolic Palace. The middle floor is occupied by
the *Sistine Chapel.* **43**

The series of courtyards in the centre of the oldest section of the Apostolic
Palace can be seen through the *Arch of the Sentinel (Arco della Sentinella)* **38**
at the base of the Sistine Chapel; its appearance as a medieval fortress has
been preserved.

North quarter

From the Piazza del Forno (38), the *Stradone ai Giardini* to the left leads to
the 18th century entrance to the Museums (*Atrium of the Four Gates - Atrio* **48**
dei Quattro Cancelli). On the other side, the Arco della Sentinella leads to the
Cortile della Sentinella, which is at the heart of the oldest section of the
Apostolic Palace.

A brief mention shall be made of an area that is normally excluded from the
tour open to visitors, but that forms an important part of Vatican City State.
This is the area north of the Basilica and papal palaces between the
Belvedere Court, which gives access to the offices and reading rooms of the **49**
Vatican Library and the Vatican Secret Archives, and Via di Porta Angelica
leading to St. Anne's Gate.

All facilities and services needed to run this small State are concentrated in **50**
this area: the *car-park* (a Roman necropolis was discovered during its
construction in 1956), the *Post and Telegraph Office;* the *Tipografia Vaticana* **51-52**
(the official Vatican Printing Office that prints all documents, in particular,

the official documents of the Pope and Holy See, in different languages); the
52 *Libreria Editrice Vaticana* (publisher and distributor of cultural and religious
53, 54 publications); *grocery store, pharmacy, health services, engineering shops*
56, 58 and the *heating plant.*

57 Before reaching St. Anne's Gate (68) note the large tower (*Torrione*) at the foot of the more recent building of the Apostolic Palace, built by Sixtus V at the end of the 16th century and now the papal residence. The tower formed the southeast corner of the fortifications of Nicholas V (1447-1455), and the impressive section to the right of the tower is still very well preserved.

59 Between the *sentry-post of the Vatican police force* and St. Anne's Gate (68)
is Via del Pellegrino (pilgrim's road). This is the last stretch of the road (Via
Francigena), which in ancient times brought pilgrims from the north to St.
60 Peter's. On the east side of the road stands the small *Church of San*
Pellegrino. Despite its Baroque façade, it is one of the oldest buildings in the
Vatican (it dates from the papacy of Leo III (795-816), and served as the
chapel for a pilgrims' hospice. On Via del Pellegrino are the buildings of
61 *L'Osservatore Romano*, the Holy See's daily newspaper with weekly
editions in various languages. Further along the same road are the *living*
62 *quarters of the Vatican Police Force,* the *tapestry restoration workshop* (run
63 by the Franciscan Sisters of the Missionaries of Mary since 1926) and the
64 Vatican Police *refectory.* At the end of Via del Pellegrino stands the *Church*
65 *of Sant'Anna,* begun by Jacopo Barozzi, called il Vignola, in 1572. It is the
parish church of the small State and the crypt contains the small cemetery of
the Vatican City.

66 Facing the Church of Sant'Anna, towards St. Peter's Square, are the
67 *barracks of the Swiss Guards.* Between the church and the barracks is *St.*
Anne's Gate, one of the main entrances to Vatican City, guarded by the Swiss
Guards.

THE APOSTOLIC PALACE

The San Damaso Courtyard. On the left is the Loggia of Bramante and Raphael, at the centre the loggia of the Gregory XIII wing, and on the right the loggia of the papal palace built by Sixtus V.

The Apostolic Palace is the name given to the series of buildings extending from St. Peter's Square to the walls of Paul III and Urban VIII at the north end of the City, where the present entrance to the Vatican Museums is located. The present chapter only describes the buildings overlooking the San Damaso Courtyard.

In the brief history of the Vatican at the beginning of the Guide, mention has already been made of the events that led many popes, from Symmachus to Nicholas III, to establish, fortify and embellish a permanent residence near St. Peter's. The oldest part of the palace is the rectangular building planned by Nicholas III (1277-1280) and partially built by him on the southern and eastern sides (see 7, plan pp. 20-21). Over a period of three centuries the palace grew around a tiny courtyard, the Cortile del Pappagallo.

When Nicholas V became Pope (1447-1455), the courtyard had already been 1
enclosed by buildings on the south side (this wing was extended into the building with the present *Sala Regia),* on the east side, and in part on the north side. Nicholas V succeeded in enclosing it completely on the north and west sides (see 8, plan pp. 20-21), while at the same time respecting its original exterior appearance of an unadorned 13th century towered fortress.-appearance of the exterior. The interior on the other hand, was renovated in the Tuscan Renaissance style. Of all the artists who worked for this Pope, one of the most active was Fra Angelico. Unfortunately, the only surviving
work by this artist in the Vatican is the small *chapel* frescoed with scenes 2
from the lives of St. Stephen and St. Lawrence. The chapel of St. Nicholas, also frescoed by Fra Angelico, was destroyed under Paul III (1534-1549).

Construction work under Nicholas V was resumed with fervour by Sixtus IV (1471-1484). He set aside four rooms on the ground floor of the building on
the north side of the Cortile del Pappagallo to house the Vatican Library, the 3, 4
foundation of which Nicholas V (a great lover of books) had enthusiastically helped to promote. (Later, the upper floors of this wing would be occupied by
the *Borgia Apartment* and by *Raphael's Stanze,* the private apartment of 5
Julius II.) The rooms of the Vatican Library were frescoed by Domenico and Davide Ghirlandaio, Melozzo da Forlì and Antoniazzo Romano. The name of Sixtus IV is above all associated with the *Sistine Chapel* (see 9, plan pp.20-

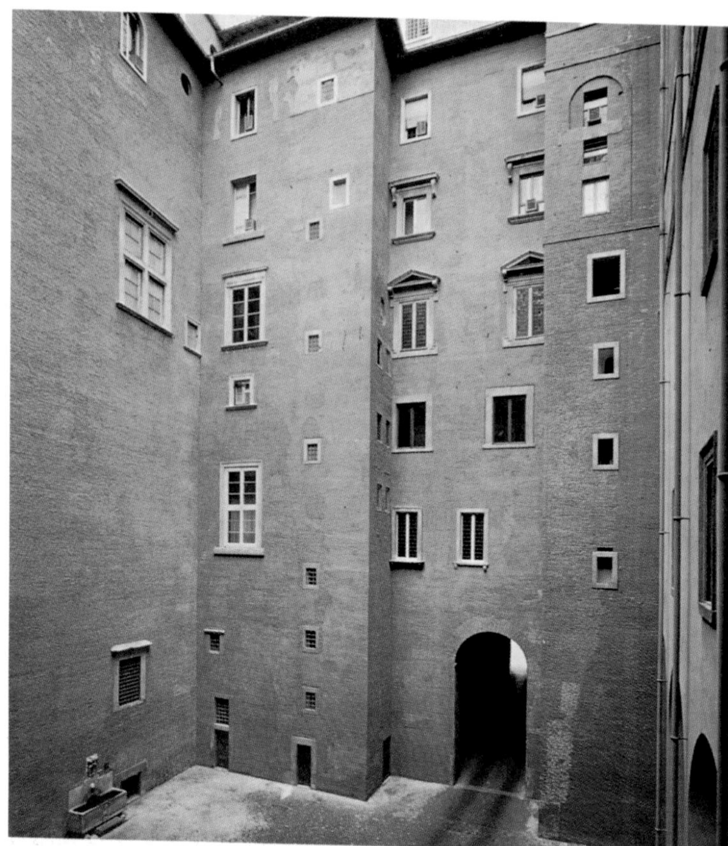

Cortile del Pappagallo (Apostolic Palace)

21), which he built to the west of the *Sala Regia* (1), on the site of an earlier *cappella grande* that formed part of the palace of Nicholas III. Originally the Palatine Chapel, the decoration of the interior was assigned to the most
6 distinguished artists at the time. The Sistine Chapel also served as the third (southwest) corner-tower of the palace planned by Nicholas III.

7 The fourth tower *(Borgia Tower,* see 11, plan pp. 20-21) was built at the northwest corner under Alexander VI Borgia (1492-1503). On the first floor are the first two rooms of the Borgia Apartment (3) and on the second floor is the *Sala dell'Immacolata.*

With the election of Julius II della Rovere (1503-1513), an exceptionally fertile period began both for the buildings of the Vatican and for the history of Christian humanism.

For most of his architectural projects, Julius II employed Donato Bramante, while for painting and sculpture he turned to Michelangelo and Raphael. Bramante planned the huge Belvedere Court (although he only completed part of the east wing — see 12, plan pp. 20-21). He also designed a
8 monumental façade for the east side (overlooking Rome) of the excessively austere papal palace built by Nicholas III. It was divided into three orders of superimposed *loggias.* After Bramante's death, work on the façade was continued by Raphael under Leo X (1513-1521).

No less fruitful, from this point of view, was the pontificate of Paul III (1534-1549). He entrusted Antonio da Sangallo the Younger with the difficult task of reinforcing the foundations of the palace for structural reasons. But Sangallo's major achievement was the almost complete rebuilding of the

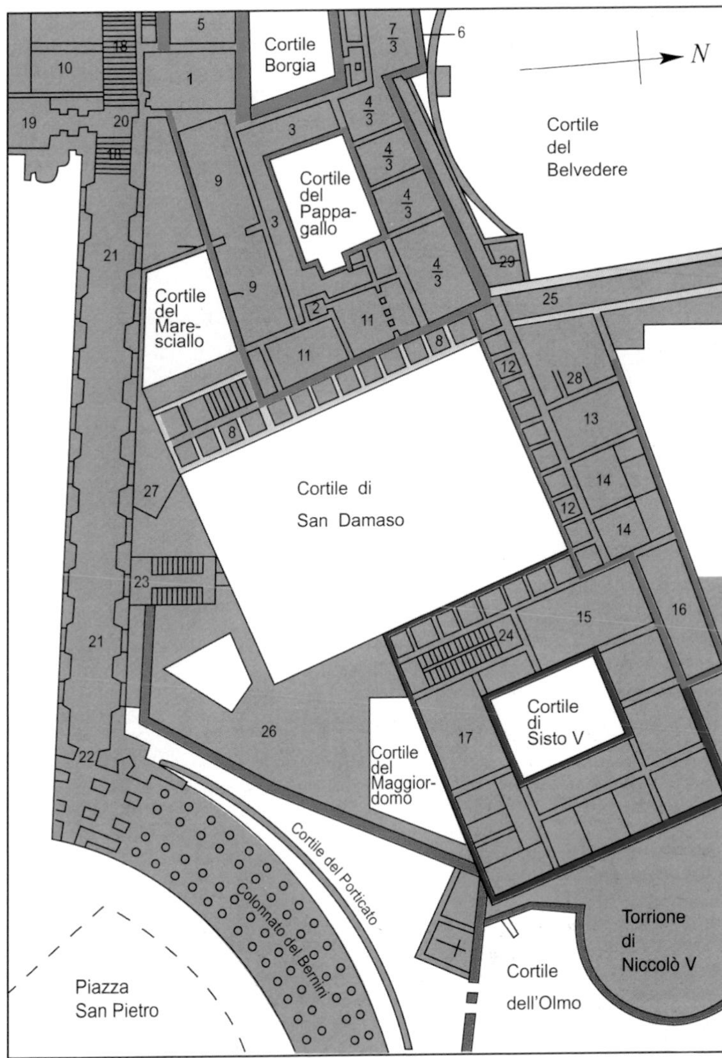

APOSTOLIC PALACE

1 Sala Regia (audience hall)
2 Chapel of Nicholas V
3 Borgia Apartment
4 Raphael's Stanze
5 Sistine Chapel
6 Borgia Tower
7 Sala dell'Immacolata
8 Loggia of Bramante and Raphael
9 Sala Ducale
10 Pauline Chapel
11 Sala dei Paramenti
12 Northern wing with the Loggia of Gregory XIII
13 Redemptoris Mater Chapel
14 Sale dei Foconi
15 Sala Clementina
16 Sala del Concistoro
17 Private library of the Pope
18 Scala Regia (ceremonial staircase)
19 Atrium of St. Peter's
20 Statue of Constantine by Bernini
21 Portico of Constantine by Bernini
22 Bronze Doors, *entrance to the Apostolic Palace*
23 Staircase of Pius IX
24 Audience Staircase

Buildings not mentioned in this chapter

25 Corridor of Bramante (now the Galleria Lapidaria of the Vatican Museums)
26 Wing of Julius III
27 Wing of Paul V
28 Building of Urban VIII
29 Building of Benedict XIV

- Medieval palace
- 16 century: Loggia of Bramante and Raphael (8); Corridor of Bramante (25)
- 16th century: Loggia and Palace of Gregory XIII (12, 13, 14, 16)
- 16th century: Palace of Sixtus V

9 southern wing of the Apostolic Palace, including the *Sala Regia* (1), where
ambassadors were once received, the *Sala Ducale* and the Chapel of St.
Nicholas (or Chapel of the Sacrament), as far as the Cortile del Maresciallo.
10 Unfortunately, the Chapel of the Sacrament with its frescoes by Fra Angelico
was demolished in the process; it was replaced by the *Pauline Chapel,* which
Michelangelo decorated with frescoes of the *Conversion of St. Paul* and the
Crucifixion of St. Peter: his last achievements as a painter (1542-1550).

The successors of Paul III generally limited themselves to completing
11 projects already underway. Between the loggia of Bramante and Raphael
and the Sala Ducale (9) is the *Sala dei Paramenti,* where the Pope dons his
sacred vestments before entering St. Peter's or the Sistine Chapel.

12 During the pontificate of Pius IV (1560-1565), Pirro Ligorio built the first
section of the *northern wing of the loggia* overlooking what was then the
"secret garden", now the San Damaso Courtyard. This work was completed
under Gregory XIII (1572-1585) by Martino Longhi the Elder, who faithfully
copied the structures and façade of the western wing by Bramante and
13, 14 Raphael. Behind the loggia is the apartment of Gregory XIII, with the
Redemptoris Mater Chapel and the *Sale dei Foconi.*

Sixtus V (1585-1590) was the last pope to promote significant building
projects in the Vatican and in Rome. He decided to build new premises for
the Vatican Library and commissioned his architect Domenico Fontana to
build them. The same architect also began the construction of a new papal
palace (what is now the residence of the Pope) overlooking the east side of
15 the Cortile di San Damaso. The building was completed under Clement VIII
(1592-1605) by Taddeo Landini, to whom we owe the splendid *Sala*
16 *Clementina,* decorated by Giovanni and Cherubino Alberti and Paul Bril.
17 This is the first room of the papal ceremonial suite, the so-called *Appartamento Nobile* (behind its rear wall is the *Sala del Concistoro),* an
enfilade of reception rooms laid out along the perimeter of the Cortile di
Sisto V, terminating in the *private library* where the Pope holds private
18 audiences.
19

During the pontificate of Alexander VII (1655-1667), the Apostolic Palace was
embellished by one of Bernini's greatest masterpieces: the *Scala Regia*, a
ceremonial staircase connecting the *Sala Regia* (1) with the *atrium of St.
Peter's.* The lower flight of the staircase is flanked on each side by Ionic
columns supporting a barrel vault. The height, diameter and distance of the
columns from the wall decrease as we ascend. In this way, by a skilful
accentuation of the perspective effect, the artist creates an impression of
monumentality that the available space, irregular in plan and narrowing
20 towards the upper part of the stairs, would not have permitted. No one but
21 Bernini could have devised so ingenious a solution. At the foot of the
22 stairway, on the right as we ascend, is the *statue of Constantine* by Bernini.
At the end of the *Portico of Constantine* (built by Bernini) are the *Bronze
Doors* (*Portone di Bronze*), guarded by the Swiss Guards.

23

On the right, after passing through the Bronze Doors, and ascending the
Staircase of Pius IX, is the Cortile di San Damaso. The courtyard is
surrounded by the building complex, which makes up the Apostolic Palace.
To the left isthe Loggia of Bramante and Raphael (8) is Julius II's
Renaissance façade of the medieval building that constituted the original
nucleus of the Apostolic Palace. The offices of the Holy See's Secretariat of
State are on the floor next to the third loggia. At the centre are the arcades
(12) of the wing built by Pius IV and Gregory XIII. To the right is the wing of
24 the palace built by Domenico Fontana for Sixtus V.

The *Audience Stairway,* which begins from the ground floor of the wing built
by Sixtus V on the Cortile di San Damaso, ascends to the *Appartamento
Nobile* and the Pope's private apartment.

plan →

ST. PETER'S BASILICA

Façade of St. Peter's

The Emperor Constantine began to build a large Basilica on the site of the tomb of St. Peter in 324. It had a nave and four aisles and was preceded by a courtyard with four porticoes (see 3, plan pp. 20-21). But it was only around 349, after the Emperor's death, that the building was completed.

Twelve centuries later, Pope Julius II had Constantine's Old Basilica demolished and replaced with a larger and more imposing building. The foundation stone of the New St. Peter's was laid in the area of the present Pier of St. Veronica on 18 April 1506. The first project for the New Basilica was by Donato Bramante, who designed a central plan based on the Greek cross. At his death in 1514, the four piers and arches, which support the dome, had been built.

Work proceeded under the direction of Giuliano da Sangallo, Raphael (who designed a church in the form of a Latin cross, with one arm longer than the other three) and Antonio da Sangallo the Younger, but progress was slow.

After Antonio da Sangallo's death in 1546, Pope Paul III appointed Michelangelo "commissioner, director of works and architect for life". The seventy-two-year-old artist reverted to Bramante's idea of a central (Greek cross) plan. The first parts to be built were the south apse of the transept, part of the perimeter wall and the drum of the dome.

Pirro Ligorio and Jacopo Barozzi, called il Vignola, succeeded Michelangelo. In 1573 Giacomo Della Porta succeeded Vignola, and it is to him that we owe the two minor domes. In 1585, Della Porta was joined by Domenico Fontana. These two architects successfully completed the dome during the pontificate of Sixtus V, between July 1588 and May 1590. In 1591 Fontana completed the lantern of the dome, and in 1593 the cross was placed on the top approximately 136 m. above ground.

In the meantime, part of the nave and four aisles of the Old Basilica remained standing. In 1602, at the death of Della Porta, Carlo Maderno became Fontana's assistant. Maderno won the competition called by Paul V in 1607 for the construction of the extension of the Basilica's nave after the original Greek-cross plan had been definitively abandoned.

The façade was completed in 1614, and on Palm Sunday of the following year all of the New St. Peter's (see 4, plan pp. 20-21). Pope Urban VIII (1623-1644) commissioned the decoration of the Basilica and solemnly consecrated it on 18 November 1626, 120 years after the beginning of work. Exactly 1300 years had elapsed since the consecration of the first Basilica.

Many important events in the history of the Church have taken place in St. Peter's in recent centuries. The First and Second Vatican Councils were held there, respectively in 1869-1870 and in 1962-1965. Ecumenical Councils are meetings in which the Pope and bishops from all over the world deliberate on important questions concerning the life of the Church. Bishops, nominated by the Pope, head the local churches, or dioceses; there are presently around 2500.

In St. Peter's, apart from presiding over solemn and public religious rites, the Pope performs canonization and beatification ceremonies, in which the Church declares a person entitled to veneration and public devotion for the exceptional Christian virtues demonstrated during his or her lifetime.

Portico

1 The *portico of St. Peter's* by Carlo Maderno measures 71 m. in length, 13 m. in width and 19 m. in height.

An inscription commemorating the inauguration of the Second Vatican Council (11 October 1962) and the coat of arms of Pope John XXIII, who convened it, are located in the centre of the floor.

2 Above the central entrance is the heavily restored *mosaic of the "Navicella* designed by Giotto for the old St. Peter's. It was commissioned on the occasion of the first Jubilee (1300). But the mosaic now visible is essentially a 17th century remake. It represents Jesus and St. Peter on the waters of Lake Tiberias and the boat of the Apostles.

3 The ceiling reliefs represent episodes from the Acts of the Apostles, attributed to St. Luke the Evangelist, which narrates the history of the first years in the life of the Church.

At the left end of the portico, to the left, is an 18th century *equestrian statue of Charlemagne,* the first emperor to be crowned in St. Peter's (on Christmas day in the year 800), sculpted by Agostino Cornacchini in 1725. At the opposite end of the atrium, to the right, is the *equestrian statue of*
3 *Constantine* by Gian Lorenzo Bernini (1670), placed at the foot of the Scala Regia (see 34, plan pp. 20-21), visible behind glass doors.

Five bronze doors lead into the Basilica.

4 In the centre is the 15th century *door of the old St. Peter's* by Antonio Averlino, called Filarete. The reliefs show Christ and the Virgin Mary, St. Peter and St. Paul, their martyrdoms and episodes from the pontificate of Eugenius IV, who commissioned the door, in the minor panels. These include the Council of Ferrara and Florence, convened in 1438 for the reunification of the Eastern and Western Churches. The borders which frame the panels show decorations inspired by Classical antiquity (heads of emperors and illustrious men, mythological scenes). It is the first work in the Renaissance style in Rome, albeit by a Florentine artist. On the inside of the left panel of the door, the sculptor has portrayed himself, being fêted for the completion of his work after his return to his hometown Florence.

5 The *Door of Death (Porta della Morte)* (1964) by Giacomo Manzù has ten panels illustrating the theme of death. On the back of one of the panels Pope John XXIII is shown receiving the bishops on the first day of the Council on 11 October 1962.

6 The next door is called the *Door of Good and Evil (Porta del Bene e del Male).* It was sculpted by Luciano Minguzzi, who donated it to Paul VI. Its twelve panels portray episodes relating to the struggle between good and evil.

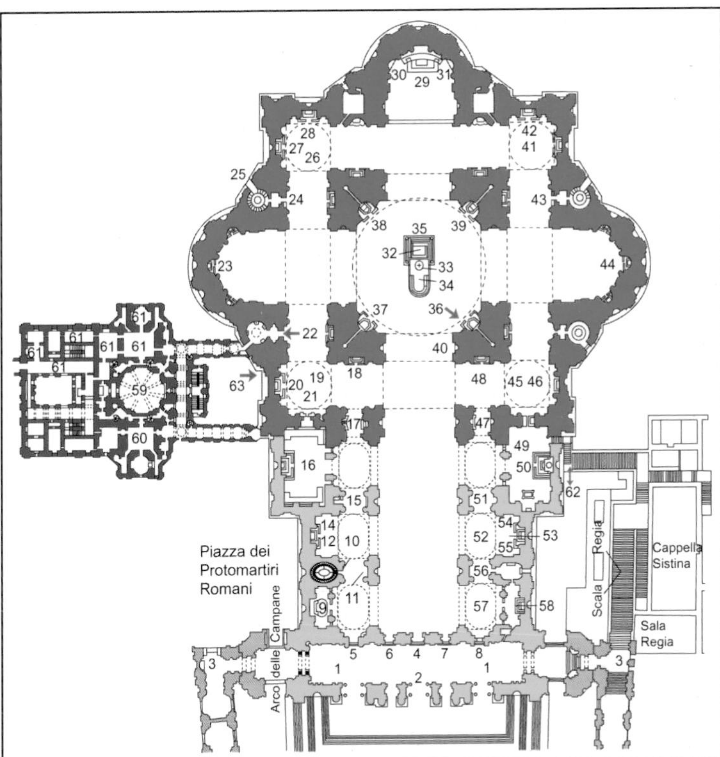

ST. PETER'S BASILICA

1 Portico by Maderno
2 Giotto's mosaic of the "Navicella"
3 Equestrian statues of Charlemagne (left) and Constantine (right)
4 Bronze door by Filarete
5 Door of Death (Porta della Morte)
6 Door of Good and Evil (Porta del Bene e del Male)
7 Door of the Sacraments (Porta dei Sacramenti)
8 Holy Door (Porta Santa)
9 Baptistery Chapel
10 Monument to Maria Clementina Sobieski
11 Monument to the Stuarts
12 Chapel of the Presentation and urn of St. Pius X
13 Monument to Benedict XV
14 Monument to John XXIII
15 Monument to Innocent VIII
16 Chapel of the Choir
17 Monument to Leo XI
18 Altar of the Transfiguration
19 Clementine Chapel (Cappella Clementina)
20 Altar of St. Gregory the Great
21 Monument to Pius VII
22 Monument to Pius VIII and *entrance to the Sacristy and Treasury*
23 Altar of St. Joseph
24 Monument to Alexander VII
25 Porta della Preghiera
26 Chapel of the Madonna of the Column
27 Madonna of the Column
28 Marble relief with Leo I the Great
29 *Cathedra Petri*, by Bernini
30 Monument to Paul III
31 Monument to Urban VIII
32 Papal altar of the Confession
33 Niche of the Palliums
34 Area of the Confession
35 Bernini's Baldachin
36 Pier and statue of St. Longinus and *entrance to the Vatican Grottoes*
37 Pier and statue of St. Andrew
38 Pier and statue of St. Veronica
39 Pier and statue of St. Helen
40 Bronze statue of St. Peter Enthroned
41 Chapel of St. Petronilla and the Archangel Michael
42 Altar of St. Petronilla
43 Monument to Clement XIII
44 Altar of St. Processus and St. Martinianus
45 Gregorian Chapel (Cappella Gregoriana)
46 Fresco of Our Lady of Succour (Madonna del Soccorso)
47 Monument to Gregory XIII
48 Altar of St. Jerome and urn of Pope John XXIII
49 Chapel of the Holy Sacrament
50 Ciborium in the form of a round temple by Bernini, and the *Trinity*, altarpiece by Pietro da Cortona
51 Monument to Matilda of Canossa
52 Dome with mosaic decoration based on cartoons by Pietro da Cortona
53 Chapel of St. Sebastian with tomb of Innocent XI
54 Monument to Pius XII
55 Monument to Pius XI
56 Monument to Queen Christina of Sweden
57 Dome with mosaic decoration based on cartoons by Pietro da Cortona
58 Michelangelo's Pietà
59 Main Sacristy
60 Sacristy of the Canons
61 Treasury
62 *Exit from the Vatican Grottoes and entrance to the dome*
63 *Entrance to the Necropolis*

■ Donato Bramante and Michelangelo Buonarroti
■ Carlo Maderno
■ Gian Lorenzo Bernini
■ Carlo Marchionni

7 On the *Door of the Sacraments (Porta dei Sacramenti)* (1965), Venanzio Crocetti portrays the seven sacraments of the Catholic Church on eight panels. In the upper left corner of the first panel, an angel announces the grace of the sacraments. This door, together with the Door of Death, was made thanks to the bequest of Prince George of Bavaria, canon of St. Peter's, who died in 1942.

8 Last on the right is the *Holy Door (Porta Santa),* which is opened by the Pope once every twenty-five years at the beginning and the end of every Holy Year or Jubilee. The Holy Year is a year dedicated to prayer and conversion; it is an occasion for Catholics throughout the world to meet and share their common faith. To mark the 1950 Jubilee, two bronze panels donated by Swiss Catholics were added to the Holy Door. The sculptor, Vico Consorti, chose episodes from the Bible that allude to sin, forgiveness (the central theme of the Holy Year) and redemption for 15 of the 16 panels. In the bottom right of the last panel is the scene of Pius XII opening the Holy Door on Christmas Day 1949.

Interior

St. Peter's has the form of a Latin cross, i.e. it has a longitudinal arm (the nave) longer than the two transversal arms (the transept), and a fourth arm (the apse), which is the prolongation of the first. The longitudinal arm consists of a nave and two aisles. Around the octagonal space of the crossing are four immense piers (36-39) that support the dome. The papal altar (32) beneath Bernini's monumental Baldachin (35) is situated at the centre of the crossing.

The Second Vatican Council was held in the nave from 1962-1965. On this occasion, special stalls were built to seat the participating bishops at various levels on both sides.

The first impression one has on entering St. Peter's is one of vastness. It is in fact the world's largest church. The lengths of fifteen of the largest Catholic and non-Catholic churches in the world are recorded in bronze letters set into the floor along the axis of the nave. None are as long as St. Peter's, which (including the walls) has a length of 192.76 m. The total width of the nave and two aisles is 58 m.

The barrel vault with high-relief stuccowork is 44.5 m. high. There are female statues (17th cent.) in white stucco representing the Christian virtues between the capitals and above the arches. The words of Jesus that according to Catholic doctrine, gave Peter and his successors the primacy as bishops of Rome appear in mosaic in Latin and Greek in the frieze of the entablature. The Gospel verses, "You are Peter and on this rock I will build my church, and the powers of death shall not prevail against it. I will give you the keys of the kingdom of heaven, and whatever you bind on earth shall be bound in heaven, and whatever you loose on earth shall be loosed in heaven" (*Mt* 16:18-19), are inscribed in Latin in the frieze at the base of the dome.

Proceeding down the nave, the lateral aisles reveal the most important decorative elements of the Basilica: the altars, the monuments of the popes, the statues of the founders of religious Orders, and the preponderant use of mosaics in the decoration (even the paintings and frescoes above the altars that were beinning to deteriorate were replaced with mosaic copies from the first half of the 18th century). Since 1727, execution and maintenance of the mosaics has been entrusted to the Mosaic Workshop, founded to complete the decoration of St. Peter's and still active in the Vatican today. Thirty-nine niches were hewn out of the pillars of the nave, transepts and apse. They contain statues of the saints – male and female - who founded religious Orders (the Catholic clergy is not only made up of secular priests included in dioceses headed by bishops, but also of monks and nuns who, by taking the three vows of poverty, chastity and obedience, become members of orders or congregations that strive for Christian perfection). Most of the statues date from the 18th or 19th century, but there are also a few from the

St. Peter's Basilica, view of the nave from the entrance.

20th century. Many merit attention, although none of them are masterpieces. With the exception of a famous bronze statue of St. Peter (40), there are no statues of popes in the nave, but there are 56 marble medallions with head portraits set into the pilasters. Other images in the aisles commemorate the popes: they are not tomb statues but monuments that have preserved the memory of the popes since the 17th century. The altars of the two second chapels (12 and 52) in the side aisles contain the mortal remains of two popes raised to the honours of the altar by the Catholic Church: St. Pius X (1903-1914) and the Blessed Pope Innocent XI (1678-1689). But most of the tombs of the 147 popes and other important figures buried in St. Peter's are in the Vatican Grottoes beneath St. Peter's. (see p. 224).

The oldest monuments, dating from the ostentatious Baroque period, emphasize the pomp and glory of the Roman pontificate, and usually show the Pope enthroned and dressed in papal vestments and tiara in the act of blessing the faithful. Often the central statue of the Pope is flanked or accompanied by female figures personifying the virtues for which the Pope was particularly noted. The more recent monuments shift the emphasis by expressing the piety of the popes: the figure of the pope is often isolated in the act of praying. An exception is the monument to Pope John XXIII (14), a composition in which the Pope is just one of many figures, albeit the principal one.

These general points should be kept in mind when visiting the Basilica. Attention will be focused on the most artistically significant papal monuments.

Left Aisle

The visit begins from the first chapel in the left aisle, the *Baptistery* or *Chapel of Baptism.* 9
The decoration's predominant iconographic subject is the administration of the Sacrament of Baptism, because, after the removal of St. Peter's throne from this chapel to Bernini's monument in the apse of the Tribune, Pope Innocent XII (1691-1700) had the baptismal font put here. Situated in the centre of the chapel, the font was commissioned from Carlo Fontana in 1692, concluding a competition in which over twenty of the best-known artists of the day had participated. Fontana used an existing precious red porphyry basin measuring 4x2 m. of pagan origin, which was thought to have come from the tomb of the emperor Hadrian (Castel Sant'Angelo), but which had later been used as the lid of the sarcophagus of the emperor Otto

II, who died in Rome in 988 and was buried in the Old Basilica. Closed by a gilt bronze cover, designed by Fontana himself and produced by Giovanni Giardini, the font is surmounted by Lorenzo Ottoni's *Agnus Dei* , symbol of the Risen Christ.

Immediately following the Baptistery Chapel is the 18th-century *monument*
10 *to Maria Clementina Sobieski* (1702-1735) by the sculptors Filippo Barigioni and Pietro Bracci. Niece of John III, King of Poland, and wife of James III Stuart, pretender to the throne of England, she died in Rome in 1735.

11 Opposite is the *monument to the Stuart family,* the Royal Family of Scotland exiled in Rome from 1689. Sculpted by Antonio Canova, it was designed in 1827 in imitation of a funerary stele in the form of a truncated pyramid and inaugurated in the spring of 1819. It is dedicated to James III (1688-1766), the 'Old Pretender' and husband of Maria Clementina Sobieski, and their two sons Charles Edward (1720-1788), Count of Albany, and Cardinal Henry Benedict (1725-1807), 9th duke of York and Bishop of Frascati. Both are portrayed in profile on the stele.

12 The second chapel is called the *Chapel of the Presentation.* On its left side
13 is the *monument to Benedict XV,* sculpted by Pietro Canonica and
14 inaugurated in 1928. On its right side is the *monument to the Blessed John XXIII* by Emilio Greco, in the form of a large bronze relief representing the Pope together with the suffering and the ill, while the mitres and figures of bishops silhouetted against the background recall the Second Vatican Council. At the centre, below the altar, lies the body of St. Pius X.

15 Against the second pillar, following the Chapel of the Presentation, is the bronze *monument to Innocent VIII* (1484-1492), the earliest and smallest papal monument in the Basilica. A magnificent Renaissance work by the Florentine Antonio Pollaiolo, it was commissioned by Cardinal Lorenzo Cybo, the pope's nephew, and is the only papal monument salvaged from the Old Basilica and reinstalled, complete in all its parts, in the New St. Peter's. Completed in 1498, it was recomposed here in 1621. The figure of the pope is reproduced twice in a single monument: the first, symbolising his imperial majesty, shows him enthroned, holding the relic of the lance that pierced Christ's side, donated to Innocent VIII by Sultan Bayazid II in 1492, while the second shows death, which is the fate of all men.

16 The third chapel in the left aisle is the 17th century *Chapel of the Choir.* Enclosed by a magnificent bronze and iron gate, the large chapel has a rectangular floor plan and is symmetrical with the Chapel of the Holy Sacrament opposite in the right aisle. It is mainly used for the choral liturgy of the Basilica's clergy, who have prayed here without interruption since the 5th century. At first they were monks, then, after the turn of the first millennium, canons. The chapel is built around four large arches, each flanked by pairs of Corinthian pilasters, surmounted by a broken curvilinear tympanum. The chapel was completed by Urban VIII, who commissioned work for the presbytery and called on the French painter Simone Vouet (1590-1649) to execute the altarpiece, where the image of St. John Chrysostom appears for the first time. The new presence was linked to the consecration of the new altar on 22 July 1626. During the ceremony, Cardinal Scipione Borghese placed the relics of the saint that had been brought to Rome from Constantinople in the Middle Ages under the altar in a black and white granite sarcophagus of the 2nd century.

17 Beyond the Chapel of the Choir, is the magnificent *marble monument to Leo XI Medici* by Alessandro Algardi (1634-1644). It was commissioned by Cardinal Roberto Ubaldini, the pope's nephew, on 21 July 1634 and unveiled to the public on 23 June 1652. Remarkable for its sobriety and composure, the monument is carved entirely in white marble. Although Algardi's choice of marble and the poise of his figures contrast Bernini's chromatic effects and dramatic style, he nonetheless adopted the essential scheme of Bernini's monument of Urban VIII, unfinished at the time. At the top of the monument is the figure of the Pope, sculpted by Algardi himself. The allegorical female figures to the sides were sculpted by his two assistants: on the left, *Magnanimity,* by Ercole Ferrata; on the right, *Liberality,* by Giuseppe Peroni.

Transept

At the foot of the left aisle, marking the point where Michelangelo's
ambulatory ends, is the *Altar of the Transfiguration*, hewn into the rear face 18
of the huge pier of St. Andrew (one of the four piers supporting the dome). The
name of the altar derives from the huge altarpiece of the *Transfiguration*,
translated into mosaic (175-1767) from the original by Raphael Sanzio (now in
the Vatican Pinacoteca). Structured like a medieval work, the altarpiece
superimposes, on two levels, two episodes narrated in succession in the
gospels of Mark and Matthew: the Transfiguration of Christ on Mount Tabor
(*Mk* 9:2-8; *Mt* 17:1-8) and the healing of the youth possessed by the devil (*Mk*
9:14-29; *Mt* 17:14-18). The original painting by Raphael, considered his artistic
testament, had an extraordinary fate. On the painter's death, the painting on
canvas hung over his bed: "the sight of that living picture, in contrast with the
dead body, caused the hearts of all who beheld it to burst with sorrow", says
Vasari.

To the left of this altar is the *Clementine Chapel,* named in honour of Clement 19
VIII Aldobrandini, the Pope who promoted its construction. Due to its size and
lavish decoration, it has been compared with its counterpart in the right
transept, the Gregorian Chapel. The original design of the chapel goes back
to Michelangelo, but work on its construction only began fourteen years after
his death, in 1578, and was concluded by Giacomo Della Porta in 1580.
Though its decoration remained unfinished, the chapel was admired by all
those who thronged to St. Peter's for the jubilee in 1600. The commission for
the mosaic decoration was entrusted to the Tuscan, Cristoforo Roncalli,
called Il Pomarancio; the pendentives, dome and lunettes were completed in
1603. The chapel's *altar of St. Gregory the Great* was consecrated in 1628. The 20
mortal remains of this canonized late-6th century pope are preserved in a
white marble Roman sarcophagus below the altar (placed here on 8 January
1606); his image is also shown in one of the pendentives of the Gregorian
Chapel. On the left wall of the chapel is the *monument to Pius VII* (1800-1823), 21
by the Danish sculptor Bertel Thorvaldsen (1823-1831). The decision to
entrust so prestigious a commission to a foreign artist, and a Protestant to
boot, caused a good deal of malcontent. The work of preparing the monument
was prolonged from 1824 to 1830; it was inaugurated on 2 April 1831.

On the chapel's other wall is the *entrance to the Sacristy and the Treasury of* 22
St Peter's (see p. 218). Above the door is the *monument to Pius VIII* (1857),
sculpted by Pietro Tenerani and inaugurated in 1866.

Through the large archway is the area of the apse of the left transept, which
is divided by three altars set in large niches. At its centre is the *altar of St.* 23
Joseph. The more prominent altar is flanked by two monolithic columns in
giallo antico, similar to those on the opposite side; the hemispherical niche of
the apse is decorated with stuccoes showing *Episodes from the life of St.*
Peter (1597-1599).

Just beyond the left transept, above a side door leading to Vatican City State,
is the *monument to Alexander VII Chigi* (1655-1667), by Gian Lorenzo Bernini 24
(1671-1678). Commissioned by the Pope himself during the first years of his
pontificate, the work had not yet been started by the time he died on 22 May
1667. After the site for the monument had been identified, it was first
necessary to remove a fresco of Giovan Francesco Romanelli and move the
already existing door forward. Bernini brilliantly solved the problem of this
door by transforming it into a symbolic entrance to the afterlife, thanks to the
theatrical expedient of the billowing marble drapery placed over the door,
raised by a skeleton brandishing an hourglass. Gian Lorenzo Bernini
prepared the design, supervised the sculptors who translated his preparatory
drawings into marble and probably intervened himself only to give the final
touches to the face of the kneeling pope. A bronze door called the Prayer Door 25
(Porta della Preghiera), by Lello Scorzelli (1972), adorned the exit of the
Basilica below the monument.

The next chapel we come to, just beyond the monument to Alexander VII is the 26
so-called *Chapel of the Madonna of the Column,* a name derived from a 15th
century image of the Virgin painted on a column shaft retrieved from the nave
of the Constantinian Basilica. Building began when Vignola held the post of 27

architect of St. Peter's (1567-1573), but the chapel was built under the direction of Giacomo Della Porta (1574-1602). The dome was the last of the four corner domes to be decorated. Placed below the chapel's altar is a 4th century *Christian sarcophagus* with figures of Christ and the Apostles; it contains the mortal remains of the canonized Popes Leo II, III, and IV, gathered together by Pope Paschal II (1099-1118). The altar of St. Leo the Great is located between two columns of oriental black granite. His remains are preserved here and he was the first to be inhumed inside the old St. Peter's. Over the altar, which may be considered a funerary monument, is the
28 large *marble altarpiece* by Alessandro Algardi (1653), portraying the historical episode of the meeting between Leo the Great (440-461) and Attila, King of the Huns.

The tribune of the apse, contains Bernini's monumental *Throne of St. Peter in*
29 *Glory* (*Cathedra Petri*), set between two columns of African marble salvaged from the Constantinian Basilica. The oak throne, decorated with ivory plaques carved with scenes of the *Labours of Hercules* is protected by a massive bronze structure. According to tradition, the Apostle Peter sat on this throne while preaching. But the archaeologist Giovan Battista De Rossi, who examined the relic, concluded that only the acacia wood frame dated back to the early centuries of the Church, whereas the parts in oak, and the ivory reliefs belonged to a renovation of the chair in the Carolingian period. On 6 February 1656 Alexander VII authorised the project for the new altar presented by Gian Lorenzo Bernini. The ancient *throne* is contained within another massive bronze-and-gold throne, 7 metres high, its backrest and two sides decorated with bas-reliefs designed by Bernini. The throne seems to float in the air and is flanked below by bronze statues representing the *Doctors of the Greek and Latin Church*. The four enormous figures, 5.35 m. high, with gilt vestments, their faces and hands the colour of bronze, are: in front, to the left *St. Ambrose* and to the right *St. Augustine*, representing the Latin Church; behind them, to the left *St. Athanasius*, and to the right *St. John Chrysostom*, representing the Greek Church. Above the bronze throne, Bernini made use of natural light from the central window of the apse and made it the focal point of a swirling glory of angels and putti, who, amid billowing clouds and glittering rays, fly round the oval stained-glass window with the *Dove of the Holy Spirit*. A typical example of Baroque decoration, the monument expresses a noble theological concept: the Churches of East and West, united in the faith of the Catholic Church, pay homage to the *cathedra* of Rome.

30 To the left of the *Cathedra Petri* is the *monument to Paul III Farnese* (1534-1549), the first papal tomb to be erected in the new Basilica, the work of
31 Guglielmo Della Porta (1549-1577) . To the right is the *monument to Urban VIII by* Gian Lorenzo Bernini. Commissioned (and its site chosen) by the Barberini Pope himself in 1627, it was only completed on 9 February 1647, three years after his death. The vitality of the monument is heightened by the soft beauty of the two female allegories in white marble, symbolising *Justice* (to the right) and *Charity*, by the fleshy putti, and by the imposing majesty of the bronze statue of the Pope.

34 Below the dome of St. Peter's is the *Altar of the Confession*, the site marking the tomb of St. Peter. The Latin term *confessio* means the affirmation of a truth to the point of martyrdom: when a martyr sheds his own blood for Christ he confesses him and proclaims his own faith by a supreme act of self-sacrifice. So the shrine raised over the tomb of a martyr or confessor is called a *confessio*: the archetypcal *confessio* is the one over the tomb of the First of the Apostles in St. Peter's. A double ramp of 16 marble steps leads down to the horseshoe-shaped *Confession*. Its walls and floor are lavishly panelled in polychrome marble, the most important work of this kind of marble inlay in 17th century Rome. In 1615 Paul V commissioned Carlo Maderno, the architect of St. Peter's to design it and work was completed in 1618. It is lit by 89 perennially burning oil-lamps inserted in elegant bronze cornucopias, designed by Mattia de' Rossi. A small apse hewn into the end wall of the exedra is decorated with a 9th century mosaic of the *Blessing Christ*.

The small exedra is enclosed by an elegant wrought-iron gate designed by Nicolas Cordier and Onorio Fanelli and decorated with two brass statues of

St. Peter and St. Paul, executed by Ambrogio Buonvicino between 1616 and
1618, and fused and gilded by Biagio de Giusti. The niche in the small
recessed sanctuary behind it (built over the site of St Peter's tomb) is called
of the Palliums because the palliums are kept there in a bronze urn donated **33**
by Benedict XIV. Palliums are Y-shaped stoles of lambswool (4-6 cm wide)
adorned with six crosses of black silk. They are made from the wool of two
white lambs blessed on 21 January in the Basilica of Sant'Agnese in Via
Nomentana. Blessed by the Pope on 29 June, Feast of Saints Peter and Paul,
they are a liturgical insignia of honour and the distinguishing mark of
metropolitan archbishops.

Above the Confession, the *Papal Altar* rises on 7 steps in Greek Hymettian
marble, set over two earlier altars built respectively by Gregory the Great and **32**
Calixtus II. It is not at the centre of the dome but displaced towards the apse.
Turned to the east, as was the practice in Early Christian basilicas, this altar
is exclusively reserved for the use of the pope or the person delegated by him.
It was built by Clement VIII in 1594 to complete the already finished part of the
new Basilica with a permanent altar. The top of the altar is formed of an
architrave in Parian marble 4.35 m long and 2 m broad. Its four sides, noble
and austere, are panelled in *pavonazzetto* marble, as are all the mouldings;
the altar is divided into three panels on the two main sides, and interspersed
with tapering pilasters on the two shorter sides; the upper part is decorated
with eight-pointed stars in gilt metal, the heraldic device of Clement VIII. The
pope consecrated the new altar on Sunday, 26 June 1594 and celebrated the
first mass here three days later, on the occasion of the Feast of Saints Peter
and Paul.

Before Bernini's Baldachin, Paul V had placed a wooden processional
baldachin over the papal altar. It was a temporary solution, hardly in keeping
with the grandeur of the Basilica. From the moment he was elected in 1623,
Urban VIII took the problem to heart, and on 12 July of the following year he
commissioned Bernini to design a grandiose ciborium. The Pope's con-
fidence in the artist was repaid by the creation of the most important structure
in bronze of Roman Baroque sculpture, which, in spite of its inventive design
and massive size – it is over 28 m. high – blends harmoniously into the
vastness of this enormous church. Far from diminishing the impression of
depth of the Basilica, the Baldachin increases it by making the apse framed **35**
by its columns seem even more remote. On 29 June 1627, Feast of Saints
Peter and Paul, three years to the day after the approval of the project, the
mighty bronze corkscrew columns were unveiled to the public. The inauguration of the completed Baldachin took place six years later on 29 June
1633.

Work on the structure and decoration of the four massive *splayed piers* that support the dome – built by Donato Bramante and completed by Michelangelo – was completed by Gian Lorenzo Bernini on commission from Urban VIII between January 1628 and 1639. The four piers were designed to contain and give testimony of St. Peter's most important relics. The existing four large niches hewn into the inner faces of the four pillars, 45 m. high with a total perimeter of 71 m., were used by Bernini to display four colossal statues in Carrara marble. The 4.50-5 m. high statues are all characterized by their theatrical pose and are the visual celebration of the relics preserved in the Basilica.

Facing the apse in the pier at the head of the right aisle is the *statue of St.* **36**
Longinus by Bernini (under its pedestal is the entrance to the Vatican
Grottoes, see p. 224). The other statues, clockwise, are: *St. Andrew* (by
François Duquesnoy, 1640), *St. Veronica* (by Francesco Mochi, 1640) and *St.* **37-39**
Helena (by Andrea Bolgi, 1640). The relics with which these statues are
associated are: the point of the lance with which the centurion Longinus
pierced the side of Jesus (he later converted to Christianity); the head of the
Apostle St. Andrew, brother of St. Peter (donated in 1966 to the Orthodox
diocese of Patras, where the saint died, as a sign of peace and to promote
Christian unity); the veil with which Veronica dried the face of Christ on his
ascent to Golgotha; and a fragment of the Cross found by St. Helena, mother
of the emperor Constantine.

Michelangelo: *Pietà*

The great dome rises above the "Confession" (*c.*116 m. over the crossing). It is one of Michelangelo's most important contributions to the Basilica. Unfinished at his death in 1564, when only the cylindrical drum had been completed, work was terminated by Giacomo Della Porta in 1590 during the pontificate of Sixtus V. Its mosaic decoration was begun in the final years of the 16th century with the huge mosaic medallions of the four Evangelists set into the *pendentives*. They are the work of Giovanni de' Vecchi, Cesare Nebbia and Cristoforo Roncalli (Pomarancio). Once the pendentives had been completed, Clement VIII preferred Giuseppe Cesari, called the Cavalier d'Arpino, to Cristoforo Roncalli to continue the internal decoration of the dome itself in 1603. The entire surface is divided into 16 ribs converging onto the lantern. The tapering panels between them are divided into 6 parts, with 96 figures enclosed in trapezoidal and circular panels. God the Father, surrounded by eight heads of angels, appears in the luminous oculus of the lantern. A choir of angels is arranged in three concentric circles, from top to bottom. At the base of the dome are images of the canonized popes buried in the Basilica; above are Jesus and the Virgin Mary, St. John the Baptist, St. Paul and the 12 Apostles. In the lunettes at the base of the dome are busts of Patriarchs and Bishops. The upper ring of the dome is surrounded by 32 gold stars against an azure blue field while an inscription in honour of Sixtus V is set into its inner perimeter: S. PETRI GLORIAE SIXTUS PP. V A. MDXC PONTIF. V (To the glory of St. Peter, Pope Sixtus V, in the year 1590, the fifth of his pontificate); it was installed by Clement VIII in memory of his predecessor and promoter of the grandiose project to decorate the interior of the dome. The dome is topped by an 18-meter-high lantern, enclosed by a miniature dome decorated in mosaic with the figure of *God the Father in Glory*, executed by Ranuccio Semprevivo in 1603-1604.

40 At the end of the nave, set against the pier of St. Longinus, is the *bronze statue of St. Peter Enthroned*. It stands on a pedestal embellished with precious

marble panelling and gilt metal. Seated on a marble throne, St. Peter is dressed in a philosopher's cloak (pallium). His left hand holding the keys lies over his breast, his right hand raised in the gesture of blessing. His right foot projecting beyond the pedestal has been worn smooth by the devotion of the faithful. Art historians are almost unanimous in attributing the bronze statue to the circle of Arnolfo di Cambio (13th century). Above the statue is a mosaic medallion portraying Pius IX (1846-1878). On 16 June 1871 the Pope celebrated the 25th anniversary of his pontificate, the first pope in history to succeed in this legendary goal. Up until then only the Apostle Peter had guided the Church for as long and, according to a well-consolidated tradition, no one else would have been permitted to reign for more than a quarter of a century.

Behind the pier of St. Helena (to the right towards the apse) is the *Chapel of St. Petronilla and the Archangel Michael,* one of the four chapels designed by Michelangelo, and the only one in which he supervised the laying of the foundation. All of the chapel's mosaic decoration is dominated by the theme of angels. The dome - the only one to alternate parts in mosaic with figures in stucco - was executed by Lorenzo Ottoni in 1725 and is covered with an *Angelic Glory* including symbolic elements, angels and seraphim. The mosaics in the lunettes describe episodes linked to the angels and the life of St. Petronilla. The mosaic above the *altar of St. Petronilla* is attributed to Pier Paolo Cristofari, Filippo Cocchi and Giuseppe Ottaviani (1728-1730). It is a faithful copy of Guercino's painting of the *Burial and Glory of St. Petronilla*, now in the Pinacoteca Capitolina in Rome. 41 42

Proceeding towards the right arm of the transept, to the left is the *monument to Clement XIII Rezzonico* (1758-1769), by Antonio Canova (1783-1792), his first work for St. Peter's. It was commissioned by Prince Abbondio Rezzonico, the pope's nephew and one of the first Roman patrons of Canova. The monument was begun in 1783 and inaugurated on 6 April 1792 during the pontificate of Pius VI. It introduced the neoclassical style to St. Peter's. Remarkable for the purity of its surfaces and the simplicity of its compositional lines, it contrasts with previous Baroque monuments in which polychrome marble was combined with bronze. The group of sculptures is uniformly carved from white Carrara marble, with the exception of the bases in *lumachello* and the two lions in travertine. It presents a dual narrative arrangement: horizontal, with the two flanking lions below, and the allegorical figures of *Charity* and *Hope* at the sides of the bas-relief on the sarcophagus frontal; and diagonal, where the position of the seated *Genius of Death* is linked with the standing figure of *Religion*. The whole composition culminates in the portrait of the kneeling pope, his face realistically portrayed. 43

The First Vatican Council took place in the right arm of the transept in 1869-1870 (the Second Vatican Council was held in the nave). It defined the dogma of papal infallibility, according to which the pope as Head of the Church cannot err when he declares truths contained in divine Revelation, or in close connection. The *central altar* of the right transept is dedicated to *St. Processus and St. Martinianus*. Their relics were transferred to the Old Basilica by Paschal I (1817-824), after they were removed from the catacombs of Sant'Agata in Via Aurelia. According to tradition, Processus and Martinianus were Roman soldiers who had been the prison guards of St. Peter in the Mamertine prison. Converted and baptized by the Apostle, they are portrayed here suffering martyrdom in the presence of their parents, at the moment when an angel from heaven brings the palm of victory. The original canvas, of which the mosaic altarpiece is a faithful copy, is the work of Jean de Boulogne called Valentin de Boulogne (1591-1632), a French follower of Caravaggio. 44

The *Gregorian Chapel*, dedicated to Our Lady of Succour (*Madonna del Soccorso*), was decorated from 1578 to 1580 during the pontificate of Gregory XIII, the Pope to whom it is dedicated. It was the first chapel in the Basilica in which both the architecture and decoration were completed. Begun by Michelangelo in 1561and continued by Vignola from 1567 to 1573, the year of his death, its structure was completed under the direction of Giacomo Della Porta and consecrated still undecorated in February 1578. The Pope also 45

commissioned Giacomo Della Porta to decorate the chapel. He was one of the most gifted artists of the time in the use of polychrome marble and executed all the marble inlay work commissioned for the Basilica till the end of the 16
46 century. Over the altar is the *Madonna del Soccorso*, a much-venerated image of Our Lady that according to tradition dates to the time of Paschal II (1099-118). This is the first of the seven privileged altars of St. Peters: altars to which the popes have granted special privileges and from which particular indulgences are dispensed.

Right Aisle

47 To the left of the Gregorian Chapel is the *monument to Gregory XIII Boncompagni* (1572-1585) by the sculptor Camillo Rusconi, executed between 1715 and 1723. The benedicting Pope is seated on a sarcophagus, flanked on the one side by *Religion* and on the other by *Magnificence* who, in the guise of Minerva, is lifting a heavy drape to reveal the relief portraying the event that made him famous: the reform of the calendar (October 1582), called "Gregorian" after this Pope. The two statues are by Camillo Rusconi; the bas-relief is by Carlo Francesco Melloni.

48 To the right, the altar of St. Jerome contains the urn of Pope John XXIII, whose body was translated here (June 2001) from the Vatican Grottoes following his beatification (September 2000). The altar contains the urn, protected by a bronze grille covered with gold leaf.

Proceed towards the entrance wall and the right aisle, leaving behind the structures of the central-plan temple originally conceived by Bramante. Most of it was planned and executed later by Michelangelo. From here, return to the extension (nave and aisles) built by Carlo Maderno.

49 The first chapel is the *Chapel of the Holy Sacrament* (to the left) in a solemn and sumptuous style. It has an elegant Baroque wrought-iron entry gate with bronze ornaments and the coat of arms of Urban VIII. Designed by Francesco Borromini between 1629 and 1630, it initially served as the sacristy. The chapel's function changed in 1638 when it was dedicated to the Eucharist. The interior is richly decorated with gilt stuccoes of the Eucharist executed by Giovan Battista Ricci from 1623 to 1627. On the central altar is the gilt bronze
50 *Ciborium in the form of a round temple* by Bernini, commissioned by Urban VIII in 1629, but only completed under Clement X fifty years later. In this work, enlivened by the contrast between gold and silver and the dark blue of lapis lazuli, the artist produced a harmonious piece of monumental goldsmith's work, inspired by architectural models of the previous century (Bramante's tempietto of San Pietro in Montorio, St. Peter's Dome, Jacopo Sansovino's
50 altar in the Basilica of Santa Croce in Jerusalem). But he reveals his Baroque spirit in the decoration of its upper part with statuettes of the 12 Apostles and the Saviour rising over the lantern of the small dome. To the sides are two large angels in gilt bronze kneeling in adoration that carry a motif dear to Bernini ever since the beginning of his career. Behind the altar is the huge
50 altarpiece of the *Trinity* painted by Pietro da Cortona (1628-1631). The typically Baroque composition, dynamic and animated by many figures but harmoniously composed, became an iconographic model much admired in its time and often imitated in the following century. It is the only altarpiece in the entire Basilica not in mosaic.

51 Set in an arch at the foot of the pillar opposite the chapel is the *monument to Countess Matilda of Canossa* (1046-1115) by Gian Lorenzo Bernini. The work was commissioned by Urban VIII in late 1633. The Pope was inspired by a special veneration for the memory of Matilda and, in the years preceding his election, had poetically glorified the heroic warrior countess in a literary work. The desire to honour her with a worthy burial in St. Peter's resulted in the transfer of Matilda's mortal remains from the Monastery of San Benedetto Po, near Mantua, to Rome. In late winter of 1644 they were taken from Castel Sant'Angelo to the finished monument made to contain them in the Basilica. One of the most powerful women of the Middle Ages and benefactress of the Holy See, her fame was thus perpetuated in the greatest temple of Christianity. Her image sculpted in marble inaugurated the series of burials dedicated to women in St. Peter's, which would later include Queen Christina of Sweden and Maria Clementina Sobieski.

The mosaic decoration of the next bay forming the vestibule to the *Chapel of St. Sebastian* was executed between 1654 and 1663, based on cartoons by Pietro da Cortona, who designed the martyrs of the Old Testament seen in the pendentives and lunettes. The main iconographic theme is the winning of redemption through martyrdom. The *dome* is decorated with the scene of *God the Father enthroned in glory over the divine Lamb adored by the martyrs bearing the palms of martyrdom.* In the pendentives are Abel and three martyr prophets (Isaiah, Zechariah and Ezekiel); and in the lunettes, six martyrdoms narrated in the Bible: the seven Maccabees and their mother, Mattatias and the apostate, Daniel and the lions, the three youths in the fiery furnace, Eleazar led to the place of execution, and the Hebrew women thrown down from the walls of Jerusalem. **52**

The altarpiece in the chapel is the *Martyrdom of St. Sebastian*, a Roman martyr venerated in the Old Basilica since the 9th century. It is a mosaic copy of the previous original fresco and oil painting, commissioned from Domenico Zampieri, called Domenichino, in March 1625, and transferred in 1730 to the Church of Santa Maria degli Angeli where it has remained ever since. The altar is flanked by two marble columns salvaged from the Old Basilica, similar to those in the opposite chapel. Below the altar are the mortal remains of the Blessed Innocent XI, brought here after his beatification on 7 October 1965. On the side walls are (to the left) the *monument to Pius XII,* by Francesco Messina and (to the right) the *monument to Pius XI,* by Francesco Nagni. **53** **54, 55**

Immediately after the chapel, to the right set against the pillar is the *monument to Queen Christina of Sweden* (1691-1702). In 1691, two years after the queen's death, Innocent XII asked Carlo Fontana to design a monument similar to the one of Countess Matilda executed by Bernini. Fontana designed the work, but entrusted its execution to the French sculptor Jean-Baptiste Théodon. The monument was unveiled to the public in 1702. The Swedish queen (who abdicated her throne) is buried in the Vatican Grottoes. **56**

The dome of the next bay is decorated with *mosaics* by Fabio Cristofari, based on cartoons by Pietro da Cortona and his school. In the dome itself is an apocalyptic scene showing the Chosen saved from punishment; in the pendentives are Abraham, Isaac, Moses and Jeremiah; and in the lunettes, the Cumaean and Phrygian sibyls and the prophets Hosea, Isaiah, Amos and Zechariah. **57**

The most famous work of art displayed in St. Peter's, the *Pietà* by Michelangelo, is in the last chapel on the right aisle (*Chapel of the Pietà*). Pietro da Cortona began the preparation of the cartoons for the decoration of the vestibule in mid-1668. The main iconographic theme of the vestibule, in keeping with the original dedication of the chapel to the Crucifix, revolves round the mystery of the Cross and subsequent salvation. In the dome is the apocalyptic vision of the *Angels who mark the forehead of those spared from punishment.* Fabio Cristofaro was responsible for the mosaic version. **58**

This chapel was once dedicated to the Crucifix due to the presence of a wooden sculpture of Christ on the Cross. Its name was changed in 1749, when Benedict XIV ordered Michelangelo's *Pietà* to be moved here from the Chapel of the Choir. The decoration in the chapel is by Giovanni Lanfranco, and keeps to the ancient tradition for an image of the Crucifix, or even a special chapel with the Redeemer on the Cross, to be placed at the entrance of a church. The chapel's decoration is unique in that it is still frescoed and has not been replaced by mosaics. The small dome of the chapel thus retains the only remaining ceiling fresco in St. Peter's. Painted by Lanfranco before 1633, it represents the *Triumph of the Cross*.

The sculptural group of the *Pietà*, representing the dead Christ in the arms of the Virgin Mary, was sculpted by the 23-year-old Michelangelo for Cardinal Jean Bilhières de Lagraulas, abbot of Saint-Denis and Charles VIII's ambassador to Pope Alexander VI. The prelate, who commissioned the group to decorate his own tomb in the ancient chapel of Saints Michael Archangel and Petronilla, died just a few weeks after the completion of the work. At the time of its commission, Michelangelo, who had arrived in Rome only two years before (1498), had sculpted little more than two statues: a lost *Cupid-Apollo* and a *Bacchus* for the banker Jacopo Galli, who also underwrote the successful outcome of the Vatican commission. Completed in 1499, the *Pietà* was immediately recognized as a masterpiece, all the more astonishing for so young a sculptor. Michelangelo's name is carved on the ribbon that crosses the left shoulder of the Virgin: MICHAEL ANGELVS BONATOTVS FLORENT(inus) FACIEBAT. It is Michelangelo's only signed work, as Benedetto Varchi mentioned in his funeral oration. Though it is one of his earliest works, the *Pietà* bears witness to the full artistic maturity of Michelangelo, who deliberately accentuated the Virgin's youthfulness, clearly dissociating himself from the figurative tradition of representing Mary in advanced age. In this way she embodies the spirit of eternal life.

In 1972, the *Pietà* was vandalized: a madman attacked the statue with a hammer and, before he could be stopped, was able to inflict various blows. That's why the group, now perfectly restored by the Vatican Museums' Restoration Laboratory, is separated from the public and protected with plate-glass sheeting.

Visit to the Dome

The entrance to the dome is located in the courtyard on the right side of the Basilica (62, see plan p. 205). Visitors can ascend by lift or on foot to the terrace above the aisles. From there to the interior of the dome it is necessary to proceed on foot.

From the terrace above the aisles surrounding the sloping roof of the nave rise two larger domes and six smaller oval cupolas with lanterns, aligned in two rows, which illuminate the side aisles. The two larger domes, rising 45 m. in height from the terrace, are the work of Giacomo Della Porta, director of works from 1573 to 1602, the year of his death. They are purely decorative, as they do not correspond to any architectural elements in the interior of the Basilica.

Four other hemispherical domes situated at the corners correspond to the four large chapels at the ends of the transept.

Forty years had elapsed since the beginning of the work. Michelangelo, repudiating work done by his predecessor, returned to Bramante's initial inspiration, but with a more vigorous and simplified conception. The decoration of the three external arms was shaped almost like a sculpture and he intended to build the largest dome in modern times on the high pedestal of the external structures. On his death in 1564, the construction of the dome had only reached the drum. It remained incomplete until 19 January 1587, when Pope Sixtus V gave the commission to complete the dome to Giacomo Della Porta, assisted by Domenico Fontana. Della Porta abided by the indications given by the wooden model prepared while Michelangelo was still alive, although he did not respect the project with absolute fidelity. Michelangelo had planned a hemispherical dome, but Fontana modified it and gave it a more pronounced curvature, thus emphasizing its vertical thrust. Once the attic had been completed, construction of the vaulting of the dome began between 15 July and August 1588. The upper ring designed to support the lantern was completed between 22 December 1588 and 14 May 1590. On 19 May of the same year, amid scenes of public rejoicing and firework displays, Sixtus V inaugurated the closing of the oculus of the lantern with the celebration of a solemn mass. Contrary to the estimated ten years, only 22 months had gone by since the dome had begun construction.

Two staircases provide access to the interior of the dome's tambour (diameter 42 m.). From here, the visitor has access to the two walkways that run around the interior of the dome. The upper walkway is 20 m. above the lower one, which is about 53 m. above the floor of the Basilica. The walkways provide panoramic views of the grandiose structures of the building and the important works of art that decorate it (see pp. 212-213).

The steep passageway between the two shells of the dome leads to the panoramic terrace at the base of the lantern, 120 m. above the level of St. Peter's Square.

Inscriptions commemorating many illustrious visitors and the Holy Years adorn the walls of the ramp on the downward route.

a

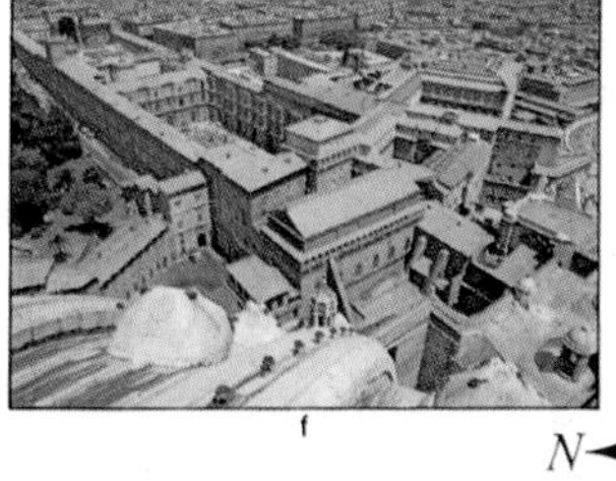
f

b

N

e

c

d

VIEW OF THE VATICAN CITY FROM THE DOME OF ST. PETER'S
(Numbers in brackets after building names refer to the text and plan of the chapter "Vatican City and Gardens", pp. 192-193)

a	St. Peter's Square
b	Palazzo del Sant'Uffizio Papa Audience Hall (7) Teutonic College (5) Sacristy of St. Peter's (8)
c	Tower of St. John (22) First Vatican Radio station (20) Ethiopian College (17) Railway Station (13) Mosaic Workshop Palazzo del Governatorato (14) Palazzo del Tribunale (Courthou-se) (11) Church of Santo Stefano degli Abissini (12)
d	Vatican Radio Offices (26) Fountain of the Eagle (31) Bronze statue of St. Peter (15) House of the Gardener (16)
e	Vatican Pinacoteca (40) Pontifical Academy of Sciences (32) and Casina of Pius IV (33)
f	Vatican Museums (39-49) Borgia Tower Apostolic Palace (3) Sistine Chapel (43)

Sacristy and Treasury of St. Peter's

The entrance to the Sacristy and Treasury of St. Peter's is located at the end of the left aisle of the church (22, see plan p. 205). It is indicated by a sign.

MAIN SACRISTY

58 The *Main Sacristy* is a large octagonal room designed by Carlo Marchionni, the architect of the entire Vatican Sacristy complex. Begun in 1776, it was inaugurated by Pope Pius VI in 1784. The large hall, 26 m. high to the base of the lantern, is the glorification of the number eight and the apotheosis of Pius VI in art. The interior is divided with giant order pilasters in *giallo antico* marble, overlaying larger pilasters in Sicilian *diaspro* marble. The passageway opening to the adjacent rooms are flanked by four pairs of fluted columns in grey marble brought from Hadrian's Villa near Tivoli, leading to
59 the *Sacristy of the Canons.*

TREASURY OF ST. PETER'S

The first of the three rooms of the Sacristy was once the Sacristy of Beneficiaries, followed by the Main Sacristy and the Sacristy of the Canons. It is now the Treasury Museum. The decision to turn it into a museum dates back to 1971 and arose from the desire of the Vatican Chapter to reorganize the rooms in which liturgical objects and gifts from private donors were displayed without any particular order since 1909. According to the *Liber Pontificalis*, the Treasury of St. Peter's was celebrated and admired for its richness as early as the Constantinian era.

A small vestibule leads to,

I I, ROOM OF THE COLUMN

1 On the left is a *corkscrew marble column* decorated with vine leaves; it can be dated on stylistic grounds to Roman artwork in the Eastern part of the Empire (3rd cent. A.D.). It is one of the twelve columns that surrounded the area of the "Confession" in the Constantinian Basilica of St. Peter. Eight of these columns were placed by Bernini in the new octagonal crossing and inserted in tabernacles hewn into the piers (see pp. 211:36-39). Two were installed at the sides of the altar on the right in the Chapel of the Holy Sacrament; one has disappeared; and the twelfth is the one exhibited in the Treasury.

2 Before leaving, it is worth noting high up on the right the gilt metal *weathercock of old St. Peter's*. During the pontificate of Leo IV (847-855), it stood on the Basilica's bell tower (demolished in 1608).

II II, ROOM OF ST PETER'S THRONE

A large elevated showcase, which the visitor can enter to observe the objects close-up, contains in various smaller showcases:

1 The so-called *dalmatic of Charlemagne* (a tunic-like vestment worn for solemn liturgies), a masterpiece of 11th century Byzantine embroidery. It is found listed in the inventories of the Vatican Chapter since 1466. It is one of the most ancient and precious examples of a *sàkkos*, a vestment of imperial origin worn by patriarchs and bishops of the Eastern Church. Figures are embroidered in gold, silver and polychrome silk against a dark blue silk background and the lavish decoration extends over the entire surface. The iconographic theme is the manifestation of the glory of Christ with the representation of Christ the Judge on one side, and the Transfiguration on the other.

A *pectoral reliquary in the form of a cross,* preserved in a gold casket 2
decorated with enamel and pearls. It is a reliquary of the wood of the Holy Cross and is known as the reliquary of Constantine because of the Emperor's image that appears in the lower left. Inside the double doors of the casket are the embossed figures of Jesus and the Virgin Mary with the Apostles and martyrs. These are examples of Byzantine goldsmiths' art of the 6th and 7th centuries. The two supporting angels are inspired by Bernini.

The *Crux Vaticana*, or *Cross of Emperor Justin II*, studded with precious 3
stones. This is a reliquary of the wood of the Holy Cross donated by the Byzantine Emperor Justin II to the old St. Peter's in the second half of the 6th century. The names of the Emperor and his wife and *socia* (partner) Sophia are carved on the arms of the cross.

Gold *reliquary in the form of a double cross,* containing wood of the Holy 4
Cross; Byzantine art of late 10th early 11th centuries.

So-called St. Peter's Throne. This is a copy of the oak-wood throne donated 5
by Charles the Bald to Pope John VIII on 25 December 875 on the occasion of his coronation as emperor in St. Peter's. The finely pierced ivory panels which decorate the legs and back of the chair and the eighteen ivory plaques illustrating the twelve labours of Hercules on the front of the chair are attributable to the school that flourished at the court of Charles the Bald. It was only in the 12th century that the popular belief gained hold that this was the actual throne of St. Peter. Although historical research subsequently established its Carolingian origin, the small throne has always been considered the tangible symbol of the authority of St. Peter's successors. That explains why the original throne was incorporated into the bronze throne of the great sculpture of the *Cathedra Petri* created by Bernini for the apse of the Basilica (see p. 210: 29).

Fragments of an ivory diptych, Byzantinizing style (11th to 14th cent.?), which 6
belonged to the decoration that the Greek Cardinal Bessarion commissioned for the Basilica (1464), together with a series of icons. On one side are Christ and the Virgin Mary, John the Baptist, Peter and Paul; on the other, two bishops and Saints Demetrius and Onophrius, much venerated in the Middle East.

III, CHAPEL OF THE BENEFICIARIES III

Facing the entrance is a *plaster cast of Michelangelos' Pietà* by Francesco 1
and Luigi Mercatali (1934); thanks to this exact copy, the original could be
faithfully restored after being damaged by an act of vandalism in 1972 (see
p. 215:57). On the left wall is a marble *tabernacle,* originally from the ancient 2
Basilica and attributed to Donatello (15th cent.). The *altarpiece* above the 3
altar is by Girolamo Muziano (16th cent.). It represents *Christ's Charge to St.*
Peter. Above the door is an oil painting of the *Quo vadis?,* by Antonio 4
Cavallucci, a Roman painter of the late 18th century. It represents the legendary flight of Peter from Rome for fear of the persecutions, and Christ who appears to him on the Via Appia to admonish him and persuade him to return.

IV, ROOM OF SIXTUS IV IV

The magnificent *bronze tomb of Sixtus IV della Rovere,* patron of the arts and 1
founder of the Sistine Chapel and the Vatican Library, can be admired both from ground level and above from a balcony. The work is signed by the artist, Antonio del Pollaiolo, and dated 1493. It was commissioned for the Old Basilica by Cardinal Giuliano della Rovere, the Pope's nephew, who later became Pope Julius II. With severe and impressive realism, the body of the pope, dressed in solemn pontifical vestments, is laid out on top of the tomb on a mattress. The artist's signature is visible engraved on the side of the mattress. The seven Virtues, placed in rectangular panels, surround the

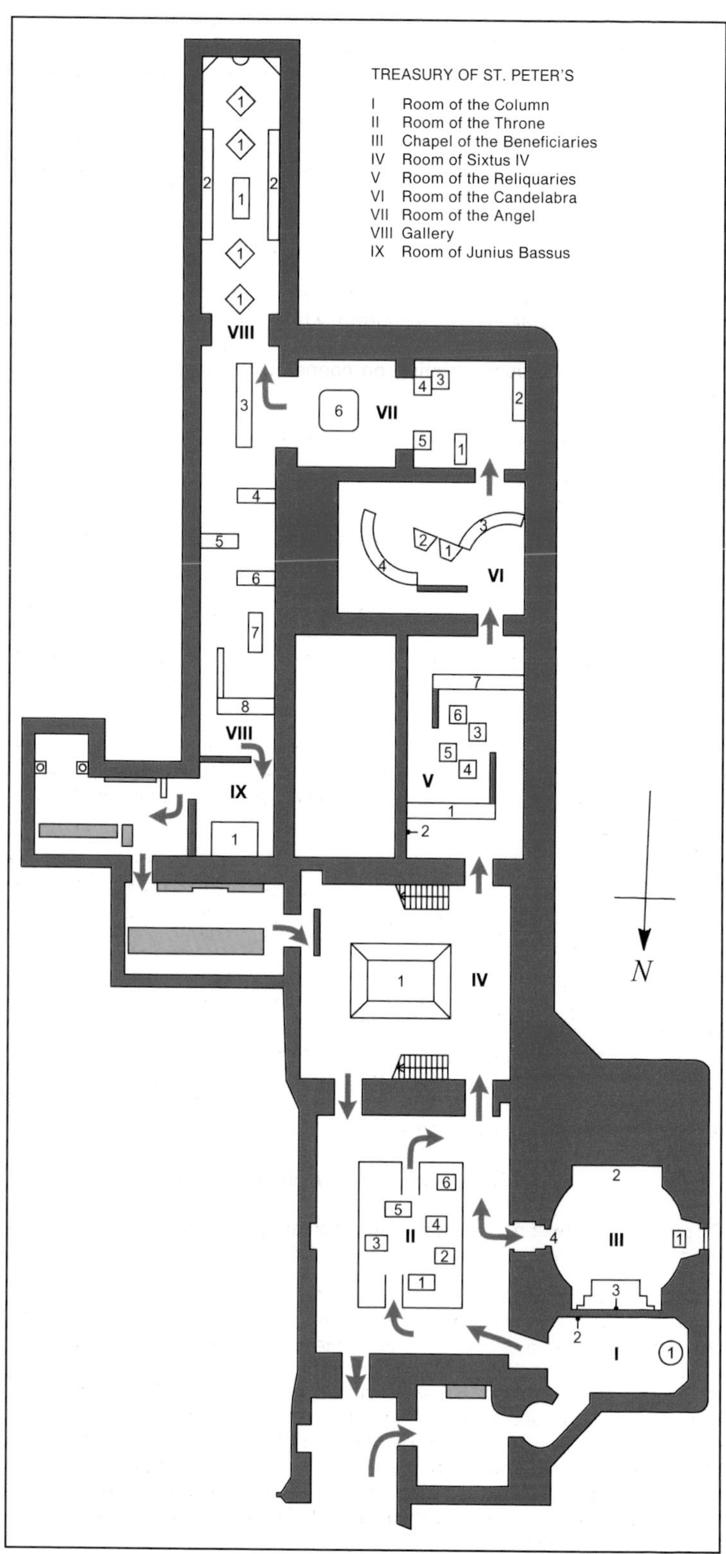
TREASURY OF ST. PETER'S
I Room of the Column
II Room of the Throne
III Chapel of the Beneficiaries
IV Room of Sixtus IV
V Room of the Reliquaries
VI Room of the Candelabra
VII Room of the Angel
VIII Gallery
IX Room of Junius Bassus
N

body of the Pope. Around his head are the three theological virtues (Charity, Faith and Hope); on the sides, the four cardinal virtues (Prudence, Fortitude, Justice and Temperance). The base is decorated with reliefs representing Theology, Philosophy and the Liberal Arts: the three Literary Arts (Dialectics, Rhetoric and Grammar), and the four Sciences (Arithmetic, Astrology, Music and Geometry), which were the seven disciplines of the medieval scholastic system, to which the artist has added Perspective, a new science.

V, ROOM OF THE RELIQUARIES V

In the large *showcase facing the entrance,* from the right are: large **1**
embossed silver frame (17th to 18th cent.), which once contained an ancient Slav icon; a wooden frame of the reliquary of St. Veronica (14th cent.?); and, to the left, a gold-ground painting on copper with *Saints Peter and Paul* (heavily restored, 14th cent.).

On the wall to the left, a *wooden crucifix* (14th cent.) from the Old Basilica. **2**

In the four following *showcases*: several reliquaries of great artistic and **3-6**
historical value, including:

Showcase: Rock crystal altar cross (18th cent.). Piscatory ring of Sixtus IV **3**
(15th cent.).

Showcase: Openwork copper spheres (12th to 16th cent.) that served as hand **4**
warmers for the canons. Reliquary of the Holy Cross, Roman goldsmiths' work (15th cent.). Reliquary of the Holy Lance (Venetian, second half of the 15th cent.), rock crystal and silver, containing the head of the lance that pierced Christ's side (*Jn* 19:34).

Showcase: Reliquary bust of St. Luke in embossed silver (16th cent.). Gothic **5**
chalice in silver and enamel; goldsmiths' work from Viterbo (14th cent.). Reliquary of Saints Leo I, II, III, and IV, 18th century casket of gilt metal with silver friezes.

Showcase: Reliquary of the Childhood of Christ, in gilt and finely worked **6**
silver (1607). Reliquary of St. Blaise: a silver tabernacle made in Naples, 1402. Reliquary of St Sebastian, gold and silver casket in the form of a Renaissance building (15th cent.).

In the large *showcase near the exit* are: two musical manuscripts written in **7**
the first half of the 16th century for the Cappella Giulia (choir plus instrumentalists), founded by Julius II in 1513 to provide music for the choral services in St. Peter's and still active today. The first manuscript, to the right, contains thirty-five liturgical compositions by various composers. The second, to the left, contains seventeen motets. In the centre of the showcase is a late 17th century ivory crucifix.

VI, ROOM OF THE CANDELABRA VI

On pedestals between two large showcases are two *large candelabra* in gilt **1,2**
bronze, attributed to Antonio del Pollaiolo (15th cent.).

The two *large showcases* contain two groups of candelabra. These were **3, 4**
used to adorn the high altar of the Basilica for solemn rites until the
pontificate of Pius XII. The *first group of candelabra,* gilt bronze with an altar **3**
cross, are the work of Sebastiano Torrigiani (*c.*1585); they were influential and long continued to inspire the forms of innumerable altar candelabra.
The *second group of candelabra,* in gilt bronze and with an altar cross, are **4**
signed and dated (1581) by Antonio Gentile da Faenza. The two candlesticks placed beside it are also attributed to him. The other four candelabra were made by Carlo Spagna (1670-1672), after drawings by Gian Lorenzo Bernini. The scenes of the Passion engraved on medallions of rock crystal set into the pedestals are by Valerio Belli.

VII

VII, ROOM OF THE ANGEL

1 In the *showcase to the left of the entrance* are the gilt bronze statues of St. Peter and St. Paul by Sebastiano Torrigiani (1585).

2 The *showcase* against the wall to the right of the entrance contains two musical manuscripts for the Cappella Giulia (the choir of Julius II), and an ancient Slav icon representing Saints Peter and Paul (9th to 11th cent.). The figures in the lower register of the painting are probably Saints Cyril and Methodius (9th cent.), inventors of the Cyrillic alphabet and translators of the Bible into Slavonic; the figure between them, in front of St. Nicholas, is perhaps Queen Helena of Serbia .

3-5 The following three *showcases* contain reliquaries, including:

3 *Showcase:* Two 18th century Neapolitan reliquaries in gilt metal. Amber monstrance (17th cent.).

4 *Showcase:* A reliquary cross, carved from rock crystal, with a piece of the wood of the Holy Cross at the centre; it is known as the "Palace Cross" (15th cent.).

5 *Showcase:* Two monstrances, one of rock crystal (17th century), the other of gold filigree (18th cent.). A silver reliquary, in the form of a Baroque altar, containing relics of Lombard and Milanese saints.

6 In the second part of the room is a terracotta *angel,* modelled by Bernini (*c.*1673). It is the model for one of the two angels of the Ciborium in the Chapel of the Holy Sacrament in St. Peter's (see p. 214:48).

VIII

VIII, GALLERY

1 To the right, the five *showcases* in the middle of the room contain a magnificent series of sumptuously decorated and monumental monstrances, reliquaries, chalices and pyxes made of precious metals studded with gems (18th – 19th cent.).

2 Displayed in the two *showcases* facing each other along the walls are tiaras and liturgical vestments richly embroidered with gold and silver (late 19th cent.).

3 Halfway down the gallery, facing the entrance, is a *large showcase* containing an altar-frontal embroidered with gold and silver, portraying St. Peter and St. Paul (late 19th cent.).

4 Further on, another *showcase* contains various monstrances, reliquaries and chalices of the 17th and 18th centuries. Here too is the silver hammer and trowel, with a cast of the hand of Paul VI, used by this Pope for the opening and closing of the Holy Door in the 1975 Jubilee Year; they are the work of the Hungarian sculptor Amerigo Tot. Also worth noting: the *York Chalice,* a large liturgical chalice of finely worked gold studded with 130 diamonds, by the Roman goldsmith Luigi Valadier, gift of Cardinal Henry Stuart, Duke of York (late 18th cent.).

5 In the next *showcase* are the Triple Crown (papal tiara made up of three superimposed crowns symbolizing the three powers of the Pope: Father of Kings, Ruler of the World, Vicar of Christ), dating to the 18th century; it was used to crown the bronze statue of St. Peter in the Basilica (see p. 213:40) on the liturgical Feast of St. Peter (29 June). The enormous clasp for a cope displayed next to it was also used to adorn the bronze St. Peter (19th cent.). Two little crowns of diamonds and pearls, donated by French Catholics to Pius XII for the Madonna Orsini in the Vatican Grottoes. Reliquary (17th cent.) containing two "Holy Thorns", thought to be from the crown of the Passion of Christ. Gold chalice, donated by King Louis of Portugal to Leo XIII (1883), a copy of the one from the church of Belem, with chased ornament representing scenes from the New Testament.

Another *showcase* with pectoral crosses of various epochs and provenance, and a pectoral clasp with a topaz of exceptional size at its centre (18th cent.). 6

In the next *showcase* we find the so-called Crown of the Immaculate Virgin, with twelve stars made of diamonds mounted in gold, donated by French Catholics to Pope Pius IX on the occasion of the 50th anniversary of the proclamation of the dogma of the Immaculate Conception (8 December 1854). Above the crown is a votive lamp studded with pearls of unusual size; it was produced in Rome in the second half of the 19th century. 7

In the *large showcase* at the end of the gallery is the monstrance donated to Pope John XXIII by Charles de Gaulle (1959). Chinese chalice and paten with fine enamelwork, donated by Cardinal Mariano Rampolla, Secretary of State of Leo XIII. 8

IX, ROOM OF JUNIUS BASSUS IX

The *sarcophagus of Junius Bassus*, prefect of Rome, who was converted to Christianity and died in 359, consists of a monolithic block of white marble, sculpted on three sides. It was found in the area of the "Confession" (see p. 210:34). The name by which it is known is incised on the upper margin of the sarcophagus, together with details of the career of Julius Bassus and the date of his death. The relief scenes are inspired by the Old and the New Testaments. In the upper row, Christ is enthroned between Sts. Peter and Paul, flanked by the Capture of Christ to the right and the Capture of Peter and the Sacrifice of Isaac to the left. In the lower row: Job, Adam and Eve, entry into Jerusalem, Daniel in the lion's den and the judgement of Paul. 1

The Vatican Grottoes

(Visiting hours: winter 7:00 - 17:00; summer 7:00 - 18:00)

The Grottoes can be reached through a passageway situated in the pier of S. Longinus under the dome of St. Peter's (36, see plan p. 205).

The numbers in round brackets in the text refer to the plan on p. 225.

The Vatican Grottoes, or Tombs of the Popes, were created when the New Basilica was built between the pontificates of Gregory XIII (1572-1585) and Clement VIII (1592-1605). They have been the burial place of popes, cardinals and kings since 1606. When the New Basilica of St. Peter was built, it was not built level with the previous Constantinian Basilica, but was raised two metres: the space between the two floors was used for burials and for displaying archaeological finds found during the construction work. This crypt (22, 40, 43), up until its most recent reorganization, was called the Old Grottoes, while the part (2) situated below the existing Basilica but outside the Constantinian Basilica was called the New Grottoes. Before assuming their present appearance, the Grottoes were subjected to numerous restorations: the most recent renovation was carried out between 1979 and 1992.

The name Grottoes was given to this crypt because the space between the two churches was so low as to give it a cavern-like appearance, as may be seen from the height of the corridor of the former exit (53). Under the pontificate of Pius XII (1939-1958), in order to make the visit to the tombs of the Popes less strenuous for visitors, the floor level was lowered and some galleries were opened to the south and north (30, 31, 52, 54) to contain most of the archaeological finds: not only Christian inscriptions and sarcophagi found during the building work in the 16th century, but also architectural fragments and ornaments from the Old Basilica and surrounding buildings.

A narrow flight of steps leads down to the small chapel (1) dedicated to *St. Longinus*. From there a short corridor leads into the *Clementine Ambulatory* (2): a horseshoe-shaped corridor from which subsidiary corridors branch out to the three other small 18th century chapels hewn out of the foundations of the four piers supporting the dome of the Basilica and dedicated to the saints represented by the statues placed on these piers. Originally these statues must have been arranged differently than they now are, since the frescoes in the corridor leading to the Chapel of St. Longinus depict episodes relating to St. Helena, in the Chapel of St. Helena they refer to St. Andrew, and in the Chapel of St. Andrew, to St. Longinus. Only under the pier of St. Veronica does the theme of the frescoes in the corridor correspond to the statue above, the only statue that is still in its original place.

The smaller chapels under the base of the piers alternate with larger chapels (open only in the morning for the celebration of Mass, the last celebration is at 8:15). Beginning from the right, the first is the *Chapel of the Patron Saints of Europe* (3), dedicated to Saints Benedict, Cyril and Methodius, inaugurated in 1981. The second is the *Polish Chapel* (4), dedicated to the Black Madonna of Jasnagora (Czéstochowa), in 1958. Facing this chapel, a passage leads to the Confession (18). The third of the larger chapels is the *Irish Chapel* (5), dedicated to St. Columbanus (1954). Further on a fragment of marble reliquary that Pius II (1458-1464) commissioned for the reliquary of St. Andrew has been fixed to the wall. The corridor continues to the *Chapel of St. Helena*.

At the end of the Ambulatory in the centre, is the *Funerary Chapel of Pius XII* (1939-1958) (7) with six niches on either side containing statues of the Apostles – once gilded – that originally stood on the ciborium that Sixtus IV (1471-1484) had built over the papal altar.The niches of Saints Matthew, Philip, Andrew and John are empty. Facing the chapel is the entrance to the *Clementine Chapel* (8), created by Clement VIII (1592-1605) from the former

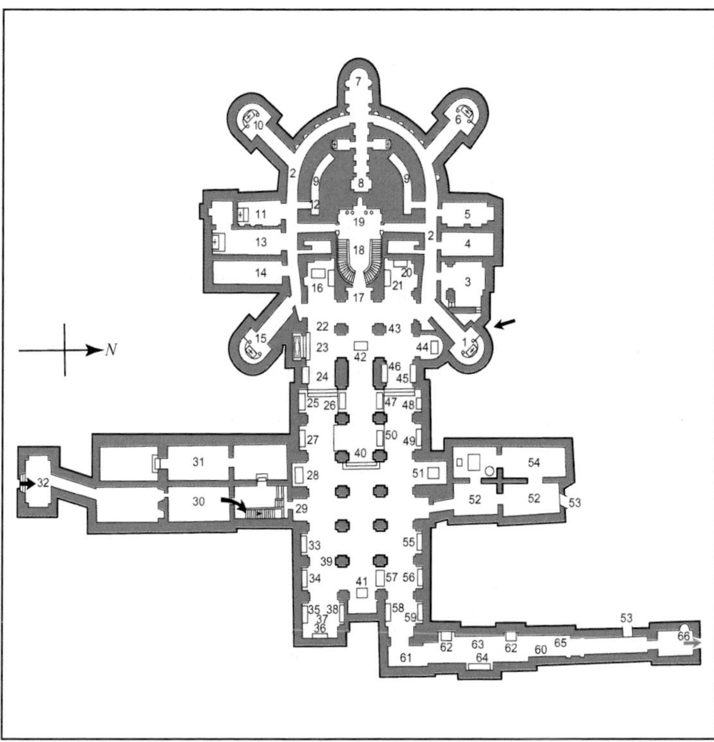

PLAN OF THE VATICAN GROTTOES

A Entrance to the Grottoes from the Pier of St. Longinus
1 Chapel of St. Longinus
2 Clementine Ambulatory
3 Chapel of the Patron Saints of Europe
4 Polish Chapel
5 Irish Chapel
6 Chapel of St. Helena
7 Tomb of Pius XII
8 Clementine Chapel
9 Semicircular crypt of Gregory the Great
10 Chapel of the Veronica
11 Chapel of the "Madonna della Bocciata"
12 Necropolis exit, formerly "Cappella della Salvatorello"
13 Chapel of the "Madonna delle Partorienti"
14 Lithuanian Chapel
15 Chapel of St. Andrew
16 Mexican Chapel
17 Plate-glass window
18 Confession
19 Niche of the Palliums above the Tomb of St. Peter
20 Chapel of the "Madonna Orsini"
21 Tomb of Pius VI
22 Left or south aisle (closed to the public)
23 Tomb of Pius XI
24 Tomb of Cardinal Raffaele Merry del Val
25 Tomb of the last Stuarts
26 Tomb of Cardinal Federico Todeschini
27 Tomb of Innocent XIII
28 Tomb of Urban VI
29 Wrought-iron gate
30 *Antiquarium* Gallery
31 *Antiquarium* Gallery
32 Entrance to the Grottoes from Piazza Braschi (from which the disabled can gain access to part of the Grottoes)
33 Cenotaph of Pius III
34 Tomb of Adrian IV
35 Tomb of Gregory V
36 Tomb of the Emperor Otto II
37 Common grave of the 17 century
38 Tomb of Julius III
39 Tomb of Monsignor Ludwig Kaas
40 Central nave
41 Statue of Pius VI
42 "Altar of the Tomb"
43 Right or north aisle
44 Former funerary Chapel of John XXIII
45 Tomb of Queen Christina of Sweden
46 Tomb of Queen Charlotte of Cyprus
47 Tomb of Benedict XV
48 Tomb of Innocent IX
49 Tomb of Marcellus II
50 Tomb of John Paul I
51 Tomb of Paul VI
52 Gallery of access to the Hungarian Chapel
53 Gallery of the old exit
54 Hungarian Chapel
55 Tomb of Paul II
56 Tomb of Nicholas V and in the floor common grave of the 16 century
57 Tomb of Innocent VII
58 Tomb of Nicholas III
59 Tomb of Boniface VIII and in the floor funerary inscription of Cardinal Benedetto Caetani
60 Renaissance tabernacle with the four Doctors of the Church and, at the centre, copy of the "Mater Dolorosa"
61 Exit gallery
62 Base of column of the Constantinian Basilica
63 Remains of the partition wall of Paul III
64 Cenotaph of Calixtus III
65 Right perimeter wall of the Constantinian Basilica
66 Marble statue of St. Peter
B Exit from the Grottoes (leading into the courtyard where restrooms and souvenir shops are located)

semicircular crypt (9) built by Gregory the Great (590-604); the altar of the chapel in lapis lazuli, malachite and porphyry was made after the excavations (1940-1950) and has a small window in the centre through which the visitor can see the 6th century walls called *ad caput* (by the head), because they are located above the burial site and correspond, according to tradition, to the position of St. Peter's head. The Constantinian marbles covering the "Red Wall" (see Necropolis) can be seen through the grate inserted in the altar wall after the excavations. The recently restored gilded stuccoes of the vaulted ceiling are by Giovanni Battista Maini (1690-1752).

Continuing round the Clementine Ambulatory is the corridor that leads to the *Chapel of the Veronica* (10). Next comes the Chapel of the "Madonna della Bocciata" (11); it derives its name from the fragment of pictorial decoration of the Old Basilica's portico on the chapel's altar, attributed to the school of Pietro Cavallini (early 13th cent.).The name derives from an episode that occurred during the Sack of Rome in 1527, when a drunken soldier, furious after losing a game of bowls, is reported to have hurled a bowl at the sacred image, hitting the face of the Madonna, who began to shed drops of blood on the floor of the portico. The stained stones are preserved in the chapel behind thick iron grating. In the chapel to the left, close to the wrought-iron gate, is the tomb of Cardinal Beran, Archbishop of Prague (d. 1969).The chapel is sometimes called the "Czech Chapel". Facing it on the left side of the Ambulatory is the Chapel of the "Salvatorello" (12), removed to create the exit from the Necropolis. A fragment of the marble decoration of the Constantinian "*memoria*" (see Necropolis) can be seen from the wrought-iron gate. Also further ahead on this side, another corridor leads to the Confession (18). On the right is the Chapel of the "*Madonna delle Partorienti*" (13), which takes its name from a fragment of a fresco attributed to Melozzo da Forlì displayed on the altar: the *Madonna delle Partorienti*. Tradition has it that women in Rome turned in prayer to the Madonna before giving birth. On the wall to the left of the chapel are two mosaic fragments: the first is a copy of Giotto's *Angel*, the second is the heavily restored original. The angel formed part of the mosaic of the *Navicella*, executed on the façade of the Old Basilica of St. Peter (1320-130), based on a cartoon by Giotto di Bondone, together with another preserved in the Church of San Pietro Ispano in Boville Ernica in the province of Frosinone. On the wall to the right of the Chapel is the bust of Boniface VIII, by Arnolfo di Cambio (1245-1310), and, in a niche, a small statue of the *Madonna and Child* attributed to Isaiah da Pisa (15th cent.) On the walls of the Ambulatory are some decorative fragments from the Old Basilica: the mosaic of the *Madonna and Child*, thought to be part of the decoration of the tabernacle of the Holy Face in the Oratory of John VII, and some inscriptions. The *Lithuanian Chapel* (14), dedicated to the Mater Misericordiae (1970), and the *Chapel of St. Andrew*, follow (15).

Leaving the Ambulatory one enters the largest section of the Vatican Grottoes, divided into three aisles (22, 40, 43) by two rows of cruciform columns.

To the left is the last chapel to be founded in the Grottoes: the *Mexican Chapel* (16) dedicated to Our Lady of Guadalupe (1992). A section of the wall was removed at the centre after the chapel in order to install the large plate-glass partition (17) through which one can see the Confession (18). The *Niche of the Palliums* (19), decorated with a 9th century mosaic portraying the heavily restored *Benedictory Christ* is here. The Tomb of St. Peter lies below the niche.

The *Pallium* is a special white wool stole with six black silk crosses sewn onto it (in the Middle Ages they were red). The wool is woven by the Benedictine Sisters of Santa Cecilia with the wool of two lambs blessed by the Pope on 21 January Feast of St. Agnese. In ancient times the *Pallium* was a liturgical vestment exclusively for the pope, who had the faculty of extending its high office to bishops. Today it is also granted by the pope to metropolitan Archbishops, as a sign of communion with the Apostolic See. Every year the new Palliums (their number varies according to the nomination of new metropolitans) are blessed by the Pope on the eve of 29 June, Feast of Saints Peter and Paul, and then in the silver urn placed over the Tomb of St. Peter. The key of the urn is kept by the Prefect of Pontifical Liturgical Ceremonies.

In its present form, the Niche of the Palliums is the work of Carlo Maderno (1556-1629), who refurbished the first monument built over the tomb of St. Peter - the famous Trophy recorded by the priest Gaius at the end of the 2nd century - discovered by archaeologists during excavations conducted between 1940 and 1950. The Basilica of St. Peter and the Universal Church revolve around this architectural and spiritual umbilicus. It is both its architectural centre (the vertical axis from the top of the dome passes through the altar of the Confession and ends on the Tomb of St. Peter), and its spiritual centre (Gospel verses about the primacy of Peter that testify to the continuity of the transmission of Christ's message from St. Peter to his successors can be found on the frieze of the entablature below the dome's impost and vaults).

The Confession (18) visible through the plate-glass window, is the synthesis of 2000 years of pilgrimage to the Tomb of St. Peter. Behind the mosaic with Christ and the purple marble panels (at the sides of the mosaic) is the Trophy. Its gilt bronze doors recall those that closed the original Constantinian shrine over the Apostle's tomb (the *Memoria*: see Necropolis). Above, behind the panel of black granite with the inscription in bronze letters, is the second altar of Calixtus II (for the history of the altars see below, Necropolis), and further above is the last altar of Clement VIII (1592 - 1605), topped by Bernini's Baldachin.

At the sides of the plate-glass partition (17): above are two marble angels that formed part of the funerary monument of Boniface VIII, sculpted by Arnolfo di Cambio (1245-1310); below, two lions sculpted for the tomb of either Urban VI or Benedict XII. Up until 1979, when the large plate-glass partition was installed, an altar dedicated to Christ the King was placed against the wall with a marble relief sculpted by Giovanni Dalmata (1440-1509) for the funerary monument of Nicholas V.The relief can now be found in the gallery (30), close to the gate (29). After the removal of the altar of Christ the King, a chapel with an altar was created in the central aisle (40) called the *Altar of the Tomb* (42). The altar table rests on a fragment of a column surmounted by a Corinthian capital. A small Cosmatesque corkscrew column was used for the lectern, while the crucifix rests on a Cosmatesque architectural fragment. After the plate-glass partition is the Chapel (20) with a large marble relief called the *Madonna of the Orsini* on its altar, attributed to Isaia da Pisa (15th cent.). It portrays the Virgin and Child in the centre with Eugenius IV (1431-1447) and his nephew Pietro Barbo, the future Paul II (1464-1471) kneeling at their feet; to the sides are St. Peter with the keys and St. Paul with the sword. To the left is the tomb (21) of Pius VI (1775-1799), who is buried in an Early Christian strigilated sarcophagus with an ancient lid and frieze decorated on the left with Stories of Joseph and on the right with the Adoration of the Magi.

In the *left or south aisle* (22) facing the Mexican Chapel (16) are some illustrious tombs: (23) the *Funerary Chapel of Pius XI* (1922-1939), completely decorated in mosaic based on designs by D'Archiardi, while the statue of the Pope is by Castiglione; (14) the onyx tomb of *Cardinal Raffaele Merry del Val*, Secretary of State of St. Pius X; (25) tomb of *James III Stuart* and his sons, the last descendents of Mary Queen of Scots; (26) red granite tomb of Cardinal Federico Todeschini (1873-1959); (27) tomb of Innocent XIII (1721-1724); (28) tomb of Urban VI (1378-1389) for which an ancient sarcophagus was reworked, while at the back of the niche is a marble high relief with the *Madonna and Child* attributed to the school of Donatello. It is followed by the gate (29) that leads to the galleries (30 and 31) that form an *antiquarium*, and to the entrance on Largo Braschi (32) opened in 1950. Returning to the south aisle (33), the empty tomb of Pius III (1503), transferred to Sant'Andrea della Valle in 1623; (34) the ancient sarcophagus in red granite in which *Adrian IV* (1154-1159), the only English Pope in the annals of the papacy, is buried; and the Early Christian sarcophagus of *Gregory V* (996-999), the first German pope. At the foot of the aisle (36) is the strigilated sarcophagus of Emperor *Otto II* (d. 983), with a large and heavily restored mosaic of Christ between Saints Peter and Paul above. On the same wall, at the sides of the mosaic, are two inscriptions: to the right the fragments of the inscription dated 1102 with the text of the donation of the Countess Matilda of Tuscany to the Holy See; to the left one dated 1267, refering to the relics transfered to St. Peter's. In front of the sarcophagus of Otto II, set into the floor, is an inscription (37) that refers to the common grave below (18th cent.) where human remains were found during work carried out under the pontificate of Paul V (1605-1621). Nearby is the burial (38) of *Julius III* (1550-155). Also set into the floor is the tombstone (39) of *Monsignor Ludwig Kaas* (1881-1952), secretary of the Fabbrica di San Pietro during the excavations of the Necropolis (1940-1950).

At the foot of the central aisle (40) is the statue of *Pius VI* (1775-1799) kneeling in prayer. It was begun by Antonio Canova (1711-1822) just before his death, and was completed by his pupil Adamo Tadolini.

In the *right or north aisle* (43) is (44) the *Funerary Chapel of John XXIII* (1958-1963) with a high relief of the *Madonna and Child* by Luigi Capponi (following his beatification in 2001, the body of John XXIIII was transferred to St. Peter's Basilica, and placed below the altar of St. Jerome, see above, p. 214). Nearby, at the beginning of the right aisle are the tombs of two queens: (45) *Christina of Sweden* (d. 1698) and (46) *Charlotte of Savoy-Lusignan,* Queen of Cyprus (d. 1487). They are followed by the tombs of several popes: (47) sarcophagus of *Benedict XV* (1914-1922), with a bronze effigy of the Pope by the sculptor Giulio Barbieri; (48) tomb of *Innocent IX* (1591); (49) Early-Christian sarcophagus in which lie the remains of *Marcellus II* (1555); and the modern sarcophagus of *John Paul I* (1978), decorated with Renaissance reliefs; *Funerary Chapel of Paul VI* (1963-1978), with the tombstone set in the floor because the Pope wanted a very simple burial; on the end wall is a marble relief of the *Madonna and Child* between angels of the School of Donatello. The following gallery (52) contains: at the entrance, mosaic fragments from the Constantinian Basilica and from the Oratory of John VII; further on, on the walls, fragments of inscriptions, reliefs and architectural mouldings; at the end of the gallery is the door that leads to the old exit corridor (53). From the gallery (52) there is access to the *Hungarian Chapel* (54), dedicated to St. Stephen, the first King of Hungary, inaugurated in 1980. Returning to the north aisle: (55) tomb of *Paul II* (1464-1471), whose funerary monument, broken up and lost, was the work of Mino da Fiesole (1430-1484) and Giovanni Dalmata (1440-1509); tomb of *Nicholas V* (1447-1455), with an inscription in front set into the floor referring to another common grave of the 16th century, and (57) the tomb of *Innocent VII* (1404-1406); (58) Early-Christian sarcophagus with unfinished reliefs in which *Nicholas III* (1277-1280) is buried; and (59) the tomb of Boniface VIII (1295-1303) for whom Arnolfo di Cambio created a sumptuous funerary monument of which nothing remains but the sarcophagus and the two angels at the sides of the plate-glass window (38); in front of the tomb an inscription on the floor commemorates Cardinal Benedetto Caetani, the pope's nephew. On the end wall of the aisle a *Renaissance tabernacle* (60) was installed recently with an inscription dated 1486. A copy of the *Mater Dolorosa* attributed to Lippo Memmi (14th cent.) was included with it. The original was damaged by shrapnel from a bomb that struck the Vatican in 1944. At the sides of the tabernacle are two reliefs with the *Four Doctors of the Latin Church* (Saints Augustine, Gregory the Great, Jerome and Ambrose). The Stations of the Cross placed in the aisle are by Gosmondi.

In the exit corridor (61) opened in 1980, the two column bases (62) on the left recall the division into aisles of the north side of the Constantinian building; between them is a fragment of wall (63) built by Paul III (1534-1549) to separate the building site of the New Basilica from the area where liturgical rites continued to be celebrated; the papal altar was placed against this wall. Facing it (64) is the empty tomb of *Calixtus II* (1455-1458), which was transferred in 1610 to the Church of Santa Maria di Monserrato. On the wall are some marble reliefs from his sumptuous funerary monument. Further ahead, to the right and left, are the remains (65) of the northern external wall of the Old Basilica with exposed brickwork. To the left, after passing the first glass door, the terminal part of the corridor (65) is visible with ancient inscriptions on the walls. After the second glass door, the marble statue of *St. Peter* enthroned (66) can be admired. It is actually a Roman statue (of a philosopher?) reworked in the 16th century and transformed into St. Peter. On the walls are fragments of architectural mouldings with geometric and floral decorations from the Oratory of John VII.

Opposite the exit is the ticket office where tickets may be purchased to ascend to the Dome. Souvenir shops and restrooms can be found on the right.

Necropolis and St. Peter's Tomb

To visit the Necropolis bookings need to be made long in advance by sending a written request, also by Fax 06/698.85518. For information and bookings contact the Ufficio Scavi/Excavations Office, open from Monday to Saturday, 9-12 /14-17 – tel. 06/698.85318.

To the left of the Basilica, after passing through the Arco delle Campane (2, p. 192), patrolled by the Swiss Guards, is the Piazzale dei Protomartiri (4, p. 192). Here, before reaching the second arch, is an inscription set into the pavement, marking the original site of the obelisk that Pope Sixtus V (1585-1590) had transferred to the centre of St. Peter's Square in 1586. In the following Largo Braschi is the entrance to the Vatican Grottoes. This entrance leads to the Necropolis below St. Peter's Basilica, also called the Vatican Necropolis.

In 1939, while work was proceeding on the tomb of Pius XI (1922-1939), Mausoleum F was found below the floor of the Vatican Grottoes. It contained cremation burials belonging to a cemetery of the 2nd and 3rd century A.D. Previous evidence of the existence of this necropolis had been found as early as the rebuilding of the Basilica in the 16th and 17th centuries.

Following this find, Pius XII (1939-1958) ordered a series of excavations. Conducted by E. Kirschbaum, E. Josi, B. Apollonj Ghetti and A. Ferrua, between 1940 and 1950, it led to the discovery of two rows of chamber tombs *(A*-R and T-Z, *theta*, *chi* and *psi)* belonging to well-to-do pagan families. The entrances of the tombs are aligned from east to west (along the axis of the future Basilica). The level of the ground drops noticeably from north to south indicating that the necropolis had been situated on a hillside. The mausolea have an entrance facing south, overlooking the valley below: this was the location of the so-called Neronian Circus, but in fact constructed by the emperors Caligula (37-41) and Nero (54-68) (see 1, plan pp 20-21). In the centre of the Circus was the obelisk that the emperor Caligula had brought from Egypt, which is the one that can now be seen in the centre of St. Peter's Square. The circus is mentioned by the inscription placed on the façade of Mausoleum A, the first to the east, still full of earth: the inscriptions tells us that the owner of the tomb, *Popilius Heracla*, wanted it to be built "*in Vaticano ad circum*" (in the Vatican close to the circus).

The mausolea, which are now approximately 80% of their original height, have walls decorated with frescoes and stuccoes and mosaic pavements. These ancient funerary chapels date between the first half of the 2nd and the end of the 3rd century. Only in the wall mosaics of Mausoleum M are Christian themes found: the Fisherman (on the wall in front), Jonah and the whale (to the right) and the Good Shepherd (to the left); on the vault are, fairly well preserved, Christ-Helios (Christ the Sun), symbol of the Resurrection.

In the 1st century St. Peter was crucified in the Neronian Circus during the persecution instigated by the emperor Nero between 64 and 67 A.D. He was buried in the Vatican at a site surrounded by pagan mausolea of the 2nd and 3rd century. The tomb of the Apostle was a simple shaft grave. The body was

---

▷ CONSTANTINIAN NECROPOLIS

(The archaeologists have named the mausolea of the necropolis after the letters of the Greek and Latin alphabets.)

1 Mausoleum A "*in Vaticano ad circum*"
2 Mausoleum M, with Christian mosaics
3 Field P. Site of St. Peter's burial
4 Red Wall
5 "Aedicula" or Trophy
6 "Muro g"
7 "Muro s"
→ « Confessione »

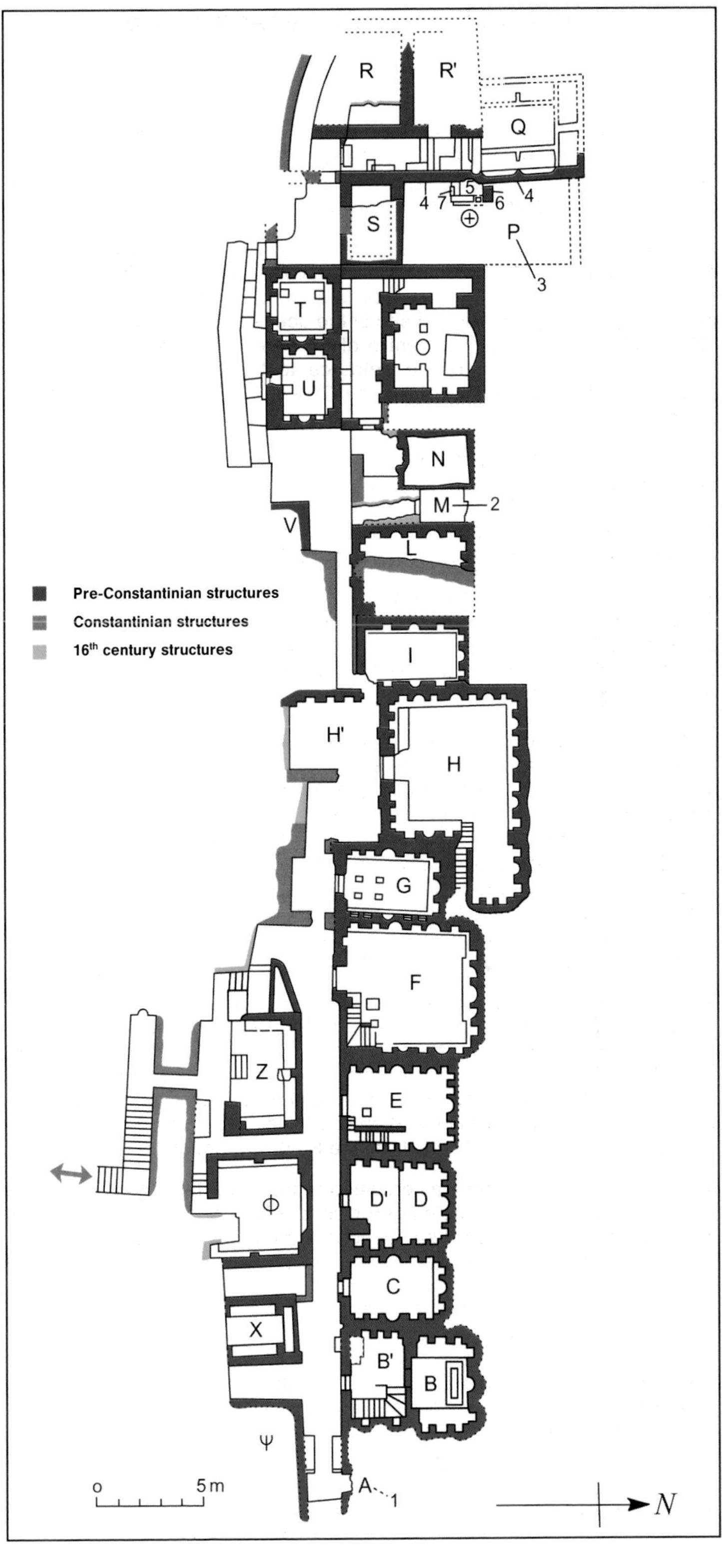

R
R'
Q
4
7
5
6
4
S
P
3
T
O
U
N
M
2
V
L
Pre-Constantinian structures
Constantinian structures
16th century structures
I
H'
H
G
F
Z
E
D'
D
Φ
C
X
B'
B
Ψ
A
1
0
5 m
N

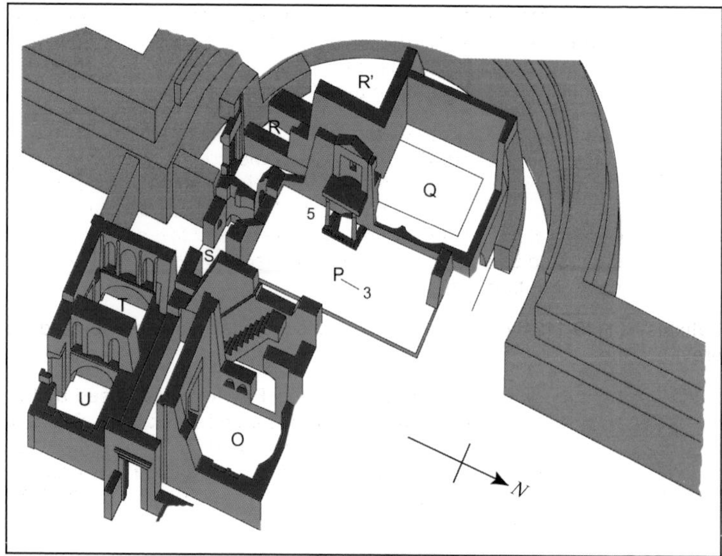

RECONSTRUCTION OF "FIELD P" AND CONSTANTINIAN APSE
Site of St. Peter's burial

3 Field P
4 Red Wall
5 "Aedicula"

Pre-Constantinian structures
Constantinian structures

laid to rest in the ground and covered with tiles arranged to form a small roof. Since St. Peter suffered the martyrdom of the cross, a monumental tomb could not be constructed for him. Numerous burials similar to the Apostle's took place in the surrounding area, which archaeologists call "Field P", perhaps those of the first successors of St. Peter.

In the 2nd century a Trophy or *Aedicula* (5), consisting of two superimposed niches separated by a marble slab, was built over St. Peter's burial, abutting onto the so-called "Red Wall" (4, due to the characteristic colour of its plaster) that delimited "Field P" to the west. Of this *Aedicula* only the lower part with two small columns (120 cm. high) remains.

In the 3rd century a wall, called "Wall g" or "Wall of the Graffiti" (6), – because it was covered with graffiti by pilgrims visiting St. Peter's Tomb in the early centuries, was built to the north of the Trophy, perpendicularly to the "Red Wall". A niche was hewn into this wall lined with small panels of marble. According to archaeologists, the remains of St. Peter were placed here after they were removed from the original tomb to protect them from possible profanation.

In the 4th century the emperor Constantine built the first Basilica dedicated to St. Peter. But to build it, he was forced to level part of the hill, fill the mausolea of the necropolis with earth and then level part of the slope that descended to the Circus below. He built three large parallel retaining walls here that were used as foundations for the Basilica. The religious problems (forced closure of the pagan cemetery) and problems of static quality (the unstable clay composition of the terrain) faced by Constantine, as well as the alignment of the Basilica, which differs slightly from that of the circus and the necropolis, show that it was the emperor's intention to build the Basilica in a precise location: over the tomb of St. Peter.

The emperor had the monument inside the Basilica built over the tomb of the Apostle, and isolated and protected it by constructing a structure around it covered with red porphyry and *pavonazzetto* marble. This structure is called the Constantinian *Memoria*. It originally had two gilt-bronze shutters; when they were opened, the Trophy could be seen. Of the Constantinian structure all that can be seen today is the rear part; it can be seen through the grate of the Clementine Chapel situated in the Vatican Grottoes.

In the 6th century St. Gregory the Great (590-604), in order to build the first permanent altar over St. Peter's Tomb, raised the height of the sanctuary and had a semicircular ambulatory placed between the two floors. The ambulatory skirted the interior of the apse and communicated with a nave, thus creating a Crypt, to enable pilgrims to arrive behind the monument. The Crypt was the first to be built in Rome. It contained the altar called *ad caput* (at the head, i.e. the head of St. Peter).

Calixtus II (1119-1124) commissioned the second altar that incorporated the previous one.

In the 16th century, when the whole of the New Basilica was raised by two metres over the original floor level of the Constantinian Basilica, Clement VIII (1592-1605) had a third altar built over the second. This is the last altar constructed over St. Peter's Tomb. Since 1633 it has been covered by Bernini's sumptuous bronze Baldachin. The papal altar is also called the "Altar of the Confession".

List of popes mentioned in the guide

Adrian I (772-795)
Adrian IV, *Nicholas Breakspeare* (1154-1159)
Alexander VI, *Rodrigo de Borja* (1492-1503)
Alexander VII, *Fabio Chigi* (1665-67)
Alexander VIII, *Pietro Ottoboni* (1689-91)

Benedict XIII, *Pietro Francesco Orsini* (1724-30)
Benedict XIV, *Prospero Lambertini* (1740-58)
Benedict XV, *Giacomo della Chiesa* (1914-22)
Boniface VIII, *Benedetto Caetani* (1294-1303)
Boniface IX, *Pietro Tomacelli* (1389-1404)

Calixtus II, *Guy de Bourgogne* (1119-24)
Calixtus III, *Alonso de Borja* (1455-58)
Celestine V, *Pietro del Morrone* (1294)
Clement VII, *Giulio de' Medici* (1523-34)
Clement VIII, *Ippolito Aldobrandini* (1592-1605)
Clement IX, *Giulio Rospigliosi* (1667-69)
Clement X, *Emilio Altieri* (1670-76)
Clement XI, *G. Francesco Albani* (1700-21)
Clement XII, *Lorenzo Corsini* (1730-40)
Clement XIII, *Carlo Rezzonico* (1758-69)
Clement XIV, *G. Vincenzo Antonio (Lorenzo) Ganganelli* (1769-74)

Eugenius III, *Bernardo perhaps of the Paganelli of Montemagno* (1145-53)
Eugenius IV, *Gabriele Condulmer* (1431-47)

Gregory I, *Gregory the Great* (590-604)
Gregory V, *Bruno of the Dukes of Carinthia* (996-999)
Gregory VII, *Hildebrand* (1073-85)
Gregory IX, *Ugolino of the Counts of Segni* (1227-41)
Gregory XI, *Pierre Roger de Beaufort* (1370-78)
Gregory XIII, *Ugo Boncompagni* (1572-85)
Gregory XVI, *Bartolomeo Alberto (Mauro) Cappellari* (1831-46)

Innocent III, *Lotario of the Counts of Segni* (1198-1216)
Innocent VIII, *Giovanni Battista Cybo* (1484-92)
Innocent XI, *Benedetto Odescalchi* (1676-89)

John VIII, (872-882)
John XXIII, *Angelo Giuseppe Roncalli* (1958-63)
John Paul I, *Albino Luciani* (1978)
John Paul II, *Karol Wojtya* (1978-2005)
Julius II, *Giuliano della Rovere* (1503-13)

Leo I, *Leo the Great* (440-461)
Leo II (682-683)
Leo III (795-816)
Leo IV (847-855)
Leo X, *Giovanni de' Medici* (1513-21)
Leo XI, *Alessandro de' Medici* (1605)
Leo XII, *Annibale della Genga* (1823-29)
Leo XIII, *Gioacchino Pecci* (1878-1903)

Marcellus II, *Marcello Cervini* (1555)
Martin V, *Oddone Colonna* (1417-31)

Nicholas III, *Giovanni Gaetano Orsini* (1277-80)
Nicholas V, *Tommaso Parentucelli* (1447-55)

Paul II, *Pietro Barbo* (1464-71)
Paul III, *Alessandro Farnese* (1534-49)

Paul V, *Camillo Borghese* (1605-21)
Paul VI, *Giovanni Battista Montini* (1963-78)
Peter of Bethsaida, prince of the apostles (martyred in 64 or 67)
Pius IV, *Giovan Angelo de' Medici* (1560-65)
Pius V, *Antonio (Michele) Ghisleni* (1566-72)
Pius VI, *G. Angelo Braschi* (1775-99)
Pius VII, *Barnaba (Gregorio) Chiaramonti* (1800-23)
Pius VIII, *Francesco Saverio Castiglioni* (1829-30)
Pius IX, *Giovanni M. Mastai Ferretti (1846-78*)
Pius X, *Giuseppe Sarto* (1903-14)
Pius XI, *Achille Ratti* (1922-39)
Pius XII, *Eugenio Pacelli* (1939-58)

Sergius II (844-847)
Sixtus II (257-258)
Sixtus IV, *Francesco della Rovere* (1471-84)
Sixtus V, *Felice Peretti* (1585-90)
Stephen II (752-757)
Sylvester I (314-335)
Symmachus (498-514)

Urban II, *Oddone di Lagery* (1088-99)
Urban VIII, *Maffeo Barberini* (1623-44)

List of artists mentioned in the guide

The artists in the Collection of Modern Religious Art mentioned in pgs. 108 and 109 are not included in this list

Vatican Press 2007